A Letter From My Father

A LETTER FROM MY FATHER

The Strange, Intimate Correspondence
of W. Ward Smith to His Son Page Smith

Edited by Page Smith

WILLIAM MORROW AND COMPANY, INC.
NEW YORK   1976

Printed in the United States of America.

1 2 3 4 5   80 79 78 77 76

Library of Congress Cataloging in Publication Data

Smith, William Ward, 1893-1968
  A letter from my father.

  1. Erotic literature. 2. Smith, William Ward, 1893-1968.
I. Smith, Page. II. Title.
HQ462.S54 1976   301.41'792'4   75-31859
ISBN 0-688-03003-3

Book design: Helen Roberts

Contents

Introduction

It was my father's strange conceit to write me a letter, the writing of which extended over a period of more than thirty years, and which, ultimately, reached ten thousand pages in length, a total of over two and a half million words. The length of the "letter" was only one of its oddities. Much of it was devoted to an account of his sexual adventures, related in very explicit detail. It contained, to be sure, a great deal of additional information dealing with his ill-fated business ventures and his lifelong fascination with politics, but anyone plunging into the nonstop narrative at almost any point could not avoid the predominantly sexual character of it.

The letter was never delivered to me during my father's lifetime but he made references to it on those rare occasions when I saw him and read brief portions during visits to Greenwich, New York, where he and his third wife had a weekend and vacation home. So I knew something of its general character long before it passed into my hands upon his death in 1968. His estate was a modest one: some hats, of which he was a diligent collector, a gold watch that had belonged to his father, a lengthy genealogy, the compilation of which took up much of the time not absorbed in writing the letter to me, a considerable number of autographed portraits of prominent politicians and theatrical figures, the letter, and a small trunk full of what might be called supporting documents.

These were delivered in several boxes and two small trunks. The "letter" was, from the moment of its arrival, something of a white elephant or, perhaps more aptly, an albatross. I poked into it more or less at random, reading the erotic, pornographic portions and feeling, while doing so, somewhat like a small boy reading a dirty book. It was a puzzle to me—as it had been from the time I first got a notion of the nature of the letter—that a father would wish to have his son read such accounts. Innumerable fathers have been womanizers. Most have attempted to conceal their philandering from their families, certainly from their children. Some have, I am sure, been the deliberate debauchers (or teachers in sexual matters) of their children, more particularly their male children. Very few, I suspect, have left such detailed and explicit accounts of their sexual liaisons. So, I asked myself repeatedly, without, I fear, producing any satisfactory answers, Why? Why the letter? Why the extraordinary emphasis on sexual encounters? And then, equally baffling, what was to be done with this white albatross? I confess my first impulse was to burn it. I have very different views on sexual matters from my father's. I am what Arthur Hoppe has called a "closet monogamist." Like Konrad Lorentz' greylag geese, I believe in "bonding," in "finding the right little woman" and cleaving to her until death us do part. I am appalled at the notion of a series of wives and mistresses, partly on aesthetic grounds—it seems so messy—and largely on emotional grounds: I could not bear all that meaningless excitation, violation of the spirit, misery, and recrimination. I believe in fidelity; in mastering one's passions rather than succumbing to them. I even adhere to the moral argument. Indeed, I am bound to because I believe that all matters are, in essence, moral, that is to say they have to do with diminishing or enhancing our humanness and thus they have to do with right and wrong. Morality, to me, is simply a kind of convenient code which prescribes most behavior so that we do not have to approach every problem *de novo,* as though it was entirely new and had to be figured out *ad hominem,* so to speak, a course which I believe to be exhausting and unnecessarily time-consuming. Virtually everything that my father did, especially though not exclusively in the realm of sex, seemed to me both wrong and personally and socially destructive, evil if you will.

So it was surpassing strange to me that I should be what I suppose many people would consider something of a prude and the son of a libertine. Such a succession is in no way exceptional, of course. Quite the contrary. It is the sons of drunkards who are most commonly teetotalers, or at least common wisdom has it so. And the sons of libertines who are often "closet monogamists," sexually repressed, homosexuals, or simply enemies of the married state. I am clearly the first of these. Certainly I am the second, to a degree, in that I have confined my sexual activities to the marital bed and, though powerfully attracted to a considerable number of women, have repressed my impulse to try to make love to them. Part of this may be simple

8

cowardice—the fear of being rejected and thus wounded in my self-esteem. After all, if you have never tried you can, like the man who has never failed, believe that had you tried you would have been found universally irresistible. But I have persuaded myself that I have a more respectable motive—to have sexual relations with another person without the sustaining structure of enduring love surrounding that act seems to me to be both a violation of oneself and of the "other." I go into these matters in some detail because, while this is a book about my father it is, of necessity, a book also about me. And part of whatever drama it may have clearly lies in the differentness of our respective temperaments.

Thus, while it is admittedly not uncommon for libertines to have moralistic offspring, it nonetheless struck me as a particular irony that my libertine father should have dropped on me this vast, imponderable, randomly obscene work in the form of a letter. So I considered, as I say, burning it. It was of no more than prurient interest to me. And the prurient is today so well attended to that I had no special need of it, granting some need for the prurient. It could hardly have any different kind of interest for my children. In fact I rebuffed their curiosity and forbade them, adults though they all are, to read it. Not on the grounds that their morals would be corrupted (their morals seem to me quite exemplary and if they were going to be corrupted they would, presumably, have been corrupted long ago) but on the grounds that I could see nothing to be gained by opening those strange, interminable, even morbid, pages to them. They could hardly live long enough to read the manuscript through from beginning to end. Therefore they, like me, would be confined of necessity to the pornographic portions. And to what good purpose?

Attractive as burning seemed, I was, I suppose, as an historian, conditioned against it. I knew of too many instances where protective widows or heirs had burned papers to protect the image of a husband or father (or, less often, mother) to be quite comfortable about burning my father's ostensible letter to me. There was some prospective historical-sociological-psychological significance to it. Beyond that it represented a substantial part of my father's odd life simply in the writing of it and, in its exhaustive and endless detail, it, in another way, contained his life, a life that seemed to me singularly futile and depressing, but a life, nonetheless, and my father's at that.

It was also possible, though it seemed unlikely then and still does as I begin this work, that it contained the answer to some riddle, some obscure mystery, having to do with my life and my relation to my father. No one can live in the middle of the twentieth century without being aware of Freud's Oedipus complex. I have never taken it as more than a kind of loose metaphor. In fact I believe that rather than wishing to murder his father and possess his mother and his father's domain, the son more typically wishes to receive from his father those gifts of mind and spirit that will enable him to find his way through the tangled forests of this strange world. But even if one rejects the Freudian system as I do, one cannot remain entirely unaffected by it. My father had never functioned for me as a real father (my maternal grandfather performed that role). I had no warm child-hood memories of a loving, caring, protecting person, or even of a stern, severe, demanding person. On those occasions when my father did appear he was almost a supplicating figure, a person who showered me with moist kisses from his full sensual lips—kisses that I found so different from the firm, warm, discreet kisses of my mother and other adult relatives, as to be rather offensive—and bestowed presents in bewildering profusion. Even then I think I felt the presents were tainted by his prolonged absences, his inattentiveness, his easy emotionalism. I sensed that he was trying to buy something cheaply— my love and admiration. With a child's shrewdness, I withheld them.

When I was three or four, I climbed on a little wooden horse with wheels to reach for some attractive object on a dresser. The horse slid from under me and I fell and cut my cheek rather severely on a wastepaper basket (I still bear the scar). I was sewed up and when my father heard of the accident he appeared in our New York apart-ment with a blizzard of toys, featuring a whole array of airplanes that were suspended above my bed. Much later I imagined he had come from one of his assignations full of remorse and shame, believing my accident a judgment upon him for his wicked behavior.

I will include further of our infrequent but strange meetings in the course of the "letter." Here I am describing my perplexity over what to do with the letter. I suspect that more than by an historian's scruples, I was constrained by this riddle I have spoken of; by the sense that someday I might need or wish to undertake the unriddling of it, so far as possible. Or might, seen in another way, perform some kind of expiation for him and for myself so that we might be united after his death in a way we had never been during his lifetime.

To be candid I should say I also considered the possibility that the letter might someday be published in some form (and thus fill out my sparse inheritance). I knew that my father had made several attempts to interest publishers in the manuscript but its length and

10

explicit language (the latter of which constituted the principal attraction for a publisher as well as the principal obstacle) prevented any serious consideration by publishers during my father's lifetime. (With the virtual disappearance of censorship, the problem of the language and the pornographic character of much of the narrative are no longer perceived as liabilities by publishers.)

In any event, for whatever combination of reasons, I forbore to burn the letter and instead locked it in a footlocker and stored it in an inaccessible corner of the barn. I mentioned it to my editor at Little, Brown. He, in turn, mentioned it several years later to my agent, John Brockman, who took an immediate interest and urged me to send him a portion of the manuscript to show to publishers. I complied, saying as I did so, that I, in a manner of speaking, washed my hands of the project in the sense that if a publisher's editor was interested he would have to do the editing. I would have nothing to do with the venture. I had meantime left the academic world and founded, with a colleague, a nonprofit corporation to do good—or what we considered good. To do good the corporation needed money. I was thus more susceptible on purely monetary grounds to the notion of publishing the letter than I had been before. I clutched at the straw of publishing the work but somehow disassociating myself from it at the same time. It turned out not to work. Several publishers were interested but shied away from the enormous editorial problems involved and, obviously, from the lack of context for the book itself. John Brockman reported this reaction to me and suggested gently that it would float only if I took responsibility for the work myself. It was, after all, a letter to me. Without, in any real sense, resolving my own ambiguities about my father's letter, I consented to try to do what I had from the beginning dimly perceived I must try to do sooner or later. I must try to exorcise the ghost of my father, that very material ghostly manuscript: the letter and the life.

I must confess that even at this stage of things I am not sure enough of my own motives to be able to say with confidence that I did not undertake what is in many ways a repugnant task in order simply to make money. I have taken some of the edge—but by no means all— off that anxiety by resolving to put the greater part of any royalties that may accrue into our nonprofit venture. But that is not enough to give me an entirely clear conscience (not that anyone should enjoy such a luxury anyhow). I still fret over whether, with all my high-sounding psychologizing, I am not simply exploiting a dirty book that my father wrote. So I fall back on what is a final argument to myself, the undoubted fact that my father would be enormously pleased. There will, after all, be a postlude to that strangely unfulfilled life. All of us search for something, a grail, a meaning, a journey through the middle earth, a Frobisher's passage of the mind and spirit, a pilgrim's progress. Perhaps my father's insatiable pursuit of sex (surely he was one of its classic prisoners) was no more than that (sex, power, money, and politics—all that is certainly thoroughly American and thoroughly human if not especially admirable), his particular grail.

* * *

My father was a striking looking man. That was my earliest impression of him—that he did not look like other men. There was, in his appearance, something compelling and exotic. As a sophomore in a college writing course I wrote a brief sketch of my father, giving him the pseudonym of Charlie Johnson. I insert it here as a measure of how I perceived him then (and later).

"He was very tall with dark hair. He had pale blue eyes. Pale blue eyes and black hair. It was a very startling combination. His teeth were long and even and yellow and slightly decayed and he showed them when he grinned (it was not so much a grin as a lewd leer). He frequently laughed, throwing back his head and giving a bellowing, trumpeting roar that started deep in his throat and came gurgling and bubbling up. It was a slightly obscene laugh. You might call it a horselaugh.

"He had a thick moustache with the ends carefully waxed, and wide, sensual lips, always moist. His eyes, not only the color, but the bold, frankly lewd way he had of staring at you, and that wide, sensual hungry-looking mouth were what struck you most; that and his laugh and his deep voice, husky with unspoken sexual implications.

"It was funny to walk down the street with him. Women followed him with their eyes. Some looked discreetly, guardedly. Others stared openly. He was conscious of it alright. He walked with a long swinging stride and talked in a loud voice, punctuating his remarks with his great obscene laughs. Usually he talked about women and sex."

I have resisted the temptation to edit these opening paragraphs describing "Charlie Johnson" though I note that my English professor circled "unspoken" in the phrase, "husky with unspoken sexual implications." I might, however, make a comment or two. Though lacking in literary merit, it still seems to me a reasonably good physical description of my father—I feel I rather overdid the laugh but that may

12

be because I haven't heard him laugh for some years now: it was perhaps his most engaging quality. Beyond that, as a late adolescent, very slow in maturing physically and uncertain of my own sexual nature, it was clear that it was the overt sexuality of my father that most fascinated me about him. I note further one important omission in his physical description. My father had the most graceful and, indeed, I am inclined to say, the most beautiful hands of any man I have known. They were slender but finely articulated with long expressive fingers, very slightly splayed at the ends. His grip or handshake combined strength with softness in a disconcerting way so that the grip of the hand was like a caress. The hands—they seemed in some way hardly to be a part of his coarseness and vulgarity—were hands that one might expect to find on a brilliant artist, a sculptor, a violinist (and, of course, seldom does). Certainly they were sensual, even insinuating hands, and to that degree in character. I remember seeing a photograph of the hands of Leslie Howard, the popular actor, that reminded me of my father's hands and made me, for the first time, conscious of their beauty. Did the hands provide a clue to the riddle of my father's strange personality? Might they be the hands of an artist manqué, of a fallen angel? There may have been something angelic in his nature—something that I missed but that women felt and that with his devilishness, his fallenness, made him irresistible to them. Perhaps it was *they* who were perpetually seducing *him,* to whom his aura of sexuality was as irresistible as their flesh to him; he created, wherever he went, this strange sexual tension, what was once called animal magnetism and constituted a respectable science and which we all know exists, which we experience daily in contacts with certain people.

That was my father in his middle forties. Age diminished but certainly did not extinguish his attractiveness to women. He and his third wife visited us in California when he was in his early seventies. In a fashionable San Francisco restaurant, while his wife and mine, my younger daughter Anne, and I looked on with some astonishment, an attractive, sexy woman in her middle or late thirties stopped at our table, put her arms around my father, kissed him and whispered something in his ear. Was she an old friend? What had she said? No, he had never seen her before. She had said, "You're beautiful." I was approximately the age my father had been when I wrote my undergraduate composition about him. That thought was not in my mind at the moment but I envied him, I think, for the first time. And I believed in the power of the aura. Most of the time I'm glad that I don't have it. I have enough trouble resisting whatever modest temptations may occasionally confront me. But it must be one of the profoundest ego-satisfactions known to man to experience the feminine world as almost totally and constantly accessible. That alone might be enough to make a man an addict. Moreover, my father failed by virtually every standard that the average American regards as important. He was an absent husband, a nothing father, an inadequate provider, a repeated business failure. In one area only was he an unqualified success—in bed, in sexual exploits. While it is reasonably clear that he had persistent and insatiable sexual appetites from an early age the same might be said of many young men, or, indeed, most young men. But it is hard not to believe that as he found himself, in part at least because of his mercurial and unstable personality, unable to succeed in acquiring that quick and easy wealth that seemed to him to be necessary to sustain the extravagant and openhanded style of living that he felt was appropriate to his persona, to his physical magnificence, he turned increasingly to the by no means inconsiderable consolations of sex. In that field he was, or felt himself to be, unrivaled.

So perhaps his letter to me can be understood as a variation of the great American success story. My father never made it. I suspect that if the money he honestly earned was prorated, so to speak, over his lifetime, it would come to no more than a few hundred dollars a year. But while his contemporaries and friends and associates were making it, he was making it with their wives, mistresses, and daughters, as well as any other stray female who wandered into his ambience.

My father was born on September 26, 1893, and christened William Ward Smith. He was always called Ward and used the name W. Ward Smith the greater part of his life. (I was christened Charles Page Ward Smith and called Page. Since my father was in such bad odor through my early youth the Ward was soon discarded, the Charles was abbreviated to "C" to prevent those who presumed from calling me "Charlie" and eventually dropped as pretentious and useless.) His father was not a distinguished or important man, an apparently competent engineer for Consolidated Edison. His grandfather, Albert Mather Smith, had been a doctor in, as I recall, New Rochelle. The family was a substantial, reasonably prosperous middle-class professional family. My great-grandfather's baby cup was a rather splendid silver chalicelike vessel; my grandfather's was less impressive but nonetheless ornate, my father's plain and modest, and mine has disappeared. I have not entirely unraveled the anthropology of the baby cups but it suggests a decline either in fortune or a decline in ostentation. There were, in any event, handsome china and silver and furniture in the family which passed into hands other than mine. Those things inherited by my father, most particularly a very fine set of Crown Derby china, were pawned in one or another of his unending financial crises.

In his later life, after he had retired from his job as an engineer, my grandfather started a business of selling wood shavings to New York state dairymen as bedding for their cows.

In my memory I see my paternal grandparents, gray and round and amiable and reserved, sitting in an oppressively dark and gloomy apartment full of velvet hangings of various kinds. They had a stuffed alligator and a steam engine in a glass case, both of which I coveted and embarrassed my mother by asking if I could have after they died, as it seemed to me they might do at any moment, they sat so still and spoke so quietly and seemed so old. I calculate now they were in their late fifties.

My father's genealogical researches which, as I have already noted, extended over a period almost as long as that occupied in writing his letter to me, turned up a host of distinguished ancestors. But distinguished ancestors are a dime a dozen, if one has the time and energy to unearth them, and this is especially true the further back one goes in history. Most of those in my father's line were seventeenth- and eighteenth-century characters, some substantial Puritans like Increase Mather (Mather remained a family name down to my father's generation), a smattering of Dutch patroons (a Polhemus, for example, after whom my younger brother was almost named), Jacob Leisler, the leader of a revolt against the ruling families of New York at the time of the Glorious Revolution in England; Blackwells of the island and the Leveriches and Elweses of Oyster Bay. A thousand distinguished ancestors, however, will not get you into the Cotillion or the Four Hundred (or however "society" is defined) unless you have money and social position. If you are a butcher your blood may be as blue as blue but you will not be included in the Social Register or invited to Mrs. Astor's ball. My impression is that my father's family, like many other similar families, clung to the very outer edge of New York society. My father went to a good private school and there he came in contact with boys whose families had the assured social status that he did not. I assume that like most ambitious young men of his generation and rather ambiguous or poorly defined social position, he desired to make a socially (and hence a financially) advantageous marriage.

Since he himself tells, in his letter, of his childhood and youth, I will confine my observations to his marriage to my mother. My mother's background was Southern, although in a manner never quite clear to me we claimed descent both from Elder Brewster, of the *Mayflower,* and the Indian princess Pocahontas (the latter was understandable because Pocahontas was, after all, from Virginia and she did marry John Rolfe, one of the early settlers, though the lustre of that descent was somewhat dimmed by the fact that an historian calculated that the dusky lady had, in 1940, 137,864 living descendants).

In many respects my mother's ancestry and immediate background were quite similar to my father's. Her maternal grandfather— my great-grandfather—had been editor of a Richmond newspaper, fought in the Civil War, was wounded and left for dead on the battlefield. He had, I gathered, been too addicted to the bottle (there were occasional dark hints of such a weakness in the blood and my grandmother was a teetotaler and member of the WCTU). My mother's grandfather on her father's side had been a schoolmaster in Frederick, Maryland.

Indeed when one got back to the seventeenth and eighteenth centuries there were distinguished ancestors galore. Carter Braxton, signer of the Declaration of Independence (and a pigheaded old reactionary), John Page, friend of Thomas Jefferson (indeed a whole swarm of Pages including Mann Page who built Rosewell, the greatest house in Virginia), and a wide assortment of Nelsons, Taliaferros, Randolphs, Carters, and Byrds. The closer one got to the present, however, the harder it was to turn up anyone more imposing than farmers, country doctors, schoolteachers or clerks in dry goods stores. The mythology of the South, however, took care of that modest status. Every Southerner who, at the end of the nineteenth or the beginning of the present century, was not notably prosperous could blame his condition on the Civil War and the damnyankees who had burned the old plantation, carried off the slaves, and stolen the family silver. Mother's family was no different in that respect from any other Southern family.

My grandfather was a poor boy in rural Maryland, determined to make his fortune. He went up to Baltimore to launch his career, but the times were bad and the only job he could get paid him five dollars a week, too little to live on. He came back to Frederick defeated. Apparently doomed to a small town existence, he devised a strategy for escape. The only member of the family with a respectable income was his adoring older sister—"Sister," as she was called. She worked in Richmond as a nurse. If she would stake her brother Willie for the time it took him to get established in business, he would provide for her the rest of her life. Before the days of social security and retirement systems the offer had a strong appeal to Sister. She agreed. My grandfather got a new start and, after a series of advances and setbacks that rivaled the adventures of Horatio Alger, he made it. He made it primarily through his sponsorship by one of the wealthiest and most powerful families in the city, the Prestons. James Preston had served a term or two as mayor of Baltimore (and was always subsequently called Mayor Preston). He helped my grandfather start a bank and was his advocate in Baltimore society. Since the Pages were known as a fine old Virginia family and the Williamses (my maternal grandmother's family) were powers in Richmond, if rather *nouveau riche,* it was relatively simple to smuggle (or usher) the transplanted Pages into Baltimore society—the Cotillion, the Monday German, the Elkridge Hunt Club, the University Club, the Mt. Vernon Club, the Colonial Dames (infinitely superior to the definitely middle-class Daughters of the American Revolution)—all those associational activities by which the elite of the city defined themselves and marked out their superiority to the crowds of ordinary merchants and businessmen pushing their way up from below and constantly scheming how they might gain a toehold on that exalted plateau. Some did it simply by the overpowering weight of money. Thus old Emerson, the druggist, happened to invent an enormously successful remedy for the nervous stomach that afflicted so many Americans from the strain of trying to get ahead, and, as a consequence, got ahead himself, although not without a fierce and prolonged struggle and some sniffs that soon dentists and such people would be trying to buy their way into the Cotillion (as indeed they soon were).

This is not the place for an analysis of Baltimore society. My only intention is to indicate that my mother's family had by hard work, good fortune, and usable family connections gained access to the charmed circle.

My mother and her sisters thus "came out," attended the proper balls and had their comings and goings recorded in the society columns of the newspapers, were enrolled in the sacrosanct pages of the Baltimore Social Register, attended the Monday German and so on. One of my mother's sister's friends was a young woman named Wallis Warfield who was thought to look remarkably like my mother, though not, the family at least thought, half so pretty.

Thus for Ward Smith my mother represented a means of ascent

on the social ladder. When Mother met him she was on the rebound from a transatlantic romance with a handsome young Englishman, Jack Goodwin, who, in the tradition of upper-class Englishmen marrying American girls, apparently expected his prospective father-in-law to make him vice-president of his bank or otherwise endower him. My father, who looked like a somewhat larger and improved version of Goodwin, talked in the most expansive way about his various business enterprises and prospects, and dropped the names of New York financiers and politicians as though they were intimate friends. Grandfather, stern, quiet, reserved, austere, with a reputation for penetrating humbug, was unaccountably charmed by this handsome New Yorker with the dazzling connections who talked so confidently of money to be made in a variety of blue-chip ventures. I can only speculate that Grandfather was still at heart a small town boy who had made good by luck and unremitting labor. Ward Smith must have opened a door for him to a fabulous world; he must have seemed a prototype of the American success story, one who could simply reach out and pluck the fruit Success that my grandfather had labored so hard to achieve. Thus, to the surprise of the family, my grandfather became a warm advocate of the marriage. His wife was unabashedly reluctant. That shrewd and suspicious lady smelled out the truth. There is little question that she divined that Ward Smith's insolent blue eyes masked a rapacious sexuality. But her daughter, gentle and compliant in most matters, had on those points she cared about a will as strong as her mother's. She was determined to marry Ward Smith.

It is necessary, I believe, to say a word about my mother's upbringing. In the class and time in which she grew to womanhood, the world was defined very largely in terms of "things not done." These varied from the most inconsequential to the most momentous. They had to do with what utensil, out of an interminable array, one ate what with. There was an addendum: the socially ambitious person worried about which fork or spoon to use; the socially secure person knew it didn't matter. The catch was that of course it did matter. How one addressed servants or what one said or did not say in the presence of servants. How, for example, one requested service. I had the incurably lower-class habit of saying to one of the maids, "May I please have some more peas or potatoes or fried chicken?" My grandmother invariably corrected me. "You do not say, 'May I please have. . . .' The servants are here to wait on you. You say, 'I'll have. . . .' " It seemed to me too subtle a point. I never really mastered it. The "things one didn't do" belonged themselves to a hierarchy. There were "things one did not do"; there were "things that were never done"—a more serious category—and "things that were simply never done!" the most heinous of social crimes. One didn't associate with Jews or Catholics with the exception in the latter instances of a few rich old families like the Carrolls and the O'Donovans; you didn't speak to people unless properly introduced, especially of course if you were a nubile female, and if you were a nubile female you never went out unchaperoned—and *all* of the negative injunctions that were imposed on young males were multiplied in spades for young females. The horror of any properly brought-up young woman was to be thought to be "loose" or "fast." There were such of course and they were whispered and gossiped about (and probably envied) and, worst of all, thought to be spoiled for any proper marriage to any decent young man. A decent young man was a young man of good family background, not notoriously loose or dissipated, who had graduated from Gilman School and Princeton (even sometimes from Harvard or Yale, seldom from Columbia and never from Dartmouth), belonged to a good club or clubs and above all, could support a wife in some degree as her dear poppa had supported her which meant, typically, a comfortable house and a cook or maid to begin with. The cook was essential, the maid optional.

There were in fact an almost infinite number of "things not done." One didn't laugh too much or too loudly, or go to church, if a woman, without a hat, or, if a man, in a sports jacket and bright tie; one spoke to one's inferiors always politely but with unmistakable condescension (lest, I suppose, they might be tempted to presume).

Just as there were utensils appropriate to every edible item, there were clothes appropriate to every social occasion. A woman who went about without a hat and gloves and, above all, a woman who smoked on the street was in great peril of being considered "loose" though she might in fact be chaste as Diana.

Above all, one did not use certain words or discuss certain unpleasant subjects. The words (and even the subjects) were coarse and vulgar and thus irredeemably lower-class: in a word, "common." "Common" was a code word that covered that hierarchy of things not, or never, or simply never, done. Those things were all "common." But "common" was even broader than that. It reached beyond the various categories of "things not done" into every nook and cranny of daily life. It was, for example, common to say "can't" through one's nose instead of "cawn't," or "ant" for "aunt." My mother tried to break me of saying "can't" by giving me a little slap whenever I erred. I had later to rather painfully unlearn it in the army where my mates thought it an absurd affectation (which, of course, it was). Similarly, one said "tomawtoes" instead of "tomaytoes." It was "common" to speak of curtains as drapes.

Leading the list of forbidden subjects was sex, or anything to do with the more personal parts of the body. A friend of mine insisted that her mother still thought babies were found under cabbage leaves when she was married. It was "common" to speak of legs; limbs were preferred. It was unacceptable or one of those dread things "simply never done" to speak directly of sexual intercourse. It was generally understood, even by delicately nurtured young women, that most men had unbridled sexual appetites. This was one of those unfortunate facts of life about which nothing could be done. It had to be endured and, like most unpleasant things, the less said about it the better.

This made for a very strange kind of world to be sure. Since sex is such a large part of life, indeed such a major preoccupation of the species, never to be able to acknowledge its existence in any direct and explicit way made for a veiled world of innuendos, hints, allusions. What was not said orally was often said with shrugs and looks and sometimes smirks. A child developed a certain expertise in interpreting these mysterious signals. If sexual matters were to be discussed in guarded monotones the children were sent from the room so that there should be no contamination of young minds.

Now I go into all of this because it was the world in which my mother grew up and the world in which I grew up as well, since I grew up in my grandparents' house after my mother and father were divorced. And if anything is clear about it, it is that it was very poor preparation for marrying a man like my father. It should also be said that it was undoubtedly the world, in large part, that my father grew up in—the late Victorian world. In fact my maternal and paternal grandparents were hardly to be distinguished one from the other even in appearance. This was much more notably the case with my grandfathers. My maternal grandmother was somewhat of a special case. But as my father's letter makes quite clear, young males had quite different resources open to them than did young females. There were, first of all, the maids, nurses, and serving girls. The number of upper-middle-class boys who had their first sexual experience with one of these often compliant lower-class females must have been legion.

So they early attained a degree of sophistication in sexual matters commonly denied their sisters. The fact that their normal sexual tendencies and appetites were perceived by the psychologically dominant female world as unnatural or beastly, or at best, unpleasant, doubtless helped to make them so and to stimulate business in the bawdy houses which flourished in every town and city.

The males of this class-age certainly did not escape, via their furtive encounters with serving girls and peripatetic strumpets, from deep feelings of guilt and anxiety about their own sexual behavior. For the most part, they unquestionably bought the notion that "nice," *i.e.* upper-class, marriageable girls had a very mild interest in sex and understood it to be an unpleasant exercise engaged in by them at least almost solely for the perpetuation of the species, ideally for the production of a male heir. Young males of my father's generation (and mine) thus divided the world into nice girls whom one married and bad (usually lower-class) girls with whom one had sexual relations. There were certainly loose girls in the "nice" category and men who were fortunate enough or bold enough to gain access to their favors enjoyed them but seldom considered marrying them. I suppose it can be said in my father's favor that he made no such invidious distinctions.

This is a lengthy but I suspect necessary preamble to the marriage of my mother and father. It was a marriage against which society had, in a manner of speaking, stacked the cards, or at least one particular deck. Beyond that, it was my mother's misfortune that she had chosen or accepted as husband a man whose sexual compulsions were abnormal, or at least whose ability to moderate his sexual drives was conspicuously lacking, a man, in fact, whose pathology was uninhibited sexuality. Whether a different man, thoughtful, patient, gentle and confident of his own sexuality, could have opened up that realm of experience for my mother I cannot of course say. What one can say is that my father was the last person in the world to undertake so complex and delicate a task. My mother was a typical feminine representative of a particular milieu, a kind of vestal virgin, guarding the fires of upper-middle-class respectability, an unquestioning acceptor of the "things not done," prisoner of a world as formal, hieratic, prescribed as that of the Brahmins or Mandarins. My father was a prancing Pan—he was apparently attracted to that image of himself; he had several Pan drawings by the popular graphic artist Willy Pogany—a Priapus.

The union of Pan and the Vestal Virgin was doomed from the beginning. It produced a great deal of anguish for my mother and intermittent outbursts of tearful contrition from my father. And it produced me and my brother, younger by five years. However much

I may have escaped in simple geographical terms (and I trust in other terms as well) that odd world in which I grew up, it nonetheless shaped me in what are generally considered the formative years of my life. I was raised by my mother and I was deeply and profoundly devoted to her. I took her "side" so far as there was a "side" to take. I accepted her picture of my father as an evil, wicked man (and though she was never very specific about what that evil consisted of, I early understood it had a good deal to do with that most unmentionable subject, sex). The world that my mother (and I, later) grew up in will seem to most readers, I suspect, a rather repugnant one. In part it seems so to me. But it was a world with its own kind of meanings and coherencies, a world that has passed and will never come again, a world I am not sorry to see go, and do not mourn, but a world in which I was reasonably happy, a world that, with all its limits, afforded many pleasures, not the least of which was exploring its boundaries and finally breaking out of it. I now know that there are worse worlds for a boy to grow up in. So I am grateful for that world and even for that strange union of which I was a product.

This is, I suspect, enough family background for the present. I will interject at those points in the letter where I feel impelled to. The story is, after all, my father's.

Finally, something must be said about the process by which a manuscript of ten thousand pages is reduced to some six hundred. In a certain sense that is manifestly impossible. If publishing costs did not prohibit it, I would have preferred to see the letter published in its entirety. That was, of course, impossible from the point of cost and would have produced a work no one could have read. It was never considered as a remote possibility by me or my publisher. Nonetheless, in what might be called existential terms, it would have much to recommend it since anyone tenacious enough to read it would experience the tedium of daily life, the strange alternations between excitement and boredom, hope and despair, the wearisome accumulation of trivia, the complex interactions of people with each other that are a part of life (but not of art) and that made up this life and, I assume, a good many others. Reading it would then have constituted immersion in an archetypal autobiography that by its very interminableness must create a new dimension of experience that would be in a sense, transliterary and transhistorical.

It would have constituted a literary "happening" corresponding perhaps to the artist Christo's stunt of hanging a curtain across the Colorado River canyon. Accepting, as I have, the practical limitations of this work, the most taxing aspect of reducing it from its vast dimensions has been to preserve some kind of proportion. The sexual episodes that figure so prominently in the book are, in the original letter, "balanced" by very lengthy sections on the minutiae of New York politics and on the ramifications of the business ventures that occupied so much of my father's time in his early years. No one can read these with pleasure or even, in many instances, comprehension but they nonetheless serve the function of making clear that, preoccupied with sex as my father was, and often in the context of business and politics (which he never really allowed to interfere with his relentless pursuit of women), it was, if a constant, not an exclusive preoccupation. In other words, as I wrote my editor at the initial stages of this venture, the challenge, in large part, was to "avoid simply producing a dirty book." I am not sure I have done so; indeed, to have done so would be, in a sense, to have triumphed over my father and over the material itself, for it is clear enough that, for reasons best known to himself, he intended to write a "dirty letter." But I hope it is more than that: a portrait of a strange man, my father, and, in part at least, of the age he lived in.

A Note to the Reader

Names have dramatic potency. My father named all the women in his life. I have chosen to use initials for last names in some cases, and in certain instances pseudonyms, to protect the privacy of those who may still be alive.

—PAGE SMITH

Ward Smith's Epigraph

". . . Until thy feet have trod the road
Advise not wayside folk;
Nor till thy back has borne the load
Break in upon the broke. . . ."
                    —KIPLING, "The Comforters"

1893-1915

Dear Page:

I came into this world without my consent, and I may or may not leave it against my will.

During my stay on earth my time has been spent, and will continue to be spent, I suppose, in one continuous round of contraries and misunderstandings.

In infancy, it was assumed, in common with all other infants, that I was sort of an angel.

In boyhood, a kind of devil.

In manhood—if I have ever attained to that degree—anything from a lizard up.

In my duties, a damn fool.

In the raising of a family, a laggard.

In the management of my personal affairs, an ass.

I early learned that if I remained out of political life, I would be shirking civic responsibility, and that if I entered the political arena, I would be called a grafter and a crook.

When I went to church I was considered, with others of the holy Episcopal flock, a hypocrite.

When I stayed away from church, I was considered a sinner whose soul was lost.

When we first enter the world everybody wants to kiss us, and by the time we depart, everyone would like to give us a good kick.

Life is a strange road, but somehow or other we all have to travel it, whether we like it or not.

With most of us it is sleep, eat, work and screw; with aught a care for mankind and the unknown.

29

That men want sympathy and understanding, and above all else an interest in the accomplishments they feel they have wrought, is a truism that is as applicable to me as anyone else, and which in part explains my reasons for writing all this down. . . .

Of my early recollections the most definite impression that I recall was the birth of my sister.

I still remember being awakened at night with a sense of much excitement and unusual activity about the house. There were strange voices and unusual noises. I was restless; the apartment seemed dark and eerie. I couldn't sleep. Finally, I was told that the stork had complied with my wish and brought me a baby sister to play with. I received that news with mixed feelings of joy and jealousy—joy that I would have a playmate in my own home—jealousy at the thought that the new baby would receive all the attention from my mother and father. I was four years old at the time.

We lived at the corner of Seventy-fourth Street and Columbus Avenue. There were steam locomotives hauling the elevated trains past our windows. The locomotive engineers would wave and throw kisses to my nurse as they passed our window. . . .

Looking back . . . there are naturally certain events in the various stages of my life that are more vivid than others, because of the emotional reaction at the time, which left an indelible impression upon my mind which a lifetime has not erased.

When I was seven years of age I was taken daily to a small private school by my mother who always called for me at noon.

One day after I arrived at school I was told that the principal had died and there would be no school that day or for several days.

Mother had left me at the foot of the steps leading up to the school proper and returned home. I became very panicky, in fact almost hysterical at the thought that I might have to remain in the school where the teacher was dead until mother came for me at lunch time.

Frantically, I raced from the schoolhouse down the street and, fortunately, was able to overtake my mother before she had gone very far. She assuaged my fear and consoled me. The horrible fright of that occasion has remained with me always.

A year later, when attending a school for boys only, I ran away from my nurse on Riverside Drive and pushed my "buckboard" all the way from Seventy-second Street to Grant's Tomb and back. This was the first time that I had ever flouted the authority of my parents or nurse. It was probably the first evidence of the contrariety of my nature and that ruthless determination of mine to have my own way at any cost.

I was early attracted to the opposite sex but not by girls of my own age. As a very small boy, I secretly worshipped my mother's first cousin, Grace Lee Smidt (Willing), who was a stunning and attractive woman, old enough to have been my mother.

The horse-drawn fire engines of the New York City Fire Department, and the fire-crackers and fire-works of the Fourths of July of by-gone days, held a special appeal for me.

As a small child, my favorite toys were fire engines, mechanical railroad trains, and lead soldiers. I think I had probably every type of toy fire apparatus that was manufactured at the time. My grandfather Ward would remonstrate with my mother for permitting me to have such toys. He feared they would be an incentive for me to set our home on fire in order to put out the flames with my toy engines.

As a youngster I was greatly impressed by my father's almost ritual display of the American Flag from our window each day during the Spanish-American War.

When Dewey and his fleet returned and sailed up the Hudson River I was taken to the top of one of the gas holders at Eighteenth Street and the Hudson River, to witness the review of the fleet. . . .

My godmother, Abbey Burt, lived in an apartment on the ground floor at 14 Fifth Avenue. The living-room had windows on the avenue. It was a horrid, gloomy, dark apartment. We went to "Abbey-dear's" to witness the return of the soldiers from the Spanish-American War. They marched up Fifth Avenue from Washington Arch—soldiers years ago marched further than they do today. There was a time when they thought nothing of marching from Washington Square to Grant's Tomb. . . .

Of the Spanish War Veterans' parade, all I can recall is the monument on Washington Square, the monument across Fifth Avenue at Broadway and Twenty-third Street (the one at Twenty-third Street was a temporary structure made of plaster) and the dark dreariness of my godmother's apartment.

The first girl of my own age that I really had an infatuation for was General Oliver Bridgeman's daughter, Anna. I had a particular passion for her legs and although I didn't see her often, whenever I did I always wanted to kiss her legs.

After Anna Bridgeman (her mother was a Kirk and her mother's mother a Tobey) there was my school teacher in the second school I attended (The West Side Private School for Boys). I was about eight

31

at the time and to me she was very attractive. I always entertained the greatest admiration and affection for her. Even after I left that school —and years later when I had reached the age of puberty and wet dreams—I would have orgasms dreaming of her. . . .

When my grandmother Ward was dying, and my mother was staying down at my grandmother's house, I often went and hid in the closet where her clothes were hanging, covering myself with her dresses, thereby gaining some peculiar sensation of her nearness from the odor of her body that her clothes still retained. . . .

When Charles Lane Poor was a Professor of Astronomy at the Johns Hopkins University, we paid his wife, Cousin Anna, a visit at her home in Baltimore. For years afterwards, my mental picture of Baltimore was a big black hole filled with suffocating smoke, an impression I must have gained from traveling through the smoke-filled Pennsylvania Tunnel entering Baltimore, which for years was a nasty experience. . . .

In the early 1900's, when we were living downtown . . . we all went over to Riverside Drive and 72nd Street to witness an exhibition of the first "horseless carriage." That location probably was selected because of the steep down grade from 75th to 79th Street. For years the Drive, with its bicycle paths, its bridle paths, its rustic walks, had been the haven of the cyclists, riders, drivers and hikers. Little we knew as we witnessed the "horseless carriage's" performance that some day the rider, the driver, the cyclist, nay, even the pedestrian, would be practically driven off the Drive by the automobile.

We were summering down on the Jersey Coast at the time of President McKinley's assassination, and we went to the special memorial services held in the Episcopal Church at Sea Girt, a service that left me with a sense of depression that I did not shake off for years.

Another summer, we went to West Hampton, to a small country hotel, the Howell House. I hated leaving Father, not seeing him at home in the evening or the morning, and I have never forgotten the stinking "four holers" back of the old hotel. The flies, the bees, and mosquitoes that inhabited those awful shacks! How I hated having to get up at night and go out into the cool night air, in order to relieve my bowels in those dirty, smelly dumps. Even the beautiful white, sandy beaches—which I can still picture in my mind to this day— didn't offset my distaste for West Hampton's "four holers" or "backhouses."

The terrific lightning and thunder storms that so frequently raged about that small wooden hotel during that summer instilled in me a real fear of lightning which I did not outgrow for many years.

Looking back on my youth, I sometimes wonder how I could have been so afraid if my mother had not been a bit nervous about the lightning too. Mother was always closing the windows during storms on the theory that lightning would not strike through glass. Then there were the discussions that used to take place in the family circle about not standing under trees during thunder storms, etc. . . .

When they first started to build the original New York Subway, I, like most other youths of the day, was enthralled by the construction work, and the excavating of Broadway. It was one of my hopes to live to see that job completed, and I often wondered whether I would. In childhood, the great question to me was whether I would ever grow up; not so much whether I would live to grow up, but whether I would always remain a child—if it just wasn't another fairy tale like Santa Claus, this business of growing up to be a big, strong man like my father. I often wondered when I first went to school whether children really ever finished school. . . .

As I grew a little older, we went to Oyster Bay to live.

By this time, Father had left the Gas Company and had gone into a silent partnership with his brother, my Uncle Gov, in the wholesale lumber business. . . .

Out of the profits of the by-products of their lumber business they had purchased their respective wives beautiful diamond rings. . . .

Before the first summer was over, Father and Uncle Gov had purchased a modest rig of their own and an old horse, and had hired a handy-man to look after the place and drive Mother and Aunt Jessie. As time went on, in the course of several summers, more horses, coachmen, footmen and gardeners were added, the house was renovated, cows, pigs, chickens and turkeys were purchased.

Then they bought a 70 foot sloop of the Lipton cup-racing type, a yacht that required a crew of nine men and drew twelve feet of water. She was a fast boat but hard to handle in a gale.

Father was an expert seaman and while short cruises were taken, the yacht was used largely to entertain friends, business associates and customers.

At Oyster Bay, the Fourth of July was an occasion of great festivity. Japanese lanterns were strung out, giant fire-crackers were exploded in barrels, in cans and under rocks. Strings of crackers were hung from tree limbs. It was a noisy—and dangerous—day. At night, we watched from our front porch the beautiful display of fire-works that President Roosevelt and his family set off from Sagamore Hill. The fire-works displayed by the members of the Seawanamka Corinthian Yacht Club, and our own generous supply of fire-works, thanks to Uncle Gov's liberality on such occasions.

I learned to swim off the end of our private pier and boat landing and often rowed my boat on the bay.

When President Roosevelt reviewed the U.S. Fleet after its return from the trip around the world, the family sailed out in our 70 foot sloop, the *Syce,* to see the review.

I was left behind on the pretext that it was too much of a blow, and the boat having an iron keel instead of lead, it was feared she might keel over. This distressed me greatly, for I was determined to see the show. The coachman wouldn't let me have my horse because of the crowds out in their carriages who were driving to Bayville and Center Island to witness the review. All other means of conveyance being denied me, I took my rowboat and rowed clear across the bay to the sand bar that connected Bayville with Center Island. It was late when I got there, but I saw the end of the review. I was so tired coming home in the dusk that at times I was fearful I would never make it. . . .

Our pew at Christ Church was but two rows back of President Theodore Roosevelt's. The President and his family attended Christ Episcopal Church at Oyster Bay every Sunday while he was President. . . .

When we were living on W. 76th Street, I broke open my first little savings bank in order to get pennies to buy gumdrops in the candy store on the corner. At Oyster Bay I was in frequent trouble with the family because of my excessive charging of candy and magazines at Mills' Stationery Store, and Snowders Drug Store. . . .

The Vanderbilt Cup Auto Road Races were the rage in the summers of 1904–5 and 6. We would drive over with our tallyho and four horses before day-break, and park along the North Hempstead Pike, which was then but a narrow dirt highway. The horses would be unhitched and taken down the road and tied at a sufficient distance so as not to become frightened at the racket set up by the roaring motors.

The racers would sweep around the dirt turn at East Norwich at 30 miles an hour. The crowd on the highway opening, as they approached, like a human gate, for them to pass, and closing immediately behind them in order to watch them tear off down the road at 50 or 60 miles an hour. Occasionally a car would lose a wheel or a tire would blow out on the East Norwich turn. Sometimes the drivers would lose control as they tried to skid around the curve, and their cars would dive right into the crowds.

It was a thrilling sight to watch those demons come down the dirt highway, through the haze of the early morning mist, with their exhausts belching fire from motors at their engine heads.

It was always autumn, and the air was brisk and sharp. The leaves were turning and these racing monsters had all the appearance of some evil spirit coming out of the dawn as they roared down the highway with huge clouds of dust behind them.

Few of the present-day cars could stand the strain of those dirt-road races. Those were the days of Chevrolet, Barney Oldfield and many other daredevils of American and European fame. There has never been anything like it since, and there probably will never be anything like it again.

I learned to drive fairly well at Oyster Bay, singly, in tandem, or double harness; even a four-in-hand.

For a month or so in the fall, before returning to the city, I would attend the Quaker school at Locust Valley—the Friends Academy—driving over and back each day. One day my whip accidentally caught a boy on a bicycle as he passed in the opposite direction. The next day he was waiting for me to lick me, but the coachman took care of that—timid and protected soul that I was.

While we still lived with Uncle Gov, I was sent out to sell my first carload of material—it was at the tender age of eleven. I was driving the high-jig with a span of horses, high steppers at that, with the coachman and footman in the box behind them. And I made a sale.

In town, we had a brougham for use in the day time, an opera-bus for the theatre or other activities at night. We also had a two-seater, and a cutter for driving about the parks and parkways in the daytime.

The most important transformation in my physical makeup took place while I was at Oyster Bay. My life there was somewhat strenuous. I rode and swam every morning and went sailing nearly every afternoon.

Speaking of riding reminds me that whenever I passed President Roosevelt out riding on the back country roads, he would rein in his horse and have a pleasant word of greeting for this, then, little boy.

From early childhood I had a passion for little girls' legs as well as women's legs. And Mother was always mortified by my insistence on crawling under the table at parties in order to kiss little girls' lower extremities.

The house we occupied at Oyster Bay was old, and the servants had their quarters in what at one time had been an attic.

For some unknown reason that I have never been able to analyze, I always possessed a great curiosity to see the maids in their bathing suits—which were fullsome garments then.

My room was on the second floor in the rear of the old house to the back of the servants' stairway.

One afternoon there was some difficulty about the safety-valve on the inlet to the water tank up on the third floor of the house.

I was sent up to make the necessary adjustments. I had just been swimming and was still in my bathing suit. When I had made the slight mechanical repair my eye caught sight—through an empty knot-hole in the partitioned wall of one of the maid's rooms—of the nude form of the waitress. To my amazement, my prick instantaneously grew quite large and hard and pressed against my bathing trunks.

I was so astonished that I went right down to my room, removed my bathing suit and gazed at the, to me, phenomenon in the mirror. I was too frightened to say anything about it to anyone. I wondered whether the erection would remain that way permanently. Fearing that it might not, I got out my camera and proceeded to photograph my erect penis in the mirror. I was not quite eleven years of age.

I took the film to the local store in the village for development.

A few days later, Mother discovered the picture when calling at the store for the usual family photographs that had been left for developing and printing.

Mother had sent the footman in for the pictures. She told me years later that when driving home from the store she was looking through the pictures of the family and the children, when she came across my self-portrait in the nude. At the time it was a great shock, for suddenly she was confronted with the unrefutable evidence that her baby son had blossomed forth into full manhood.

From then on, I possessed an unsatisfied curiosity to know why my mother and father slept together and other men and women did not.

I also became aware that the strange sensation which always accompanied the erection of my cock was one of the nicest feelings, in fact the nicest feeling I knew. It was nicer than sleeping, eating, or doing something I liked or wanted to do.

Night after night, as I lay in my bed, I racked my confused and troubled brain for some explanation of it all, and what most frequently occurred to me as a solution was the notion that mother and father pissed on one another as they slept together.

Night after night, I dreamt of men and women peeing over one another and leaving puddles in the bed, and when I would awaken I would find that I had wet the bed with my own sperm—in my dreams I had "come!"

This happened many many times. It happened so regularly that there was no apparent effort or thought or desire on my part to masturbate.

After my first experience I would often sneak up to the maid's quarters and peep through the hole in the wall after they had been in bathing, and watch them dress and undress—I would always get a hard-on.

For a while in the early fall and the spring, I commuted back and forth to school in New York. In those days I would always be in the old 34th Street ferry house on the Long Island side in time to see Mildred Poor, the niece of my cousin Charles Lane Poor, as she passed through the station to her train, week-ends, for Southampton. What a kick I used to get out of just watching her, she was so lovely.

One day I met Nan B. in the Long Island Railroad Station. She was a girl from Cold Spring Harbor. I saw her often and was rather hot for her.

We frequently met in the old cemetery at Jamaica, near the railroad tracks, and in a boat-house of Nan's father on the shore of Cold Spring Harbor. In the boat-house we would take off all our clothes and then play with ourselves—I with her pussy and she with my cock. In the cemetery, we would excitedly expose ourselves to one another, but only our privates. She was very passionate and so was I.

My father was chairman of the Board of Directors of the North Shore Bank while I was still in school. Every Monday night he would attend the Board of Directors meeting at Oyster Bay. Often I would ride down with him from New York and wait in the railroad station while he went to the meeting.

When I had enough money with me I would engage George Bennett, the local liveryman, to drive me over from Oyster Bay to Cold Spring Harbor while Father was at the bank attending the Board of Directors meeting.

By this time George was sporting an automobile along with his horse and buggy rigs, and the auto made it possible to get over and back in time to be at the station ahead of Father.

At Cold Spring Harbor I would visit Nan B. Such visits usually consisted of tongue sucking and playing with one another, when invariably we would both "come." In those days I didn't know enough to put my cock in her cunt, and she apparently hesitated to rape me.

Why Father ever thought a kid would sit in a railroad station alone at night for two or three hours reading magazines or newspapers, I don't know.

At first I did stay in the station but it wasn't long before I became restless and got the idea of driving over the hill to see Nan.

Nan's parents bought an automobile (motor cars were few and far between in those days) and on different occasions I would take the train down to Syossett where she would meet me and take me driving. It wasn't the air we were seeking. She would drive up lonely woodland roads, where she would park the car in the woods. There we would expose ourselves to one another as we made passionate love.

The first time I ever saw Nan nude was when she took me to the bath house. She proceeded to leave the door of her dressing room ajar (while she took her things off and got into her bathing suit) for me to see her naked body. It made me very passionate, and while she was undressing I jerked off.

As time went on, she talked much of marriage and I acquiesced. Somehow or other Mother and Father learned of the affair—I always suspected that George, the liveryman, snitched—and were able to interpose many obstacles in our way. Through the bank, Father exerted pressure on Nan's father, who had credit at the bank for his ship-building business.

Nan's cunt was the first pussy that I ever had my fingers on, and the sweet memories of those exciting occasions remained with me for many many years.

I spent a good deal of time playing in Riverside Drive. When I wasn't going to school Mother would take us there in the morning and the nurse would take us there in the afternoon.

Mother developed in me a terrific aversion to caterpillars and little worms that were to be found in the parkside, and to all manner of insects and bugs. She was fearful that we would be contaminated by the other children who played in the park, so she always kept us away from them for fear, as she said, that we could catch diseases.

Mother was quite a snob and never wanted us to have anything to do with any children that did not come from the most aristocratic families or whom she considered our social equal.

As a kid my bladder must have been almost as weak as that of the diabetic dog of Eugene Field fame, for I was invariably having to piss, which was always a matter of great distress and embarrassment to my mother and nurse, who surreptitiously sought trees or cartwheels where I could relieve myself unobserved.

The interesting thing about my peeing proclivities in childhood was the fact that from maturity to this day I have held my water for hours upon hours at a stretch without any discomfort or desire to piss. And this, in spite of the fact that I drink quantities of water at meals, sometimes as many as fifteen or twenty glasses at a time.

Your mother, Ellen, after we were married told me that the Page family often wondered how I managed for hours without going to the bathroom to pee. I'd be with your mother for an entire day at a time before, during and after meals, without ever going to the bathroom.

I never had any desire to go. Twice a day was usually enough—in the morning when I got up and in the evening before I retired.

When very small, Mother got tickets to take my sister and me to see *Way Down East* at the Old Academy of Music. . . .

All I ever remembered of that show was the door of a cabin opening and closing while the wind howled outside and snow swept through the door jamb every time anyone entered or left. It must have been exciting as I wet my breeches.

Father was meticulous about his appearance, very orderly and tidy about everything he did. That was also true of my grandfather Smith. Mother, while a very beautiful woman and a smart dresser, was very careless and untidy about everything, which was also true of her sisters.

All my life I have had spells of disorderliness, with complete disregard for my own personal appearance or the tidiness of things about me. Then there are periods when I am scrupulously careful about my appearance and extremely fussy, exacting and orderly concerning everything about me.

The second show I went to see, when I was a year or two older, was *The Wizard of Oz* with Montgomery and Stone. What I remember most about that show was the Straw Man, the Tin Man, and the girl with the black lace panties and black silk stockings who danced in the show. Here again I disgraced myself by peeing in my pants during the play. This show was given in the Majestic Theatre on Columbus Circle. . . .

Occasionally for one reason or another my mother would leave me with her sisters overnight. I was left at the 45th Street house for some weeks when Elise was born.

I was just four then, and I slept in the bed with my Aunt Lucy. Much to her discomfort, I would wet the bed at night. As a matter of fact, I developed quite an urge for her which I felt very strongly from time to time, particularly during my adolescence. I was always peeking up her dresses to see what I could see.

Two things about my stay with her at that time apparently impressed her. First, my declaration that "grass was the earth's whiskers," and second, "She was so lovely, how could God have ever let her out of heaven. . . ."

One summer, Mother took us up to Milford (see the picture of Elise and myself in the donkey car). . . . Up in that country the beggars were always coming around with trained bears with poles that performed for pennies.

Four things stand out about Milford: First, the town jail on the main street, with the drunks always calling through the bars. That used to frighten me a good deal.

Next, the little summer house up on a hill just back of the town where I strolled with Mother and Father one Sunday afternoon while they left Elise behind with Aunt Lucy and Aunt Aline at the Bluff House.

It was in this summer house where I propounded a most important, to me, question, a question that had been puzzling me for some time: Was there a Santa Claus, or wasn't there? the answer much to my regret was in the negative. I suspected the worst, but it was a shock learning the truth. . . .

I was nearly eight when I learned the truth about Santa Claus which proves what a gullible kid I was. . . .

I went to Rugby Military Academy on West End Avenue and 83rd Street, where they had a cavalry troop.

It was my great ambition at Rugby to get to be a member of the Cavalry Troop. All through my school life I had a desire to get to a military school which had a cavalry troop. But my father never could afford to send me.

In the early years of my schooling, I had an ambition to be a

40

West Pointer, an ambition which was cultivated by my father but which never materialized.

From Rugby, I went to Poly Prep for a winter. . . . There, each afternoon, the coachman would call for me with the team and I would drive around Prospect Park before going home. If there was snow on the ground the cutter would be brought and I would drive around the park or down Ocean Parkway before coming home to study.

I never liked Poly Prep. It was too big. I felt lost. I seemed to have trouble with my lessons. I didn't get on well with the other boys. They resented me because they thought my parents had money. I had been brought up under too-sheltered circumstances to be able to get on well with such a mixture of boys in such large numbers as there were at Poly Prep. I belonged to a debating class, but do not remember much about it. The principal thing I remember about Poly Prep, and which stuck with me for quite a while, were the marching songs for the athletic teams, especially the football team.

[My father went from Poly Prep to Calisan School and, when that folded, he attended Berkeley School.]

After the panic of 1907, when Father sold his home in Brooklyn and gave up the joint tenancy with Uncle Gov of the house at Oyster Bay, we moved to New York to the old San Remo Hotel on Central Park West. . . .

At the age of eleven I started selling for my father lumber, baled shavings, and sawdust in carload lots, to retail lumber yards, feed dealers and to dairy farms, week days in the summer time and on Saturdays in the winter time.

At Berkeley School I was on the senior football, basketball, tracking and fencing teams. I was manager of a tennis team and helped coach the baseball team.

I was a member of the crack Infantry Company of the school, which entered many competitive drills. I also belonged to one of the Gatling Gun Battalions.

The nervousness, the tension, and the excitement of a competitive company and Gatling Gun Squad drills that we entered into in the State of New York, winning first prize in every instance, was greater than any of the thrills enjoyed in playing on the various teams.

Football as we played it then was pretty rough, although I'm not at all certain but what the personal injuries sustained were greater in basketball.

Somehow or other, I was never able to accomplish much with

41

small balls, such as tennis and baseball (except my own testicles, and they mostly got me into trouble). This I also found to be true later on, when I took up golf while Secretary to the Governor of New York.

I shall never forget my old boxing instructor at Berkeley, an ex-prize fighter who would maneuver me into a corner of the gym and refuse to let me out of the corner until I punched my way out.

While my grandfather lived, I eagerly made it a point to obtain good marks in mathematics. He, an excellent engineer, was anxious for his grandson to excel with the figures. At no time during his life did I fail to lead in my mathematic classes, usually obtaining averages of from 98 to 99 in geometry, algebra, arithmetic, etc.

I also did well in Chemistry and with Physics.

Languages stumped me, although I was very fond of German. I traced my pro-German sympathies prior to our entry into the World War to the liking I acquired while at school for my old German Professor, Dr. Paul Adrian Scharff.

Dr. Scharff was a typical German martinet and gave me sufficient demerits for dittoing a German sentence I was supposed to write out twenty-five times, to break my record of perfect deportment which I had maintained during my entire schooling at Berkeley, and for which I was given a special honor medal each year.

In the light of my unruliness in later life it is hard to believe that I ever could have conducted myself as the perfect little gentleman should.

Perhaps Dr. Scharff's handing me what I considered the unde-served demerits in such large numbers that it was impossible for me, no matter how hard I worked, to get them off or bring back my average in deportment, changed my attitude considerably on the conduct side of my life—just as the death of my grandfather lessened my interest in mathematics.

We had a drawing teacher at Berkeley, a Miss Hyde, a rather sporty bitch. It was generally assumed that some of the older boys were having affairs with her.

The senior class room was on the ground floor facing both West End Avenue and 72nd Street. The school building was on the southeast corner. Opposite, on the northeast corner, lived the Aldrich family. All my last winter I was having quite a flirtation across the width of 72nd Street, with Maude Aldrich, one of Spencer Aldrich's daughters. . . .

Next to the Aldrich house on 72nd Street was a boarding house in which lived a rather attractive woman. I should say she was about

35 years old at the time and lived alone. About her only activity was riding at Durlands Academy on West 66th Street. Most of the senior class flirted with her regularly, in fact spent a good deal of their idle moments doing so.

On one occasion when several of us were standing near one of the school windows we opened our pants and showed her our stiff cocks. We waved dollar bills to her and then laid them on top of our penises.

For some unknown reason we never met her. She never managed to be out when we were out and we either didn't have nerve enough or were not ingenious enough to meet her by calling.

Ten years later when Secretary to the Governor, I was in the Horse Show Ring at the New York State Fair at Syracuse with the Governor and the Horse Show Commissioners, when much to my embarrassment this same woman of the Berkeley days rode past on a splendid blue ribbon-winning animal and bowed to me most cordially. Later that day I met her when she was presented to the Governor and we reminisced on the conduct of ubiquitous school boys.

She hardly seemed a day older than she appeared when we were at school, and was just as attractive, but for some reason she did not appeal to me physically or excite me the least bit then.

On the West End Avenue side of Berkeley was a school for girls. Attending that school was a particularly attractive Jewish girl from Savannah. The whole school was after her. There were frequent fist fights to see who would take her to the movies at Loewes Sherman Square.

While we all knew this girl and took her to the movies, and exposed ourselves to her in the window, she reciprocating from her school window across the street by showing us her cunt, I don't think any of us ever made her. I know I didn't, because I didn't get my first "piece of tail" until quite a few years later.

One night Mrs. August Belmont brought Vivian Martin to Berkeley School to entertain the senior class. "That was a night!"— Louis Mouquin's Uncle Henry, then the owner of Henri's Restaurant, supplied the refreshments, and what pastry!

During the festivities some of us went across the top of the roofs of several houses on 72nd Street to a girls' school in the middle of the block, where we sneaked into the room of one of the boarders on the top floor. The girls were in their nighties. What a time we had loving them. Nothing happened—no one got a fuck. On our way back to school, one of the house owners took us for burglars and called the police, but by the time the police arrived we were all back eating French pastry and ice cream.

For some years after that I had quite a distant crush on Vivian Martin, going to all her plays, and sending flowers and mash notes to her dressing rooms.

At the turn of the century, women's skirts were so long that when they had to run it was necessary for them to pick them up quite high. This was true even when they crossed the streets.

It was a favorite stunt with two or three of us—the bright well-brought up young men of nice families and good schools,—to stand on street corners and call to the women crossing, to lift their skirts higher, and to remark to one another in loud voices that we would like to see "it" "clear up," and similar brilliant statements, and to feel very hellish about it all.

Once in a while on blustery days, we would wander down to the Flatiron Building to watch the wind blow the women's skirts about, exposing shapely ankles or a bit of hose.

Sometimes after making such bright remarks to the passing girls we would, out of fear of being arrested or bawled out by some hardy dame, run a block or so to get away from any trouble that might arise.

While going to Berkeley, and playing football, I met a girl in the subway one afternoon on the way home from Van Cortland Park. She was a Jewess named Amy Green. Her father was in the jewelry business and she a student at Wadleigh High.

Although she was somewhat older, I always took her to the school dances. I learned lots about the art of kissing from her.

My mother did not approve of my interest in Amy but, as she always did for peace sake, she invited Amy to our home, entertained her, and chaperoned her on several school parties. It was a burning adolescent affair while it lasted and it lasted quite a while.

At the San Remo Hotel I had my room decorated with seductive school banners and the college posters that were so popular in those days.

My sister Elise frequently brought her girl friends home in the afternoon. There was one girl who was older than my sister but not as advanced as Elise in her studies. This girl, whose name I do not recall, would slip into my den where we would feel one another all over.

Loving in those days consisted principally of kissing, passionately tight embraces, and coming in my pants. I understood but little of the actual sexual function.

44

My enthusiasm for professional baseball was very keen. The famous pitcher Christy Matthewson was my idol. I attended the World Series by waiting in line all night with breakfast and lunch put up by my mother so that I would be sure of a seat in the bleachers. The thrills of those games were real thrills. I would bite all my finger nails off down to the flesh at every game.

Years later, at a World Series opening game, I walked across the ball field behind the band with the Governor of the State of New York, the Mayor of the City, and the best dressed woman in New York, the fashion editor of *Harper's Bazaar,* Helen Koues, and sat in the box of honor, without experiencing anything like the thrill or joy that I felt at the World Series game which I saw after waiting in line all night with my fifty cents and my lunch.

At that time in my imagination I was having a violent love affair with my cousin Millie Ford, whom I saw occasionally. In later years Millie's older sister, Rosette (Ford) King—now herself a divorcee—spent much of her time conspiring with your mother against me, and telling Ellen of her suspicions as to my amours. . . .

For many years the boys at Berkeley had published a monthly school paper, but it had not been successful. In fact it had always lost money. It carried over a deficit from year to year of printers' bills, etc.

My last year at school I was elected business manager of the paper, the "Berkeley Folio." I sold enough advertising to pay off all the back debts amounting to more than $500, permit the editors to get out the best school paper that had ever been gotten out in that school and to leave the publication with a balance in the treasury of $1000 to the good at the end of the year.

The final issue, the May number in 1911, was a booklet that compared favorably with any college year book of the time, particularly as to advertising linage. . . .

Like all boys of my day, I loved the *Buffalo Bill Wild West Show.* I liked the Circus too, but that I outgrew to the point where it bored me. But I never outgrew the thrill of the *Buffalo Bill Wild West Shows* during their entire existence.

How eager I always was to see Buffalo Bill's shows, and how frightened I would be when I got to them! More than once I pissed in my pants from fright and nervousness witnessing the exciting capers of the Wild West performance. The Indians and the sham battles always got me. . . .

* * *

45

Besides having flat feet, or fallen arches, my teeth were crooked, and a great deal of time and money were spent on straightening them. They were of rather a chalky substance which added to the difficulty.

I never minded going to Dr. Whitman's, wearing plates for my fallen arches, or doing my foot exercises, but I loathed the dentist and still loathe all dentists. The dentist Mother took me to had a dingy office and I thought he took a particular delight in hurting me as much as possible. My teeth were always bad. All my life I've been troubled with abscesses. Whether or not the braces put on my teeth in childhood in an effort to straighten them helped weaken the bone and hasten decay, I will never know. For years I've worn upper and lower bridges, dating back as far as 1920 (at 44 I had all my upper teeth removed and an upper plate put in).

When we lived on 74th Street I was operated on the second time for my tonsils. I had had my adenoids removed in a previous operation.

As was the custom in those days, the operation was performed on me at home. When I came out of the ether I felt so fine that I let out a yell which brought on a severe hemorrhage, and I damned near bled to death. . . .

Dandruff in an aggravated form has been a bug-bear all my life. When I was between 15 and 16 years of age, the barbers predicted that if I didn't have my dandruff cured, all my hair would fall out before I was twenty-five—the dandruff was never cured, and my hair today is as thick as it ever was, and that's some thick.

Lawrence Groat, a school mate, who lived at Cauldwell, N.J., and I went around a great deal together.

Larry introduced me to a girl that lived up on St. Nicholas Avenue and 180th Street near where he lived.

I met her first at a party given at the Hotel Montclair, in Montclair, N.J. There was an observation platform on the roof of the hotel, and we went up there to look at the New York skyline, but instead I looked at her cunt and she at my cock.

I took quite a fancy to this little bitch, and called on her many times at her home in New York.

On one particular occasion, when I undid my pants, and showed her my tool, she took my cock in her hands, caressed it and played with it most tenderly and affectionately.

This was the first time that any girl had ever jerked me off or that I had ever had my hand up inside a woman's cunt.

She excited me so, playing with me, that I came all over the piano keys, which were near where we were standing—she had a busy time getting those keys washed off before her mother and father returned home.

The next time I called, she had a thing of rubber which she placed over the end of my stiff prick, to keep the cream from getting all over the furniture when she jerked me off—I shot a pretty healthy load, and she was more concerned about the furniture than about our clothes.

Although I saw much of this girl, for the best part of the year, I never screwed her—maybe I didn't know enough, or how.

Father's work at the Gas Company as Superintendent of the 18th Street Station was of such a character that particularly on bad winter nights, he found it necessary to remain at the office or be on call at home, so we had one of the very early telephones. It was a huge arrangement nailed up on the wall, with batteries in a box on the floor, and you had to crank it to make it work. It was even cruder than the arrangement that one still finds today in some of the remote rural districts of this country.

After finishing school, I went to work for Father. He had a secretary called May F. During his absences from the office, and in fact whenever we were alone, May and I would make love. May was the first woman that I ever completely undressed. For years I was very devoted to her. I always suspected that Father was, too.

When business picked up, Father hired another girl, Florence H.

I took her to the old Hans Restaurant on Park Row one day for luncheon.

She was a ritzy bitch. When we returned from luncheon, the odor of liquor on her breath was very strong. Della Hugg, Father's cashier, always an old maid at heart although married twice, reported Florence's condition to Father, and he watched us closely thereafter.

One morning he caught us in the mailing room. I was lying on top of Florence on the mail sacks. They were dirty, but softer than the floor. Nothing had happened, except that I had come in my pants. But Father decided to take, instead of the bull by the horns, the bitch by the forelock, so to speak, before we got to screwing, so he fired poor Florence. What justice!

When I was ten I was so large for my age that it was impossible for Mother to buy me any ready-made ribbed boys' long stockings to go with my short trousers—knickerbockers for men, for sports wear or otherwise, were not then the style. In fact, they were unknown, unheard of.

47

Since I flatly refused to wear stockings similar to those worn by women, there was nothing left to do but put me in long pants.

Shortly after the auspicious occasion, I went out selling lumber, baled shavings and sawdust for Father, especially after school hours and on Sundays and holidays.

About the time I finished school, Father and I had a fuss over some girl of mine that he objected to, and so I set up in printing and stationery for myself.

I sold stationery to my friends and relations, and printing to customers of Father's. I had a small office at 29 Broadway, and a little room at the old Hotel San Remo on Central Park West and 74th Street.

Copies of some of the jobs that I printed as well as copies of labels and stationery will be found in my scrap books.

From this, I became active in the wholesale wax paper business, putting up special rolls of 24 sheets, about 16 x 22, under the trademark label "Ward's Sunshine Brand." I sold these rolls to stationers in cartons of two or more dozen rolls to a carton. The stationers in turn sold them to school children for wrapping up their sandwiches in order to keep them moist until luncheon time at school.

These rolls of wax paper were a real novelty then, parents previously having been accustomed to wrapping their children's luncheons with wet napkins or cloths.

I sold large quantities of wrapping paper and thin sheets of wax paper in case lots to the retail florists in New York City for wrapping their flowers. . . .

Larry Groat went with me to Bayhead, N.J., the first summer after I finished school for a two weeks vacation.

My mother and sister were already at Bayhead. In fact, they had been spending the summer there.

We stayed at the Grenvil Arms. Also staying there were two or three families from Baltimore, and the Hydes from Plainfield, N.J.

Helen Hyde was a cousin of Elise's friend Helen (Montgomery) Orrick, a girl from Trenton, N.J. Helen once told me that the way to win a woman, particularly a woman popular with men, was to affect at all times complete indifference to her obvious charms. That is damned sound advice but hard as hell to follow, and if followed doesn't always work.

On our first day at Bayhead, Larry and I took a walk along the boardwalk where we spied two girls. Feeling kittenish and desirous of attracting the attention of the girls I pushed Larry off the board-walk several times.

At first they giggled, and then became most indifferent to our pranks, behaving just as all girls do under such circumstances.

Later, back at the hotel, Larry and I were introduced to one of the girls, Virginia Page, of Baltimore, and her mother, Mrs. William Carter (Chisholm) Page.

It was some time before either Larry or I were able to get Virginia to introduce us to the other girl, her sister, Ellen Page. In fact, she neglected that little detail for several days.

I had been brought up in the High Episcopal Church, going regularly to St. Mary's in New York. I was almost a religious fanatic —I did, and still do, all things in extremes. There appears to be no middle course for me. There never has been—I must either be either all one way or all the other.

When I met Ellen Page and rushed her I was going regularly not only to early morning services but to 11 o'clock services as well. At the time it distressed me greatly that she did not attend both services.

Shortly before I met Ellen, I met Helen Hyde. These two girls were a study in contrasts. They were both debutantes. Both Junior Leaguers. Helen in New York—Ellen in Baltimore. They had both lived abroad, and had had part of their education over there. They were both society leaders in their respective cities. Helen was strong, active, energetic, athletic, a wonderful horse woman, a perfect shot, a wonderful hunter, and oh, boy! how she could swim. Your mother, on the other hand, was typically southern. Her Virginia and Mary-land ancestry and habits were spread all over her. She was slow, sleepy, quiet and languid about everything. I do not suppose that Ellen was ever proficient in any sport. It was even difficult for her to concentrate on driving a Ford flivver.

Day after day, while I was at Bayhead that summer, Helen Hyde and I would drive over in her car to a place where they had riding horses back of Point Pleasant. We would ride miles and miles cross country at full gallop. It must have been hell on the horses, bringing them in just all wringing wet and worn out—some young lovers are that way—prone to ride their *horses* hard. After the ride, we would jump into Helen's car and race the Pennsylvania R.R. train, beating the locomotives to the crossing, back to Bayhead. Before we were hardly dry ourselves from our ride, we would don our bathing suits, plunge into the ocean and swim the whole length of the Bayhead boardwalk and back. More than once after such a swim I would see stars as I stepped out on the beach.

Recalling Ellen's lack of concentration while driving a car reminds me how often I heard you as a small boy in Morristown shriek in alarm at your mother: "Mother, you're on the wrong side of the road!—Mother, don't you see you're going to drive up on the sidewalk! Mother, don't you see the red light!" etc. etc. Ellen, coming to with much amazement, would be much annoyed with herself and you. She invariably went by traffic lights. Only the patience and consideration of the Morristown traffic cops prevented her from being a constant visitor to the traffic court.

At the Grenvil Arms there was an old man of eighty, named Keeler. He paid your mother much attention. He was a man of means. He showered her with many presents. The colored porter at the Grenvil Arms still talks about those days. I tried to keep pace with Keeler. He asked Ellen to marry him. He promised her a beautiful home, trips to Europe and anything her heart might desire in the way of material things.

I extended my vacation two weeks, commuting every day between Bayhead and New York—the round trip a four hours journey —just in order to pay court to your mother.

Toward the end of the summer, I began to lose some of my intense religious interest. The Keeler competition and your mother's purely passive interest in the church seemed to cool my religious ardor.

In the fall, when I visited Ellen at Sudbrooke, we quarreled over the fact that while she had promised to marry me, she was at the same time engaged to an Englishman named Jack Goodwin.

Goodwin was dropped from the running after he wrote Mr. Page and asked him if he would give him (Goodwin) a five dollar-a-week job in Mr. Page's bank, The Calvert Bank of Baltimore, Md.

While I had been far from perfect in my thoughts, I had not screwed any woman up until the time I knew Ellen. But after we agreed to disagree at Sudbrooke, and the engagement was defunct, with the resultant heartbreaks which always follow such decisions, I decided I should go about more with women who could "learn me."

I don't know which of the love severances was the severest; my first break with Ellen or the time that Marjorie Drake of Kingston turned me down (may her soul rest in peace).

Eventually I picked up with a woman whose name I have forgotten and who was much older than I. She was the mistress of Finley S., the husband of Helen G. It was this woman who was my seducer.

I still remember my mixed feelings of emotion on that occasion —the burning passion that she aroused in me, and then—when the realization of what had actually happened dawned upon me—the fear.

I was thoroughly frightened after it was all over, because for years Father had told me of the terrors of venereal diseases. Told me of the men and women that his Uncle Dr. Gouverneur Smith had shown him in the alcoholic ward at Bellevue, shown him when Father was still a boy. Men and women rotting with syphilis. Men and women whose hands, legs, eyes, ears and other parts of their anatomy, were being eaten away, as they lay decaying in their cots in the Bellevue ward.

I was afraid—afraid, yes, terribly afraid, that something awful might happen to me from the result of that first intercourse.

From that woman's bed I went directly to Dr. Williams, the family physician, and told him of my sexual debauche. He gave me some salve to rub on my cock and also injected some liquid in the opening at the head of my penis.

He told me of the experiences he had had with syphilitic patients. He said he would never screw a woman who had ever been screwed before. That no matter how careful the doctors were, or how soon the disease was treated after the infection, that it would come back to plague one through life, either in the form of insanity in later years, or being passed through the wife to the child or children, unto the third and fourth generation.

Doc Williams observed that it was a ball-bearing universe—that the world would not revolve if it were not for the stiff pricks—that all boys were born with cunt on their brains and were not real boys until they had wallowed in the mire—that girls, too, were given to having thoughts of cocks in their heads most of the time.

He told me that no matter where I was, or what I was doing, I would always unconsciously find a woman amongst all the women in a group that I knew instantly and instinctively I could screw if I so desired. That I could recognize the fact by simply looking into the woman's eyes. He nicely predicted that in the end that would be my downfall. That I would be attracted to those weaker women, that I could not resist them, that I would take them. I fear his analysis and predictions have been true so far in my life.

Dr. Williams also told me that night that because of my height many women subconsciously would assume that my prick was in the same proportion to the rest of my body. A fallacy because men's pricks have no relation to their physical size. Small men often have large instruments and tall men often have small ones. In this I hasten to add that I am not speaking for myself—to the best of my knowledge my instrument has, to say the least, always been considered adequate.

With my sexual escapade behind me, I became intensely interested in Jacob Riis and the social welfare work he was doing. I read incessantly those books that dealt exclusively with cures for the type of social ills that existed then in the overcrowded East Side. I avidly read:

Books on prostitution
Books on the slums
Books on political government
Books on economics
Books on philosophy
Books on psychology
Books on psycho-analysis
Books by Freud, Jung, etc.
I gradually absorbed the doctrine of Karl Marx.
I became a devoted follower of John Spargo (the faker).

The more I read and the more I studied, accumulating my own library as I went along, the more I doubted and questioned the religious faith of my childhood.

My first year out of school I was chairman of the Heavenly Rest Church Committee for the welfare of the young boys of the parish. This committee concerned itself largely with the young boys living in the vicinity of the Heavenly Rest Parish. . . .

Elise was confirmed at St. Thomas's and there I met Dr. Ernest Stires, the rector, now the Bishop of Long Island. . . .

I went to Dr. Stires and told him of my doubts, my questions, my misgivings—I asked him to explain the unexplainable in the doctrines and teachings of the Episcopal Church. His answers were weak, unsatisfactory, unconvincing.

Stires told me I must accept certain statements at their face value, that I must not try to delve into the past too deeply.

Stires' inability to proffer some hope . . . which I could grasp, was the straw that broke the camel's back. That drove me far afield from the faith of my mother—a faith the belief in which was so great that I had gotten out of a sick bed as a child, while we were living in Brooklyn, to be carried (at my own request) to the church around the corner from us, in order that I might be confirmed in the Episcopal faith.

There is nothing in the world more comforting, more satisfying, more wonderful, more beautiful, than a perfect faith in the teachings of one's own church.

While we were living at the San Remo, I had an affair with a girl named Jane. She was one of the telephone operators at the old hotel. I screwed her only a few times, but I experienced real joy and pleasure in her simple society, especially in her little room on lower 8th Avenue. And it was many years before I shook the scent of her out of my system.

There was a French waitress at the San Remo who often walked with me around the lake in Central Park at night. She would play with my prick as we sat on the park bench, kissing my tool and balls all over. I believe she was the first woman who ever kissed my penis. I loved playing with her wet, hot cunt. She used some cheap, insidious perfume on her pussy. She was the most passionate girl I had met up to that time. Finger-fucking her in the park was a real joy, and how she loved it!

There came to the San Remo a girl and her mother. Shortly after her arrival she picked up an acquaintance with Elise, with the result that we met shortly.

Mother and daughter lived in an apartment on the floor above us. I often walked with her to the elevator or up the stairs to her apartment, stealing a kiss on the way—what a thrill it gave me.

One day, after she had been in the hotel a week or so, I called on her and we loved. She was very passionate. She went perfectly wild and frantic when I touched her. Her hair came down—she clung to me—she rolled over and over on her mother's bed—she pretended to be greatly frightened for fear that her mother would catch me. I didn't screw her—I wonder why? Perhaps she was too excited—perhaps she was too frightened. Nevertheless I didn't. I was afraid. Her terrific passion unnerved me. Then, too, she was so near home. Knew my sister, my mother, and our friends in the hotel.

This voluptuous bitch suggested that we exchange love messages, that we use an intricate code in doing so. This surreptitious nonsense was kept up for a while through sly means and fervent love. My God! what a hot baby she was!

One day her mother set up a howl. Accused me of having sexual relations with her daughter and raised hell. That episode was enough for mother and father. They determined that I must go away. So I was sent to North Carolina, to work in a lumber mill at Edentown.

They claimed that I had been neglecting business, being wholly interested in my studies and girls.

At Columbia University I was taking night courses in Economics, studying railroad transportation, and politics.

With the cooperation of Professor G. G. Huebner of the University of Pennsylvania, and with many other leading authorities including former Secretary of the Interior, Franklin Knight Lane, I wrote a monograph known as "Car Shortages and Surpluses."

The purpose of the monograph was to make a comprehensive study and offer a suggested solution of the car-shortage and surplus problem that then confronted the country, particularly during certain seasons of the year.

I also attended lectures on Socialism at Carnegie Lyceum, many of them given by John Spargo. While attending the lectures at Carnegie Lyceum, and a few days before I left for the South to work in the lumber mill, I picked up a very beautiful girl on a Fifth Avenue bus.

She lived at Riverside Drive and 97th Street.

She was a Ziegfeld Folly beauty—in the first Ziegfeld Show— she came up out of a pie in the center of the table wearing very scanty attire.

The girl's name was Julian B., and I went home with her.

She had a very attractive apartment. I was unsophisticated. I didn't understand a lot about life. I don't even to this day. She took me to bed with her. She was without doubt the most ravishing beautiful young creature I had ever laid eyes on. She screwed the very life out of me, time after time, and when we finished I was dead to the world.

A day or two later she was taken to a private sanitarium for some treatment which was never clear to me.

She gave me to understand that there was a man very much interested in her, who was older and who had a lot of money.

I didn't have any money. I never have had any, and I don't suppose I ever will, and at the time that seemed to let me out of the picture.

Then I left for the lumber mills. From Norfolk, Va., on my way south, I sent Julian a postal card. . . .

I don't know why this fits in here, but I suppose it is the connecting thought between Julian and the Follies which calls to mind the theatre. Father and I were in the habit of attending all first nights together, usually sitting in the peanut gallery—they had them in those days. They were the second or third balcony. We were especially fond of George M. Cohan and his shows—*The Seven Keys to Baldpate; Forty-Five Minutes from Broadway; Yankee Doodle Here I Come,* etc. William Gillette was our favorite—*Secret Service; Held by the Enemy; Sherlock Holmes;* and others of his very interesting repertoire. William Faversham in *The Squaw Man;* and Cyril Maude in *Grumpy,* were other favorites of ours in those days.

On the way south to North Carolina, I took the boat as far as Norfolk. There were a lot of Tammany Hall politicians on board, going to Woodrow Wilson's first inauguration in Washington via the water route. Wilson had beaten Teddy Roosevelt and Bill Taft in 1912 for the Presidency. I had been active in that campaign. How big and important the men who ran the political organizations in those days seemed to me then.

I placed a sort of halo above them all. They seemed so far away. So unapproachable. All whom I came to know in later years intimately I found in so many instances lacking in the essentials I thought they possessed, utterly stupid about so many things in life and politics.

My idols then were such men as Frank Munsey, George Perkins, Elon Hooker, Van Valkenberg, Fred Davenport, Sr., and a host of others—all turned out to have feet of clay.

In many cases their careers had been 90% luck or opportunity; 10% ability.

How bungling they were about so many things, but I admired them then even if I grew to scorn them later.

But why should they be scorned? They were like all of us—mere creatures of happenstance.

There are a few clippings among my personal effects of my activities in behalf of Colonel Theodore Roosevelt's Presidential Campaign.

I admired Senator Hiram Johnson with almost as much fervor as I worshipped Colonel Theodore Roosevelt, Sr.

But there is only one out of the whole Bull Moose crowd that today still stands head and shoulders above all others in the field of politics and state-craft. That one, unfortunately for the nation, has not for many years graced a seat in active political life. That one is none other than former Senator Albert Beveridge, the most brilliant and able statesman of his day (Beveridge was still living in 1926 when these pages were written). . . .

* * *

On our arrival at Norfolk, we drove up to the old Jamestown Exposition grounds. Then our guide took us into the red light district where for the first time I saw houses of prostitution—"cribs."

The guide pointed out the cribs where you could get fucked for 50¢ and the ones where it cost $5.00; the houses where you could get niggers and the houses where whites and blacks mixed; houses where they made a specialty of frenching and the houses where they staged shows, daisy-chains, etc.

At many of the cribs the whores were standing in the doorways with little on, drumming up trade from the sailors and the passersby on the streets. At night it was not so bad, but in broad daylight it was a most unsavory and uncouth sight. In New York I have picked up many women of the streets—women who in those days plied their trade on Broadway, Sixth Avenue and Fifth Avenue—just as they do today; hounded from street to street by the police when they don't pay up, but permitted to do their business unmolested if they pay the proper authorities.

I have never screwed such women, but have always had them jerk me off when going with them to their rooms or even while standing in dark doorways or alleyways on the street.

Fear of disease always prevented me from fucking street-walkers.

Larry Groat and I often when picking women up on the street would walk off to some dark spot or areaway (there were many such when high stoops were in vogue) and have the cunts lift their skirts while we slipped a silver half-dollar or a dollar bill into their twats.

In all the times that Larry and I pulled that stunt, I do not recall one street-walker who ever objected to our frolicsome procedure.

There was a street-solicitor named Dater—an appropriate name —who was listed in the telephone book. She lived on upper Broadway. I always thought she took dope.

Her specialty was to jerk me off in her highly perfumed lace handkerchief. Her apartment was a busy spot. I doubt if I ever went there when there were not at least three or four other men there losing their loads at the same time in other rooms with different girls. She was the first woman I ever fucked between the tits.

At the lumber mill in Edentown, N.C., I had to be up in the morning at 5 o'clock to ride the logs.

When I first went to the mill I had to go out to the timber camp, handle the saw and the axe, then to the river, where the logs were bound together and shot down the rapids. Riding the logs was the most nerve-racking and dangerous work I have ever done. One false step and you're through.

After working in the woods and riding the logs, I went to work first in the sawmill and then in the planing mill.

In the sawmill and planing mill, we started to work at 8 o'clock in the morning, quit a half hour for lunch, and finished at 6:30 in the evening.

In my shack I slept on straw. Had a box for a chair, another box for my desk, and one for my toilet articles.

On Sunday, we congregated in town and there I learned that the leading white citizens had no hesitation in fornicating the black women thereabouts at their pleasure.

The postmaster, for example, had anywhere from five to six black babies a year left on his doorstep, yet no one criticized him, least of all his wife.

If a black man rapes a white woman south of the Mason-Dixon line, or makes any advances towards her which she repulses or accepts, he is shot at sight.

The justice of this southern point of view on negro-screwing is hard for northerners to comprehend. What is right for the whites should be right for the blacks, where sex is concerned.

In those days of prohibition in N.C., before we had National prohibition, I was often taken for a blind-tiger detective—a federal agent on the hunt for local liquor stills.

Huge quantities of liquor were shipped into this dry state almost daily, by the express agencies, from adjoining states. This was the packaged or more expensive type of liquor, not the local brew. I was not happy in Edentown. It was so hard to get on with the local talent. They were insulted so easily. Everyone carried a gun. It was always a gamble who would be quickest on the draw. I didn't stay there long enough to find out. But I stayed there long enough to learn about North Carolina Pine from the stump to the freight car, and to learn the life of a mill hand in a mill town, dependent on a company store.

The nigger mill hands were usually in hock to the company store for calico with which they had paid for their "hump."

On my return north, I stopped over at Baltimore and there I called on Rufus Goodenow, Jr. who was then the president of the Canton Box Company. I negotiated a contract between Rufus' box company and my father's company for the entire by-product output of the Canton Box Company.

Business completed, I dined with Rufus at the Maryland Club.

After dinner, he sent me in his car to the Union Station to catch the 8 o'clock train to New York.

While waiting for the New York train at the station, my urge to telephone, as usual, got the better of me, and I had the girl operator at the public phones in the station call Ellen—out of sheer cussedness, I guess.

When your mother answered, I chatted with her for a while. She invited me to call. Without a moment's hesitation I accepted.

I changed my Pullman reservation to the midnight train—by so doing I changed my destiny.

The visit was formal. I caught the midnight back to New York.

Two or three weeks afterwards, I wrote Ellen, and then, after a respectable length of time had elapsed, I received a polite reply.

From time to time, as business took me to Baltimore, I called upon her. In the spring, we gathered a lot of settlement children together, children whom she had been looking after in her Junior League work, and carted them all off to the circus in the "original" Baltimore taxis.

The first year I met your mother at Bayhead, the Pages went to Sudbrooke in the fall and lived in a boarding house. But this particular summer they took a house in Sudbrooke, a nice old place as I recall it.

One evening while walking down by the Jewish country club, I again asked Ellen to marry me, and to my surprise she consented.

It was the last evening in July of 1914. The following day I called on her father at his bank. Told him that I was going to marry his daughter and asked for his consent—it was the day that the World War broke out.

My visit with Mr. Page was very pleasant. Nothing occurred that would separate it from a most casual business chat.

All that summer and the next winter, I practically commuted between New York and Baltimore, going down to Baltimore on the Congressional Limited of the Pennsylvania Railroad, coming back on the Midnight.

On one of my visits to Baltimore I called for your mother at a party. She was in evening dress. When we got to the Page home I protested that her decollete was much too low. She countered with the statement that her mother had approved of the cut, to which I replied that if Mrs. Page had approved of such a low neck dress she was an immoral woman.

The two Rosalies who were listening at the head of the stairs became enraged—told your grandfather Page. He became infuriated at what he considered a slur on his wife's name—sent for me to come to the bank. When I called he said I must never enter his house again—no one could speak so disrespectfully of his wife—blah, blah, blah.

I was not to phone, write or see Ellen again.

That night I became greatly depressed at the thought that I might lose her. Dick Oulahan, Jr. the son of *The New York Times* correspondent in Washington, a boy who had gone to school with me, took me and tried to comfort me. Finally my mother came to Baltimore, called on the Pages and patched it all up again.

Ellen often said she was not at all interested in the affairs of the heart that I might have had before I knew her.

One evening while we were sitting on a bench in Mount Royal Square, I started to tell her about the Baudin affair, and that my indiscretions had occurred between the time our first understanding was terminated and our friendship renewed.

When I realized how she was taking it and how upset it made her, I passed it all off lightly, telling her that she had misunderstood me—that I had not meant to convey the impression that I had ever actually stayed with a woman—simply that I had made love to her. This cleared the atmosphere.

Perhaps I should not have rectified it. But that is something I shall never know.

It has always been my idea that a man has no right to ask of a woman any more than he is able to give in return.

I never questioned your mother, nor did I want to know whether she had ever had an affair with any other man before she knew me.

Subsequent events proved conclusively that she had never been with anyone before she married me.

She on her part always labored under the erroneous impression that I had never had any experience before our honeymoon.

There was a manicurist in the barbershop in the Emerson Hotel in Baltimore by the name of Pearl G.

Pearl was very anxious to come to New York. Several times after having spent the evening with Ellen and having become worked up to a high degree of excitement, I had taken Pearl for taxicab rides and screwed her.

The barbershop in the old Manhattan Hotel in New York was the finest barbershop in town, and was the most difficult one for either a barber or manicurist to get a job in. One of the girls quit to live with a prominent banker, and I asked Ellen if she would object if I gave the Emerson Hotel manicurist a letter of introduction to the owner of the Manhattan Hotel barbershop.

Ellen approved. I gave Pearl the letter of introduction and she landed the job, which she kept with them and their successors for nearly twenty years.

Besides being a good screw, Pearl was one of the best manicurists I ever had do my nails.

Everyone in the Manhattan Barber Shop suspected that Pearl was my mistress, but as I continued to go to the same manicurist I had always gone to before Pearl came into the shop, that suspicion was soon dispelled.

From the San Remo Hotel, we moved to an apartment on the northeast corner of Riverside Drive and Eighty-Fourth Street—120 Riverside Drive. This was done primarily to have a guest room for Ellen while she visited New York during our engagement.

While living on Riverside Drive, I had occasion to use the subway almost daily.

It was terrible then; the people were packed in like sardines—and I mean sardines. They didn't have the Lexington Avenue lines then. Only the one subway, north and south.

One day in the subway jam, I was pushed so close to an attractive female that I could feel her cunt up against my cock. I got so hot that I came in my pants.

Returning one evening from the office, I took the train at Wall Street and got off at 72nd Street. I was jammed in the doorway of the express, face to face with a lovely creature, who put her hand down, opened my trousers, took out my cock and played with it. My coat and her clothes covered the procedure. Naturally I came, over her clothes and partly over mine.

I left the train at 72nd Street, and I had got upstairs and was cleaning myself off in the washroom when I discovered that while this beauty was jerking me off she had also picked my pockets of all the cash therein.

I had many "feeling" parties with various women in the subway. Some girls I got to know quite well, and have known for years.

I can't recall any woman ever having made the slightest objection when being played with in the subway, although today it is a dangerous proceeding—liable to arrest.

Many of them entered into the "spirit of the occasion," purposely rubbing themselves up against me.

Several times I've had men, particularly in the doorways of the subway trains, try to play with me. When such advances were made I have not repulsed them—when they felt my cock I felt theirs in return.

60

The amount of that sort of immorality that took place in the subway trains in those days before the congestion was relieved by the new subways, and may still exist, must have been tremendous. . . .

A considerable amount of the toilet immorality has been eliminated by closing the men's and women's toilets early in the evening and keeping them closed during the night.

I have often wondered how many young girls have felt a man's prick for the first time in the subway train, how many young boys have had their cocks sucked, or been buggered in the public toilets of the subway stations.

It isn't possible to visit these public toilets without finding men standing around either masturbating, or in the act of abusing one another.

I met the beautiful Emma S., the present eminent socialite, Mrs. Hamilton P., in the subway, while rubbing my hard cock against her cunt.

Emma lived on West 72nd Street at the time with her sister, and we were both going downtown to our offices on the same train. Emma played with me and I played with her.

We became fast friends and have been devoted to one another for years. Before I was married the second time, Emma used to come to my office frequently after she was through work for a drink and/or a screw. She worked for the Harrimans and my office was just across the street.

Elizabeth C., the present Mrs. William I., another social registerite, was a subway pickup, and by subway pickup I mean I met her when I felt her cunt in the subway with my hand, and she played with my cock. At the time Elizabeth was Courtlandt Nicoll's secretary. Afterwards she became secretary to Paul D. Cravath. I've known Elizabeth many many years, and in that time have screwed her often. She was always a good lay, but was particularly effective when she used to come to me at the Plaza Hotel for quick screws while I was Secretary to the Governor.

In Detroit, the barbers at the Statler Hotel, years and years ago, gave their customers cards to houses of prostitution.

In one of the houses I visited, the walls were all of glass. The girls entered the room one after another, nude except for a light lace throw-over, and strode past the customers.

After picking out a girl, you went upstairs and were entertained in any manner you desired.

For $50 you could see a circus—men and women fornicating—blacks and whites—men sucking women—and women frenching men.

By frenching I mean women taking men's cocks in their mouths and sucking them off. Frenching is a favorite with the Jews. Jewish men are noted for preferring to have their cocks sucked instead of screwing. Many Jews pay Christian girls liberally to suck their cocks. Particularly if their wives have an aversion to cocksucking, although today Jewish women are becoming more and more adapted to their husbands' desires in this respect. The Madame of any house of assignation will bear this statement out.

Some of the girls in the Detroit house would love one another. Others would have men go down on them.

This was also true of the red light districts of Richmond, New Orleans, and San Antonio, Texas.

In New Orleans, and the Texas towns, women solicited their trade in automobiles, driving up alongside the curb and inviting their prospective customers to take a ride. Once in the car, you would be taken to their house of prostitution, where you paid your money and got your tail.

On the Hudson River night boat I met a grass widow, by the name of Jane B.

Jane was a splendid character, managing her own insurance business, supporting and educating her two children. She was probably one of the best liked women in Syracuse.

Jane was unfortunate in having a worthless drunkard for a husband.

I grew very fond of Jane B. and often visited her on my trips through the state of New York, going out to her lovely cottage on Onandaga Lake.

There was Mrs. B., who built up a flourishing inexpensive photographic establishment, with many branches in New York City as well as throughout the country, thirty-two in all.

Mrs. B. was one of the most passionate women I have ever known.

One time I met her in New Haven on her way back from her Boston branch. We went to the Taft Hotel where we spent the night, having our dinner with much champagne served in our room.

That woman literally devoured me. When she got through I don't suppose there was a place on my body that had not been bitten. I was black and blue all over.

We dined in the nude, fucked during the meal, and afterwards.

How she fucked me and sucked me! I was crazy about her, and in fact so nuts that she could have done almost anything she wanted and gotten away with it.

After dinner we had a party in the bathtub, and again just before dawn as we arose to catch the New York sleeper.

We took one of the Boston to New York trains and engaged a drawing room. There we had another party en route to New York. She certainly used me up.

I wasn't worth a damn for several days.

I saw a good deal of her after that from time to time, generally meeting her in the tea room at the Prince George. In the darkness of that seductive, heavily shaded room we would play with ourselves under the tea tables.

During this period of my life, 1915-1917, I masturbated a good deal.

One of the women that I finger-fucked in the subway was a model in a wholesale dress house. I got to know her fairly well, calling on her frequently and screwing her often. Then I lost track of her.

Recently I met her on a Fifth Avenue bus. She was married and had growing children. She has a home over at Fort Lee. I can't remember her name, but she has become quite settled and suburbanitish in appearance.

One of the other girls I picked up in the subway I screwed in the motorman's booth on the rear end of the last car of the train one night going uptown.

Another girl that I picked up on a Fifth Avenue bus had a passion for wearing black lingerie, which appealed to me greatly. We were getting along very well until I discovered she had a lover who was keeping her, and that she really didn't have the job she claimed she had. She lived in 16th Street in one of those old houses that were remodeled; her name escapes me as I write.

On a business trip to Chicago via the Pennsylvania R.R., between Harrisburg and Altoona, I picked up a woman who got on the train at Altoona and rode to Harrisburg.

It was late at night and we were alone in the observation car. We had a few drinks of liquor.

When the train stopped because of some block the rear-end flagman went back with his red lanterns.

Going out on the back platform to see what was happening, the cool air, plus the alcoholic stimulation, plus the sexual excitement, did the trick. I hurriedly lifted her skirt and shoved my old prick into her as she stood with her back against the door of the car. The flagman was never out of sight, but he was oblivious to our pleasures as he walked down the tracks with his back to us—what a nice, juicy fuck she was!

In the summer of 1915, your mother and her family went to Madison, Conn. . . .

That summer, Ellen and I quarrelled on the beach at Madison.

I threatened to commit suicide. Ellen registered such indifference that there was nothing for me to do but to go out into the water with my clothes on. When I got out up to my neck she suggested that it might be well for me to turn around and walk back again, which I proceeded to do. The cold water had brought me to my senses, which helped her no end in adequately calling my bluff.

That fall we were married.

I was anxious to be married in time to get to Lake Mohonk before it closed for the season, so I suggested that we be married in September.

That was not satisfactory to Ellen.

She wanted to be married in October.

In order to be married in October, at a time sufficiently early so that we could make Lake Mohonk before the season closed, it was necessary for us to be married on a day when she began to be unwell.

I doubt if there was any event in my life that impressed me as little as the whole marriage ceremony, and for that matter any marriage ceremony.

I had not read the marriage service since a child in Sunday School and was not familiar with what was contained in the Episcopal Service.

The wedding was at the Page home in Baltimore. The house was packed. My father acted as best man.

Town Topics, the social scandal sheet of the day, in recording our engagement and wedding, continually referred to me as a person of great wealth, when all I had was the small salary of $3000 annually that I received from father's firm.

No matter how broke I may be, even to this day, people think of me as affluent, unless they are my intimates. . . .

As I stood before the improvised altar of palms and flowers— I hadn't the slightest idea what the service was—I merely repeated after the clergyman what he said verbatim. I did not make much of a go of it. The time that I really slipped, however, was when I said, instead of "with all my worldly goods I thee endow"—"with all THY worldly goods I thee endow."

1915-1920

We left for our honeymoon on the afternoon train over the Baltimore and Ohio for New York, having luncheon by ourselves in our drawing room on the train.

I was eager to caress your mother, being very excited, but I didn't get very far. She was very nervous and very tired. . . .

In New York we took the Montreal Express which was stopped at Poughkeepsie for us.

At the river front a motor boat was waiting to run us across the dark Hudson to Highlands.

After landing on the west shore, we went by motor car to Mountain Rest and then by horse and buckboard to the Lake Mohonk Hotel.

It was midnight when we arrived. The log fire in the fireplace was burning brightly in our attractive tower room overlooking the valley.

For some time I had been much concerned about my masturbating. Afraid of what it might be doing to me, what effect it might be having on me, although I had never, and have never, heard of anyone dying from it.

I had been abusing myself considerably as well as screwing many women. As I wanted children, I was fearful of the effect all this screw- and masturbating might have on my offspring.

While I tried hard to restrain myself from masturbating I never completely succeeded.

When the Lake Mohonk Hotel closed, we returned to New York, and it was not until we got to the St. Regis that I possessed my bride.

I made a pretty awkward attempt for a connoisseur.

When I finally succeeded, with great agony to us both, such a violent hemorrhage occurred that we became greatly alarmed, and I sent for Dr. Williams.

The doctor attributed the hemorrhage to the fact that the act occurred too soon after menstruation.

For several days Ellen was in such a serious condition that she was under the doctor's constant care. . . .

The first winter of our marriage we lived at the old Netherland Hotel on the corner of 59th Street and Fifth Avenue.

From the Netherland Hotel we went to live in a boarding house on 58th Street, an attractive old place, long since torn down, directly across from the apartment house Mother and Father were living in. We stayed there for quite a while and then moved to 550 Park Avenue, where we took an apartment and furnished it with our own furniture.

During our married life together, with but one exception, I never had intercourse with Ellen except when wearing a condom. I disliked condoms and never felt complete satisfaction with one on.

It was in the old boarding house on 58th Street that Ellen finally consented to have a party without a condom, so we might have a baby.

One try was sufficient, and you were born the following September in Baltimore.

From 550 Park Avenue we moved to 981 Madison Avenue so that we would be nearer the park for you, and anyhow we had to move from 550 as they were tearing down the apartment.

When you were born the war was still raging, but I was not in it.

I had taken an active part in the Preparedness Parade at the suggestion of my father. . . .

One day, after luncheon, as we were walking down Broadway together, Father asked me why I didn't drop in and see if they had formed a lumber trade division or a division of the parade of the Traffic Club, to which I belonged.

We were in the lumber business and I was an active member of the Traffic Club of New York, which organization was composed of the commercial and industrial railroad traffic managers of New York City. I was handling the traffic end of Father's business at that time, in addition to doing his advertising. . . .

They elected me a member of the executive committee of the parade, representing the Lumber Trade. . . .

I . . . marched at the head of the parade with the Grand Marshall and the Executive Committee in the early morning when it started.

Later in the afternoon, after the Lumber Trade had covered the line of march, I had command of half a dozen different trade divisions, which meant that I had to cover the whole line again for the third time.

The hardest march was the first one in the morning, when we were all dolled up in our cut-a-ways and high hats.

Photographs appearing in the *Evening Telegram* of that day show me in the front line with the leaders of the City's commercial, industrial and professional life who were on the Executive Committee.

At the time this country had not declared war, but the feeling for preparedness was running strong, regardless of the "peace at any price" antics of Woodrow Wilson and William Jennings Bryan.

Although of pro-German sympathies, I was an ardent advocate of preparedness.

When the war finally came, and we entered, I registered with the Draft Board. Because of my cowardly nature, and my inherent fear of personal conflict, I applied for exemption on the ground of having to support my wife and child, Ellen certifying to this necessity. My fallen arches would have disqualified me for active service, anyway.

This action, in which my father and mother encouraged me, was the first big error in my life. I should have gone as a volunteer private, and for years that fact haunted me. . . .

During the Preparedness Parade I had become very closely associated with Karl Behr, the tennis star. In fact, we were together in many activities during that period.

I organized the Lumber Trade Recruiting Stations of the Citizens Preparedness Organization which Colonel Charlie Sherrill set up after Governor Whitman had appointed him Adjutant-General for the State of New York. . . .

In the fall of 1917, Karl Behr and I organized the Mitchel Torchlight Parade and had five columns of fire companies converging on Madison Square Garden.

We put more men on the streets that night for John Purroy Mitchel than the total number of votes he received in the Borough of Manhattan.

The parade was an idea I sold Sam Koenig and Collin Woodward, who was in charge of the mass meeting of the Garden. Sam Koenig was Chairman of the New York County Republican Committee.

By having the parade, I felt sure we could pack the Garden and have big overflow gatherings outside. I enlisted Karl Behr's support, and we made a good job of it.

After the procession was under way, and the marchers were converging on Madison Square for the overflow meetings, I learned that the political party workers were not filling the old Madison Square Garden. The attendance was not coming up to Collin Woodward's expectation. So I turned many columns into the Garden until it was packed.

After completing the arrangement at Madison Square and the

Garden, I went up to 59th Street, where I met Colonel Theodore Roosevelt, former President of the United States. He had been speaking for Mayor Mitchel in Queens. I took the Colonel in my car down 3rd Avenue along the line of march. We drove down slowly. The roar of the applause that greeted the Colonel was tremendous rolling down the avenue, as he rode along the line. I will never forget it.

In bringing the former President to the line of march, the chauffeur was speeding, as is customary on campaign nights, and Roosevelt suggested that he drive with less haste. T.R. felt that to have any car he was in run over anyone would be most unfortunate.

As we approached the Garden, a Police Captain jumped on the running board, and Roosevelt went wild with enthusiasm over the Captain.

The Colonel had not seen the Captain since the Spanish-American War, when he had been one of the Colonel's Rough Riders.

In his excitement over meeting the Captain, the Colonel kept ordering the chauffeur to drive on. Much confusion was created as Teddy insisted upon discussing, with outbursts of exuberance, a fire that had taken place during Roosevelt's term as a member of the New York Police Commission.

The former President recalled by names the women and the children whom the Police Captain had rescued from the fire when the Captain was but a patrolman.

This delighted the officer, who was as excited over Roosevelt as Roosevelt was over meeting him.

We entered Madison Square Garden amid wild cheering and proceeded up the center aisle to the speaker's platform.

The speaker who was talking had no chance to continue. The crowd wouldn't let him. They demanded "Teddy."

The thrill of this momentous occasion has always remained vivid. While as a child I had sat in the pew back of the Colonel in the Church at Oyster Bay and had spoken to him when he called to me as we passed on the bridle paths near Sagamore Hill, I had never before had quite as close contact with him.

To me, like to thousands of others then, he was "our Teddy," the great hero of the day, whom I had always worshipped from afar.

During the course of Roosevelt's speech in favor of the re-election of Mayor Mitchel, and while denouncing "Red Mike" Hylan for his association with the anti-American and pro-German society, word came that Mitchel had arrived and was waiting outside.

After consulting with the Colonel in a whispered undertone I sent word out that the former President would be at least 15 minutes before finishing his speech.

I was seated beside the Colonel on the platform, where I kept in close contact with all that was transpiring.

Hardly two minutes had elapsed after sending word to Mitchel before the Colonel finished speaking.

Someone in the topmost gallery had yelled the query "What have *you* done to help win the war?"

Stopping abruptly in the middle of his speech, calling upon the crowd to be quiet while he answered the heckler, and warning the police not to throw the heckler out, the Colonel made his famous reply to the question as follows: "I applied to the exclusive Committee on Admissions for permission to participate in this war, in command of a regiment which I agreed to recruit. The exclusive Committee refused my application—they didn't like my politics, but I have given what to me is even dearer—a greater sacrifice than the giving of myself—I have given my sons who have gone forth to defend the honor of their country—one of my boys could not wait until we declared our intentions, but went and joined the French forces overseas before we entered the war."

Everyone knows what a sacrifice the Colonel had made because the son that was nearest and dearest to him, Quentin Roosevelt, was shot down and killed in a plane while flying over the German lines.

Knowing that there could be no other climax to his speech as dramatic as the one he had just obtained in replying to the heckler, Roosevelt turned and sat down amid the roar and yells of the crowd. A hurry call was sent to Mitchel and he appeared on the scene. . . .

That year I prepared for Mr. Willard Straight, a partner of J. P. Morgan, a complete study and analysis of the freight congestion in the harbor of New York.

That report I filed with Mr. Straight and from it, eventually, the plan for a joint Port of New York Authority to control the movement of all the railway and steamship lines entering the harbor of New York and the distribution of the freight and passengers, as well as the vehicular traffic was drawn. . . .

With the first Liberty Loan Campaign out of the way, Karl Behr and I pitched in and designed the first War Saving Stamp Posters which were ever printed.

The design that we used was afterwards altered from the Eagle to the Torch of Liberty.

Frederic W. Allen, the junior and the New York partner of Lee Higginson and Co., a large and old-established banking firm of Boston, was appointed War Savings Director for Greater New York.

In the organization which was set up in Allen's private office at Lee Higginson and Co. on Exchange Place, and afterwards moved to 51 Chambers Street, I was placed in charge of the organization of all the sales agencies, some 75,000 all told, in the Greater City.

I was also given charge of the trade divisions or the Commercial, Professional and Industrial groups, which brought thousands upon thousands of employers and employees into the campaign.

Hundreds of War Savings Societies were organized by me in the commercial and industrial units. . . .

I had to build these divisions up from nothing to 150 different commercial, industrial and professional groups.

I had charge of all the trade publicity on the subject of War Saving Stamps and Liberty Loans throughout the United States and continued to direct that publicity until George Creel's Bureau of Public Information was organized in Washington directly under the President. . . .

We had a meeting of the Milk Division one afternoon and I jokingly suggested that the milkmen should call up the dumbwaiter shaft each morning and inquire as to how many thrift stamps or War Saving Stamps the housewife wanted with her milk.

In those days New York Apartment houses abounded in dumb-waiters, or elevators, pulled up and down shaft by servants, housewives and delivery boys. Under present-day construction, the dumb-waiters are rapidly becoming extinct, service elevators being installed and deliveries being made direct to everyone's door.

Arthur Ferguson, the W. S. S. Director of Publicity of Greater New York, liked the story and released it.

Nearly every newspaper in the country carried it, which goes to show how a small feature story originating in New York rapidly spreads throughout the country. New York City is even better than Washington for the distribution of general news or propaganda; in fact, New York is better than any other city in the country. You can frequently get a story going out of New York, but can seldom get one coming in. . . .

Another feature which received a lot of publicity was when I arranged for Bird Millman to walk a tight-rope which I had hung from the base of the George Washington statue on the Sub-Treasury steps across Wall Street to the window of J. P. Morgan's private office.

From her perch on the tight-rope, Bird Millman in costume sold many stamps and succeeded in creating much publicity, both in the still pictures and newsreels, to say nothing of the news columns.

Miss Millman wore the costume that she always used in the circus. We got one amusing picture showing the Reverend Mr. Wilkinson, "The Bishop of Wall Street," standing beneath Miss Millman gazing up her shapely legs, ostensibly in the act of purchasing thrift stamps.

We set up tents in 59th Street and Columbus Circle, at Union Square, at Park Row, also one in Borough Hall, Brooklyn. Inside, in each of these tents—the outsides of which were draped in mourning— we placed a coffin, and in the coffin we put an animated figure of the Kaiser. As you gazed down upon him in all his glory, the picture would suddenly change and you would see merely a skull and bones.

At each tent we had a band which, day in and day out, played the funeral march, while mobs bought large strips of stamps in order that they might drive tacks into the Kaiser's coffin.

In order to drive a tack in the coffin, it was necessary to purchase a dollar's worth of thrift stamps.

All day long there were long lines waiting their turns to drive tacks into the coffin.

The business people occupying offices and stores within hearing distance of the band complained bitterly of the constant playing of the funeral dirge.

Eventually we dispensed with the band but the crowds continued to march past the Kaiser's coffin, driving in thousands of nails day after day until the Armistice.

On one occasion Houdini got into his strait jacket and shackels and was suspended by ropes midway in the air from the tower of the old Madison Square Garden.

In this position he extricated himself and slid down the rope to the delight of the onlookers.

This stunt collected large crowds, produced much publicity, and was successful in selling many stamps.

Throughout the campaign, we put on a daily performance of one kind or another at the top of the United Cigar Store window display projection in front of the Flatiron Building. . . .

* * *

As mentioned before, I first met Elizabeth C. (Mrs. William I.) in the subway. I again met her at Mineola where she was waiting for a friend at the Long Island R.R. Station.

The Mineola station was a conspicuous place, but we walked behind the station where she played with my cock, kissing it, while I finger-fucked her.

A few months later I met her again in the Concourse of the Hudson Tubes at 33rd Street, that is, the runway between the Pennsylvania Railroad Station and the Hudson Tube Terminal.

I did not recognize her at first, and my trousers were open with my old crowbar standing right up. My cock thought I was picking up something new and fresh that I had not met before.

Elizabeth squeezed my bare prick with her hand as she gave me a kiss there in the Concourse. Some might call this exhibitionism. I had on my overcoat so no one could see what was happening, except Elizabeth.

At Madison, Conn. Nina Wilcox Putnam, the authoress, had a home. What a weird creature she was. Although a great friend of Dave Cummings, my Russian-Jewish assistant on W.S.S., I had never met her. I picked her up one summer on the New Haven Railroad train between New York and Madison. After that, on week-ends I would occasionally steal away from "Thrift Cottage" for a bit of Nina's ass in the grass.

Until I was 25 or 26, the sight of a woman's garter, or a woman in a bathing suit or a bit of lace drawers, would set me wild with passion.

There was a model named Betty, a beautiful thing that lived around the corner from 981 Madison Avenue. During the summer while Ellen was in Connecticut, Betty would visit me, often late at night. Our apartment was on the ground floor, and I would watch for her passing and let her in without her ringing. This generally was when she was returning from some wild artists' party.

One night when we were fucking, she told me that my penis reminded her of a crowbar—she asked me if I had been eating oysters. She said that never in her life had she felt anyone my size, that it made her feel full up, like she was going to burst inside—to her I felt like a stallion driving right up into the big hole in the middle of her.

At that age, such statements naturally pleased me. In fact, they would at any age.

During the summer of 1918 you took your first step.

What an adorable baby you were. What fun I had with you, week-ends.

After we were married, your mother's physical attractiveness for me waned.

I felt most of my passion for her before I married her, particularly one day when we were down at Beltsville, Maryland, on a picnic. We were in the woods alone. I have often wondered why I did not attack her then. I had great respect for her and a naive adolescent belief that one didn't really suggest or do anything off color to the girl one was going to marry and who would some day be the mother of one's children.

The Page family were so strict, so conservative, that they objected to almost everything we did or wanted to do.

In later years, their other sons-in-law who came into the family after I did were much more brazen in their wooing than I had ever dared to be, and yet were not criticized or hampered by the Pages nearly so much as I had been. But that's the penalty of any ice-breaker, particularly in a nest of females.

When contemplating matrimony, remember that the male should fix his affections upon a girl who is of good family, whose parents are alive, and who is three or more years younger than himself.

The young lady in question should preferably be born of a highly respectable family, possessed of wealth, well-educated, and with many relatives and friends of social position and standing.

She should also be beautiful and of good disposition, with lucky marks on her body—good hair, nails, ears, eyes and breasts—neither more nor less than they ought to be, and no one of them entirely wanting.

She should not be burdened with a sickly body.

The man, of course, should possess all of these qualities himself before seeking them in the female—and then you have an ideal union.

At all events, a girl who has already joined with others, i.e., lost her cherry—is no longer a virgin—should never be loved, for it would be reproachable to do such a thing under the old concept of marriage. Today there may be exceptions, but there are few. . . .

Valera [an actress] was a Canadian girl. Her mother travelled with her on the road, which made things difficult. I had been keen about her for some time, and in Chicago the inevitable happened. It was in her apartment on Michigan Avenue. Her mother was out.

We were alone. My stored up burning passions broke over the dam, and the damage was done—I literally devoured her beautiful body. I lost all sense of time, thought and judgment.

Officially I was in Chicago on Government business, but I was out of the picture for days in my delirious devotion to Valera.

I finally came to my senses and set forth once more. A peremptory telegram . . . to get going brought me back to life.

I left Washington on a nation-wide tour after the first of the year, 1919. I first went to Boston, where I addressed a big meeting in one of the local theatres.

What a disconcerting experience that was. It was the first time I had appeared as the principal speaker before so large an audience. I had talked to large groups and introduced prominent speakers in Carnegie Hall and other places during the W. S. S. campaign in Greater New York, sometimes addressing three or four meetings a day of four or five hundred each, but here I was the lone performer, representing the United States Government, before 2,000 people. . . .

Then Springfield, Illinois, and Kansas City.

What a mob there was in Kansas City, where I addressed all the girls in the Loose-Wiles Biscuit factory.

I then crossed the country to the coast. On the train west I met a little girl from Akron, who was going to Los Angeles to work for the Goodyear Rubber Company, in the new plant they were constructing there.

When all had retired on the train for the night, I crept into her berth, which was just across from mine. After I had buried my devil in her hell, I fell asleep. When I awakened it was late, but with the aid of a bit of filthy lucre I enlisted the help of the Pullman porter in getting back to my berth, which avoided all complications. . . .

In San Diego, at the U.S. Grant Hotel, in the room adjoining mine, was an army colonel and his lovely wife. They fought most savagely.

When he was out of the room she would hold long conversations over the telephone with some man in San Francisco.

We met quite by accident in the corridor outside our rooms. It was a simple matter to unlock the connecting door—what a screw she was! There was a girl who had learned her army tricks full well, and what I learned about screwing from her stood me in good stead for sometime to come. . . .

I turned east from Seattle to Minneapolis, coming back over the Chicago-Milwaukee & St. Paul. On the train was a most attractive bitch, and nearly every man aboard fell for her seductiveness.

By a percentage arrangement with train and Pullman conductors, she occupied a drawing room, the bed of which was made down. To that room she took her customers one after the other. She started with the Pullman cars—the Observation car first—and finished in the day coaches.

All day long on the road to Spokane she worked that train. When she got off the male passengers gathered on the station platform and serenaded her with "She's a Jolly Good Fellow," etc. It was the most obvious case of railroad prostitution that I have ever seen, but it was not an unusual performance in the cross country travel of the day.

From Minneapolis, I went to Chicago, then back to Washington and New York. When I arrived in New York I resigned from the organization. . . .

After my return to New York, I picked up a girl named Mildred L., the mistress of a book mart proprietor. I first saw her with this elderly man at the theatre—the old Casino on Broadway.

The old bastard went out for a smoke between the acts, and we flirted. She was a very beautiful creature. She did modeling on the side.

I followed them to her home in a taxicab. They took an old horse-drawn victoria. The buzzard left her at the door of her apartment house. When he had gone around the corner, I drove up in the taxi—she was still waiting, and I went upstairs to bed with her.

I became very attached to Mildred and we spent a good deal of time together. Once when I was trying to collect a bill from a client who was living at the Hotel Pennsylvania, we stayed at that hotel for several weeks together.

Mildred had a gorgeous body and a good mind.

On one occasion when I was in financial distress, she drew $1000 of her whoring money from the savings bank to tide me over.

Later she introduced me to the wife of a lover of hers—a most passionate woman with children. That married bitch was a disturbing factor for some time.

Mildred picked up with a coffee salesman, but not with much success at first. He was an Englishman and in the beginning he cost her a lot of money. As time went on he gave up coffee selling and took to peddling stock in the Radio Corporation of America. Radio was in its infancy and having trouble to get financed. People didn't have much confidence in its future.

Against my advice, Mildred put $500 into the company's stock.

Eventually her original investment made her quite well to do. By 1926 the Englishman was an important official in the company and she was riding around with every luxury.

When I arrived in South Bend, Indiana, the chairman, old man Oliver of plough fame, was out of town but I was entertained by his secretary. She was the real director of the Indiana campaign, anyway. Thirty minutes after I had arrived I was fucking her in her private office.

During the New York War Savings Campaign I picked up a girl at Forest Hills named Lydia G., a great tennis fan.

She was with Street & Finney in their make-up or layout department.

For years I played with Lydia's "mary." We would go to the movies where we diddled one another as we watched the picture. She was very passionate and we would both come while apparently watching the picture.

It was not until years afterwards while driving on Long Island in the Governor's car, that we finally got together. She was a good fuck but it didn't last long. Why she had deprived us of that pleasure for so long a time I never did know.

In Bridgeport, Conn. a Mrs. O'Rourke was in charge of the Women's Committee for War Savings.

I saw her quite often and used to drive with her around the country outside of Bridgeport.

She was always in fear that her husband would find out about us. One night he came home unexpectedly. What a time I had getting away. Going over the back fence, which was of barbed wire, I tore a long piece out of my pants, but considered myself fortunate that I had not been caught by the husband.

Eventually this O'Rourke woman became quite a nuisance, particularly when I was in Albany, although it was bad enough when I was in New York.

In New York, she would come and sit in her car outside the door of my apartment on Madison Avenue for hours waiting for me to come out.

In Albany, when the motion picture censorship legislation was

76

up for consideration, she tried to bring pressure of a personal nature on me in order to have me use my influence against the bill. Her husband had large interests in the industry which she feared would be adversely affected by the passage of the proposed legislation.

Fortunately, I had guts enough to tell her to go to hell. And her threats evaporated into thin air without damage to anyone.

In Philadelphia, I visited a whore house where I had a girl of my choice sit on the side of the bed. While in this position I had the mistress of the house come over and bare her bosoms. I also made her lift up her petticoat as far as the pit of her stomach. She placed her legs as far apart as possible. I then seated myself in front of this lovely perspective.

One of the other girls then came and laid herself upon the first in the same position, so that it was the altar of generation which offered itself to me instead of the girl's face. Then they placed their attractions on a level with my mouth.

A third girl on her knees before me excited me with her hand while a fourth girl played with her fingers on the first where I was to strike with my cock.

This last girl apparently excited the first girl into insensibility. What she was doing to the first girl, I also did with each of my hands, the right and the left, to the two other girls.

When I was thoroughly excited by my own lewdness I approached the first girl and everyone followed me endeavoring to enflame me more.

I had all my hind parts stripped naked, and one of the girls took hold of them, omitting nothing in order to irritate me, rubbing her hands all over my bottom, my asshole and my balls, covering me with kisses, making use of everything I had.

Completely on fire I rushed upon the first girl.

These wanderings determined the psychic.

As I uttered terrible cries in the last moment of my intoxication everybody surrounded me, everybody waited on me, everyone was working to double my *exstasy* which was finally obtained in the midst of these strange episodes of lust and depravity.

In Philadelphia we had at the New York Shipbuilding Yard one of the best War Savings Societies ever organized in the United States.

There was a wonderful woman near Philadelphia, Mrs. Percy Madeira, Jr., the former Margaret Cary of Baltimore. She lived at Rydal, Pa. . . .

There was Beatrice M., a secretary in Father's office, who always went up to the store-room on the roof of the building when I went to get supplies, and there she would suck me off.

She was some gobbler. She was quite young and inexperienced and was always worried for fear that by sucking me off she might get with child. This apprehension on her part was largely caused by the fact that she always swallowed my juice.

When I was Secretary to the Governor, Beatrice decided to get married. One day when I visited Father's office she rode uptown with me—we were in the Governor's car with a police motorcycle escort—and told me that she was glad of the opportunity of seeing me because of her approaching marriage. It seemed she was afraid that because she had sucked my cock she had lost her virginity and that her ability to have babies might have been affected.

I reassured her, and when last I heard of her, she was the mother of three or four bouncing kids—by her husband.

Years later I met a woman who was engaged to Henry Schatzken. It seems that she had come to the office with Miss M. when Miss M. got the job. Schatzken's wife-to-be was a brunette and I had engaged Miss M., the blonde. I didn't pick Beatrice on her looks. I picked her because she was the better stenographer of the two—maybe.

A month or so after I returned to New York from Washington, Manny Straus, a promoter whom I had met during the W. S. S. Campaign, suggested that I organize the Lumber Trade division for the Actors' Fund of America.

Manny thought it might be a nice gesture on my part, in return for the help the theatrical profession had given the lumber industry in selling government bonds and raising money for the various war drives.

I consented to do this and before long I found myself in complete charge of the whole campaign.

Dan Frohman was president of the old Actors' Fund. After organizing the lumber trade I organized all the other trades and set out to raise a million dollars for the Old Actors' Home on Staten Island.

I had frequent clashes with old Frohman, whose brother was Charles Frohman, the producer. Charles had been lost when the *Lusitania* was sunk. Maude Adams was Charles' mistress.

Frohman couldn't do very much with me because I was giving my services as a volunteer. The fund was paying Manny Straus $25,000 yearly for consultation services.

We planned a nation-wide Actors' Memorial Day.

Some idea of the extent of this campaign can be obtained from scrapbooks I have kept on the subject. . . .

John D. Rockefeller, Jr. and his father took the occasion to contribute $50,000 each, although neither of them had ever been inside a theatre up to that time.

Another high spot of the meeting was when Ethel Barrymore and I made a trip to the Old Actors' Home on Staten Island. They made movies of us there pinning ribbons on the old actors and actresses, which movies were shown throughout the country.

The trip to Staten Island depressed Ethel Barrymore very much.

At the time she was presumably happily married to young Colt, a broker whose father was head of the United States Rubber Corporation.

Talking to the old actors and actresses about her mother and her father—many of them had acted with her parents—she became a bit morbid. On the way back to town she confided that she feared, in fact was sure, that she would spend her last days in a home for down and out actors and actresses. At the time she was at the height of her career— a great success in *Declassé* at the Empire Theatre—the wife of a wealthy financier—the daughter-in-law of a rubber baron.

She was very anxious to get an unusually wide, red patent-leather belt, which I was able to procure for her from the novelty division.

We gave a breakfast one morning at the Commodore at which over 400 people were present. The speakers at the breakfast were: Williams Fellows Morgan, Charles Evans Hughes, Mrs. Oliver Harriman, Mark Klaw, "Big Bill" Edwards, and myself. (See photograph of Justice Hughes, Mrs. Harriman, Mr. Frohman and myself.)

At that breakfast we raised over $60,000.

At a meeting of the Lamb's Club one evening over which I presided and where Major General Edwards was the guest of honor, and La Guardia, Curran and Judge McCook attended, I observed in the audience a girl who had lived across the street from our 981 Madison Avenue apartment.

On more than one occasion I had stood in the window of the apartment, jerking off for her benefit. Sometimes she would pull up her dress and show me her hairy cunt and lovely legs which only tended to further excite me as I masturbated.

When I first noticed her at the meeting I felt her presence might be disconcerting, but it did not alarm me, and later someone introduced us and we stepped aside and laughed and joked over our past conduct.

She lived at home with her parents, and had come to the meeting with her father, who was a member of one of the commercial and industrial committees that I had organized for the drive.

Later that night I got her away from her father, took her to a hotel room around the corner and screwed the bitch—she was Jewish.

Ibañez, the famous Spanish author, was in this country during the Actors' Campaign. He was quite the lion of the day. His book *The Four Horsemen of the Apocalypse* being among the best sellers, if not the best, appealing especially to the women.

I arranged with him for a meeting at the Lyceum Theatre.

I sent out invitations to all the women in the social register, inviting them to hear Ibañez speak on the stage of the Lyceum Theatre and to attend a tea afterwards in honor of the author in Mr. Frohman's studio on top of the theatre.

The mob of fashionables was so great and so terrifying in their deportment and determination to hear Ibañez and to meet him at the reception and tea, that we had to call out the police reserves to maintain order.

The meeting was a great success. Frederick Wallace, a Deputy Police Commissioner, Ibañez and I addressed the gathering—a packed house. Ibañez spoke in Spanish.

We raised a great deal of money at the meeting. The meeting in the theatre on the ground floor over, the fun really began.

There was only a small elevator to Frohman's studio atop the theatre. The alternative was a climb of many flights of stairs.

The fashionables, the society women—the well-trained and brought up females of New York—would not await their turn for the elevators, but jammed the stairway, pushing and pulling police and firemen aside in their mad rush to shake hands with the famous author or to get him to autograph a bit of paper.

The serving of tea was out of the question. I've never seen such a sight in all my life. It produced a raft of publicity and added tremendously to the momentum of the campaign. . . .

The night the campaign ended, I gave a dinner to all the correspondents, photographers and artists who had cooperated in the drive. We engaged half a dozen women to dance in the nude. Liquor flowed like water. During the night we kept the telegraph instrument in my office open in order to get returns from other cities throughout

80

the country, especially the Far West, and in cases where benefit performances were being held on ships at sea, which were wirelessing their returns in.

About 2:30 in the morning I went up to my office and found Pehryn Stanylaws on a woman across the top of my desk fucking hell out of her while the telegraph operator was calmly working on apparently oblivious to the screwing.

Among those present at the dinner were James Montgomery Flagg, Harrison Fisher, Bill McGeehan, Grantland Rice, Heywood Broun, F.P.A., Claire Briggs, K.C.B. (Beaton), and many others of note.

A cartoon of that dinner is to be found among my papers. It shows an old pocketbook being thrown open wide and liquor, chickens, dancing girls and song bursting forth.

During the Actors' Fund, I met at Bay Head, N.J. Margaret Carey Madeira who had for years been a great friend of your mother. She had two charming little boys. Margaret was a very interesting person. She had been responsible for much splendid and progressive legislation passing the Maryland state legislature and becoming the law of that state. Although of pronounced Socialist tendencies, Margaret had married the son of one of the most prominent capitalists in the State of Pennsylvania, a coal baron.

I became keenly interested in Margaret and after Ellen left for a visit to Baltimore with your grandparents, the Pages, I returned to Bay Head on several occasions and visited with Margaret, going off alone with her on week-end sailing trips.

Our friendship was very wonderful and beautiful—a friendship I shall always cherish. For years I never passed through Philadelphia without communicating with her in some way or other. Often I would stop over, meeting her at some place where we could talk quietly and discuss the events of the day. There was a small library or museum just off Broad Street where we often met, feeling particularly safe there from prying eyes.

Margaret was the one woman of whom your mother ever displayed the slightest jealousy or even objected to my interest in—yet I never had sexual intercourse with Margaret Carey.

About this time I picked up a girl named Elizabeth D.—now Mrs. P. Elizabeth lived in the cellar of a tenement on Charles Street, New York. She was engaged in social work and was considerably broken up over the fact that the man she had lived with for several

81

years—a very attractive fellow, according to her—had married an older woman immediately upon his return from the war (a woman of large means), throwing Elizabeth over completely.

Elizabeth was a pioneer on Charles Street. No one of intelligence and good breeding and education had lived there for many years prior to her setting up her home there in the basement of a tenement, an apartment which was most attractively arranged.

The day I picked her up I went home with her, and what a fuck she was—screwing her was a real novelty. She was a past master in the art of fornication.

To my great distress, the next day she told me that I had better see a doctor—that she was not at all certain but that she had gonorrhoea; a pleasant thought to entertain—a bit of a shock at least.

It seemed that Elizabeth in order to learn about her former lover had, on several occasions prior to our affair, permitted her lover's best friend to screw her.

I called Stanley Howe and he brought me a prophylactic which he had had while in the army. Then I went around to see my doctor. The doctor gave me a preventitive treatment, and nothing happened.

It finally developed that "Liz" had simply had a slight irritation, probably a touch of Leucorrhea from insufficient screwing.

In spite of the inauspicious start of our affair, I grew very fond of Elizabeth. A sincere friendship blossomed and lasted for years. I never screwed her again, but I visited her often at all hours of the night and day, telling her of my affairs of the heart, describing my experiences with other women, explaining their reactions and mine.

When troubled over some petty row or disagreement with the girl of the moment in my life I would go to Elizabeth for advice and she would straighten me out, invariably suggesting some happy solution of the imagined difficulties. For the last ten years I have had no trace of her.

In *Vengeance of the Gods* there was an actress who, in the play, seduced the young Jewish daughter of the whore house proprietor. The exquisite creature played the part of the lesbian of the whore house—the head prostitute. I told Elizabeth about the seductive beauty, adding that if any girl ever made love to me in the ravishing manner in which Dorothea Nolan played the part in that excellent performance, I would be perfectly willing to call it a day, for to me that would be the ultimate. It developed that Elizabeth knew Dorothea Nolan well. She stoutly contended that Dorothea in real life was not a lady-lover, but was, in truth, crazy about men; and she promised to introduce me.

A year or more went by. Dorothea had had a touch of t.b. and had gone west to Colorado.

When Dorothea returned Elizabeth arranged for us to meet.

By that time I was in love with another—a woman named Florence M.

But Elizabeth had raved over the beautiful tan that Dorothea had acquired all over her body while out in Colorado, emphasizing that not a particle of Dorothea's lovely person had been left untouched by the sun's rays.

The eventful day arrived. Being in the chips at the time, I sent one of my cars to the stage door of the theatre where Dorothea was playing after the matinee. I also sent her a large bunch of orchids.

I awaited her arrival at Elizabeth's. I had often been disappointed in the contrast of an actress before the footlights and at the stage door. But somehow or other I expected more of Miss Nolan.

So when she appeared it was quite a set-back. She was short, dull, unattractive, and sexless. On the stage she had played the part well of what appeared to be a tall, sleek, seductive amorous female vamp slinking stealthily through each scene.

I took Dorothea to dinner and was bored to death. After dinner she returned to the theatre for her night performance.

After all the build-up, I felt I should go through with it—so I took her to Barney's after the evening show.

There was not the slightest thing about her or her personality that resembled even remotely the character on the stage. When I took her home she undressed to show me her body; and it was beautifully tanned—and I might have succumbed then and there had I not had before me the contrast in my memory of her on the stage and her real self.

She gave me one of her pictures, and I suggested that I would like one in the nude. Whereupon she went and had some made while fully clothed, which I rejected and heartlessly refused to pay for—she had fooled me; they were merely theatrical pictures and not in the nude. In the quarrel over the picture I stopped seeing her—she was a mediocre lug.

Through Elizabeth I met a little French girl named Loyola, in whom I became much interested. When I first met Loyola I wanted to keep her as my mistress. I stocked her empty larder up with green

83

and dry groceries. She was having an affair with some girl friend and put on the act with me of being a virgin. I did not believe her and it annoyed me. Subsequently I learned that she had lost her cherry years before; but she was so keen about her room-mate at the time that she wouldn't let a man come near her.

She wrote me several letters from time to time, but it was impossible for me to become interested in her again—once the spark is lost it can never be regained. Cold love will not stand rewarming.

Colonel Arthur Wood—nephew-in-law of J. P. Morgan the first, and Police Commissioner of New York under Mayor John Purroy Mitchel (now President of Rockefeller Center) and I with a committee of gentiles, raised $250,000 for the Jewish Federation Building Fund from a headquarters we established at the Pennsylvania Hotel.

When the Gentile Committee drive was completed, R. J. Caldwell invited me to help him with a drive for the Near East Committee of Cleveland H. Dodge.

We had our Near East headquarters for Greater New York in a private house on Madison Avenue between 39th and 40th Streets.

I re-established most of the Actors Fund crew and we staged a mass dinner at the Biltmore, where we showed the horrible conditions of deprivations in Armenia and other countries of the Near East.

A great deal of attention was attracted to our headquarters and much news comment obtained by a display from our windows of the flags of all the nations that comprised the Near East group, many of which had never been seen in New York City before.

Attending the dinner atop the Biltmore were a thousand guests. The speakers were Jane Addams of the Hull House, Hon. John Skelton Williams, Comptroller of Currency, General John Pershing, Herbert Hoover, Henry Morgenthau, the ambassadors and ministers from the Near East countries, Hamilton Holt, and others. Although radio was not known then we limited each and everyone to five minutes. We cut the speakers off with a white warning and a red final light.

We raised $750,000 that night.

We also had a luncheon at the Bankers' Club, where the only thing served was the amount of rice ration that was allowed daily to each child in the Near East. This luncheon was most effective and produced results in money and publicity.

My Near East scrap book tells in detail of these meetings and the others of that campaign. . . .

84

Florence was my secretary during the Near East campaign.

During that drive I tried to keep myself as far removed from the detailed activities as possible, and for that purpose had my private office on the top floor away from everyone.

In the evening after a hard day's work Florence and I would slip into the large closet in my room. There we would embrace violently—love, caress and fornicate.

We did a good deal of fucking during that campaign. She went with me from the Near East to the Hoover-for-President Committee; then with the Red Cross. For a time I lost track of her. Then, sometime in 1926, I received an announcement of her marriage.

Guy Emerson, one of the owners of the John Price Jones publicity organization, was doing some work through the Jones outfit for the Hoover Committee, and he asked me to help out.

Hoover's war record appealed to me greatly and I agreed to pitch in. I first got Robert Fulton Cutting to accept the chairmanship of the Hoover-for-President Committee for Greater New York, and then I proceeded to organize local Hoover-for-President committees or clubs in various southern and western states from coast to coast, from Canada to Mexico. This was in 1920.

While away on my trips about the country I left the detail work of the New York Committee in the hands of Bert Hall. Hall's father was an I. C. C. Commissioner.

Just prior to my becoming interested in the Hoover campaign I had met an actress named Jane Haven. She was struggling along in Vaudeville. Jane had a 2 x 4 room in the Roaring Forties. The partition that separated her dingy room from the next room was so thin that we never dared have a party for fear the next door neighbor would hear the whole works, particularly since I was not noted for my quietness—the light screwing was out.

I was very depressed at the time and with very little cash. We would frequently cook meals on the single gas burner in that small room—they were meager but good.

When I started out on my tour of the southern and western states for Hoover, Jane went along in the drawing room with me as far as Washington. Being full of the campaign work that lay before me, I was completely devoid of any physical urge for Jane.

When I wakened in the morning I found her sleeping on the floor of the drawing room. She explained that I had been so brutal with her during the night that she decided to sleep on the floor—she had come on the trip with expectations of a pleasant evening. In my preoccupied state of mind her physical urge created a ruthless intolerance in me which made sleeping with me as well as cohabitation impossible.

On my second trip through the South, Dick Patterson (Richard C. Patterson, Jr.) went with me as far as Alabama.

On the way south we picked up a sweet young thing on the train and took her into our drawing room. After we had both jazzed her she told us that she was going to visit New York in the summer. She promised to look us up, wanted our names and addresses—I told her Dick's name was Stanley H. Howe, and gave her Stanley's address.

That summer the young lady arrived in the big city and looked Stanley up at the Brevoort. He invited her to the hotel and had quite a time, although he had no idea who she was or where she came from. After Stanley had given her a good fucking with his famous sword, she told him how much he had improved in technique and size since he had screwed her on the train. And that yarn was a great blow to Dick's fornicating pride.

My trips for Hoover took me down through the South and out through the West as far as El Paso.

While I had been across the border at San Diego, it was at a time when there was not much activity in Tia Juana, but in 1920 Ciudad Juarez, the Mexican border town across from El Paso, was in full blast. . . .

Thanks to Woodrow Wilson's vacillation and weakness in dealing with our southern neighbors, Americans in Mexico, particularly the women, were then being sneered at on the streets and in public places, not infrequently openly yelled and hooted at.

While enjoying a bit of light alcoholic stimulant in one of the saloons we were summarily ordered out of the joint and directed to return across the border by the proprietors and local police. Investigation as to the cause of this action disclosed that the Yaqui were on the war path and about to attack the town.

I couldn't stay to watch the attack from the American side, but it was quite a skirmish while it lasted, the Yaquis being driven out after a short exchange of Mexican shot and shell. . . .

While in Ciudad Juarez, we visited the Cribs—where the village whores were dispensing their favors—and the bull fights. I had heard much about bull fights but I had never seen one before. Suffice it to say that it was the most abhorent sight I have ever witnessed, before or since. I saw two helpless old horses, blindfolded "nags," gored until their very insides were falling out and dragging on the ground as they

86

feebly endeavored to carry on. The toreador's job seemed to me a well protected one in comparison with that of the poor horses. After two horses had been horribly gored I left the ring—it was too much for my sensibilities to sit and watch the helpless horses so unfairly destroyed.

The Mexicans seemed to enjoy the entire proceedings hugely— and with much gusto applauded all the thrusts of bull and man. You will find bull fights much more entertainingly described by writers of note, so I will not attempt to set forth here the fine parts and details of that bloody sport. . . .

In Houston I met an excellent screw, a girl named Claudia whose memory haunted me for several years.

Thanks to Claudia, I had my first experience with a Drive-yourself-automobile, in Houston.

I had organized the local club, visited with E. A. Peden, a leading industrialist and great friend of Hoover, called on the local Republican leaders, and had some free time for myself before filing my night wire report to the New York Hoover Headquarters.

They had drive-yourself automobiles out in that part of Texas first, I suppose because you could not get very far away with a car in those days—the roads were not passable.

I rented a car and Claudia and I took a ride out to a solitary part of the country—and we didn't have to go far from town to find a lonely spot. Then we parked the car, and there tasted of that eternal joy on the back seat with top down in the hot sun of the late afternoon. What a lovely screw she was. It took me a long time to get that cunt out of my mind.

Later we drove back to the hotel. Her room was across from mine. I entered and we again gave in to our passion which knew no bounds as far as she was concerned.

Months later, while she was attending the Ann Morgan School in Chicago, we again met. That was during the Republican National Convention in June. And I certainly sweated my balls off fucking her in the dressing room of the Morgan School, in the Chicago heat. It was one of the real reliefs from the ardors of that Convention. There are some hot letters from her in my files. She sure could take it, and did she love it!

Copies of many of the wires and reports during that trip are to be found in my files. . . .

When I returned to New York I found that Royal Victor, senior partner of Sullivan & Cromwell, was in the saddle directing the Hoover campaign from behind the scenes.

It seemed the organization under Captain Lucey, Guy Emerson and John Price Jones had been going badly, and Victor had been called by Hoover to straighten things out. . . .

Victor had me attend the first few meetings—which were a complete waste of time—in order to report the happenings to him. Years later Victor told me that during the convention Barnes always referred to me as "that sinister young politician. . . ."

It was my habit every evening to take a bath and put on my dinner coat, which seemed to refresh me. There is nothing more wearing and tiring than wandering about corridors of hotels talking to delegates and visiting them in their various headquarters at a political convention. All day long you attend the convention and then all evening long you pound the marble floors of the hotel corridors well into the early hours of the morning, particularly when you are on the sort of scouting work to which I was assigned.

The Friday prior to Harding's nomination, at a time when it was generally conceded that if the convention went over into the second week Herbert Hoover would be the next Republican candidate for President, Victor called me into his office in the Auditorium Hotel —Hoover Headquarters—about midnight. He gave me two thousand dollars in marked money and introduced me to two colored men who were representatives of the Georgia Peach—the colored man who was head of the Georgia delegation—(They had called to see "Bill" (William L.) Ward of Westchester at the Blackstone Hotel to discuss the sale of the Georgia delegates and other southern delegations to the Hoover camp. Ward was asleep, and Harry Barrett, Ward's assistant and Secretary of the Westchester Republican County Committee, sent them over to Victor.) Victor did not think it wise for him to visit the negro leader and delegates for such a purpose, so he assigned me to that task.

Leaving the Auditorium Hotel with these two colored men, I met Jim Haggerty, political correspondent of *The New York Times,* just as I crossed the sidewalk on Michigan Avenue to enter a cab. Jim seemed surprised to see a Hoover man thus comporting himself and inquired as to my destination. I told him he hadn't seen me and I would tell him all in the morning. The hour was late, in fact too late for the *Times,* had Jim been inclined to comment.

The taxicab stopped in front of an apartment hotel on the South Side. From the windows Wood and Lowden banners were hanging.

With much ceremony I was ushered into the suite of the Georgia Peach.

I found him propped up in bed, wearing the best of silk pajamas and covered by a silk counterpane. Many secretaries or hangers-on waited upon him and answered his every beck and call.

I gave the gentlemen who had brought me to the hotel several hundred dollars apiece as evidence of good faith.

After introducing me to the Georgia Peach the two steerers departed, leaving me alone with the King Pin of the southern delegations. When we were alone the Peach to my amazement disclosed the surprisingly large number of delegates to the Republican National Convention that were for sale. He put a price on each delegate or delegation per ballot.

He told me that the purchasable black and white delegates from the South and some states in the North had been watching the Hoover management with keen interest because William A. Ward—one of the old-time Republican wheel horses—a boss of importance in New York State and the nation, a compatriot of Boss William Barnes of Albany—was in the Hoover Camp. These colored gentlemen assumed from this fact that at the proper time the whole convention would swing to Hoover.

They were anxious to be in line when the switch came.

The price was $1,000 per delegate vote per poll of the convention and $2,500 per roll-call for the boss of each delegation that was for sale, and $5,000 per roll-call for the Georgia Peach himself for his services. The Georgia Peach even named men in the New Jersey delegation that were for sale.

He suggested that he might do a little better for us with the Mississippi crowd and get us the six delegates there for $7,000.

I made a deal with him to deliver as per his list and I gave him a thousand dollars to prove to him that we meant business. It was agreed that after I raised the necessary cash we were to meet in the morning outside the Coliseum on the side that was little used. It was understood that I was to pay him for the votes of his controlled corrupt delegates just before each roll-call.

After completing the arrangements to buy these votes, approximately 75, and which, if purchased, would have been enough to stop the Harding onrush that morning, I went back to the Blackstone Hotel to Victor's bedroom and told him the story. It was nearly 3 a.m. by that time.

Victor at first thought the thing to do was to buy the votes—that if those votes were for sale and others were buying them, we had better buy them for ourselves.

Apparently the negroes that historical Friday night had earlier heard garbled rumors of what had been decided in the "little room full of smoke"—Harding was to be nominated on the morrow—and confusing their H's had mixed Harding with Hoover. Giving credence to their assumption was the satisfactory fact, to their minds, that "Bill" Ward was in the Hoover corner. . . .

We proceeded to Judge Nathan L. Miller's room. Miller was a member of New York's "Big Four" having gone on the delegation when Elihu Root, Sr. had declined. Miller had a long New York political record behind him, having climbed right up to New York's highest court, the Court of Appeals, with an enviable record for great ability as a jurist.

I had met Miller for the first time shortly after we arrived in Chicago. I had helped him correct and proof-read his nominating speech, which he delivered to the Convention when putting Hoover into nomination. . . .

The morning of the day that Miller delivered his nominating speech Dick Oulihan, Washington correspondent of *The New York Times,* an old friend of mine whose son had gone to school with me, told me that the real spontaneous demonstration of the convention would be when Herbert Hoover was put in nomination. At the time I pooh-poohed that—laughed at the idea. The Hoover managers had only fifty tickets for the galleries. Those fifty were all the tickets available for the legion of Hoover workers attending the convention. How fifty lusty lungs could make a dent in that auditorium—that any Hoover demonstration could be staged that would be effective, seemed impossible.

Those fortunate Hooverites who had obtained tickets, upon arriving at the Coliseum, were besieged with requests for Hoover banners by the general public who were already there. We quickly sent to Headquarters and secured a large supply of Hoover flags. We had to send for all we had and then we didn't have enough to go around among the people, all of whom we never heard of before. Most of them seemed to be Chicago people and had had no connection with the organization—they were independent Hooverites.

As I said, the delegates, after the stupendous applause that greeted Miller's entrance upon the platform, listened quietly while the Judge praised Hoover. Three-quarters through, Miller put out his

90

hand before him and pleaded with the delegates to bear with him just a moment longer. Then pandemonium broke loose. Miller hearing his own voice re-echo back to him all through his speech had thought it the howls of the delegates, had not known it was the amplifier throwing his own voice back at him from above.

At the conclusion of Judge Miller's address putting Hoover before the Convention, the wildest demonstration of the Convention broke loose, and it would have continued for well over an hour if a woman who was not in the scheduled line-up for seconding speeches had not rushed forward to the platform and demanded to be heard in behalf of Herbert Hoover's candidacy.

It took some time before the crowd would even quiet down for her. They would not quiet down for the men seconders. They didn't want more speeches—they just wanted to cheer Hoover.

The crowd was with Hoover, but the delegates were not. The demonstration was valueless except as an indication of Hoover's popularity with the people.

Returning to the purchase of delegates, when we reached Judge Miller's room and wakened him, Mrs. Miller had to take to the bathroom before we could come in.

We told the Judge what had happened. He cautioned that we must not purchase these votes for Hoover. It was Miller's contention that because of the type of man Hoover was it would be political suicide for the former Food Administrator if it ever transpired what had happened—that others might buy votes and get away with it—but not Hoover. So it was agreed that I would communicate with the colored gentlemen, telling them that I would meet them as per our tentative "binder" arrangement in the morning with the money.

Victor was to arrange to have a Federal Judge, U. S. District Attorney and Federal Marshal available. The moment the marked money was passed by me to the leaders and distributed by the heads of the colored ring, all were to be arrested and the Convention halted. Hoover was to come to Chicago by special train, demand a purge of the rotten delegates (refusing the nomination himself) before the Republicans should proceed to the nomination of a President and Vice-President.

We conferred all morning and after the Convention was under way, Messrs. Oscar Straus, Julius Rosenwald, Royal Victor, George Barr Baker, William R. Wilcox and I paced the floor of the Black-stone Hotel, trying to decide what to do, or not to do, and frequently conferring with Hoover over the long-distance phone (Hoover being the only one of the candidates at the Convention who was not in Chicago).

Finally we had the money all ready and everybody set. Oscar Straus was selected to go to Will Hays, Chairman of the Republican National Convention, and Chairman of the Convention, and tell Hays we had the evidence against the corrupt delegates.

This was to be done after I had passed the money. Then the U. S. District Attorney in Chicago, and the police officers were to arrest the crooked delegates and bring them before a Federal Judge, charging them with the crime.

Victor had instructed me the previous day to keep a detailed record of all my movements and to do or say something unusual to each person I met so that they would recall definitely the time and occasion of meeting me.

It was agreed that upon the completion of the arrests, Will Hays was to be told that Herbert Hoover was on his way to Chicago in a special train; that he would not be a candidate himself, but that the Convention would have to be purged of the rotten delegates and that new candidates would have to be put in the field.

Oscar Straus went to Hays with the message of what was happening.

I passed the marked money.

The arrests were never made. Hays pleaded successfully with Straus and Hoover (over the phone) that it would be better to nominate Harding on the Republican ticket in spite of the corruption than to have four more years of Democrats in control of the government.

Hays sold them the idea that to disclose to the public the corruption, to disband the Convention and later reorganize it, would spell ruin for the Republican Party in the coming National Election, and would strike such a blow that it would be years before the party could recover.

I doubted Hays' sincerity and I always believed that the Party would have gone on to a greater victory had such a house-cleaning been permitted to take place.

That interesting and exciting incident closed by Mr. Hays, the Convention went on to nominate Warren G. Harding for President, and by a fluke Calvin Coolidge for Vice-President. Together they swept the country that fall.

At that convention Hiram Johnson was offered the Vice-Presidency, and refused. If Johnson had accepted he would have become President when the apparently robust Harding died a few years later, thereby satisfying a life-time ambition. . . .

In the Chicago Hoover Headquarters was a girl, Madeline Loomis, whose father was Treasurer of the Chicago, Milwaukee and St. Paul Railroad. Captain Lucey, the official head of the Hoover outfit, and I played around with her quite a bit. We never anticipated that she would be more than a Chicago amusement. Because of her father's position, the young lady always found it possible to travel as much as she liked, with railroad transportation free, particularly in the direction of New York, and eventually she became quite a nuisance and a bore. She had little consideration for Lucey or myself —phoning either our offices or our homes for us at all hours of the day and night.

After the Republican National Convention of 1920 I returned to New York, George Barr Baker and I returning together, and became associated with the New York Life Insurance Company. . . .

I joined the New York Life the last of June, 1920, and in the month of July wrote more insurance than any other agent of theirs throughout the country and was awarded a special testimonial for my efforts. I was in the 44th Street Branch, just off Fifth Avenue— William Royal (son-in-law of the then Vice-President, and afterwards President and Chairman of the Board of the Company—William Buckner) was Agency Superintendent. . . .

[During this period my father founded the Valley Stream Bank at Valley Stream, Long Island.]

We opened the Bank in what had been the corner saloon or "gin mill." At that time there were only five or six stores in Valley Stream, although it had then as now the best and most frequent train service of any town on Long Island outside of Jamaica. What the excellent train service had been unable to do, a bank was destined to achieve—showing what an important factor a bank is to any community.

We limited the stockholdings to not more than two shares to any one person.

We started business with $25,000 capital and $6,250 surplus. The shares were $125 each—$100 to capital; $25 to surplus. We bought a secondhand safe and fixtures—everything was the most inexpensive. . . .

The first day we opened for business we took in over $100,000, mostly in mutilated bills that the truck farmers had hidden in their cellars or up their chimneys.

Most of it was cash. A small portion checks on the Lynbrook Bank. And the cash was largely all mouldy.

When we packed the money for shipment to the Federal Reserve Bank in New York via the late afternoon mail train, the farmers couldn't understand for the longest while why we didn't keep it in the safe; some of them may still be wondering despite our painstaking explanations of how a bank functions, etc. . . .

You may ask why did I go to Valley Stream to start a bank, or why did I want to start a bank? What was the purpose? the point?

Well, Father. My father had been very active as Chairman of the Board of the North Shore Bank of Oyster Bay. He was constantly insinuating that I was improvident, indifferent about money, careless about my personal finances, knew nothing about the value of a dollar, etc.—that money meant nothing to me—the value of saving was meaningless—that I couldn't keep my own bank account—that I was slovenly, untidy, had no system about my work, etc.—no interest in figures, etc. etc.

I was a good salesman—knew a lot about railroad traffic, freight movements, rates, etc., but had a natural bent for advertising and publicity, but there I stopped.

Your mother and grandfather had the same idea. Everyone pointed to his job of putting the Calvert Bank together as a great achievement.

Of course, they were perfectly right about me.

So I thought I would show them—fool them. I would have a bank, the best, the most conservatively run and successful for the depositors on Long Island. So I did.

At one time I even flirted with the idea of a chain of banks on Long Island.

—and sufficient stock control of Calvert Bank to have a large voice in its management, and assure control for you and Marshall.

—and I bought a few shares as a starter with that idea in the back of my head.

But I didn't follow up on it, and had to let the stock go for a loan.

I attended the Republican State Convention at Saratoga in August, 1920. I went there with Harry Goddard and Al Cox, Jr.

(both now Federal Judges for the Southern District of New York) and Karl Behr (the former tennis champion—now partner in Dillon, Read & Co.). We only remained for 24 hours but had a very interesting hell-raising time.

The present highly-honored, venerable judges of the Federal Court, Goddard and Cox, threw a water pitcher through the transom of my room, gave my loudly colored striped neckties (for which I was noted at the time) to the negro bell-boys, and made one of the bell-boys slide down a fire escape rope outside my bedroom window.

We played a lot of rough tricks on one another the day we were at the Convention, more like schoolboys than men.

Judge Nathan L. Miller had written me a letter (which I still have) stating that he would not be a candidate nor accept the nomination under any circumstances.

Regardless of Miller's disavowals . . . we nominated [him] for Governor. . . .

After the Primary and sometime about the middle of September, Royal Victor sent for me to come down from Jamestown, where I was vacationing with your mother and you, to confer with him and Miller at the St. Regis.

He told me that the organization was not making any attempt to support Miller's candidacy.

Victor got hold of Louis Marshall and Hoover, and with Miller we mapped out a plan of action to bolster the Miller campaign.

From the outset the organization Republicans, not only of New York City but throughout the state, were only interested in assuring the success of the National Ticket, that is, to elect Warren G. Harding and Calvin Coolidge for President and Vice-President respectively, and James W. Wadsworth for United States Senator.

The Republican organization was perfectly willing to sacrifice Miller for Smith if by that sacrifice they would succeed in electing the United States Senator from New York and carry the state for the presidency.

It always has been more important to New York State and National Republicans and to Big Business to carry the Empire State for its Republican candidates for U. S. Senator and for President than it is that the slate should be carried for Governor.

It was expedient for those whom Miller had helped in the Republican National Convention—namely, Hoover, Victor and his associates—to see to it that in return for that assistance no stone was left unturned by them to assure Miller's success.

To me was assigned the task of visiting all the former County and City Hoover Food Administrators in the state and enlisting their support of Miller.

I also was charged with the task of determining in each community I visited whether the Republican leaders of that district were actively supporting Miller along with the rest of the ticket.

Further, I had the job of attending many of U. S. Senator Jim Wadsworth's political meetings upstate and making notes of his references, if any, to Nathan L. Miller's candidacy for Governor.

I had to report to Miller personally on his campaign train from time to time, giving him the results of my findings.

Religion always plays an important part in American political campaigns.

When I traveled over the country for Hoover in the Spring of 1920: In Tennessee, they were "agin" him because he was a Catholic. In New Mexico, they were against him because he (Hoover) was anti-Catholic.

In the Spring campaign often I had met the religious question frequently. I queried Hoover—as to what faith he professed, if any, and he wired that he was a Quaker, that his wife was a Quaker, but that a friend of theirs, a Catholic priest, whom they both had known for years, had married them. This was done outside the realm of the church.

I was paid $2,000 for this work, which covered all my expenses for three weeks, Royal Victor, Louis Marshall and Herbert Hoover chipping in with Miller to make up the kitty.

In covering the State of New York in behalf of Miller I met with some of the same sort of religious bigotry that I had met with when campaigning for Hoover.

In Buffalo, they were having street fights on the subject of Al Smith's and Miller's religious beliefs. Miller's full name being Nathaniel Lewis Miller gave currency to a report in Niagara County that he was of Jewish extraction. . . .

During the Miller drive I took Hoover up the State of New York on two separate occasions when he delivered addresses in Rochester, Buffalo and Syracuse.

In Rochester, Eastman, the Kodak man, entertained Hoover, but snubbed Christian Herter and myself. Hoover had dinner at Eastman's house, but as soon as the meal was over he excused himself and returned to the hotel where we were staying. He came to my room and remained there the rest of the evening until train time.

Hoover said he couldn't stand Eastman and he saw no reason for being bored to death with such a confounded ass.

In Buffalo, we met former-President Taft. He occupied a little room in the old Iroquois Hotel, without bath. He was pounding away on a typewriter with his coat, vest and collar off, and his sleeves rolled up, in order to get off his daily syndicated article—an analysis of political happenings throughout the country. The American people show little regard or respect for the highest office within their gift when they fail to provide some sort of pension or compensation for their ex-presidents so that they may retire in dignity. That a man who has occupied the position that Taft occupied—the highest in the gift of the people of the United States, should have to eke out his livelihood in his old age by pounding a typewriter in a small hotel room is a disgrace to the nation. . . .

The meetings that Hoover addressed seldom averaged over a couple hundred, and they were mostly women—the balance were local and County members of his old Food Administration. At Hoover's behest those Food Administration members turned to almost as a solid body and worked for Miller—I know, because it was part of my job to check up on them. Women everywhere, regardless of political allegiance, simply adored Hoover. This was primarily due, I believe, to the fact that the Chief (as Hoover was known to his staff intimates and affectionately referred to by nearly all members of his far flung War Relief and Administration outfits) personified their patriotic expressions during the War. Nevertheless, even with such a small audience, it was difficult to hear Mr. Hoover past the first two rows at any meeting. At these gatherings I would invariably stand in the back of the room and wave frantically to indicate to him that he wasn't being heard and for him to try to get his head up and speak louder.

He never did, or never could, or never would—in later years the radio saved him. The amplifiers in the big halls did the trick of getting his voice across for him, but he always was a monotonous "reader." . . .

Miller was swept in on the Harding landslide.

During my Miller-for-Governor activities I attended a matinee of *Welcome Stranger*. There I spied and flirted with Pauline W. After the show I followed her taxicab and met her outside her home.

After a short chat she invited me up. We had tea. Then I left. That night I returned and became greatly enamoured of the lovely creature. Pauline was one of the first girls I had known who resented having intercourse with me when I wore a condom. Needless to say, I appeased her distressed feelings immediately by removing the obnoxious bit of skin rubber.

During the entire gubernatorial campaign I saw a great deal of Pauline on week-ends.

When I met her she was living in an apartment up many flights of stairs on Lexington Avenue. In October she moved to East 57th Street between Park and Lexington.

Pauline enjoyed giving afternoon teas. She was playreading for Sam Harris at that time.

That fall and winter she had the part of Marianna De Puyster in *Little Old New York*. Genevieve Tobin was the star. . . .

My first affair with Pauline was but the beginning of a very passionate attraction, which for a time I feared might get the best of me.

It was Pauline who taught me the thrill of observing the congress in the mirror. From her I learned to love the body and how often, oh, how often, did we spend hour upon hour in burning caresses of each other's flesh, always surrounded by mirrors in which we witnessed our mad lust. Hers was the first cunt I ever loved with my mouth. Eventually our mutually perverted attractions became so great that I only wanted to have her suck me off while I was sucking her. She was slender of body, in fact skinny, but oh! so sensual.

It got so that I could hardly go a day without gobbling her at least two or three times.

We spent days and nights together in her apartment.

During this period in my life, in addition to my passion for sucking her very soul down through her cunt, I had a mad desire for eating lady fingers dipped in hot chocolate.

Her apartment was attractively furnished. Her bedroom radiated sex appeal and warmth.

We were much together and although she had been writing a play when I met her, she did very little writing during the period of our sensual debauch.

On some occasions she would play with me as I sucked her off and she would take the juice from my cock and together we would rub it all over our bodies.

Often we would bathe together and would fornicate while in the tub full of water.

Each week-end after my trips up through the state for the gubernatorial campaign of Miller I would come back to the city to stay with her.

On Saturday night we motored to Lakewood, putting up at Seton Hall, an old inn that was run by some Germans—weird sort of people—way out in the woods near a golf course.

The trip down in the stillness of the night was filled with charm and seductiveness.

We went to sleep that night in each other's arms.

Sunday we played but two holes of golf, and then back to our room and to bed where again we gave full vent to our passions. Oh, God, how I did love that female's cunt. There was something about Pauline that at times seemed just to drive me mad with passion and yet in my cooler moments I had to admit that she was a jinx, for a stay of any length in her society usually resulted in some misfortune coming my way.

That Sunday evening in Lakewood we strolled down a dusty old country road to attend the evening prayer in the farmside meeting house or church.

The quaintness and simplicity of the service, the unpretentiousness of the edifice, to say nothing of the homely honesty and sincerity of the preacher and his tiny flock was in strange contrast to the worldly-wise, fascinating, seductive creature at my side. The simple service truly humbled us and left us with a memory of sweetness and peace despite the sordid squalor of our perversions—and excesses.

What beautiful spiritual and base thoughts we mortals can have at almost one and the same time—chaos and peace intermingled—but then that seems to be the only life we know.

The next day late, after many reversions to our sexual delights, we motored back, in our chauffeur-driven car, to the city.

The entire time we were at Lakewood with car and driver we had taken but one short drive and that just over to the ocean at Bay Head, New Jersey.

The campaign over—Miller in by the skin of his teeth—we went on loving until Christmas.

Then Royal Victor called me to his office one day with an offer from Miller to serve as Executive Secretary to the Governor.

With that offer came the realization that it would mean the severance almost immediately of our wild completely abandoned sexual relations.

It was Pauline's decision that I must accept, which I did, and it eventually put an end to our debasement.

No doubt it was for the best. Regardless of Pauline's beautiful mind, her brilliant brain, and her womanly cleverness, I would ere long have slipped into mental as well as physical decay.

She was the most ravishing, devastating creature that ever entered my life up to that time. Pauline was always jealous of my family—my mother, my father, my wife and my child. . . . She wanted me to cut loose from all entanglements.

She fed my ego with suggestions of my potential greatness and genius, unadulterated bunk, to urge me on.

After going to Albany I was only able to visit her on several occasions far between and then only late at night. Because of the exacting demands Miller made upon my time, the visits were short—but very sweet. There is never much real satisfaction or pleasure in hurried encounters, for male or female—although the male, of course, gets much more out of quickies than the female.

In the winter of 1921 while Pauline was playing in Chicago I took the "Century" (20th Century Limited—New York Central crack Chicago flyer) one Friday afternoon to spend twenty-four hours with her on Lake Michigan, returning by Monday morning on the east-bound Limited, in order to be back on the job the first thing the beginning of the week.

It was in Chicago that I told her Ellen was pregnant and that our "second" would be due in mid-summer.

This concrete proof of my, as she called it, infidelity to her seemed to drive her frantic.

She threatened to, and in fact attempted to, destroy us both. Before I left her to go back to Albany she had calmed sufficiently for me to feel reasonably sure she would do nothing drastic—boy! oh boy! those were tight moments—in more ways than one. Or I should say, in more ways than they should be.

I was always glad that I waited—until after we had loved in one long and marvelous embrace, wherein I thought our souls would be mutually exchanged as she drew me in her mouth and I drew her down with my tongue—to tell her the news about the expectancy. That wild embracing and maddening passion, burning caresses that kept us all-involved for hours, took years to forget—to wear off.

The explanation that I gave her of the happening, to-wit: that it was while I was being nursed back from the flu, convalescing, etc.—that in a weak moment we had—the rubber was old—there must have been a hole—and there we were—and no amount of effort had successfully brought about a miscarriage—did not seem to soothe her troubled soul.

For a month or so after that, when I was living at the Fort Orange Club, I phoned her at midnight—and with passionate loving murmurings we would come down the telephone wire, she playing with herself on her end of the wire while I jerked off on my end of the wire.

Later, when I had left Albany and we were both in New York, I went to see her at the Murray Hill Hotel. That night we went to see the first edition of the *Chauve Chauris* [Souris] together and liked it very very much.

At the theatre that night it dawned upon us both that what was past was past and could never be brought back.

The baby would be arriving shortly and we could never recover that which had been so wonderful to both for several years—such an important and all-absorbing part of us both.

I saw Pauline after her return from abroad, the fall of 1922, and on several occasions after that. A romantic soul, she was always eager for us to travel together in Europe—a dream many women I have known have indulged themselves in but few have had that pleasure, I regret to say.

Each time we met on those now infrequent occasions I was impressed with the futility of attempting to turn back the hands of the clock.

Florence G. was a nurse—a training nurse—at the Lenox Hill Hospital whom I met while living at 981 Madison Avenue (just around the corner from the hospital). We saw much of each other and one day after loving around but no fucking, finger or otherwise, we decided to take a boat trip over the week-end—no, we didn't take the Albany Night Boat—but one nearly as bad, the Night Boat to Fall River that travels by the Sound.

We had the bridal suite. Before going to the boat we stopped at the Brevoort Hotel on lower Fifth Avenue, run by a Frenchman, Ortieg. We drank much and took much liquor with us. When aboard the Sound steamer we went straight to our room, and it was not long before we were abed. Much to my amazement, surprise and chagrin, Florence claimed she was still a virgin. Somehow, through stupor and with a drunken desire to be self-righteous by a display of much virtue, I refused to take her maiden-head—I abstained from rape, believe it or not!—one of the few regrets, sexually speaking, that I have had in life—a regret perhaps that might, on the other hand, well have been remorse had I stolen her cherry that night.

The regret, I suppose, is occasioned primarily by the fact that she chose the life of easy virtue, not content with one man at a time—

she went in for the attention of many. It was after our boat ride that she let a well known attending doctor take her virtue.

A year or so later, when I had left New York for Albany, I received a note asking me to call. I found her in much style and luxury in a swanky Park Avenue apartment. While she had graduated with honors from Lenox Hill, she found the art of satisfying the lust of horny males much more to her liking. She was big enough, however, to afford me an opportunity to make up in some small measure for that which I had passed up that eventful night on the Fall River liner by letting me crawl in between the sheets, "on the house" as it were. With difficulty I refrained, repressed my urge, kept my pants buttoned. She had been denied me that night on the boat, so I would not fuck her after she had become promiscuous.

There was a girl in the show *Irene*. I sent her flowers and bought her silk stockings. Captain Lucey, who had been the nominal head of the Hoover organization—the same that went playing around the Loomis girl with me in Chicago—decided that he wanted a party for some oil men at the Waldorf (on 34th Street and 5th Avenue then). So I took the *Irene* girl, Mabel G., and some other cunts that I knew to dinner in Lucey's suite at the Waldorf.

Everyone drank a good deal of liquor and the evening had hardly gotten under way when the girls, during my momentary absence from the room to take a leak, proceded to get into a hair-pulling fight because of counterclaims they felt they had upon me. So the party broke up disastrously. I beat a hasty retreat when it got to the throwing, biting, scratching and kicking stage. After I left it settled down somewhat, but the boys never got what they hoped for —the dopes! Any one of the girls in that emotional state would have been real hot stuff, tops.

Berenice T. of the Dry Goods Economist is not to be forgotten when enumerating my luscious cunts of bygone days. She entertained me most pleasantly on many interesting occasions in her petit boudoir during the summer of 1920 before I met Pauline W.—she was older, but what she lacked in youth she made up for in the know-how.

1920-1924

I organized the William Ward Smith Corporation in the fall of 1920 with the expectation of selling insurance in all its forms, as well as rebuilding my old stationery business.

Herbert Baker was to be active head of the company. We were no sooner incorporated and about to set off on our way than Victor called me and told me that Governor-elect Miller was anxious to have me for his Executive Secretary at the Capitol.

I had had no thought or desire of holding political office, either elected or appointed, and was completely taken by surprise.

Had I served my country in a military way during the great War, I probably would have entertained ambitions for the post of Secretary of the Navy in some presidential cabinet, but I realized that by my cowardice, or perhaps it was my reluctance to serve as a private in the ranks, I had eliminated all possibility of enjoying public office for many years.

When the suggestion was advanced it was a new idea but I liked it and accepted. As a matter of fact I was quite thrilled.

I visited Miller in Syracuse at his home office, Christmas week. He asked me if I had had a college education. When I replied in the negative, his answer was that he doubted if it would make such difference, as he too had had his training in the hard school of experience. He was a lousy speller; so was I. His handwriting was atrocious; so was mine. . . .

I will never forget (I was still at the impressionable age, just turned 27—you had just turned three—I was the youngest Secretary that had ever sat in the Executive Chamber) Al Smith, the Governor (retiring) of the Empire State receiving me in the Executive Chamber with his feet propped up on his desk, in the presence of his legal counselor, Jeremiah O'Connor, who sat facing the Governor in the same manner—feet on the Governor's desk, coatless, in his shirt-sleeves. . . .

On the ride up to Albany from New York, your mother and I invited the Chairman of the State Committee, George Glynn, to dine with us in our drawing room. Your mother, of course, was full of her Junior League liberal—I should say pink—ideas about Government and was always ready to give the "dyed-in-the-wool" conservative Chairman an argument. She had me on pins and needles—I was constantly kicking her shins under the table trying to shut her off.

My ego was boosted considerably after I went into office—what vain mortals we creatures be—to see big placards in the subway cars bearing a copy of a proclamation prepared and attested by me and signed by the Governor, urging the citizens to support this or that activity, such as the American Relief Administration, which proclamation was displayed in every street railway, not only in New York City but throughout the state as well. . . .

Early in January, 1921 we had planned to pay a visit to Lake Placid, but the League of Women Voters notified the Governor of a half-promise to attend their annual convention. They reminded him of his contingent informal promise by accusing him of going to Lake Placid in order to avoid addressing them. This was sufficient to turn most any trick with Miller. He gave up the trip to Placid and stayed in Albany to tell the girls what he thought of them.

This was that memorable occasion when he arose from a sick-bed to assure them that, as an independent body, unaffiliated with any recognized political organization, they were a menace to society. His ire had been aroused by their attacks on Wadsworth and himself during the previous fall campaign. He not only did not like the League of Women Voters, but he was feeling sick. . . .

During the Governor's confinement to the mansion with nervous fatigue and eye trouble it fell to my lot to pay many visits to New York, conferring with George McAneny, LeRoy Harkness, Travis Whitney, William Prendergast, Judge Francis Scott, Mr. Outerbridge, Judge Mayer, Jo Hedges, and Lindlay Garrison in the preparation of the Governor's proposed New Transit Bill. . . .

Miller believed that a unified transit system in Greater New York—or at least he so confided to me—would make it possible to give a comprehensive service with interchangeable free transfers . . . from one end of the city to the other profitably for a single five cent fare. He also believed that if managed along the proper sound business lines of those days that the fare could be reduced to two and a half or three cents a ride. Because of the Governor's ingrained judicial temperament he steadfastly refused to make such a statement for the press until such time as his new Transit Commission could complete its study and analysis of the entire system and render a report, which report, he felt, would bear out his contention. He wouldn't prejudice the work of his pet commission and commissioners by pre-judging their work publicly. . . .

The Port Authority was another of those achievements put through in Governor Miller's administration.

One afternoon while walking in the park with the Governor I suggested that it might be a gracious compliment and political expedient (in that it would cramp "Red Mike" Hylan's style) if the Governor were to appoint Al Smith upon that board as one of the New York State members.

I suggested that it would be necessary for the Authority to deal with the railroads and various corporate interests entering the Greater City, which would bring forth severe attacks upon the Authority and Miller, unless someone like Al Smith were on the Authority board.

Miller agreed, so we went to a corner drugstore, found a telephone booth, called the Executive Chamber and had them get Smith immediately. The Governor talked with Al a few minutes and he accepted. . . .

It worked well. Smith became an enthusiast and devoted much time and interest to the plans for improving the facilities of the port. I don't suppose it hurt his trucking business with which he was so closely affiliated at the time. . . .

In the first session of Miller's administration there appeared in Albany, in addition to Anderson of the Anti-Saloon League (afterwards sent to Sing Sing for tax evasions) and other professional reformers, one Canon Chase. With Chase was a Republican District Captain from Brooklyn—a woman. These two proceeded to present to the Governor what they considered evidence of salacity in the moving picture field, showing posters that were displayed at the cheaper class of houses and telling stories of the obscenity that was being displayed upon the screen. . . .

Thanks to the influence of the Catholic Church and the activities of the two, the bills had Mrs. Miller's hearty support.

At a meeting in the Executive Mansion (regardless of Mrs. Miller's wishes), it was decided between the Governor and the Legislative leaders that the bill would be killed; that the only legislation that would be passed would be a resolution creating a committee to investigate the advisability of censorship.

105

The moving picture people were hysterical at the thought of any censorship legislation.

Will Hays, who was then the Postmaster General of the United States, as well as Chairman of the Republican National Committee, brought every political pressure that he could bring upon the Governor and the Republican Legislature to prevent passage of the bill.

The motion picture legislation which was riding a sort of reform wave throughout the country was in part responsible for Will Hays' appointment as so-called Czar of the Motion Picture industry.

The day following the conference in the Mansion, where the plan for a commission to investigate was decided upon, I was introduced to William Brady, the theatrical producer, in the lobby of the Ten Eyck Hotel by George Franklin, the Republican State Committee's upstate publicity director.

Brady invited me up to his room for a drink. In prohibition days it was the usual custom. With Brady in his room were several motion picture officials.

After a few drinks they came to the point—when one of them offered me one hundred thousand dollars to oppose the passage of the bill. When I declined with thanks, they raised the ante to two hundred thousand.

Sam Koenig once told me, years afterwards, that they had offered him fifty thousand dollars which he too had refused.

At the same time they went after "Bill" (William L.) Ward, the Republican leader of Westchester, who was a man of large personal means, owned the Birdsall-Ward Nut and Bolt Co. He played politics for joy as well as profit.

Ward and I told the Governor what had happened and it was determined there and then (in order to save the administration from a public scandal, or talk of bribes given and received—whether the principals took the money or not the go-betweens would have cashed in if the bill had been killed by claiming to the motion picture executives that the money had been paid to all of us—if it had not been for the [bribe] attempts the bill would have been killed).

Two days after the Brady offer Harry Rosen, one of the largest writers of insurance in the world, (he had been an alternate delegate at Chicago) called me on the phone and offered to give me either three hundred thousand dollars in cash or a permanent job with a moving picture corporation which he professed to represent, at fifty thousand dollars a year. I thanked him, and also had the pleasure of recalling how ungracious he had been when I, as a representative of the Hoover organization, had met him at Chicago, and also how obnoxious he had been at the time I was connected with the New York Life office at the same time he was, and at which time I led even him in the writing of insurance.

Mrs. O'Rourke, the married woman from Bridgeport, Conn., whom I had played with some years before, attempted to bring pressure to bear of an entirely different sort. In those few days the motion picture people brought about their own doom, due to their supposition that all men in public life were corrupt. If they had kept hands off, the bill would have died a natural death, but eventually public opinion would have demanded something of the sort. Personally I was always opposed to censorship of any kind.

[My father accompanied Governor Miller on a highly publicized tour of the state's prison, reform and mental health facilities. He wrote a very detailed account of the trip. The following excerpts give a brief but vivid picture of the conditions in these institutions.]

The most revolting and horrible . . . sight of all [on the tour of investigation] was the hospital for the defective children at Newark, N.Y.

There the most ghastly deformities were seen—those poor contorted monstrosities of imbecilic children would make Bob Ripley's "Believe it or Not" sideshows of revolting freaks look like a bevy of bathing beauties. There wasn't a normal body amongst them, twisted and misshapened, every one, eyes out of focus, mouths open and drooling, huge heads, abnormal heads, on Lilliputian bodies, deformed limbs like toothpicks on big fat children, hands, fingers, feet in gruesome shapes—some fingers or toes missing—some more than the usual in number, some who couldn't hold their heads up, couldn't walk—crawled about in the dirt like fantastic grubbing animals of another age. Flies everywhere, crawling all over these revolting sights, that mostly couldn't even be trained to use toilet facilities but instead preferred to piss and shit in their pants, immune to the flies on them thicker than those around sticky paper or a hot horse turd on the highway—a sight you could never forget—a harrowing nightmare—the most terrible distortions of the human race—minds mostly blank, but some lightning calculators, some photographic able to recite perfectly anything seen, written, no consciousness of the spoken word. And all this largely, in fact invariably, the result of mating venereal-diseased parents. . . .

The Manhattan State Hospital on Wards Island in the East River,

New York, a stone's throw from Randalls, was the most dilapidated and unkempt in the state, and perhaps one of the oldest.

Incidentally, the founding fathers didn't seem to have this insanity problem—perhaps they were all crazy.

Manhattan was rickety, over-crowded, a veritable fire-trap of wooden shacks, the haven for the poor who all wanted their relatives at Manhattan State on Wards Island because of its accessibility to New York City.

According to the doctors and hospital superintendents, and the case records, the majority of the thirty-six thousand cases of dementia praecox that were in the New York State Hospitals for the insane in 1921, were directly or indirectly traceable to syphilis, either contracted by the individual or inherited.

As we went about, the doctors or superintendents or stewards would show us the brains of the deceased patients which had been preserved in alcohol with all the creeping vine-like markings of the ravages of syphilis on the brain clearly visible. . . .

Excellent work was being done then, and I assume is still being done, in rehabilitating, improving, and building-up the health of the patients in the New York State Hospitals for the insane. A great handicap to more effective work is and has always seemed to have been the crowded condition of the hospitals. In nearly every hospital at one time or another, as population increases faster than building, the crowding has necessitated the using of corridors for dormitories when all else was packed to overflowing.

Occupational therapy in 1921 and 1922 was already working wonders, particularly in those hospitals where the soldiers were segregated. It seemed especially adapted for the young men who had been drafted or served. . . .

The only institution that ever really upset us was the Rochester State Hospital for the insane. The Superintendent's wife was herself insane and living in his quarters, which were part of the main hospital building and it was not nearly as clean as most of the other hospitals we had visited. Nearly all the others in the state have detached houses for their superintendents, the houses, while on the grounds, being set quite apart from the main buildings.

At Rochester the patients, as a whole, were a more hopeless lot— more unkempt—the odor of disinfectant was stronger—the number of wild disorderly old women who tried to reach the Governor with a tale of woe and denunciation of the superintendent were legion. The straitjacketed cases were many and more than a few were being bathed or soaked in warm water to keep them quiet. They did what they had to do right wherever they happened to be and that added to the odoriferousness. . . .

The stories of the strife at Bedford [the state institution for women] would fill many volumes if ever truly and frankly set down by a sympathetic superintendent.

One fortunate thing is that while there a majority of the girls undergo treatments for venereal disease—which is more prevalent with the black girls than the white.

Sex perversion in prison for all sexes is a problem even tougher than in the U. S. Navy.

The slighted girls have their pals who also take offense at the treatment a neglected white girl has received, and the new favorite having her following which is resentful of the castoff's gang, the war is on—biting, scratching, hairpulling, beating, kicking and batting around. Frequently the nigger friends of the black lady add their two cents, and there is such hell to pay that even state troopers can't quell it at times. A female spurned is a fiery bitch at best, but when it's by one of her own sex she is Hades personified. . . .

At Bedford, N.Y., the great difficulty with the prostitutes housed in the Girls Reformatory there is degeneracy.

When the daily press reports an outbreak, an escape or a bad fight between girls it is nearly always certain to be a Lesbian feud over some favorite.

On the bare plaster walls were written such choice rarebits by the girls as "If that nigger son-of-a-bitch dirty wench doesn't stop sucking Kate and suck me I'll rip her god damn cunt out." The walls were covered not only with vile messages of perverted sex but with crude drawings of women's cunts and of girls sucking and loving one another as well—nothing was left to the imagination; it was all there in the frank and unblushing raw—poetry of the most obscene nature addressed by one girl to another and signed with their first or pet names was written everywhere—on doors and floors as well as the walls. A liberal education in erotica.

Most of the jealousy that is the forerunner of the riots is over the attentions of the nigger girls for the white girls. A white girl is in high dudgeon, seized with uncontrollable rage when her colored lover drops her for some other woman. . . .

The mastication habits of the guests of the Old Soldiers Home at Bath interested me no end, medically speaking, for as a child I had

109

been told that in order to digest my food I must chew it very carefully—I must not eat hurriedly or else I would be very sick. If that theory were true I should have died long ago, and there would not be a single living inmate at Bath. Those old soldiers, ranging anywhere from seventy to ninety years of age, as soon as their dining room doors open, rush in and set themselves before the food that has already been placed on the long dining tables, and much more rapidly than it takes me to tell you they take large pieces of beef and vegetables and literally fling them into their toothless mouths and swallow it all in one grand gulp; and they all appear to be in excellent health and look as though they were going to live forever—they actually lick their platters clean with not a chew in the bunch. Their exercising is almost nil—they potter over a few childrens games or flower beds and the like. The bare fact is that their failure to chew does not seem to affect their digestion a single bit—maybe it's the saliva that saves the day for them. I can still hear my mother "CHEW YOUR FOOD, WARDIE, CHEW YOUR FOOD OR YOU WILL BE SICK! CHEW YOUR FOOD, WARDIE," and then I think how the old boys at Bath live on, and when the time comes for my teeth to go I suppose I will live on and there will be no adoring mother to say "Chew your food, Wardie"—for there will probably be no mother and, of course, no teeth to chew with. . . .

At Sing Sing, the old Death House was the outstanding feature. I had always had a notion that the execution room would be most horrifying. As I followed Warden Lawes through the court yard my shoelace, as was its wont, became untied. He opened a small side door of the dilapidated prison. The door opened into a large room. I entered and placed my hand upon a nearby chair in order to balance myself as I tied my shoelace. As I finished I asked the warden where the death house was located, and he replied that I was in the death house and that the chair I was resting against was the electric chair.

The revelation didn't shock me—my many contacts with death sentences and the frantic, grief-stricken families of those about to fry had given me an immunity to the death house horror.

The autopsy room did not bother me either.

The section next to the autopsy room, where the condemned await their turn at the chair, was pretty appalling. First of all, the walls were so thin that not only could they see the condemned march off to the chamber but they could hear the entire performance. To cap it off the autopsy, performed immediately afterwards with an electric drill on the skull, was always plainly audible. The condemned wait

110

their turn in large cells like box stalls—rows of these cells faced one another in double tiers—and were so arranged that every occupant could see all the others except the ones directly above. This has all been changed now, and a most modern death house adorns the hillside at Sing Sing—one that was planned by Lewis Pilcher, the State Architect under Miller.

Before a man goes to the chair, a direct open wire is established between the Warden's office and the Executive Chamber. This is done so that in the case of a last-minute decision on the part of the Chief Executive to commute a sentence or stay an execution, the Secretary can so advise the Warden. . . .

The best and only sound argument that I know of in favor of capital punishment is the fact that life sentences usually mean that the prisoner will be free in ten or fifteen years.

That capital punishment does not have a deterrent effect upon crime is pretty generally conceded by criminologists.

The prisoners cooked the meals and waited on the Warden's table at Sing Sing. My luncheon there was my first experience with the receiving of smuggled notes for the Governor from prisoners or patients waiting on table. At Lawes' table I was the recipient of many myself, that is, addressed to me personally, beseeching me to use my influence with the Governor to secure their pardon or a pardon for some other fellow criminal. There were plenty there that didn't like Lawes or his methods.

Even in those early days he risked the Executive's disfavor with his wild urge for personal publicity.

At Auburn we found women prisoners—in, not for prostitution but for crimes of sundry and varied nature against the peace of their respective communities. Women are much more of a problem than men, eternally getting into rows and disturbances, and for some unknown reason, although there unquestionably is much sex perversion among men, apparently the percentage of mutual attraction between women is much greater.

At Auburn they had found that the most effective way to dispel a feminine outbreak was to turn the hose upon the charming damsels and give them a good soaking, which invariably quieted them instantly and sent them like drowned rats scurrying to their cells in complete subjection. . . .

While the women are bad sexually, the men in prisons are no paragons of virtue. At Clinton Prison—the Siberia or Alcatraz of New York—when we were passing through on inspection I not only saw men masturbating in the exercise yard, but jumping one another as well, while the others went about their affairs unconcerned. . . .

Many people felt that Miller was almost inhuman, yet I have found him playing with you and his own children on the floor of their playroom, setting up their toys and getting much pleasure and joy from his association with them. There was nothing of the prude about him in any way. He liked attractive women—liked his liquor—knew a dose of syphilis from a dose of clap, and did not hesitate to discuss same. I doubt if he ever missed a shapely leg or any of the other feminine allurements that attract and hold the attention of most men. He liked social gossip and scandal. He would frequently, in the presence of Mrs. Miller, ask me about the latest gossip in *Town Topics* or the other scandal sheets. Yet in business he was hard, ruthless. A great egotist, he had little patience with the weaknesses and human frailties of his fellowman. He expected all around him to be supermen. He was too cold and calculating to radiate any warmth on the public platform. Miller was an autocrat, with an iron will that insisted upon absolute rulership, and disliked being hampered or fettered by restrictions; his mentality was arbitrary and masterful, backed by sound judgment, common sense, cool deliberation, and an entire absence of any human sympathy or emotion that might conflict with the performance of his duty; a man of superlatively constructed mental machinery, functioning with the highest degree of efficiency; able to accomplish the maximum of great results, but with the ruthless efficiency of a machine, and devoid of any element of human feeling in the execution of his work; he had a complete absence of the element of love in his nature, and an incapacity for making friends through emotional instincts, although capable of drawing people closely to him in sheer admiration of his dynamic force of character, his honesty, and his matchless intellect. He was mentally alert and quick to grasp new ideas; vigorous and enthusiastic in whatever he undertook; he had excellent organizing ability; was a splendid executive; and was capable of carrying whatever enterprise he started to a successful finish; his was a bold, brave and indomitable spirit. . . .

Regardless of his own desire, ambition and qualifications and the kind words and encouragement of his friends Miller knew that his wife's blood and [Catholic] religious creed stood firmly and clearly between him and the White House and that there could never be an "On to Washington" for him.

It embittered him—although he never would admit it.

Often when the Governor, Mrs. Miller, your mother and I were alone together out at the country club—after the day's work was done —for a round of golf or supper, I would relate a brief resume of the day for the edification of the women and whenever I would mention that some important caller had been in emphasizing the Governor's presidential availability, Mrs. Miller would invariably remark, although no comment would be forthcoming from the Governor: "Nathan can never be President of the United States because of me."

I always felt that because the Governor fully realized the potent truth of Mrs. Miller's statement he proceeded to act and administer his office as if he had no intention of running for re-election or any other office.

The Catholic Church made him tough—not the belief that he had a mandate from the people. . . .

While Miller's administration was unquestionably one of the most economical and well run that the State of New York has ever had, excepting the administrations of Theodore Roosevelt and Charles Evans Hughes, it was not a popular administration, largely because of Miller's almost willful disregard of popular opinion. . . .

Miller did what he thought was right and what he promised the voters he would do, come hell or high water. . . .

When Jesse Phillips resigned as Superintendent of Insurance, Nathan Miller offered the appointment to me. The McCall brothers, Darwin Kingsley, President and Vice-President Buckner of the New York Life, were most anxious to have me accept.

I suppose they thought it would be fine to have a former salesman as the Superintendent of Insurance, passing upon their "ifs" and "ands." Had I accepted I probably would have leaned over backwards to be tough on them.

I felt there was more fun in being Secretary to the Governor than head of one of the many departments—as Secretary I was in on everything; as a department head you are only in your own department. Anyway, I had never liked the insurance business. That decision was a mistake. Had I accepted the appointment I would have gone from that job into a good executive position with one of the first-line companies and had a job for life; died in my tracks, an irascible old man, a nervous wreck with a sizable bank account—and life would have been much easier for you and Marshall. . . .

Miller was very extravagant in his household affairs and in his personal traveling.

While it was possible for me to reduce the expenses of the

Executive Chamber by more than $50,000 annually below the previous Al Smith administration, it was necessary both for the Governor and for me to expend large sums out of our own pockets to defray his luxurious traveling costs.

Miller entertained royally at the Plaza and the St. Regis, and it cost money.

On one of our trips to New York he learned from the new Military Secretary Coogan that we had been spending a good deal more than he had any idea of, and for the first time since I had been with him he brought his critical guns to bear on me.

I resented it and told him that I felt that it was impossible to do anything with him from the standpoint of his own personal expenditures—that whenever I tried to economize on the suites at the Plaza or other hotels he found fault; that Bill McCarthy and I had repeatedly cautioned him about reckless spending. He and his wife and daughters were always buying theatre tickets and riding around in hired automobiles which had to be paid for at $5 and $7 per hour, and they were always expensively entertaining their personal, business and political friends.

My father and I put up several thousand dollars for Miller's expenses which he never repaid—not that he might not have done so, but rather than get into an argument on the subject we never presented them.

Miller was the type that always felt that he was paying a good deal more than he should have for everything, although always insisting on paying.

When he realized that he was greatly exceeding his traveling expense appropriation, he attempted to make me the goat.

He never practiced personally what he preached. All other items in the Executive Department were way below previous years and the appropriation. The explosion took place in January and after much argument I insisted upon resigning. So it was agreed that I would quit after the thirty-day bill period of the second legislative session.

George Aldrich, one of the big leaders in the State at the time, thought that it would be bad for me and bad for Miller if I left, but I got myself into such an hysterical state of mind that it was impossible for me to reason sanely or to remain.

I immediately moved my private office to the extreme end of the Executive Chamber—as far away from the Governor's office as I could—so that I would no longer have to be in close daily contact with him.

This action on my part caused much comment in the press, and was finally silenced by the statement that I had moved to other quarters in order to devote most of my time to the preparation of material for the Governor's use in his debate with Governor Allen of Kansas. Miller was against the St. Lawrence Canal project—Lakes to the Sea—

Our families maintained pleasant relations up until the day I left, and later, at the request of Mrs. Miller when she and the Governor came to New York. Your mother introduced the girls into the Junior League and saw that they were elected members. And that was no mean task, although Mrs. Charles Sabin, Mrs. Tony Sarg, and Mrs. Cortland Nicoll cooperated with her. They almost didn't make it and would not have but for your mother's heroic efforts. . . .

Miller was very free with his money and was always lending money to his associates on the bench.

A few days before I left Albany, the Legislative Correspondents presented me with a handsome mahogany cane with a silver band bearing an inscription commemorative of the occasion. It was the first time that they had ever made a presentation as an organization, or as individuals, to any Governor or Governor's Secretary, or to anyone else on Capitol Hill, an honor that I shall always cherish, perhaps the one I cherish most. Miller wanted to attend the presentation but they wouldn't let him come. Somehow it always seemed more of a slap at him than a boost for me—am I ungrateful?

That summer your mother went to Madison, Conn. I stayed with my mother and father in their apartment in New York City most of the time. Your Grandfather and Grandmother Page were sharing the cottage and part of the expense, although most of the burden fell on me. As usual, I couldn't get along with your Grandparents Page, especially your grandmother, so I was not in New Haven with your mother when [your brother was born].

The deliberate interference of the Pages in my domestic affairs from the very outset tended to disrupt our relations and to make trouble between your mother and me. And when I say the Pages I include Rosalie and Virginia as well as Mr. and Mrs. Page.

While attending the State Fair at Syracuse on Governor's Day, I met Virginia S., whose husband was president and principal owner of the L. C. Smith Typewriter Co. They occupied a charming home opposite the Governor's on Oneida Street.

Several weeks later, when attending a party at Mrs. S.'s home in company with the Lieutenant-Governor and the Adjutant General of the State, I met her again. She had a lovely figure, with fair youthful breasts and a peculiarly full bottom. She looked the picture of health.

The full cheeks of her behind excited me intensely—I do not know why. There was much drinking and finally, behind the couch in one of the living rooms, we had our congress. Before the last sperm had passed on its way, another couple came and sat on the sofa to enjoy life's greatest ecstasy.

That night I went on to New York. On my return, several days later, she called me on the phone to say she thought something was the matter with her. She wondered if I had any trouble. I told her no. She inquired if I would be willing to see her doctor, and I agreed. He called. I told him that I was perfectly clean and let him make an inspection for himself. He took a test and found there was not a sign of gonorrhoea, although he told me that he also had taken cultures of Virginia's and failed to find any germ there, but she had a slight irritation and some discharge.

I called General Leslie Kincaid's nephew in Syracuse immediately. He introduced me to his doctor who, although it was four days late, proceeded to inject powerful preventives in the end of my cock. Net result—he brought on an irritation but could find no sign of the dreaded bug.

Shortly afterwards, the situation cleared and before long we were back at the old game again. Her husband was having an affair with his secretary, and frequently I would spend most of the night with her in her house. Parties were usually going on downstairs, while we would use a guest room for our affair on the floor above, for loving by that time had progressed much beyond the parlor stage. On some occasions I had one of the State Police officers stand guard outside Virginia's home to warn me of any unexpected return of friend husband. Leaving in the cold gray dawn I would have the 20th Century stop at Syracuse so that I could keep my engagements in New York or Albany.

The station agent would call the state troopers through a police booth on the corner telling them that the 20th Century was coming into the yard. They would knock on the front door gently and I would rush down pulling on my pants, jump into the police car and rush off to the station with the troopers.

After I resigned I frequently saw Virginia in New York, usually at the Ritz or the Carleton House where she stopped with her mother, Mrs. George K. Virginia's father was a wealthy brewer, George H. of

116

Syracuse. On one occasion we motored up to City Island to see her husband's yacht before it was put in condition.

Virginia didn't like to climb ladders—it made her dizzy. It was a big yacht, and it was quite a climb. Her married sister Leonora Warner had accompanied us and she volunteered to go aboard and check up on the linens and a few other items. So the captain took us through the boat.

A few months later her step-father advised me that, in a suit for separation Virginia's sister Leonora was bringing against her husband, her husband had entered a denial and counter charges wherein he had submitted an affidavit of the chauffeur saying I had screwed Leonora on the trip to City Island. The truth is Leonora wanted us to get a boy friend for her. We were not successful in finding the aviator she wanted, so she went along with us anyway. I did screw Virginia in the car while Leonora watched but I never touched Leonora.

At Colonel K.'s request I called on Judge Robert McCurdy Marsh, who was then sitting in the Supreme Court and before whom the case had come, and told him some of the grounds which had not been mentioned in the suit as reasons for desiring the separation, namely, that Leonora's husband insisted upon being sucked off each night when he came home. It was Leonora's contention that he would drop his pants off, sit on the side of the bed and make her get down on her knees before him. Sometimes he would have her sit on the side of the bed while he stood before her.

They must have done some screwing in their day because they had two strapping sons to prove it. She professed to abhor the sucking practices of her husband. Perhaps she wanted to be sucked.

We had a waitress in our State Street house. I noticed that she seldom wore an underskirt and that you could see her legs through her dress. One week-end when I was alone at home, as she went up the rear stairs to her room I observed she had fine ankles and I divined that she had shapely limbs. While she was placing some things on the kitchen shelf the lifting of her arms raised her bodice and showed small round breasts. Apparently she hoped I would notice. Already my blood was lava and my mouth parched with desire. I took her into the living room and pressed her head down on the arm of the sofa and kissed her. Her lips grew hot. At once I put my hand down on her cunt. She struggled, which I took care should bring our bodies closer. And when she stopped I put my hands up her dress and began caressing her sex again. It was hot and wet and opened readily. I begged her to undress. I wanted to see her nude body. She had no corsets on. Then

117

I lifted her and carried her upstairs onto the bed. I drew up her clothes and opened her legs and was in her. There was no difficulty. In a moment or two I came but went right on poking at her passionately. In a few minutes her breath went and came quickly and her eyes fluttered and she met my thrusts with signs and nippings of her sex. All the while she became more and more responsive, until suddenly she put her hand on my bottom and drew me to her forcibly, while she moved her sex up and down awkwardly to meet my thrusts with a passion I had hardly imagined. Again and again I came, and the longer the play lasted the wilder was her excitement and delight. She kissed me madly, forging and thrusting her tongue into my mouth. Finally, she pulled up her chemise to get me further into her, and at length, with little sobs, she suddenly got hysterical and, panting, burst into a storm of tears.

The pay-off I afterwards learned was that she had been a prostitute in an Albany whore-house and only took up general housework for "the Master" when business got dull and the cops persistent.

There was the Night girl that George M., the Republican State Chairman, brought to Albany. He met her at the Belmont Race Track. She soon became the whore of that political town. Bill McCarthy was much excited one afternoon because I took her out to a roadhouse for tea and liquor and much conversation—only conversation. She was too promiscuous and I knew about her many affairs so my sex was not aroused.

I met in New York while I was still with the Governor, Margaret R., a school teacher, who was more or less up against it. For a while she lived with Grace Humiston, and then with Rose Little, who had a public stenographic office on the corner of Christopher and Sixth, where she used to type manuscripts for Kenneth McGowan and McVeigh. On one or two occasions I spent the night with Margaret. She claimed to be a virgin, said she had never been screwed, so I left her alone. I heard from her often, however, receiving bits of poetry and requests for recommendations for jobs at teaching.

Rose Little was a friend of Elizabeth Dinsmore. One day when I called Elizabeth her husband answered the phone and told her I was on the wire. When Rose heard my name she exclaimed "Why, that's Margaret's married boy friend." It seems that Margaret had asked Phillips before he married Elizabeth Dinsmore, to marry her. She had approached several others with a similar request.

She proposed to marry any single man who would marry her and leave the fellow at the City Hall as soon as the Clerk had performed the ceremony.

Her story was that she was in love with a married man (I was it) and wanted to have a baby by him—wanted him to take her virtue. She wanted a name for her baby but she didn't want to be raped by her groom.

Until Elizabeth broke the news, amidst gales of uproarious laughter, I never had any idea of the little bitch's scheme for my presenting her with a semi-bastard. But I took good pains after that to see that she did not succeed with her lovely little plan.

Miss L., a stenographer in the Executive Chamber when George Glynn was Secretary under Whitman, was transferred, before I reached Albany, to one of the other State Departments in New York City.

When the Motion Picture Commission was created she was put in charge of that department's Personnel.

One night George, who was then Chairman of the Republican State Committee, staged a dinner party in the private office of the State Committee, at which Miss L. was present. The Republican State Headquarters were in the rear of the National Republican Club. While her husband waited in the reception room of the club, she left the dinner table and went with me into George Glynn's private office which adjoined the main room. We were both quite lit up, and there on the floor of Glynn's office I screwed her. I always believed that George had hoped I might have a long affair with her, counting on her to obtain information from me that would be of value to him, but it did not work out that way. George really was an awful ass, he opened the door once and walked in, watched us fucking on the floor for a few minutes, then strolled out again. And everyone in the state knew she was George's mistress.

At the Ten Eyck Hotel one night Rockwell Cole, General Leslie Kincaid's Secretary and Publicity Director, and I picked up two girls from Haverstraw who were passing through town. It was in the summer. One of the girls' name was Laird. We took them up to my office in the Capitol to impress them with our importance and screwed them then and there. The Laird girl was Oliver Harriman's secretary. She bombarded me with communications to have wrongs in Haverstraw righted—or what she thought were wrongs. The hell of that episode was that she was ever after complaining about this or that. For years she kept in touch with me but I suppose she found other fish in Haverstraw she thought important.

On a New York Central train westbound one day I met a girl named Mildred M. She lived in California on a ranch. Her family were important here. She had a brilliant mind and was discontented there, but determined to stick it out. We had an affair in my drawing room, and corresponded for a while thereafter. There was something very attractive about her. She was married and had children.

For years I had worshipped Helen K. To my mind she was everything that personified womanliness and godliness. Although I had never had the courage to pay her much court, I did see quite a bit of her while I was Secretary to the Governor. She entertained me at her home often when I was in New York.

One night over the phone she told me that instead of marrying a very attractive man in Boston who was madly in love with her, she was going to marry an old millionaire in Philadelphia—some fellow with a stable full of hunting horses, etc., a widower much older than herself—but that she would continue with her Hearst *Good Housekeeping* Editorial contract until it expired. It has long since expired and been renewed. I suppose the thirty-five or forty thousand she received gave her a feeling of independence.

I expressed my keen disappointment over her decision to take the older rather than the younger man, and was so upset that I declared my full intention of going out and getting tight. I was with the Governor at a Lincoln Day dinner of the National Republican Club being held at the Waldorf Astoria at the time. As soon as I could get away and tuck the Governor into bed I phoned her again to pour out my distress over her matrimonial plans. She gathered from my thick and rambling speech that I had gotten very tight (I was tired but I hadn't been drinking) so she invited me up to her apartment at that unusually late hour for her to have a farewell chat. . . .

In order to make good on the illusion of drunkenness that I had created on the phone, I had to take a fair amount of alcholic stimulant aboard before I went up to her apartment.

The maid opened the door for me (she had gotten the girl up for the occasion—made it look more respectable).

She entered the living room in a most charming negligee. She had never interested me sexually in all the years I had known her— somehow I had never thought of her in that way. She had always been on a pedestal above all such craven desires. Her seductive negligee plus the liquor was sufficient for me to discover charms never before unfolded. My sex instincts were ravishingly aroused. I had always assumed she was a virgin. I should have known better—they don't grow anymore. I expressed a wild desire to see her nude. To my amazement, instead of ordering me out of her lovely home that had such a definite air of virginity about it, as if it forever had been unsullied and

120

untouched, she sat up on the couch where she had been lying beneath me, smiled and said, "Here I am, I can deny you nothing," as she let the negligeee slip from her. She showed me herself nude from head to stockings. As I had guessed, her figure was slight and lithesome, with narrow hips, but she had a great bush of hair on the mouth of her Venus. Her breasts were round but not so firm as others I had had. She was very pretty and well formed, with slender wrists, ankles. After I had kissed her breasts and navel, I placed my sex into her passionately. The ecstasy of that fornication is one I shall never forget. I was totally unprepared for any such passionate reactions as my attentions provoked.

I have never seen her but once from that day to this, and then only for a moment. My mother and your mother, and your Aunt Elise, frequently ran into her and she always inquired about your old man.

Women are strange creatures. It is not unusual for them, when going to marry one man, to screw another on the eve of their launching forth—also under great emotional stress (such as the sudden loss of someone very near and dear to them when their eyes are flowing over with uncontrolled tears) they will spread their legs apart for the handiest man available.

Helen hadn't had an easy life. She supported her father from the time she was sixteen until he died, brought up her sisters, introduced them to society and married them off. She started with the *Ladies Home Journal* in Philadelphia—sort of made a place for herself—and then Hearst picked her up for *Good Housekeeping*. She did much to make that publication a great success. She inaugurated the personal shopping service for readers with special emphasis on xmas shopping. It went over big—the advertisers were convinced of the real reader interest and pulling power of the circulation.

At one time Helen was Fashion Editor of both *Harper's Bazaar* and *Good Housekeeping,* but under different pen names.

Well, she married the buzzard in Philadelphia. I have a sneaking suspicion she thought he might die while she was still fairly young, but he didn't.

Occasionally I hear from her, but very formally, about something of interest in the publishing world.

Several girls that worked for her as secretaries worked for me afterwards—Helen was ruthless, and determined to succeed.

She once told me that as you ascended the ladder of success you must cast off those friends who do not contribute to your future as

121

you go along the road—it seems hard but it is necessary if one ever is to get anywhere—there are only so many hours in a day and days in a week and weeks in a month and months in a year, and if you are to get along as you make new friends who are helpful you must discard the old ones—the hangers-on—as you go.

In private life dear Helen is Mrs. S. Laurence B. of "Greenbank Farm" Newton Square, Pa.—oh! she was a well-bred lady—Colonial Dame, social registerite, and everything that goes with it.

While we were working in Syracuse, the girl who did our mimeograph work gave herself to Walter Berry and me one night in her office, after we had finished a busy hectic day. She was a pretty good desk screw—wet deck and all. I don't know why I mention her, except that it was a nice way to top off a busy day—and those days were busy.

On the Executive Chamber Staff was a girl named Irene M., who had worked there through one administration after another since Theodore Roosevelt's day, when she had come in as a file clerk at $600 annually, and worked up to stenographer, and a good one at that. George Graves, who had come in at the bottom and worked up to Assistant Secretary, was her brother-in-law. In all the time that Irene had been there, there had never been a breath of scandal about her fair name.

A week or so before I left the Executive Chamber, it suddenly occurred to me that she might be responsive. While I had been hard on her, at times driven her ruthlessly, yelled at her, swore at her and cursed unmercifully (as is my wont when things go wrong), I somehow felt she liked me a little.

I had made her chief stenographer and raised her pay—she was an excellent shorthand reporter and executive.

Well, I played the hunch—one night, late, out in the outer office, I took her in my arms—my hand played with her sex—she said she was a virgin, but she was willing that I have her. I was leaving and as hot as I was, I had her pull me off rather than destroy her virtue, and possibly knock her up.

For the next few nights—or until I left—we managed to get some loving in. Irene was sweet and I always felt lousy about that episode. When I did go, they tell me she completely broke down and had to go home for a week or ten days. I think she was one of the few who really missed me. . . .

After Miller had refused to turn McArthur over to the New Jersey authorities to be tried for rape, his lawyer, Emil Fuchs, a former magistrate of New York and owner of the Boston Braves, invited Ed Schoeneck (a former Lieutenant-Governor of the State of New York) George Glynn (the Republican State Chairman), Ralph A. Day (the Prohibition Director and dress manufacturer), one of the up-State Supreme Court Judges, and myself to have dinner with him at a speakeasy on 48th Street. I was late in getting there, but they had Hawaiian music and several very attractive girls who danced up on our table, showing their cunts, after we were all pretty well liquored up. Following the dinner we went to an apartment on 72nd Street. When we arrived it was very quiet, no one there. But shortly lovely girls began coming in, one after another. In my state they all looked lovely.

We continued to drink and to dance. The girls' garments were thin and they rubbed their bellies right up against us.

With a lot of liquor aboard I wandered (in a semi-despondent mood) into one of the bed rooms with a lovely little piece and found a revolver in a bureau drawer, with which I amused myself—I suggested suicide. They finally got the gun away from me, and the party was safe again.

When I came back into the room the girls were gradually taking off their clothes as they danced around with the others until they were all nude. Then the men took their things off and everyone danced naked.

Most of the men were so excited that they lost no time in unsheathing their swords right in the center of the dance floor, fucking the girls while everyone watched.

In the midst of all this revelry a charming tidbit in a "come-on" negligee, who had an apartment across the hall, dropped in and extracted a promise that as soon as her lover left I would come over and go to bed with her.

After that we all went into one of the bed rooms and put the twin beds together. Formed a human chain, one upon the other; men on girls, girls on men. At the tail end of the chain, or the final link, was the nigger maid. That was some picture to take home and pass on to future generations or degenerations. Despite my drunken stupor it made a lasting impression.

The maid knelt at the foot of the bed, while the last white girl held her head between her legs, and Emil Fuchs got down on his knees and fucked the nigger wench from behind.

The first girl took Ed Schoeneck in her mouth, and then the others all in turn were sucking one another, loving their titties. When the performance was getting started, the little neighbor from next door came in and took me away. As I was about to mount the bitch all the liquor I had consumed got the best of me and I passed out of the picture.

When I recovered, I decided that we must all go down to Reisenweber's, where, at five o'clock in the morning, I trailed a vision in blue into the ladies' dressing-room and stripped her.

Why that night I did not get a dose of syphilis or gonorrhoea is more than I could ever figure out.

Your grandfather and grandmother, especially grandmother, were very shocked that summer (1922) over my alleged misconduct with the trained nurse your mother had for [your brother] when she came back from the New Haven Hospital.

On several occasions, when I was up there over the week-end, we would go swimming and she, a playful young thing, would climb all over and about me as we frolicked in the water. She was young, full of fun, and there was nothing out of the way about it—the water was too cold for me to get a "hard" on.

Dr. Pile, a summer resident who lived next door, had a very attractive nurse girl for his children. On the sly he was slipping her a piece when his wife wasn't looking. No one suspected any interest on my part for the maid, but there they would have had something real, for I did find my way into her belly on the Madison sand one dark night—no moon.

That was the summer I got you to jump and didn't catch you, hoping you would swim to keep yourself up.

[I remember the incident very well. My mother had just knit me a sweater of which I was very proud. While I stood on the pier my father, in his bathing suit, stood in the water below me, exhorting me to jump. I protested that I could not swim and, further, that the water would ruin my new sweater. He assured me that he would catch me. I jumped; he deliberately let me land in the water and struggle to remain afloat for what seemed like an interminable time before retrieving me. He belonged to the sink or swim school. On an earlier occasion when I was four he had thrown me into a swimming pool on the same principle. I was almost ten before I overcame my fear of the water.]

During the winter of 1922–23 in New York I met Evelyn N. She was a show girl in the cabaret at Shanley's. We stayed one night at the Brevoort Hotel and I kissed her feverishly but she contended I was quite a novice and proceeded to teach me some of the fine points that I should have known. I met her often, and in fact for some months followed her about the country when she was on tour with road com-

124

panies. She was a good sport. She finally married the manager of Jimmie Hodges' road show. Evelyn was a swell kid and I was always very fond of her.

In Morristown that same winter I met Helen B., a friend of your Uncle Eddy and Aunt Elise. Helen was an old sweetheart of Haley Fiske, Jr., and the mother of three or four children. Helen would have lunch baskets made up at the country club and we would go off for the entire day in the woods.

One time she had a date with Haley to meet him at the Madison railroad station of the D. L. & W. at high noon. Well, we drove over to Madison in the morning right after her husband left for New York. At first I was going to New York on a later train, but I parked my conspicuous cream-colored Cadillac roadster in a garage and drove off with Helen in her station wagon. We planned to return in time to meet Haley at the train.

Station wagons not only are inconspicuous in the country but the side curtains make identifications difficult—and there is always lots of room (when the extra seats have been taken out for baggage).

We parked up a little-used road about three miles from the station and somehow or other got so all-fired het up that we forgot about Haley's date.

Late in the afternoon, Haley, who for hours had been on a personally conducted sleuthing tour, caught up with us in the woodland road and drove alongside in his hired taxi. To his chagrin he found me on top of the very passionate Helen B. on the floor of her station wagon, clothes in great disarray—mostly off—her hair tumbled down around her bare shoulders. As I got up my load was plainly visible in my condom. (I still have one of her garters as a souvenir of that wild occasion when we had been screwing our silly heads off.) Haley was ferocious—so excited at the picture he beheld that he could hardly control himself.

I suggested that he get in the station wagon and drive us back to Madison where I would get my car (Helen could gather her things together and primp up a bit on the way), and I would leave them to work out their own little problem.

This Haley very gallantly did, driving right into the garage.

Helen was not pretty, nor did she have a beautiful body, but she was passionate and had something about her that was compelling and insistent. I met her surreptitiously almost daily for several months, and then she went to Europe with her children for quite a long stay—to be rid of Haley and myself, she said. In one of my exciting picnic outings I feigned insanity in order to win my way about some minor matter and was so convincing that Helen thought I had gone raving mad. I don't think she was ever quite sure after that whether I was or not, and of course I never really was certain in my own mind how close to the line I was—and am.

We moved to Morristown, N.J. from Connecticut in 1922 and I went into business for myself selling hay and lumber by-products for my own account and for father, traveling all over New Jersey and Pennsylvania; and that gave me a great deal of liberty to get in some fine outside work.

I met a girl from Boston named Baker on Fifth Avenue one night. She was in her car and I in the Cadillac. We struck up quite a friendship immediately. She was peddling thermometers for some well known thermometer instrument manufacturing company.

We took a trip down through Pennsylvania, along the Delaware Water Gap, and back to Newark by way of Morristown. We stopped over the week-end at the Robert Treat in Newark. We did not hit it off very well although a congress did occur.

Several days later she told me she had gonorrhoea—had gotten it from me. She wanted a large sum to visit her doctor for treatments. I told her that she couldn't have gotten it from me, but that if she had it I would be glad to have my doctor treat her. She agreed to this until it came time to make the appointment for him to see her, then she backed down. I saw her once or twice after that at Barney's but never did I fornicate with her again. She was a stick-up artist. She was a hostess at Barney Gallant's for a while after she lost her thermometer job. When I learned she was up to her old tricks, I had Barney kick her out on her dirty ear.

I suppose I better get the women business well along so that I can catch up with the rest of the story—all my life women and my perpetual "hard ons" have kept me from doing real constructive work for my country and myself. It's all been for cunt.

I frequently commuted between Morristown and New York, and on the trains I met a few—a weakness with me, trains and stations and boat and hotel rooms. One girl lived in Orange. She afterwards moved to Madison. We would get off the train, wander into the countryside and fuck.

There was one from Madison and one in Summit. They were interesting cases, and I might as well tell about them.

And there was Othello, an actress—she calls herself Ophilia or

126

something like that, plays character parts—ladies maids, etc.—in the movies. She was a nymphomaniac—couldn't wait to get to the wayside bushes, would want it in the telephone booth or toilet of the station waiting room.

On one of my trips I met Mary M. of Summit, mother of four fine boys. She was a tormenting creature, lived in a beautiful house with her father-in-law and had a lovely place in Newport, R.I., called "Haddon Hall."

When I called, Mary would come down to meet me in a diaphanous black negligee (my piece de resistance) and show me pictures of herself in varying moods of abandonment. I never put my prick into her, although on many occasions I came all over her. The reason for the consideration? At the height of her passion she was given to spasms or fits and would roll on the floor. Then her father-in-law would come in and we would work over her to bring her around. She had her points, she wanted it badly but was afraid of it. She had a girl friend who stayed with her at times, and on one occasion she insisted that we fuck while she watched. Another time when she had nearly all her clothes off she fainted and her father-in-law came in on that too. He was an old man in his dotage, and the situation didn't seem to bother him much.

There was an attractive girl in Morristown who worked in the Internal Revenue Department. She was the daughter of one of the leading butchers in the town. I had watched her pass the Morristown Inn four times a day every day while we lived there.

After we had moved out on Mt. Kemble Ave. and then back to the house on the other side of the town, I would see her at a distance, but I never knew she saw me—she gave no sign that would indicate she was ever aware of my existence.

Learning by chance that she was about to be married (I had found out long since who she was) I called her from New York and arranged to meet her. Although it was the first time that I had called her up, and I was careful not to say who I was over the phone, she seemed to know. We arranged a date. Everyone was away at my house, servants on vacation, etc. I was thrilled.

I sent flowers and candy to her office anonymously early in the day.

Then at 10 o'clock at night I met her on a lonely road on the outskirts of town. It was raining hard. She got in quickly without a word and I drove her to my home. Before I left the house I had lit the fires (the night was damp and raw) and they were all burning—

everything perfect, flowers and all as they should be. We had hardly spoken a word. I gave her a few drinks, showed her some of my choice erotic literature and suggested that I show her the rest of the house, particularly my study on the top floor.

When I kissed her as we started up the stairs, her lips were cold, but by the time we had gotten up she had thawed a bit. All the time she had not said much.

As we entered my room she took over, quietly shutting the door after us, and to my utter surprise she almost immediately drew back her outer robe or raincoat, which she had refused to take off downstairs. She had nothing on under the coat and stood before me stark naked.

She threw the garment on a chair and it fell on the floor. She stooped to pick it up, turning her bottom to me as she did so. I kissed her on the bottom and caught her up to me with my hand on her wet sex. She turned and said: "I have washed and scented myself for you. How do you like this bush of hair—I was so ashamed as a girl I used to shave it off—that's what made it grow so thick. It is so ugly, don't you hate it?" she inquired, "or rather, don't tell me if you do. Tell me you love it." I asked her if she were ready to take me inside or if I should kiss her first and caress her pussy to excite her—women take longer to get excited than men.

Hell, she (the bride-to-be) wanted everything I could or would do to her, she said. God! she was rotten ripe, soft and wet. She frankly admitted that she had been wanting me for months and months, ever since she had first seen me looking at her from the hotel porch. This was all said under her hot breath while I was racing to get my clothes off.

When undressed I laid her on the bed and made her draw up her knees until I could see the holy of holies, the shrine of my idolatry.

Her legs and bottom were well shaped without being statuesque, but her clitoris was much more pronounced than the average. And the inner lips of her vulva hung down a little below the outer lips. I knew I should see prettier pussies, but what of that. The next moment I began caressing her with my hot stiff prick. Slowly I pushed my penis into her full length and drew it out again to the lips, then in again, and I felt her warm loving juice gush as she drew up her knees even higher to let me further in. When my thrust grew quick and hard, as orgasm shook me, she writhed down on my prick as I withdrew, as if she would hold it, and my seed spurted into her she bit my shoulder and held her legs tight as if to keep my sex in her. We lay a few minutes both

128

in bliss. When it was over she made me swear never to speak to her again, or call her on the phone. This was what she had waited for and all she was to have. And so it was. She was married two days later. She came, she tasted, she went out alone into the dark to her mate-to-be for life.

A buxom girl named Nan helped an aunt run a tea house on the White Horse Pike out of Summerville. I stopped there once or twice for lunch and telephoned the New York office and Morristown from there. One day I learned to my great discomfort that Bernice, the woman who ran the place, as well as a friend this girl had picked up, had taken the trouble to motor over to Morristown in order to see where I lived and learn more about me.

One night, returning from Philadelphia, I stopped at the Inn close to midnight for a bite. Originally a dozen or so of us attending a cattle sale had planned to stop there for midnight supper, but that party was canceled by phone before I reached the Inn. I was late coming, the others either got drunk en route or had to go home.

When I drove up, Nan told me that Bernice's lover was with her, and that we had better not go in, so she got into my car and we drove a few hundred feet up the highway, where we parked. The inevitable happened. She too was to be married shortly and I did not hear from her again except for a notice of her wedding to a Survey Engineer working on the highway.

One night when I was attending an executive committee meeting at the Valley Stream National Bank, your mother called me and asked if I were coming home or staying in New York. She wanted to know if I knew a girl named Nan—? I hadn't heard the name for so long that I didn't remember—so answered in the negative. I told her I was coming home but she asked me to phone her as soon as I left the bank.

On my return to New York I called your mother and learned that some man had telephoned asking for me. He said he was a friend of Nan and her husband.

When he learned he was talking to your mother, he told her I had often visited Nan, and had had intercourse with her, and accused me of raping Nan. This mystery man said Nan was going to have a baby and that the baby was mine and there would be hell to pay. Ellen asked him who he was and he refused any information. She told him she did not believe the story and he told her she could confirm it by calling Nan, whose address and phone number he gave her. Your mother called up Nan and she assured Ellen that she was not going to have a baby by me or by her husband or by anyone else. Nan swore that she had never been screwed by me and volunteered to come over and see us and confirm the fact. Your mother arranged for Nan to come over the following morning for luncheon—a ride of fifteen or twenty miles. When she arrived, in the presence of both of us Nan told her story. Henry Uterhart advised me to get a sworn statement from her and to give her one in return. She agreed and we exchanged affidavits denying we had ever had intercourse with one another. Nan attributed the telephone message to the jealousy of a former lover who was trying to break up her home. Nan was very nervous and upset throughout; your mother calm, cool and collected. And was I on the spot. Then the maid served a light lunch and Nan went on her way. We never saw or heard of her again—that unsavory incident was closed. . . .

Another D. L. & W. pick-up was the fashionable Mrs. Fred [Phyllis] M. of Convent. I would meet her on back country roads and she would always have some dirty pictures or books with much filthy conversation about her daughters (she had three aged 9, 11 and 16). She would talk about their cunts and breasts and inflame my passions with all sorts of screwing ideas.

She wrote me long love letters to a small post office near Morristown—why I never knew.

If my car were parked in a garage or outside a store she would have her chauffeur drive around and around the block until everyone caught on. Several times she was enraged when I couldn't make a date with her and she would trail me to some lonely spot and find me parked with Helen B. Then the sparks would fly. What those two girls wouldn't call one another wasn't worth calling.

Phyllis would play with me while I fondled her pussy.

One time when your mother was away, Mrs. M's daughter Dorothy came to the house on Mt. Kemble by the back way. I had left the rear door open and had the fires all burning. It was broad daylight but a car parked at the rear of the house could not be seen from the road.

I lay on the bed upstairs in the nude.

She came in through the door and wasted no time coming right upstairs.

She opened the door to my room, rushed over to the bed in great excitement, threw herself upon me smothering me in kisses. In a moment she was up again slipping swiftly out of all her clothes. When

130

she was completely undressed she came back to me and I began kissing her, touched her sex, caressing it gently while kissing her. In a moment or two her love milk came. I lifted her up on the bed, anointed my prick with vaseline and then parting her knees and getting her to pull up her legs, drew her bottom to the edge of the bed. I told her that it might give her a little pain at first and that I wanted to give her as little as possible. I slipped the head of my cock gently, slowly into her. And at the very entrance I felt the obstacle. I lay on her and kissed her and let her or mother nature help me out. As soon as she found that I was leaving it to her, she pushed it forward boldly and the obstacle yielded. She exclaimed, and then pushed forward again roughly. And my organ went into her to the hilt. Resolutely, I refrained from thrusting or withdrawing for a minute or two, and then drew it slowly to her lips as I pushed Tommy in gently and again she leaned up and kissed me passionately. Slowly, with extremest care I governed myself, and pushed out and in with long, slow thrusts, though I longed to plunge it in hard and quicken the strokes as much as possible. I knew that the long, gentle thrusts and slow withdrawals were the aptest to excite a woman's passions. In two or three minutes she had again let down a flow of love juice and I kept on with the love game. I came ever so many times, passing ever more slowly from orgasm to orgasm before she began to move me, but at length her breath began to get shorter and shorter. She held me to her violently, moving her pussy the while up and down against my man-root. Suddenly she fell back. There was no hysteria, but plainly I could feel the mouth of her womb fasten on my cock as if to suck it. That excited me fiercely and for the first time I indulged in quick, hard thrusts until a spasm of intense pleasure shook me and my seed spurted or seemed to spurt for the sixth or seventh time.

The mother had introduced me to the daughter and I was getting letters from the daughter at the same post office as I got them from the mother. The daughter was on to the mother but the mother wasn't on to the daughter, at first.

It was a mess when it was through—they call that seduction. Anyway, I must on with the tale of the M. gals—mother, daughters and mother's sister. You may have known the girls, but they all were older than you. Dorothy, Phyllis and Helen. The mother's name also was Phyllis.

The day following the affair with the daughter—the seduction or rape—the daughter returned with her mother and her aunt (her mother's widowed sister) and was I worried. I thought they had come to raise hell over the previous day's performance, but I was wrong—they had come for a three ring circus—mother, sister, daughter.

They all stripped and loved one another. Then we got into bed together and I fucked them all in turn, leaving the daughter to the last.

The daughter had told the mother about the day before and instead of being aggravated she had come over with her sister to get in on the show.

One time after that I was with the mother in her car back of Summit. We both stripped. Some old woman saw the performance through glasses from her house down the road a bit and raised the very devil. She came running and screaming, threatening to call the police and using very vile language. Maybe she wanted to see more, or play too, or perhaps her old man was impotent and she wasn't getting enough. Anyway, we hurried on, hoping she wouldn't be able to take the license number. It was slightly awkward, with our clothes all off.

Dorothy the eldest daughter attracted me very much and as time went on and the mother discovered that I was paying more attention to the daughter than to herself she got very jealous.

Several times she caught the daughter meeting me at night in a field or wood near her home, where she herself had met me for a quick piece on the grass.

Finally she got so jealous that she threatened to shoot me if I didn't leave Dorothy alone.

One night when she caught us red-handed—right in the act—she brandished a gun and was going to shoot us both—so I decided to let it all go.

Then she made a damn nuisance of herself calling up trying to get hold of me, and all the time following me everywhere. . . .

Writing is inferior to reality in the keenness of the sensation and emotion, and it grows monotonous when discussing sex, because it is quite difficult if not impossible to show the tiny and ineffable difference of feeling which difference of personality brings with it in fornication. . . .

Some girls' feelings, long-repressed, flame with the heat of an afternoon in July or August, while in the other one feels the freshness and cool of a summer morning, shot through with the suggestion of heat to come. And even such comparisons are inept, because it leaves out of account the effect of one's beauty, one's great eyes, or the rosy skin or superb figure. Then about one there might be a glamour of

132

spirit, while the other would never give a new note that did not spring from passion. In one you could feel a spiritual personality, and in the other you felt the thrill of undeveloped possibilities.

I devoted most of that summer to Grace H., whom I met coming in from Fort Lee, N.J. I was pretty much up against it then financially, so most of our fornication was in the doorway of her rooming-house. I have never known a woman who would let herself go so much. A few years later her young daughter came to work for me on a temporary basis and she, too, was most passionate and eager for her tail.

Grace worked for the New York Central in the Pullman Reservation office. Her boss and the girl on the same night trick would fuck in the office and several times the boss was careless where he left his condoms which was most embarrassing to all hands.

Grace's hearing was seriously affected by her work—the earphones on her head all the time while at work affected the drums.

One time when I got hold of a little dough I took her to the Brevoort Hotel for a night, and she said I didn't nearly come up to her expectations apropos of my own advance billing.

Grace had an older daughter who was a trained nurse and some of the stories she told about the medical profession were hot stuff.

A girl named B. lived in the Y.W.C.A. on 35th Street or 36th Street east of Lexington Avenue. She had a friend named Mrs. C. who lived on Washington Square, north side.

I spent one evening in that apartment with those two passionately perverted creatures. It damned near consumed me. I lost track of those two lesbians, or should I say bi-sexual bitches. I often thought a brief encore would have been nice, but I couldn't find them.

I met Kay C. of *George White's Scandals* at Barney's one night. Everyone was very tight. I was telephoning and she came into the little room where the booth was located. Just to look at Kay made me hot—and I opened the fly of my dinner suit and took out my cock. She lifted her skirt and showed me her cunt, and laughed. I left the phone, grabbed her and fucked her there and then on the sofa. It was all over by the time Barney got around to seeing what was going on. Well, the upshot of that quicky was a fast friendship that lasted for years.

I am getting ahead of my story, but Kay deserves it.

On several occasions I took her to Sands Point Casino or Beach Club, where she would go swimming, late October, in the coldest kind of water. Although she knew that I was involved with someone else, she always was a good sport, and when I went to Florida, she rode with us one week-end as far as Hamlet, N.C. We had been up all night, with much drinking at Barney's, and other places, and went straight to the train, where we continued to saturate ourselves with champagne.

When we passed through Baltimore en route south, we were all completely disrobed. Mrs. Page didn't come to the train (your mother and Virginia were in Europe at the time) but she sent a note by the chauffeur and the Red Caps, addressed to Mr. Ward Smith's party, Orange Blossom Limited. At that particular moment we were smashing all the glasses we could corral with bribery by throwing them at the door knob as a target to see if we could hit it. This performance went on after each toast to the beautiful nude Kay, who would then dance the "black bottom" on the table for us. If Mr. and Mrs. Page could only have been seen their son-in-law then!

Later that winter (1925) Kay went to Jacksonville with me when the show was playing in Philadelphia. That was some treat. At Hamlet she danced the Charleston on an express truck at 1 a.m. in nothing but her panties. It almost paralyzed the negroes who were loading ice and water on the train. In my drawing room on the way south she would dance the Black Bottom or Charleston on the card table for the benefit of the porter and the maid.

On our arrival in Jacksonville, Florida, we went to the Hotel Windsor where Frank Butler, my local partner, got us pretty tight. We went out to Vista del Rio, my development on the Mundy property at South Jacksonville. While our backs were turned Kay stripped, ran down the embankment and started swimming the St. Johns River. It was a thrill but it scared us to death. We were fearful that she would be sucked under by the quicksand. I took a movie of her and after much persuasion and the promise of a bit of liquor she came ashore, OK.

On our return to New York we put up at the Brevoort for several weeks to recuperate.

Kay was one of the best-built girls George White ever had, and that is saying something. She was a swell, lovable girl, out of the West, a good sport, a true friend, one of the nicest girls I have ever known in the show business. No gold-digger, Kay.

She and Helen M. both were show girls in *George White's Scandals,* and lived together on 59th Street in the Plaza Annex. That was before Helen was known outside the small show girl group.

Helen left George White for a job as hostess in a mediocre night club, speak-easy era. A Jewish boy friend with Tammany connections landed it for her—more money more opportunity.

From there her next step was a club named after her on 54th Street between 7th and 8th Avenues, where she sat on the piano and sang. I liked Helen but never cared much about her as a singer.

Well, here I am getting far too far ahead of my story—for it was from that night club that I set off one night on a most eventful trip to Washington.

One night at Barney's, after Kay and I had returned from Florida, Betty Maurice, one of the hostesses, expressed some doubt that we had been there. I dragged her into the ladies dressing room and proceeded to take off my dinner coat and shirt and exhibit my sunburn. When I had finished that display she inquired if I had anything more to show, whereupon I stripped completely nude, much to Kay's and Betty's delight, to say nothing of the maid's. The old crow-bar was standing up quite rigid. Betty played with my balls while Kay went down on me, and I played with the colored maid's pussy. Women's dressing rooms or toilets have always been one of my great weaknesses.

On one of my visits to Washington to confer with the Comptroller of Currency about the King's Park Bank, I picked up two girls and took them for a taxi ride along the river bank. I remember that I gave them a few bills and proceeded to play with each girl's pussy, while they in turn played with my balls and cock, a stunt I always got a kick out of.

I knew a French seamstress named Louise. In her apartment, one night, I dared her to strip naked as I was going to do, and she laughed and said she would be undressed first; and she was.

She was very slight, with tiny breasts, a flat belly, and straight flanks and hips. As I held her naked body, the look and feel of her exasperated my desire. I still admire Kay C.'s riper, richer, more luscious outlines. Her figure, though, was nearer my ideal. But Louise represented a type of adolescence destined to grow on me mightily. In fact, as my youthful virility decreases, my love of opulent feminine charm diminishes and I grow more and more to love youthful outline with the signs of sex rather indicated than pronounced. I lifted Louise into the bed and spread her legs to study her pussy. She made a face at me, but as I rubbed my hot sex against her little button, she smiled and lay back contented. In a minute or two her love juice came, and I got into bed on her and slipped my root into her small cunt. Even when the lips were wide open it was closed to the eye,

135

and this and her slimness excited me uncontrollably. I continued the slow movements for a few minutes but once she moved her cunt quickly down on mine as I drew out to the lips and gave me an intense thrill. I felt my load coming and let myself go in short quick thrusts. It soon brought on my spasm of pleasure, and I lifted her little body against mine and crushed my lips on hers. She was strangely tantalizing and exciting, like a strong drink. After she had used the syringe, we went to bed again and had the time of our lives. Lying between her legs, but side by side, an hour later, I dared her to tell me how she lost her maidenhead. She admitted having caressed herself, or played with herself, ever since she was ten. At first she could not even get her forefinger into her pussy. Then she was able to work up further and further.

Outside of Barney's, the two cabarets I always enjoyed most were "The New World" at Atlantic City and Baron Wilkins' at Harlem. Night after night I went to Barney's, spending money lavishly, with women all about me. Sometimes they would go home with me to my apartment on 11th Street, three or four together, where Louis, my valet, would have cocktails and an early morning breakfast ready for them. *[My father had his own apartment in New York during the years that my mother lived in Morristown.]*

The four walls and the ceiling of my bedroom were all covered in glass and there, nude, the girls would play with me while I would fuck them in the ass, the cunt, mouth or between the tits.

Dorothy K., a virgin, came with me one night to 11th Street. She stripped before me as I lay in bed, leaving on nothing but her chemise. I asked her to take it off, which she did, and as I touched her cuze, she wound her arms around my neck and kissed me. To my surprise, her sex was very small and well formed. I had always heard that people of her type had far larger genitals than others. But the lips of Dorothy's sex were thick and firm. Obviously she had not been fucked before. I told her what would happen and that at first it would hurt, but she still persisted in urging me with the statement that she did not care—she wanted to taste of the joy of the depths. She opened her legs. The next moment my sex was caressing her clitoris. She drew up her knees and with one movement brought my sex into her and against the maiden barrier. Dorothy had no hesitation. She moved her body lithely against me and the next moment I had forced the passage and was in her. I waited a little while and then began the love game. At once she followed my movements, lifting her sex up onto me as I pushed her and depressing it to hold me as I

136

withdrew. Then when I quickened she kept in time and so gave me the most intense pleasure, thrill on thrill, and as I came and my seed spurted into her, the muscles inside her vagina gripped my cock, heightening the sensation to an acute pain. She even kissed me more passionately than any other girl, licking the inside of my hot lips with her hot tongue. Then I went on again with the slow in-and-out movement, she followed in perfect time, and her trick of bending her sex down on mine as I withdrew and gripping it at the same time excited me mightily. Soon, of her own accord, she quickened while gripping me until we both were spent together in ecstasy. Never was there a more attractive figure. Her form had a curious attraction for me. Her breasts, small and firm as elastic, stood out provocatively. Her hips, however, were narrower than others I have known, though the cheeks of her bottom were full. Her legs, too, were well rounded. Her feet even were slender and high-arched. In a few moments I was in her again, and again she kept even better time than at first and somehow the thick firm lips of her sex seemed to excite me more. Instinctively I quickened and as I came to the short hard strokes she suddenly slipped her legs together and under me and closing them tightly, held my sex in a firm grip, and then began milking me—no other word conveys the meaning—with such skill and speed that in a moment I was gasping and choking with the intensity of the situation. My seed came in hot jets, while she continued the milking movement, tireless, indefatigable. She wound her arms around me and mounted me. Dorothy thought only of me and seated herself on me and then began rocking her body back and forth while lifting it a little at each movement, so that my sex, in the grip of her firm thick lips, had a sort of double movement. When she felt me coming, as I soon did, she twirled half round on my organ with a new movement, and then began rocking herself again, so that my seed was dragged out of me, so to speak, giving me indescribably acute, almost painful sensations. It was thrilling with her every movement.

1924-1926

While we were still in Morristown Senator Schuyler Meyer called me and said he wanted to organize a chain of country newspapers. He had been State Senator from the 17th [District] during my time at Albany but had failed of re-election the year Miller was defeated.

I had been the treasurer of Schuyler's senatorial campaign committee and had devoted much time to a canvass in his behalf. In the north end, or Jewish end, of the district they felt that Joe Steinburg should have had the nomination that year and so Joe's friends had helped to defeat Schuyler. I enlisted Miller's support in Schuyler's behalf because Schuyler had supported Miller's legislation and Miller felt he should reciprocate. I also supported Schuyler in his Club House battles.

I liked his idea and together we visited many country newspapers that spring. Then Schuyler went away for the summer and nothing happened.

In the fall I decided to organize a bank at Kings Park. For some unknown reason I had always cherished a desire to have my signature upon paper currency of the United States. (All national banks for years were banks of issue and if they elected to exercise their right to issue they could do so by depositing bonds with the Government and receive in return paper money bearing the name of the bank and the signature of its cashier and president.)

When Schuyler returned to town and found that I had made considerable progress in organizing the bank and had obtained an option on the principal corner in Kings Park from State Senator George Thompson, he asked if he could not serve as attorney for the organization and join with me in the Building Company I was forming.

I agreed and together we first organized the Schard Corporation, the "Sch" being the first three letters in Schuyler's name and the "ard" the last three of Ward.

Next we organized the bank and selected directors for the Kings Park Bank Board from the Board of the North Shore at Oyster Bay, the Valley Stream Bank at Valley Stream, the Bank Board of the Bellome Bank at Bellmore and the Hempstead Harbor Bank at Roslyn. It was my idea to tie together the five banks into one control group. . . .

During the Schuyler Meyer 1924 campaign for leader of the 15th assembly district I met a woman named Ethel H., a trained nurse at the Roosevelt Hospital. She came from upstate (Glens Falls), and was living in one of the election districts under my supervision. She consented to run for the County Committee. She was a registered Republican—I came across her name when we were searching the registration lists for likely sympathizers.

Ethel H. had a beautiful body, but was quite phlegmatic at times. She was always willing and ready to be fucked. She harnessed a bad disposition which she would unloose if she felt she was being neglected at any time. I saw quite a good deal of her for a while. After the campaign was over she would come to my office and do many favors for me.

One time when I met her in the Christopher Street Station of the Hudson Tube, we stepped into a phone booth together and there, after a little feeling around, I took up her skirt and shoved my cock into her belly. The surroundings, the circumstances and the difficulties of the position did not prevent emission of the seed.

On one occasion at the office, after all had gone away for the day, a little French woman who was peddling ties through the building, stripped and lay on the floor. Ethel H. got undressed with me. Then I opened the door so she could see the French girl playing with herself. That performance gave Ethel an idea for a little party of her own.

At Christmas time she decorated her apartment with greens, disrobed and draped her body with holly and mistletoe just above her belly. So I had to play house with her. There wasn't a position or sexual perverted act that I did not try with her.

At one period when I was hard pressed for dough, she signed a series of accommodation notes for me in blank. However, she was never embarrassed by that performance.

Jimmy Caulfield, an Assistant Secretary of the Republican State Committee, took a liking to her and saw her for some time after my interest had been attracted elsewhere.

Minnette L., who lived at the Hotel Seville when Mother and Father lived there, was an oversexed Jewish spinster. She was living with her mother and brother. He was a fairly good architect.

Minnette came into the campaign and ran for County Committeeman with Mrs. Delafield, old man Priestly (a dealer in oriental goods (dope) on 57th Street), and myself.

Minnette was in the insurance business and eager to do anything that would help her meet people.

She was forever inviting me up to her apartment, when her mother was out, "for tea."

She was a burden. Unless I played with her enough and she received sufficient attention, she would sulk and make a nuisance of herself. She was always watching to see if I was working some other girl in the district.

Minnette, after she was elected, stuck to the regular organization, becoming an election district captain—and a very busy body in the 15th.

A Mrs. Beatrice R., who had been active in organizing the "Dugout," a club for ex-World War Veterans, was having a difficult time with her attractive husband. In order to keep up her interest in the campaign, I found it necessary to discuss matters of strategy with her in her boudoir on more than one occasion.

Crete K., who lived next door to the Hotel Seville, had been on the stage. Her husband was sales manager for Onyx Hosiery. She was lively and attractive. Visiting her for hurried consultations was always something choice—something to be highly desired—made vote-getting a pleasure.

The women in my section were all enthusiastic workers, and contributed much to my successful vote-getting activities. In those days I never left for tomorrow what I could humanly accomplish today. My motto—"Satisfy the feminine vote."

On the way out to a campaign meeting for Schuyler Meyer one night, I was taken with the look of a woman who was passing the hotel as I came through the door. I followed her up 58th Street and picked her up at 7th Avenue where she stopped to get a street car. She was "taking herself" to the theatre. She gave me her phone number (a private wire) and a fictitious name. I gave her my office number and the nom de plume of William Simpson. Then she went her way and I on mine to the political meeting.

Although I well knew that it was better to fall into the hands of a murderer than into the dreams of a lustful woman, I called several times in the evening, but had no success in reaching her. . . .

Then one night I caught her in. She gave me her address and

correct name—Florence W. M. She lived [with her young daughter] on the same block with Father and Mother, that is, one block over east, between 6th and 5th Avenues, a walk-up. I dropped in after I left the Lenox Hill Club. She was dressed in black satin, which always excites me. We talked aimlessly for awhile and after a bit in a burst of uncontrolled wild passion I laid her on her day bed—we didn't stop to undress. Her legs were tormenting in seductive stockings. Jesus, what a fuck she was. She had my blood boiling. I nearly fainted with ecstasy—I came and came and came, until I thought my head would burst.

Florence's body was slender and soft, lovely to touch and she knew a trick or two when it came to grabbing onto a cock with her cunt. She used a black lace handkerchief to wipe my cock off with and that only inflamed me the more.

She never was as hot after that night. As the attachment took hold, I came to realize that her piece de resistance was playing with herself.

[Among my papers] you will find the diary of a trip we took down east that August, and a diary she had kept before she knew me, and an account of the moneys she collected from different boy friends from time to time. You will notice your old father's initials creep in for the first time on the 9th of April, 1924, with $15. That was just after the Primary campaign.

Then my political activities having slackened and my return to the business world being gradual, I had time for selected amours.

It took nearly two months for her to get going, or for me to get into the saddle, for I do not appear as a contributor again until June 24th. From then on I was stuck—the Sugar Papa.

Shortly after that spring primary was out of the way we opened the Kings Park National Bank. Kings Park being a State Hospital town was largely Irish Roman Catholic and word had been spread that I was a Ku-Kluxer. Monsignor York came to the opening, prayed for us and made a speech in which he lauded me to the skies. That set me right with the Catholics. I was elected President, and Senator George L. Thompson was elected Chairman of the Board.

The bank went ahead very rapidly, as had the Valley Stream Bank, which bank when I resigned in July of 1926, was as large an institution (more than $2,500,000 on deposit) as Mr. Page's bank has been with its five or six branches when I first met your mother.

Our perspectives vary so through life. In earlier youth I looked with awe upon the president of an institution the size of the Valley

Stream Bank, but I never could take my position as Chairman of the Board of the Valley Stream Bank or of the Kings Park Bank heavily. While the people of the community considered the head of the bank a post of great honor and importance, I always felt I was playing a game. It was a playful stunt of mine while Chairman of Valley Stream Bank, especially when out with the Directors at a speakeasy hot spot where I was known to draw checks for the evening entertainment— food, girls and liquor—on toilet paper.

When President of Kings Park Bank I would take the sheets of banknotes, four to a page, ask for scissors and a pen, cut the bills apart and sign as President.

The directors were all human beings when you knew them, although they carried hard-boiled masks with which they greeted the world.

I had the nucleus of a powerful banking chain on Long Island. George McLaughlin, the State Superintendent of Banks, tried to block my activities by granting charters for state banks whenever or wherever he learned that I was getting one for a national Bank. . . .

How did I finance the banks, the building, the women?

Well, for Kings Park (Valley Stream was popular local subscription—one share to a person except the prospective board members who had five qualifying shares each) we sold stock to officers in other banks, to a few of the local people, including the Jewish general store owner.

With the exception of the qualifying shares for the directors, the balance of the stock was in a Voting Trust for five years. The Trustees were George Thompson, Bill Reisert of Valley Stream, and myself.

I hocked some of my Voting Trust shares through your mother with the Calvert Bank; some with my own father who loaned me the money for my director's shares, and bought some for himself. Then a few of my business friends in New York bought stock, hoping thereby to obtain a line of discount at the bank.

The people locally in Kings Park couldn't afford to buy much stock.

The Kings Park Bank was opened in the local hotel—a corner of the dining room being railed off—on Jan. 17, 1924. . . .

The day we opened the bank building we had entertainers down from New York, gave little savings banks and flags with each new account opened, had a contest with prices of radios, etc. for the stockholders or depositors who brought in the most accounts. Then we numbered each account and put all the numbers in a hat at the end of the day and the lucky numbers to be drawn got the prizes.

The Schard Corporation that built the building gave Senator Thompson a mortgage for half the purchase price and raised the balance and the money to build the building by selling debenture notes to the Lynbrook National Bank, the Valley Stream National and others whose directors and officers were friends. Hempstead Harbor at Roslyn bought some too. . . .

Florence M. was very exacting. I would visit you, your mother and brother on Saturdays and Sundays, spending the week in town (during the Meyer campaign, the organization of the Kings Park Bank) with Mother and Father.

Finally Florence balked. She contended that if I could spend the week in town while she was busy at the office, and tire her out at night, I should spend the week-ends when she was free. So my trips to Morristown grew less and less.

Father caught on to my playing with Florence who was at that time employed as an assistant to a public stenographer specializing in legal work for the big law firms in Wall Street, Helen Younker.

He objected strenuously. One day he issued an ultimatum that I either go back to your mother and give up Mrs. M., or leave him— he wouldn't have me in the business any longer.

After a terrible row, I left Father and opened up an office for myself in the same building, 29 Broad (this was the second time I had gone out for myself), where I proceeded to do business in securities and bank supplies, etc. I also had a small income from the banks. . . .

During this performance I went to Miami with [Clark] Davis on several occasions while he was organizing his Citizens National Bank.

After my second trip the land boom fever started to get me and I gambled in Florida sand. I made three or four purchases, using the five or six hundred dollars in each case, and came out with clear profits of from five to six thousand dollars a lot.

When calling on Manley, who was president of two of the leading Miami Banks and head of the Witham system and the Bankers Trust Company of Atlanta, Ga., he assured me that for every thousand dollars I put up with him for binder he would get me six thousand back within ten days. I gave him a grand and a half for myself, and one and one-half for Davis. Davis's investment was a loan from me.

Florida was a madhouse. Coleman du Pont was running around coatless and hatless screaming Boca Raton.

Francis Sisson, vice-president of the Guaranty Trust of New York, was buying here and there and boasting of the dough he was making.

All New York City's financial world seemed to be there playing.

The telephone operator at the Fleetwood went out in the morning with $500 and came back at night with $15,000. . . .

The affair with Florence, the divorce from your mother, the Florida boom, my frozen assets—the collapse of my own boom—the Mexican Government negotiations and propaganda plans.

Now we are in the fall of 1924.

Florence moved out of her apartment on 58th Street where she had been living with a girl friend, Helen G., and took a place by herself on 11th Street between Sixth and Seventh, the top floor, owned by a nice Italian doctor, who lived on the ground floor with his wife.

Helen G., Florence's room-mate, was fairly promiscuous as well as being double-gaited and preferring girls to men. She was Treasurer of Forhan's Tooth Paste Company, and the mistress of the vice-president.

While they were still living together Helen would sometimes get home early—although it was usually long after I had left—and watch us fuck.

One night when I got very tight I fucked Helen from the rear while she went down on Florence.

The affair with Florence burned fiercely for several months and then died out gradually. . . .

Florence continued a wonderful screw, greatly excited and interested in fucking, until she began to negotiate for the Younker business. Then she rapidly lost her enthusiasm for screwing. It was the business that really came between us.

I met Florence in March. In April she borrowed $15 (as recorded in her diary). It was to pay the balance on a lamp she had purchased at an auction.

Her steady admirers, as her records show, were handing her out plenty of dough at the time, in lots of $150 and $250 a month sometimes. But in March outside her stenographic salary she only netted $90 for fucking.

In May of 1924 her ass brought in $300.

144

At first I was very poor pickings; my earnings were low, my home expenses heavy.

Florence's diary sets forth some of the fucking parties before she met me. It partially reveals what a stenographer thinks about when she mixes business with pleasure in an effort to provide herself and child with home, board and education, and get some fun out of life, in a big city.

At first I lived down the street in a rooming house, then across the way in an apartment house where I had a room in the apartment of a young couple.

I spent most of my time, day and night, at Florence's across the street.

She had a passion for tea rooms—for meals. We seldom cooked at home. She liked to dress and go to the theatre. Demands of customers who wanted overtime work often interfered with her plans; she would have to work until twelve or one in the morning sometimes, getting out briefs or testimony. . . .

It was in the summer of 1925 that Florida started to shape up the bank and real estate deals.

Davis had some friends who had a large tract of land near Orlando. They came up to New York in July of 1925 and tried to get me to underwrite their property with a syndicate at a million dollars. Pending at the same time was a proposal of Manley's (the president of several local Miami banks) for me to organize a syndicate to buy and sell a whole square block on Flagler Street.

I agreed to undertake the job if they would advance me sixty thousand dollars in cash before I started, with a minimum guarantee of ninety thousand dollars whether all the money was raised or not. They accepted my proposal for cash on the line and Judge Marsh was engaged to prepare the contract.

While Bob Marsh was getting the papers ready, I consented to inspect the property for one thousand cash—the most I ever got out of them was two hundred and fifty; the balance of $750 is still owing.

Oh, I almost forgot! They gave me a big party when I inspected the place; a tremendous feed and a barbecue—venison—they had the whole animal there. It was too gamey for me, but I put it down, thinking of the dough to come.

The Flagler Street deal fell through too as the bubble burst in August. You were too young to know much about that Klondike.

Much has been written, much will be written, about the Florida boom, the gambling, the plunging in real estate, the wild loose women. Florida in the hot tropical sun and the cool night moon was really something to write about.

After waiting a week or more for a reservation, I finally secured a compartment on The Seaboard for Miami in July, 1924. It was my first trip to Florida. For some time I had been negotiating with the Comptroller of Currency to get permission for Clark Davis to organize his bank. Now with the Comptroller's consent in the bag, we set forth together to round up stockholders, officers, etc.

The train was crowded with Jews. I wouldn't have been surprised if someone had pointed us out as the only Christians aboard. The "chosen" were all rushing southward in a mad quest for easy riches.

The trip as far as Jacksonville was uneventful as we rolled slowly through the barren southland. Poor nigger and broken down white trash shacks were scattered here and there along the railroad crumbling to dust.

When we passed through Baltimore, you and your brother came down to see me at the train—your mother was in Europe at the time. When they called "all aboard" you excitedly exclaimed: "Daddy, if you don't hurry you will miss your train, which would not be nice for you but would be very nice for us."

Like all trips south in the summer, it was beastly hot and we had our meals served in our room in order to avoid the objectionable Jewish element on board. I tried to forget the heat and the Jews by reading *The Monk and the Hangman's Daughter* and *The Fugger Letters—1568 to 1605.*

The meals on the Seaboard were excellent, quite superior to anything on the Pennsylvania. Their deep-dish peach pie was something to write home about. We had a waiter who was a jolly negro and a porter who was a perfect riot. An hour out of Savannah a storm broke and cooled the air considerably. Davis was good company. . . .

It took us almost as long to make Miami from Jacksonville as it had to get to Jacksonville from New York.

Thousands were pouring into Miami daily. Some came for home-making purposes, but most of them came for speculation, hoping to make a fortune from real estate deals.

The diner was so crowded on the Florida East Coast our second morning out that people were standing three deep waiting for breakfast.

The main streets of Miami were jammed with people. The only

146

stores along the main streets and many of the side streets were real estate offices. The city was overrun with automobiles from all over the country.

The streets were so packed with cars that they insisted on a speed of 30 miles per hour to get the traffic through.

Dozens of small town skyscrapers were literally racing heavenward; some never to be completed. $5,000,000 worth of building contracts were let there the first day we arrived.

The bank clearances were $500,000 daily in 1924 and $6,000,000 daily the first half of 1925.

It was a madhouse. They enacted an anti-jaywalking ordinance one day, and when a man crossed the street against a red light the next day, a cop shot him.

Everyone was buying and selling in a wild frenzy.

The majority of the winter hotels were open and doing a land office business at rates far in excess of their winter rates.

Fifty new families were starting housekeeping within the city limits each day. That did not include the suburbs. An accurate record of this was kept by the Health Department for the Chamber of Commerce and was taken from the statistics of the number of garbage permits granted daily.

We stayed at the Fleetwood Hotel, Miami Beach (really on the bay). $25 per day for room and bath; no food. In the dining room you were lucky to land a can of grapefruit for breakfast—there was a real shortage of food.

Only Fifth Avenue on Easter has crowded streets comparable to Miami's in July, 1925, but the people were more like those packing the streets on Fifth Avenue below 23rd Street where the cloak and suit makers foregather to gossip, at noon. The crowded conditions were such that on Flagler Street they arrested any pedestrians who stopped to talk to a friend or greet a business acquaintance.

No notations of deals were permitted on the sidewalks.

Most of the male populace went about hatless and coatless, with pad and pencil in hand, which created an appearance similar to the Produce or Curb markets.

The presence of women traders reminded me of the women bookmakers at Saratoga during the racing season.

In spite of the mushroom growth, the traffic was handled very well, pedestrians and vehicular traffic moving only on the lights.

Next to real estate stores, banks predominated, and their facilities were not nearly sufficient to care for the demands.

Most of the banks were working under great handicaps for space, both for their personnel and for their customers. Their growth was almost as phenomenal as the growth of real estate values and the city itself.

One institution had $5,000,000 on deposit in 1924, and by 1925 they had resources in excess of $27,000,000.

I did not notice a single shop that summer of the type that caters to the winter or summer vacationist, such as one sees at Newport, the Hamptons, or Bar Harbor. The few that had been there were all being operated as offices by the real estate mongers.

On the first of June, Clark Davis had bought a piece of property for $4,000; the day we arrived Mark Newman, a local realtor, offered him $16,000—$12,000 in cash—for a client.

A large part of the trading was done on options or binders, as they were called, which were disposed of before maturity. The transactions were so fast that people could not wait for recordings and deeds—they just dealt in binders.

On the big deals you would find the well known New York financial figures.

For the first week or two that I remained there organizing the new National bank with a capital of $1,000,000 and a surplus of $500,000, I avoided the bug like the plague, but when everyone— conservatives, bankers and business men from the North—were rolling it up, I began to get the fever myself. So I organized a New York corporation to deal in Florida real estate, and Davis and I started to work on a $1,500,000 syndicate.

I bought the Miami Beach lots from Manley for Davis and myself, as I mentioned before.

The telephone system in Miami was completely demoralized; I often waited as long as thirty minutes to get an operator in on the line to answer. The hotel operators would drop in their tracks from exhaustion. Many households had had applications for phones in for over a year without results. It often took the best part of a forenoon or afternoon to get Miami Beach from Miami on the phone. And the job of driving across the Causeway was almost as bad.

The barber shops in Miami, like in many small towns in the South, were open to the street; reminded me of the orangeade dispensaries in New York. Manicure girls were working at their tables placed on the sidewalks, waiting on customers and dealing in binders at one and the same time.

Even in the department stores the clerks were busier buying and selling real estate than dry goods.

1896

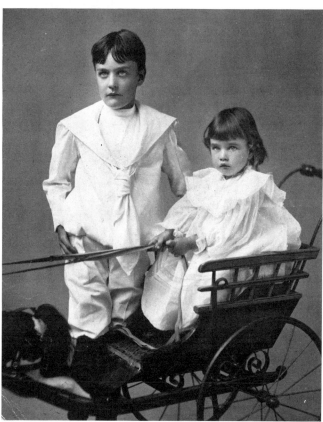

With Elise, 1901

1910

Ellen, 1916

With Ellen, 1916

1918

1919

With John D. Rockefeller, Jr., and Daniel Frohman, 1919

With Daniel Frohman, Supreme Court Justice Charles Evans Hughes,
and Mrs. Oliver Harriman, 1919

With Al Smith, left, congratulating Nathan Miller, who defeated Smith
in the New York gubernatorial race, 1920

Ellen, 1920

1922

With Governor Nathan Miller, 1922

With unidentified associate, Florida land boom, 1926

1926

Melba, c. 1928

The prize development was Coral Gables. I have never seen anything like it before or since. Their club house and open air cabaret were most attractive, especially in the moonlight.

Coral Gables, a complete city—municipal buildings, electric light plant, paved streets, sewage system, trolley lines, fire department, movie house, golf courses, and homes galore—literally rose up out of a swamp wilderness in a few years time. It was breath-taking, the enormity and the freshness of it all.

The architecture at Miami was the Spanish-Mexican type exclusively, that is, as far as the new buildings were concerned. The older homes were of the usual wooden type of structure found at seaside resorts. In spots it reminded me very much of southern California. Many of the houses in lines and appearance were like the dobe houses of New Mexico.

Irwin Mills, a very mediocre New York Jew whom I knew, was there when I arrived. I ran into him in the hotel lobby. He had been there four weeks and had cleaned up $20,000 cash.

Most of the people cooked entirely by electricity and their ice-boxes were equipped with machinery for the manufacture of ice.

My initial investment was $5,000 all told. And in two days I had sold for $15,000.

The way I got the cash to start. I would draw a check on one of my banks and then have my bookkeeper in New York send them a note of Ethel H.'s or Stanley Howe's or George Bell's, or The Floard Hay Company (which I organized that summer in New York to deal in alfalfa hay) to the banks for discount and credit to my account. The proceeds would cover my checks and then some.

On an ascending market it was simple, because I used profits to retire notes and pay interest and discount charges. On a descending market I issued more notes.

But you squirm when it runs the other way. If I gave the Kings Park Bank a note of George Bell's for $1,000, when it came due I would give the Valley Stream Bank a note of George Bell's for $600, the Bank of Hempstead Harbor a note of Ethel H. for $500. Then I would pay George Bell $1,000 when it was presented in New York with the cash received from the new discount at Valley Stream and Hempstead Harbor Bank, and so on and so forth. At one time I had $300,000 pyramided that way—never a question asked, my credit was so good.

After the first trip I returned to New York to look after my affairs, but I stayed on only a week or two.

Then off to Florida again.

The hay company I organized with dummy officers in Syracuse, and had its office there and bank account in Fayetteville, N.Y. I called it Floard—Flo out of Florence and ard out of Ward. The New York office was at 200 Broadway, but all the circularizing was done from 29 Broadway by the staff there, as was the bookkeeping. . . .

To Father, Florida was always a cypress swamp where you caught fever when you went there to buy timber. He couldn't see Florida except as a place to buy lumber and as a place for the Seminole Indians to live. He liked St. Augustine because his grandfather Major Elwes, who died of the fever down there in the Indian Wars, was buried there in the Soldiers Burying Ground, but then he liked the old Flagler hotel, the Ponce de Leon.

People were coming to him telling him how well I was doing but he kept on his own sweet way, never once coming down to see my office.

On my second trip down to Florida during the boom, Clark Davis's brother C. W. Davis awakened me in my state room when the train arrived in Jacksonville, with the announcement that he had a real estate proposition that was a honey.

He told me it was over in South Jacksonville about two and a half miles from the center of Jacksonville. And Jacksonville was the largest city in Florida—the railroad and shipping hub of the state and all railroads and highways north, east and west; it was twelve miles from the Jacksonville-Atlantic beaches on the ocean and right on the St. Johns River, 24 hours from Penn Station.

It was owned by a wild animal trainer, who had gone around the world thirty-six times and into 38 different countries with his circus animal act and his wife as cashier.

The property was on the Dixie Highway and St. Augustine roads. The land, according to Davis, was twelve feet above the river and a perfect drainage, no marshes or swamps, all high and dry.

He said the place was called Hollywood Park by Mundy, the owner.

Well, I was intrigued—a development of my own was looming— it was a few miles north of the famous San Jose development with its Vanderbilt Hotel, just south of Granada. . . .

C. W. Davis wanted a check for five thousand for a binder; the total price was $160,000.

Well, I was fascinated with the property and its location. I gave Davis the five grand (that would mean another note). The river at that point was two miles wide and you could see the Clyde Line steamships passing on their way. Sleek yachts and luxurious house-boats slipped silently past the property at all hours of the day and night.

On arrival in Miami I rejoined Davis; bought and sold sand as the shekels rolled in.

The day I arrived on the second trip I bought a lot for $1,000 and the next morning at breakfast sold it for $4,500.

Twenty-four hours after I put up the binder on the Jacksonville property I received an offer of $15,000 more than I had paid for same.

I sold out rapidly in Miami to consolidate my interests in Jacksonville.

Again I came back north. I organized a syndicate to take Vista del Rio off my hands, leaving the corporation just to manage, sell and operate the property.

The participations were for ten thousand each. Mundy had taken back a mortgage for $100,000.

Jerry Wood (who had been Lieutenant Governor) bought one participation. Davis, his brother, and Frank Butler bought one between them. I bought one and got two for organizing. The Superintendent of 29 Broadway bought another. The Deputy Comptroller of the State of New York, another.

Shortly thereafter I had another offer of fifty thousand more than I had paid. A month later, as our plans for laying out the development took shape, Charlie Dawes' sister offered us $660,000 for the property—a clear profit of $500,000—but the rest didn't want to sell. They wanted to develop. We all thought we would clean up a million and a half on the developing deal.

After the fifty thousand profit offer was turned down, I offered the rest $30,000 apiece for their ten thousand dollar share interests, but they wouldn't sell—and that was after the bubble had burst in Miami.

While in New York in January, 1926 for a day or so, I bought and sold one parcel of land that Clark Davis was handling. I came out of the deal with $5,000 cash in my pocket, and all I did was sign contracts and execute them—we had the property sold when we bought it. The deal took place in the Hotel Plaza. It was just a matter of going from one suite to the other. . . .

Somewhere along the line one of the subsequent owners claimed I was wholly fictitious, that I had never existed, etc. But he was wrong; I existed; I was in on the so-called Ryan Brownstone deal and made $5,000. . . .

✿   ✿   ✿

Getting back to the trip I took to Florida, when your mother and Virginia were in England—and Kay Chapman came along. I had sold a half interest in a lot I had paid ten thousand for to Barney Bricks, a headwaiter in Barney Gallant's, for $20,000.

A funny thing about the Florida boom was that people who couldn't get away to go there were begging those who did go to take their money—buy, buy, buy, anything. They didn't know, and didn't care, what you bought and sold for them. They wanted quick money!

I never went out to lunch in New York with anyone but what they threw money at me to take to Florida.

Well, this lot was good. It was across the way from the Nautilus Hotel, near the Polo field; had a splendid view and was next to the Jimmie Cox place. It was a good piece of sand.

A fellow named Keeler gave me mortgages—brought them in without my asking for them ($10,000 worth of first mortgages on good old Brooklyn property) and practically forced them on me. Afterwards Judge Marsh gave him some worthless stock in one of my holdings for it (the Judge did it knowingly) and took the mortgages, cashed them and kept the money for his legal services.

Senator George L. Thompson had $20,000 on deposit in the Kings Park Bank. Returning from one of my trips and attending Directors Meeting at the Bank, he gave me hell for not drawing on him for the twenty grand and investing it in Florida property. And he meant it. I didn't do it; it was too risky; he was too old and it was his all. But he never thanked me for saving that loss.

I stayed at the Pancoast Hotel; room cost $100 per day without meals—their dining room wasn't open. The Pancoast was on the beach.

[Just as the bottom fell out of the Florida market my father sold his interest for $20,000.]

I had been trying all that day to get your mother and Florence on the phone. Finally I had them both at the same time—your mother in one booth and Florence in another. By that time your mother had returned from abroad, bringing me a copy of James Joyce's *Ulysses* (I already had one copy and had read it). She felt she had been very amiss to bring that in. I had sent her a list, the money and the name of the store in Paris to get me a certain erotic [book] (for a friend who was a college professor) but, womanlike, she had used the money for other purposes. I think she rebelled at the thought of bringing in erotic literature.

Well, the two calls got me all mixed up, and I told Davis, in my cups, that I was going to sell everything, chuck banks, real estate and all, and go away for all time, especially from women. So he bought my last piece of Miami property. And I was out.

Being out of Miami, I proceeded to the promotion of the Vista del Rio property. The people in Jacksonville were all permanent residents—income-producers.

I had the property laid out, surveyed and staked.

Had a Spanish professor at Columbia name the street.

Dedictated a corner, on the river bank, as a Public Park to the City of South Jacksonville.

Made a deal with a squatter to relinquish his rights for a bigger piece of land elsewhere; bought a house on the highway for a sales office; placed flags along the highway; had the main streets plowed out. . . .

The sales house was attractively decorated and remodeled. . . .

All this kept everyone very busy getting ready for the big sale to come in January, 1926.

In May, 1925, Arthur Ham, vice-president, called me up to come to luncheon with him. We met in the 200 Fifth Avenue Restaurant.

Some promoter had come to him with a gadget called Vagex. It was a douche nozzle of non-corroding metal; prongs like fingers that opened up after it was inserted into the vagina, thereby stretching the walls and giving a smooth surface for the spray to wash. A soothing powder was used for the solution, $1.00 a bottle (cold water some doctors say is as effective). The Vagex instrument cost $5, and was to be used after intercourse by the females of the species as a birth controller.

It looked good. We were to put up $10,000 each. Between us we would control the company. The inventor would have a third and we one-third each, giving us two-thirds against his one-third.

I took the matter up with Judge Marsh in June, and in July drafted a memo for a certificate of incorporation. I was going to get my dough out of notes.

It was to be a surgical instrument company, to manufacture, buy, sell, import, export, deal and trade in any and all kinds of surgical instruments, appliances and apparatus, physicians' and hospital supplies, drugs, medicines, chemicals, druggist sundries and toilet articles.

Well, it dragged along. The inventor and some previous financing he had received became involved. Arthur stuck to it, and lost his $10,000 investment.

153

I never got going because the promoters couldn't get along.

I do not know a woman that ever saw it but what wanted one. We had a lot of fun with them while we were negotiating—giving away samples to amenable girls. . . .

[The same summer Lewis Straus, a partner of Kuhn, Loeb & Company, sent a promoter named Elt Brock to my father to enlist him for a trip to Mexico to investigate the possibility of a major investment in a white pine forest in the mountains of Durango. In my father's words, "Rank upon rank they stood, tall, clean-growing stalwarts, their feet unencumbered by undergrowth, arrogant in their indifference to puny humanity and its works." Much of the long train trip through New Orleans to San Antonio and then on to Torreón, Mexico City, and, finally, Durango, was spent in a kind of Tequila-soaked haze with visits at various stops to local whorehouses. He wrote some perceptive accounts of Mexican life and mores. After visiting the timber stand, my father and Brock advised against its purchase in light of the difficulties of getting the lumber to a railhead and the uncertainties of Mexican politics. A British timber firm subsequently bought the lumbering rights and took "$300,000 a year out of it after they had paid off all the grafters, soldiers and bandits."]

Before your mother left for Europe she made one remark that always stuck in my craw, when refusing to live with me as man and wife until she returned from Europe.

We were in an apartment over Mother's and Father's at the Seville on West 58th Street. She was sailing with your Aunt Virginia the next day.

"Wouldn't you feel safer with one woman who was true to you alone than going around with all the poisonous women whom you do not know anything about? Isn't a woman who is entirely yours worth more than women that are anybody's? Being the only man in a woman's life should mean something."

I admitted the virtue of her statements. But when she returned in the fall it was obvious we couldn't make a go of it any longer.

She had seen Jack Goodwin, had had a wonderful time with him in England where he burdened her with all his woes and domestic troubles and how he and his wife couldn't get along.

So we agreed to a divorce for $18,000, I to buy her a home in Morristown and put $250,000 in trust for you all. As part of the deal I agreed to give your mother a trip to Paris, arranging with Henry A. Uterhart to handle a Paris divorce for us on a retainer. I too had to go to Paris (under the French law) to be served. She was to go in February, 1926.

In September, 1925, Frank J. Williams in the *New York Post,* then the daily journal of the Wall Street plutocrats wrote a yarn under his series "Younger Men of Wall Street." "Born with a silver spoon, W. Ward Smith by hard work adds to his gold—launches projects from his 'play office'." It was to help with Florida promotions.

1925 was an active year for me more or less.

I had a small Xmas on 11th Street—set the tracks up at Morristown for the last time. I went out the day before Xmas, got everything ready and then went back for Xmas with Florence and her daughter Mary Jane.

After I left Florence's, I went to Barney Gallant's night club, where I sat up and drank my silly head off, feeling very sorry for myself, while the girls tried to console me. Then I got in the chariot and coasted over to Morris County. I frightened your brother to death playing Santa Claus. Had a row with your mother, who insisted that I take the mask off. If I hadn't your brother would never have confused the two personalities with the, to me, unfortunate result.

I returned to New York later in the day and had a second Xmas dinner with Mrs. M. She was very exacting and irritated me no end.

During the holidays you and your brother were brought in by your nurse to see me, first to the office and then to the 11th Street house, where I had a small tree and electric train for you.

In January (1926) we started the big sales drive on Vista del Rio at South Jacksonville.

I brought a carload of models, and I mean carload. I had a private car, ten models, Bill Reesert, a director of the Valley Stream Bank, Florence (who cramped my style) and my own Japanese servant, a secretary-stenographer, an adventurer, a former head waiter at the Sands Point and Milton Point casinos, by the name of La Brossie, and my own publicity man, Walter B. Maier. . . .

I had one hell of a row with Florence when she tried to jump off the train because I stayed too long (conferring) with two of the models, who were lesbians, in their drawing room.

The models were brought for the purpose of putting on a Fashion Show for the Junior League of Jacksonville at Vista del Rio.

I contributed one thousand dollars to the local Junior League for their infants' home.

We had a leading caterer from Jacksonville serve the refreshments for the Fashion Show which was widely publicized and we

155

had a very large attendance. The Dixie Highway traversing the property was so blocked that the police were called out to handle the traffic.

We drew crowds out there day after day, and with great pressure sold a handful of lots.

We had a sales office in Jacksonville on the main street in a store, and that office as well as the one out on the property were well staffed.

The sales were successful, but not successful enough.

We sold one house to Elsie Janis. I sold that myself.

We concentrated our sales force on Jacksonville, but they were all tied up with their investment in the south, but when the bottom dropped out at Miami, West Palm Beach, etc. the Jacksonville people like the rest of the country were left holding the bag—our development had gone on too late.

Those that did buy couldn't keep up their payments, and we couldn't lay streets, put in underground conduits for electric and telephone cables, water mains, sewer pipes, street lights, etc.

So we called it quits.

The girls did a fashion show for the Mayor in the Jacksonville Park—some charity of his.

We were very strict with the beauties, docking them for laundry, long distance calls, etc., and when they took time off for boy friends without permission. We allowed them $5 per day for meals, if they didn't eat at the hotel.

They put on a Pirate Show in line with our publicity.

When the sale was a flop we shipped the dames back by the Clyde-Mallory Line, with Bill Reesert in charge. While Florence and I motored south to Miami . . .

Dorothy P., a manicurist friend of Florence M., was also with me (in the summer of 1925) the night that I set off for the South with Kay C. When I left Dorothy at her home she was so tight she tried to gobble me at the door.

Although we had teased one another often we had never gone the limit—I was always afraid she might not be clean.

One day in the summer of 1925 Dorothy rode with me up to the Kensico Reservoir at White Plains, where I made nude pictures of her in the woods, both still and movie.

There are no illegitimate children. Babies are always for legitimates. Ask the mother.

We never see today quite as we saw yesterday—so what?

As the sales didn't come in and the bills piled up, Miss Meltis, the bookkeeper in New York, slipped into kiting the various checks under my expert guidance. . . .

[None of my father's financial manipulations, however, could do more than delay the day of reckoning.]

When I froze up altogether, the latter part of January, the Bank of Hempstead Harbor was holding overdrafts of the Schard Corporation and Foard Hay Co. for $27,600.22.

The fact that my assets were frozen and it looked as if I was doomed enraged your mother.

Your grandfather and grandmother Smith offered to help her and to take care of you and Marshall during the emergency, if your mother would come and live with them in New York and stop abusing me. This your mother refused, and my mother and father were adamant—they would pay the bills, but they wanted your mother and you children with them. . . .

In 1926 Cornelius Vanderbilt, Jr. and I contacted again. Up until we both hit the rocks in 1926 we had not seen one another much except on and off occasionally over a period of five or six years. Being in town and bachelors, and in financial distress, we drifted together. He had an apartment on Fifth Avenue across from his grandmother, between 57th and 58th. She was on the west side in her palatial mansion—he was on the east side in a renovated graystone house (third floor rear, furnished).

John B., Tom B., Erin M. were steady visitors.

At that time I was very busy with Constance P., Lillian C., Imogene R. and Edith M. (whom I had met through Neil), also Kay C., Helen M., Dorothy P., etc. So Florence's physical indifference didn't disturb me overly much.

In addition, there were always a host of girls who drifted in and out of Neil's—a screw for a night, never to be seen again, like ships that pass in the night.

Neil, although not drinking himself, enjoyed midnight parties, especially those that wound up in Harlem.

A study of his complexities was revealing. He was always seeking something that I had long since determined could not be found—the ideal type of woman with whom he could have a semi-permanent affair.

I met many women at Neil's. Some of them had known him only for a day; others for the matter of a week or two, and others for longer periods. Most of them were women of rare beauty; some had unusual intelligence. All of them paid great court to him.

Both Neil and Charlie Chaplin seemed to attract all women. That was particularly true of Charlie. Women made damn fools of themselves over him.

Charlie was often at Neil's parties, as was Horace Liveright.

The girls who visited Neil's apartment were more than eager to have an affair with him—something to brag about.

At one party a lovely creature—a model—who after dancing in a voluptuous manner with me, rubbing her belly against my cock and thoroughly arousing me, took me into Neil's bathroom for a cocktail. Tommy B. and Neil were already in the bathroom preparing drinks with their girls. There was much hugging and loving, when suddenly the girl and I were stretched out over the toilet seat and tub with me on top of her, her dress over her head and my cock out, fucking her then and there. This excited Tommy and Neil so much that they fucked their girls in the bathroom, standing up.

Many of the girls that rushed Neil contended they were virgins.

One night in Small's up in Harlem, we had a table on the dance floor, where white women with their colored partners, or vice versa the colored women with their white partners danced by in passionate embrace ("still-screw" they called it), while practically standing still on the dance floor, going through all the motions of complete, tense fornication. When some of these mixed couples passed our table, Tommy Brodix and I would grab at the women's behinds sticking our fingers in the crevice of their asses. Some liked it so much that they held their partner back and would not move on, hoping for more. It made us all quite passionate. When we got up to dance I was so hot I came in my pants.

One of the girls at the party, Betty B., a good friend of Neil, early in the morning removed her shoes, opened my trousers, took my cock out, placed it between her lovely feet and jerked me off.

Fairies and lesbians or homos often came to Neil's parties and had a great time chasing one another about the place.

The lesbians were usually trouble-makers, being infuriated if boys attempted to make their sweethearts.

Neil loved to cook scrambled eggs for everyone and then sit in the center of the living room floor and retail at length grim details of the horrors of the World War as he had experienced them. Most of such stories were pure creatures of his vivid imagination.

A friend of Neil's, Morris V., son of Madame de Gamma, was a frequent visitor to Neil's. He would get horribly drunk and troublesome.

On the regular staff at the office were my permanent secretaries Mrs. M., Miss P. and Miss O., as well as several of the file girls, who played with my cock from time to time jerking me off.

After the Florida smash-up I had Miss Melton close my office at 29 Broadway and I opened a single room office down on Whitehall Street in the Swedish Steamship Building, where the bookkeeping department, auditors and accountants worked on my books with the lawyers.

One little bitch, after working for me several days, teasing me to death, playing with me and sucking me off, left without a word, that is, failed to show up. She was a file clerk. Then a man called up, said he was her husband, etc.; wanted $5,000 to shut up; said I had forcibly raped his wife; claimed to work on the *Brooklyn Eagle*. Well, we investigated, found that he was a blackmailer living with the girl. We trapped them and got them both to sign off or go to jail.

Somehow I seemed to have been always chasing rainbows. For years I sought the woman who would be at once passionate, steadfast, intelligent, interested in all the world, with a sufficient keenness to occasionally want to taste life outside her domicile. The finding of someone compatible and whose personality and intelligence was on a par with mine, whose sex interest was sufficiently developed to be maintained after a period of close association, had proven well-nigh impossible.

Most women during the period of courtship show signs of much affection and sex interest, but after they have acquired their man and are certain of his devotion and capacity for love, their sex or physical interest declines, as their domestic and home interests increase, until the home interest is all-supreme and the physical is almost, if not completely, obliterated.

I have tasted of free love and married life, and have had my existence with mistresses, but the result has always been the same.

The sex interest has invariably waned.

Perhaps if I were to completely analyze my ruthlessness, I would find that therein the secret lies. . . .

I, at times, have found it necessary to fight a certain cowardice, a fear within me of meeting issues. While that fear always exists, yet I have always noticed that when I meet facts face to face, the difficulty or the danger I most feared evaporates. For example:

I have dreaded certain situations in life with a sickening horror so great that I have never wanted to see or speak to anyone again.

I have been so afraid that I have gone to bed and stayed there afraid, entertaining the most horrible thoughts. Often I have wondered if my fear complex was traceable to a false vanity.

I have never been able to completely analyze my feelings on occasions which have been to me critical periods in my life.

When I determined to resign as Secretary to the Governor and Miller and I were finally agreed, the thought of the humiliation of an unfavorable newspaper account of the affair drove me to such depths of despair that for days and nights I sincerely contemplated ending my life. And then, when the event took place and the exchange of our formal letters was published in the papers and the legislative correspondents presented me with a beautiful cane, a symbol of their affection and esteem, there was nothing to be concerned about.

In fact, many people wondered why I had stayed so long under such a ruthless cold bastard as Miller.

But the days and nights prior to the announcement were a living hysterical hell to me.

During the World War, the "fear" that I might be drafted before I could persuade Secretaries McAdoo, Leffingwell and Pierre Jay to let me accept a commission in the Motor Transport Corps, was a perpetual nightmare.

Bringing things down to date, while I fear personal contact, I must admit that I always gain by same. And yet realizing that, I still tremble with fright at the contemplation of a personal conversation with a new, or even old, acquaintance. At the time that the Bank of America officers, whom I had been gunning for because of certain Florida deals, suggested in order to get even with me to the National Bank Examiners that they have a special examination of the Kings Park Bank, when Miss Miller got the bank checks twisted the Kings Park Bank was cleared, I was in holy terror, yet the bank proved to be in excellent condition, particularly as to my accounts.

I owed the Valley Stream $10,000 and the Hempstead Harbor $25,000. . . .

When the bottom dropped out in Florida, I found myself in Jacksonville much in need of funds with Vista del Rio creditors closing in on me, so I took a trip to sea.

That was a poor move and no relief. It only frightened my associates the more and it did not have the effect on me that I had sought.

My fear at times was almost more than I could stand.

When I arrived in New York after my postponement and got the Company's creditors together and met the various bank representatives face to face, the situation was not nearly so ghastly horrible as I had pictured it would be.

Fear, fear, fear! But more about Fear later.

I want to first tell you about my transactions that actually brought about the financial fall, thanks largely to the Bank of America's squeeze play. Then about the divorce proceedings with your mother, and my next trip to Mexico. . . .

[In the spring of 1926 my father's rickety financial structure began collapsing around him—his "house of cards" as he himself put it. My mother, who had traveled to Europe with her sister, Virginia, was suing for divorce. Mother wanted a trust of $250,000 established the income of which was to be used for the education of my brother and myself. In addition she asked for alimony payments of $8,000 per year and the house in Morristown, New Jersey, in which we were then living. She asked for complete custody of my brother and me. My father was to have the right to visit us "from time to time within their home, or at any point within the state in which they reside."

My father countered by suggesting a clause in the divorce agreement which would stipulate that in the event that my mother remarried, he was to have the children half of each year.

In the midst of the divorce proceedings and an action in bankruptcy forced by his many creditors, my father decided that it was time to improve relations between Mexico and the United States and that he was ideally suited for the task. Relations between the two countries had been embittered by the avowed intention of the Mexican government to expropriate large American oil holdings. My father's notion was to secure a large public relations contract with the Mexican government (then under Calles) to promote a favorable image of that country in the United States. He met a fellow venturer, Arnold Robinson, in San Antonio, and the two traveled on to Mexico City together.]

On the train was an attractive German school teacher. I laid her. In fact, she came into our drawing room and spent the night in my berth with me, which disturbed Arnold no end, but he was too drunk to care much.

There was a Spanish boy aboard who wanted to lay quarters on the table from the edge inward, and see who had the longest cock. The cock that could cover the most quarters would then get all the quarters. It was a cute idea of his, because he had a phenomenal tool, like a stallion. He took all the quarters, but I beat Arnold. . . .

[In Mexico City] Bert Smithers, President Calles' stooge, and

161

Robinson were much impressed with the argument in favor of a subtle propaganda campaign for the Mexican Government in the United States and they agreed to take the matter up with President Calles. We also discussed the question of how to encourage wealthy citizens of the United States to invest money in various enterprises in Mexico.

Smithers, Arnold Robinson, his father, brother, and John Marchmont comprised the Mexican Engineering & Development Corporation of New York and Mexico City, in which Calles had a large interest. . . .

The first night we were in Mexico City we hired a horse-drawn Victoria and visited the red light district (after a native fellow dining in the restaurant thinking I was laughing at him had drawn a gun to shoot me). We went to the French, Spanish, Mexican, English, Italian and American whore houses.

At the French house the girls put on a show that appeals especially to the Mexicans—they rubbed their cunts together until they were so exhausted with excitement that they nearly passed out altogether.

The Spaniard on the train had told us of a woman who fucked five men at once. She charged one peso to participate and two to watch. We paid the two. She was a dirty, fat old thing and it was a hell of a sight—like looking over a pig sty at a lot of sows and boars.

She took one cock in her cunt, one in her asshole, one prick in her mouth, and one in each hand.

If she could have, I suppose she would have taken one between the tits and two between her toes.

An oddity of that phenomenon: All the men came quickly and at the same time. So the show did not last long. The native boys participated, while we watched.

Being short of money I returned second-class from Vera Cruz to Havana. . . .

I had a big stateroom to myself, a room for four people, but there was no one else in the room. It was a Hamburg-Amerika liner, the small type that call at South American ports. It was on "D" deck, inside.

Second class from Vera Cruz to Havana was $20 American dollars less than first. . . .

My financial plight had given me an awful attack of nerves. I slept very little on the trip to Mexico City and none at all to speak of while there—my nerves were all gone. . . .

On board the ship from Vera Cruz were a troupe of horrible

midgets, traveling second class, and most of them eating at my table or the one next to me.

That trip got me down. I was very sick; couldn't hold food on my stomach. The ship was hot as hell and rolled and pitched. I had only $30 to get from Havana to Jacksonville. At times, with worry and nausea I saw stars.

I didn't have a bath the entire trip, so I must have smelt badly. I let my beard grow, took bromides frequently, a habit I acquired from Florence M.

I counted the hours, not the days, from Vera Cruz to Havana like a prisoner tapping of his time. . . .

The deck was dirty and it smelt of dirty people. . . .

At night I would listen to the music and watch from our deck the dancing on the other side—"the first-class side of the ship." I was lonely, depressed, almost mad with despair. At night I often left my room, went up on deck, planning to jump into the Gulf of Mexico. Then the fear that the sharks which had been plainly visible by day would still be there to attack me—that I would try to swim and battle them—would drive me back from the rail.

It would have been so easy to have given the sharks a feast, and yet I didn't—I was afraid.

In the afternoon they would serve tea, coffee and German buns.

If I had gone I would have left enough insurance to clear all and leave you a nest egg. Yet I didn't jump. Why? I rationalized. Because one policy for $25,000 had to run two months longer and another premium had to be paid before they would pay on suicide; in fact, May 19th was the date.

My room was just over the driving shaft of the ship, in the stern, with its beat-beat-beat. My head would throb and throb and throb until I would nearly go mad.

The ship was only 14,000 tons, and I was 2nd class.

How fast the mighty fall. Four months before I was traveling south in my private Pullman car.

The man sitting next to me at the dining table had hands all covered with some sort of rash—in many places open sores.

Thanks to the bromides, I slept a lot day and night.

The napkins and the table cloths were not changed on the voyage. The flies and dirty people, midgets and all, almost drove me nuts.

At times I thought my head would burst, it ached so. . . .

The people at the table spoke only German or Spanish and that helped. . . .

In order to land at Havana you are supposed to have $50 in

cash on your person. I had only $30 as I have said, so that worried me now. . . .

I was so despondent that I wrote Florence a letter telling her to have my books of clippings—Near East, Actors Fund, W. S. S. Campaign, Vista del Rio, Governor Miller, etc.—sent to Brock to be turned over to you.

I didn't have the money for a deck chair so I had to sit on a second class bench, or stand up, or walk the deck, or go to bed. The trip took about 76 hours, and that was 76 hours of torture.

The midgets had a birthday party—the youngest was 24—so they had much wine and singing.

Each night, even on that old tramp, the first-class passengers dressed for dinner—not the 2nd.

It all made me very class-conscious.

There was no hot water. You couldn't see in the mirrors; the little ship bobbed about like a cork.

As a matter of fact, the food was rotten.

That trip was one mad nightmare.

Well, we arrived. The Germans wakened me at 5:30. I washed as best I could; then packed. Breakfast at 7:15. Sighted Havana at 7:30; dropped anchor in the harbor at 8 a.m. . . .

On that one trip from the U. S. A. back to the U. S. A. five doctors inquired as to my health, five immigration officers cross-examined me, and my bags were searched five times.

The little boat to Key West of the Peninsular and Occidental Steamship Company was clean. I had a nice outside cabin and the people mostly spoke English. The ship fairly reeked with drunken Americans, however.

The harbor of Havana was very attractive; the streets extremely narrow. The city was not nearly as well laid out as Mexico City.

When the inspector wanted to know how much I had, I said $500, and they never asked me to show it, thank God.

Fortunately the lunch on board was part of the fare. The sea was calm, the air clean, the boat swift—a relief from the German ship.

At Key West I went to the best hotel, beard and all, broke. Then I sent wires to C. W. and Clark Davis for dough.

The dining room was attractively lighted by candle light. There were only a few at dinner. Across from me was a stunning woman— maybe it was my beard that drew her attention.

164

Upon inquiry I learned she was a Metropolitan opera singer named Starrett.

I was surprised that anyone would look at me twice with that beard.

After dinner I phoned her from an outside public phone. She seemed to know who it was. She came down, met me and we went for a stroll in the moonlight down to the pier head.

Breakfasted, lunched together. Then money arrived and I booked passage on the steamer with her to Tampa.

She was a charming, lovely creature, especially alluring under the moonlight on the Gulf. She was sympathetic and understanding. Intrigued by the beard, I guess, a new sensation; or maybe singers come in contact with bearded men, so it was no novelty.

Anyway, she was met at Tampa by her agent—and that was goodbye to another ship that had passed. It was wonderful while it lasted.

[After some detailed discussions of his efforts to extricate himself from his financial difficulties, and a review of the horrors of his trip back from Mexico on the German ship, my father reverts to the theme of "fear."]

Fear, fear, fear of meeting facts face to face and conquering them.

It almost made me mad at periods in those turbulent times, and yet in my saner moments I knew that if I would come face to face with a situation, no matter how bad it was, somehow my quick brain would find a way.

Regardless of how terrible anything has ever appeared to me I have always been successful in finding a solution.

There are times when I do not know the word fear, when I do not hesitate to attempt anything that I want to do.

The thing I feared in Jacksonville and Mexico was bankruptcy and the attendant disgrace thereto, and yet I knew somehow that if I took the bull by the horns, that no matter how great the liabilities might be, they could be overcome.

These clearly defined contradictions in myself are hard to explain. I suppose, perhaps most of us are full of contradictions. That is why many can so well play the role of Dr. Jekyll and Mr. Hyde.

Kay Cr. lived in a cellar on 13th Street. I had met her from time to time in the Village and occasionally I called and chatted freely, but no sex—she didn't attract me physically. She taught drawing in some private girls school, and made hand-painted postcards at home. One evening she expressed the startling wish to sketch me in the nude. And from then on it was impossible to escape from her passionate embraces for many a moon. It was so easy to slip the cellar latch and nestle in amongst her big tits—they hung down almost to her waist. While she was ideally built for fucking between the tits, she preferred it between the legs.

[In October, 1926, the final divorce papers were agreed to. The principal point of contention was the issue of visitation—when and under what circumstances my father would be permitted to see my brother and me. Some of these terms follow:]

1. The mother shall have the custody and control and the right to direct and supervise the education of said children but this is not intended to impose upon her the expense of their maintenance and education.

2. The father will not seek by any means, whatever, direct or indirect, to interfere with such custody and control or with such right of direction and supervision of education.

3. On the third Saturday of each of the months of March, June, September and December, in each year, in the manner and subject to the conditions set forth in paragraph 4, the father shall have access to and the right to visit the children between the hours of ten o'clock in the forenoon and six o'clock in the afternoon.

4. Said right to visit shall be exercised by the father at and around the customary residence of the mother and her said children, whether such residence then be in Morris Township aforesaid or elsewhere. It shall be made without interference by the mother or any agent or employee of hers, or by any member of her family (including her parents). Should any such visit be prevented or interfered with by the mother or by any agent or employee of hers or by any member of her family (including her parents) or should the father request the privilege in writing and the mother consent, the father may take either or both of the children away from the premises of such residence, but in any such event the mother may, if in her judgment the best interests of the child or children require it, appoint a nurse or other representative or representatives to accompany such child or children. The written request by the father referred to in this paragraph shall specify the intended purpose and destination of the expedition and the father, upon obtaining the mother's consent to such expedition, shall not vary the same.

166

5. Upon the occasion of every visit, the father shall surrender the child or children at or before said hour of six o'clock in the afternoon of the day of such visit. Should he take either or both of the children away from the premises of such residence as provided in paragraph 4 hereof, the father shall return the child or children at or before said hour of six o'clock in the afternoon of the day of such visit to said residence or to such other place as the parties may have agreed upon for their mutual convenience; except that if the visit shall have been prevented or interfered with, as above specified, the return may be withheld for a time equal to the duration of such prevention or interference. . . .

[*Aside from the divorce proceedings, most of the summer of 1926 was taken up with ambitious plans for the Mexican Information Bureau, as it was prospectively called. It involved endless conferences, letters, wire-pulling, contacts with Mexican officials, including, of course, Calles, and much infighting among the half-dozen individuals by now interested in the enterprise. The idea was certainly not an implausible one and my father drew up lengthy and persuasive plans for the Bureau. But the scheme bogged down in rivalries, maneuverings and red tape. My father's affair with Florence M. continued to be a major preoccupation during this time.*]

I had gotten a Russian wolfhound for Florence M.—"Valdo." She showed him everywhere, and won many ribbons. I had bought him from a breeder at Huntington named Riley. The dog had been a 1925 Xmas present. He went to Florida with us, and looked well with Florence. . . .

He played in the *Countess Maritza*.

When I was living at the Brevoort, recuperating, Emma S., Kay C. and Rose S. called on me, as did Ethel H.

One day Rose took a room next to mine, and in the evening she opened the door between and came in, with her mane of hair about her shoulders and a long dressing gown reaching to her stocking feet. I got up like a flash. She had already closed the door and bolted it. I drew her to the bed and stopped her from throwing off the dressing gown. I asked her to let me take off her stockings first. The next moment she stood naked before me. A flickering flame of a candle cast arabesques of light and shadow on her beautiful ivory body. I gazed and gazed. From the navel down she was perfect. I turned her around.

Her bottom even was faultless, though large, but the breasts were a bit too large for beauty. I could think only of the bold curve of her hips. I put her on the bed and opened her legs. Her pussy was ideally perfect.

At once I wanted to get into her, but she pleaded with me to lie in bed beside her for awhile, saying that she was cold and wanted me to warm her. I got in, pulled up the sheets and began kissing her. Soon she grew warm as my middle finger caressed her cunt and I rubbed my sex against her, moving it up and down slowly. As soon as the head of my cock entered her, her face puckered a little with pain.

As I had a long afternoon before me I was the more inclined to forbear, and accordingly I drew away and took my place beside her for further caressing.

She told me that while waiting in bed for the time to piss, and thinking of me, that she had felt a strong prickling sensation in the inside of her thighs which she had never felt before.

Now that she was with me the prickling sensation and the front part of her sex burned and itched so much that she must touch it.

I persuaded her to let me, and in a moment I was on her, working my organ up and down on her clitoris, the porch of Love's Temple. A little later she herself sucked the head into her hot, wet pussy, and then closed her legs as if in pain, to stop my going further.

But I began to rub my cock up and down on her quickly, letting it slide right in every now and then, until she panted and her love juice came and my weapon sheathed itself in her naturally. I soon began a very slow and gentle in-and-out movement, which increased her excitement steadily, while giving her more and more pleasure, until I came, and immediately she lifted my chest from her breast with both hands, and showed me her glowing face. She had come too with me. I felt her trembling all over. When the love juice flows in unison, it is a perfect blending and the highest of exhilaration.

After I left the Brevoort I went back to my apartment at 47 Horatio Street. . . .

I meant to tell you about an experience I had on Election Day— the first year of the voting machines.

A call came to County Headquarters that the Democratic captains were going into the booths with the voters. So I hopped into my polo coat, stepped on the gas, pinned on my deputy attorney general's badge, and rushed to the red school house in the Italian district at Spring and Lafayette Street. I went alone.

When I got there I entered the voting section in the gym, spoke to the Republican captain. I wasn't there a minute before the Democratic inspector took a voter inside the machine. I protested to the board, and then to the cop. The cop wouldn't bestir himself. I called the officer's attention to the election law printed in big letters on the wall that "when a voter could not see, was crippled, or didn't understand, he or she could ask for help, and then two inspectors, one from each of the two major parties would accompany the voter into the booth."

I had hardly finished quoting the law and demanding the arrest of the board when I found myself out on the street, the victim of an Italian flying wedge—it had been swift and effective.

Cursing and swearing was of no avail and amid boos, catcalls and charges of "silk stocking," "high hat," I dashed around the corner to police headquarters and got Inspector Coughlin to give me two men from the bomb squad, and drove back.

When I returned, Judge Eddie McGoldrick (whose sister had worked for me in Albany), a staunch Tammany Democrat whom Miller had appointed to the Supreme Court Bench, was there, as was another Tammany leader, Judge Olvany, and a dozen cops. They were very pleasant, expressed regrets at the misunderstanding, assured me all would be well, that the men had not understood. After a drink with them all at a "speak" around the corner I went on my way. There was no more trouble there that day.

Of course, the first year there were all kinds of calls, even from districts where there wasn't a single registered Republican vote. Of course the Democrats were paying off but they did need holes in the curtain—they knew all the voters were Democrats. So they gave them a couple of bucks each or cigars for coming out and voting. The handouts would be made sometimes on the corner nearest the voting place, sometimes in the polling place. The reformers would shout fraud. We would rush out only to find it an airtight Tammany stronghold in the slums—no need to steal there. Father told me that in the days when they were good the Democrats would push Republicans (in close districts) out of line, and the cops would make them get on the end of the line, and if the voters could stick it out they would still be at the end of the line when the polls closed. . . .

One night in late November Arnold R., who was a heavy gambler with his brother's money, having won on a football game insisted upon going to Harlem to the "Barons," the toughest spot there. He had a thousand dollars when we started out.

He threw the money away—the nigger girls stripped in the act— their men partners screwed them right on the floor. It turned into a hell of a mess, Whites screwing Blacks, customers, performers and all, with Arnold throwing money right and left to anyone who would fuck or suck.

With the aid of several of the best colored girls we got him to their apartment, where he bought them cheap lingerie for high prices.

I left the place at 6:30 a.m. with $400 of his to keep for him.

I looked in his room. There he was stripped, on the bed with his cock standing up and a black girl kissing it. She was naked too. He said he was getting used to fucking black meat preparatory to marrying Tinena C. As I closed the door and left, the bitch started fucking him—she was on top. . . .

1927

In February, 1927 I met a young matron, (Mrs.) Dorothy S. who understood much of my reaction to life.

She was married to an American living in Mexico.

I was with her for quite a while before I realized the effect she had on me and how responsive she was to my desire.

I took her to Florence's studio, where I removed her clothes gradually and photographed her nude.

She was very passionate and I adjusted a set of mirrors in the room so that I could photograph us both together, she with my penis in her mouth. She went down on me and I fucked her.

After I made the pictures, I sat down with my legs stretched out.

She placed herself astride my thighs, crossing her legs behind my back and placing her vulva opposite my member which after slowly stroking she finally guided into her vagina.

She then placed her arms around my neck while I embraced her sides and waist and helped her to rise and descend upon my prick. This is frequently called "pounding on a spot" and how wild and passionate one can get in such a position.

She was an excellent stenographer and typist.

I saw her frequently after the first party and had many parties.

I remember one time in my room while we worked together, she turned over on her stomach and raised her buttocks with the help of a cushion and then I approached her from behind and stretched myself on her back, inserting my tool while she twined her arms around my elbows.

What a luscious screw she was!

EDITOR'S NOTE: While these last pages about my affair with Dorothy S. are written in the past tense, they were written by Dorothy herself from my dictation. She nearly wrote it with my prick in her mouth—we did most of our work in the nude. So she took this letter to you. It will have to be rewritten because we were both very hot when we wrote it, this March, 1927.

And so, 1939

The original copy was so sloppy that I had it copied in 1939 by a man who has known me for years—and there is none better at the typewriter. I hope to write the period 1927 to 1939 shortly.

The first section of this epistle having been retyped in the summer of 1939, although having been written in 1926, and the second section, pounded out in the summer of 1937, also having been retyped and proofread, I am continuing the balance of this self-exposé from 1927 to date, and that "to date" shall be the time at which I turn my last sheet around the typewriter roll.

So, on this 3rd day of September, in the year of our Lord One Thousand Nine Hundred and Thirty-nine, I continue, and as I do so the radio brings forth the ominous news that the world again stands on the edge of a great cataclysm.

The conflagration from the approaching Armageddon is destined to be more devastating than anything in the past.

And so I say "Peace on earth, good will to men," as it was in 1914, so shall it be now again.

Prime Minister Neville Chamberlain has just announced that a state of war exists between Great Britain and Germany—from the French radio comes word that the British have taken the pride of the German merchant marine, the *Bremen*. The British Admiralty denies it.

From London the Minister of Information has just flashed the

171

word that the steamship *Athenia* with 1400 refugees from the coming struggle, 314 of whom are said to be Americans, bound from Belfast to the U. S. A., has been "torpedoed without warning" by a German submarine and sunk.

The war in Poland has already been on for two days, the fighting actually starting at 5:45 a.m., Friday, September 1, 1939, when a shell from the 11 inch guns of the German training ship *Schleswig-Holstein,* riding in Danzig harbor, heralded the War by an attack on the Polish ammunition dump on the Westerplatte Peninsula at the mouth of the harbor.

It is twenty-one years, 9 months and 21 days since the end of the World War.

Ten years before this day, on September 3, 1929, Prime Minister Ramsay Macdonald had spoken before the Assembly of League of Nations, announcing the progress of negotiations for Naval Disarmament between Great Britain and the United States, which pronouncement was a forerunner of his visit to the President of the United States on the banks of the Rapidan River.

Herbert Hoover was still a popular resident of the White House. The Dow-Jones stock averages had reached an all-time high. Peace and prosperity had formed the backdrop of our national life.

On that day, ten years ago, the *Graf Zeppelin* landed safely at Friedrichshafen after having circled the world.

Passengers were still taking a Pennsylvania Railroad sleeper from New York to Columbus, Ohio, and flying by day from Columbus to Waynoka, Oklahoma, where they took a Santa Fe sleeper to Clovis, New Mexico, and continued by air to the West Coast. The first all-air trip Coast-to-Coast was five years hence, and Melba [my father's second wife] and I were passengers on that inaugural flight.

Commander Byrd was not yet an admiral and was waiting in the snow of Little America, preparing for his subsequent flight to the South Pole.

The Empire State Building was still a project on paper. . . .

The evening dress reached just below the knees in front, though on both sides they had panels that reached to the floor. Eve [my father's third wife] had not yet been launched on her career as one of the country's leading designers. The clothes of that day with V necks and long waists and helmet-like hats, fitting tightly right down to the nape of the neck and flaring out back of the ears, made the young woman of fashion in 1929 look as if she were equipped for an open cockpit aeroplane ride rather than for the street.

172

While some moving pictures were listed as talkies, just about as many were silent. Mary Pickford was being billed as the perfect screen voice, "100% talking" in *Coquette*. *Our Modern Maidens* with Joan Crawford and Rod La Rocque, *The Lady Lies* with Claudette Colbert and Walter Huston. *Bulldog Drummond* with Ronald Colman. *Say It with Songs* with Al Jolson.

On the legitimate stage, Eddie Cantor in *Whoopee* and that evening *Sweet Adeline* opened in New York. *Street Scene* and *Journey's End* were both in high favor with the playgoers.

That day, ten years ago, the American people reached their great economic divide, and started downhill into the depression.

U. S. Steel was 261¾; American Tel & Tel 302½; General Electric 391, the equal of 97¾ on its present status; Radio 98⅛; Consolidated Gas 180¾; Westinghouse 285⅞.

The 18th Amendment was still in force and well informed students of politics argued convincingly, and I was one of them, that a few dry states could block repeal indefinitely. The speak-easies were the craze.

Lindbergh had been married but several months. His wife had just had her first solo flight.

Bill Tilden was about to win his last American Amateur Championship. Bobby Jones and Babe Ruth were in their heydey.

All Quiet on the Western Front led the best sellers. Ernest Hemingway's *A Farewell to Arms* was at the binders.

The familiar names were: Bishop Cannon, Texas Guinan, Senator Hefflin, Mabel Walker Wildebrandt, Hugo Eckner, Dolly Gann, Mayor James J. Walker, "Doug and Mary," Legs Diamond.

Samuel Insull was at the height of his career.

The Chrysler Building was under construction.

Shirley Temple was a baby four months old.

The first cables had just been strung across the Hudson for the George Washington Bridge.

The last surviving veteran of the Mexican War had died.

Calvin Coolidge was living quietly in Northampton, his life's work behind him.

The first Tom Thumb Golf Course was about to be installed in Miami.

Walter Disney had just brought out his first *Silly Symphony*. 16 mm was still his principal outlet.

Amos n' Andy had been on N.B.C. but for a fortnight and were taking a day off for rest.

Hervey Allen was writing *Anthony Adverse* on his farm at Casanova [Cazenovia], N.Y.

Franklin Delano Roosevelt was busily carrying out Al Smith's power policies in the Executive Chamber at Albany.

Dr. Francis E. Townsend had not been heard from.

Henry Morgenthau, Jr., Alf M. Landon, and Harry Hopkins were unknown.

The CIO, Rockefeller Center, Joe Louis, Bruno Richard Hauptman and Donald Budge were unheard of.

Few well-informed Germans were taking Hitler seriously. He was still only the leader of a small though growing faction in the German Republic.

I had just completed a trip around the world and was trying to straighten out my Mexican mining problems when in a mix-up with an old army horse, high up in the hills of rebel-infested mountains of Durango, Mexico, I had smashed the head of the acatabelum and had damn near died from peritonitis.

And now, ten years later, having fairly well weathered the depression, we have another war, which presages well to be another world affair.

In 1931, in *Nomad* [a magazine edited and later bought by my father], I predicted that war would have to destroy the surplus of mankind created by the machines. I reiterated this in . . . 1934, as follows:

> The virtues of the modern Machine Age have proven a boomerang and are destroying Western Civilization. The saturation point of production can be reached so much faster than man can consume, the world over. In other words, the machine in the home, on the farm, in industry and in business, has brought about an over-population in this age of mediocrity.
>
> Japan, our warrior-like neighbor in the Pacific, was over-populated long before she began to ape Western ways, so the sons of Nippon have been forced to seek other territory for their gainful expansion and the livelihood of their people, but before they have reached such a saturation point, even with their new territory, they will have been forced to war in order to reduce their population and expand their territory so as to balance their ledger.

The all-absorbing debate which will now rise forth in this country is to go to war or not to go to war; to lift the embargo provisions of our Neutrality Act, or not to lift them.

To go to war would result in abolishing unemployment, banishing the W.P.A. and Work Relief by absorbing the jobless in the army, the navy, the air corps, the gun foundries, the munition works and the fortifications, as they have done in Europe—that is the price of the Machine Age.

If we eventually enter into the conflict which is just starting, the American debt and taxes being what they are, the change-over to such a way in our national life would compel a gradual surrender to the Hitlerian, Mussolinian and Stalinian economic heresies, and our national enthusiasm for arms and unity would sacrifice the very liberties which such an effort on our part would be intended to defend —another triumph for the machine.

To fight for Democracy that has ceased to exist, even in France and England, would be to spell the doom of Democracy in the Western Hemisphere.

This will be a war of Central Europe. Since Charlemagne bequeathed his empire, these lands have been fought over, captured and recaptured by every race now fighting, and as often as pawns in a continuous chess game.

In our Colonial times, whenever they fought over there we fought too, as in the French and Indian Wars, not because it was our business but because we belonged to them.

That's why the Father of our Country, George Washington, warned against foreign entanglements.

Wars and conflicts have come and gone dozens of times and we have kept out of them.

Since this nation was founded Britain has built her far-flung empire by conquest, conquest all over the world, conquest which snapped up strategic outposts and areas of trade.

Part of this time that that snatching was going on, we regarded Britain as a rival rather than as an ally, as in recent years.

We have watched the British take India, seize the Cape of Good Hope, take South Africa in the Boer War, grab part of the Dutch possessions in the East, pick off Malta, a strategic base in the Mediterranean, fight the Chinese and establish footholds in the Far East.

The English have devoted more than a hundred years from 1814 on to conquering her African empire. France, too, has not been idle. During the glorious reign of that renowned British monarch, Queen Victoria, the following foreign conquests come to mind:

British war on Afghanistan; British Opium War in China; British war in Punjab; French conquest of Algeria; French and British War in China; French, English and Spanish action against Mexico during our Civil War; British seizure of Cairo; French conquest of Indo-China; British conquest of the Soudan; British war in South Africa.

Germany was busy, too. Russia and Japan were busy. Everybody on the other side was grabbing whatever was loose and possible.

Except in 1812 and 1917, we stayed out, devoting ourselves to our own growth while the wars went on.

Maybe we can lick the Machine Age if we stay out. We have a better chance of maintaining our democracy, the liberty for which your ancestors and mine came to this country and gave their blood, if we do.

I think we sometimes lose sight of the fact in our admiration for ideologies, or for political programs or parties, that they are merely the expedient instruments of clever individuals who wield them for their own selfish ends in attaining power over their people and the peoples of other countries.

I am afraid the ideologies follow the trade routes.

Men and nations are always fighting for something they haven't got and think they ought to have.

The Jewish Communists in New York, and 95% of the Communists in New York are young Jews, were a little stunned by the Russian-German deal.

I look to see Russia, Germany, Italy and Japan all in the same pot. They want what they want and they have developed the fighting power to get it while John Bull and La Belle France have stood by twiddling their thumbs.

When you have lived in a realistic world you are not overly surprised when one day a nation puts men to death for suggesting negotiations with a neighbor and then the next day enters into those negotiations. So it has been, and so I suppose it will be until the end of time.

First you will have to eliminate the greed and the jealousies that remain dormant, if not active, in the breasts of those who have not for the possessions of those that have.

Gradually all the fine talk and all the ideologies to the contrary where humans are dealing with humans simmers down to the survival of the fittest, just as with the beasts in the jungle. It's a hard truism to face, but the more I see of life the more I am convinced of it.

There are very few people interested in Communism, very few Leftists, very few actively engaged in promulgating these heresies who have anything to lose by their interest in or their professions of belief in a particular dogma.

176

Invariably they have something to gain economically. They are the "withouts" hoping to be the "withs" without too much effort.

With you, the situation is different. Your sincere battle for your political and economic beliefs will be at the definite sacrifice of economic security that can be yours for the asking. But so it was with John Reed.

Jewish parents tell me that their children have found Communism an outlet for intellectual activity and a substitute for the lack of gainful employment.

A Jewish parent born in humble circumstances rising to affluence in American industry gives his children educational and social advantages which he in his youth never heard nor dreamed of, and thereby totally unfits him for following in the parent's footsteps in the industry or business in which the parent makes a living.

And so what do all the educational advantages that we have to offer in the United States lead to?

My laundryman comes from Odessa. He barely speaks English understandably—just enough to get by in his job of picking up and delivering laundry. He claims he makes a poor living at his work. He is a gray-haired old man, but he is satisfied to pick up the laundry and deliver it, sending it out to the Wet Wash and getting it back, and having his colored wenches and modern machinery iron it.

The laundryman's son went to City College. He graduated with honors. He hangs around the house most of the day and attends Communist gatherings in the evening. His father doesn't approve because his father is living better here than he ever lived in Russia or his parents before him.

His father feels that the American system has done much for him, but there is nothing for his son to do but get into trouble with the fanatics, preaching what they do not know. But then he philosophizes "maybe it is better Abie he should talk a lot than he should gamble and drink and get mixed up with bad women and bad boys and maybe steal and maybe go to jail."

Then I take you to my tailor. He also comes from the Ukraine, as did my old girl friend Mrs. G. Here again we find a son, an attractive looking likable well-turned out and presentable young man. He has had a college education too. He divides his time between Leftist meetings and his father's shop, occasionally making a delivery for his old man. But he is very much a fish out of water. All his boy friends, and many of his girl friends, are lolling at home and attending political powwows at night, plotting and planning in their childish misguided

177

way to overthrow the scheme of things which have given them a liberty, a freedom and a scale of living the like of which their ancestors never dared dream of.

And then my mind turns back from the laundryman, the tailor, the successful dress manufacturer or the Jewish banker, to the little Chinese boys in Peking who haunted the hotels patronized by the American and British tourists or other points of interest to the visitors about the city, and in a sing-song chanted—"Give me ten cents please, thank you very much."

These Chinese boys had been educated by the American missionaries into American ways of doing things and converted to Christianity. They had attended the educational institutions maintained by missionaries in China and been taught the higher and the finer things of life, of the American luxurious way of living, of our higher standards of living—all for what? To become beggars. They were misfits; they had no place in the Chinese scheme of things. They were educated for something that was non-existent in China, even in the modern China of today. There was nothing left for them to do but beg or join the army and become cannon-fodder.

Such is the waste of advancing civilization, culture and the Machine Age.

There is a great surplus of highly trained, well educated American youth in the United States totally unfitted and unsuited to take their place in the productive activities of the nation. Again it's the machine age that's to blame. Again it may be that a war will be the solution. It is a travesty on the advancement of mankind in this enlightened hemisphere that no solution has been found to use the surplus man-power released by the machines for anything but cannon-fodder—and that is just as true of the totalitarian states.

We seem so wise, we have great waves of self-satisfaction in the achievements we think we have wrought in the development and progress of the human race, and yet I have it on the authority of my doctor, a leading medico of New York, that in faraway communities having little or no contact with the outside world—where living conditions are intolerable, sanitation nil, the perfect medical profession's idea of breeding ground for tuberculosis—the dread disease is on the wane. And this has lead the doctors to conclude that during the last decade the human race has been developing an immunity to tuberculosis, and that the development of that immunity has not in any way been the result of the precautions, the preventatives and other anti-tuberculosis activities for which we for years have been asked to buy stamps at Yuletide to help maintain.

It is the contention of these same medicoes that the White Race will gradually develop its own immunity to syphilis, cancer, heart disease, infantile paralysis, etc.

Before proceeding to set down my own activities from 1927 on, there is one question upon which I want to express my own personal view, and that is the Semitic problem which has caused such profound distress throughout the ages.

I, like many other Christians, have had many close friends, male and female, among the Semitics, men whom I admired greatly and whose ability I respected and friendship I prized, and women whom I have loved dearly. But as a group, I have recognized certain qualities which in toto are repellent to our point of view and to our historical background; and that I shall develop briefly in the next page or two.

I have made it a studied point all my life to follow as closely as possible those tenets of my ancestors who came to these shores seeking religious and racial freedom.

In making that point I have strenuously endeavored to entertain no religious or racial prejudices, in fact, I have leaned over backward to be free of them. Color and creed have been no barrier to my extending individual hospitality and friendship, but I do acknowledge academically that there are certain factors that set up a wide cleavage between the various peoples of such different racial and religious viewpoints.

There is no use denying that there is a Jewish problem—especially in great industrial centers.

Laura, our Finnish maid who recently arrived from Finland, tells us that there are few Jews there but those that are there own and run the merchandising stores.

The Jews have an ingrained feeling for Jewish cohesion which transcends all loyalty to or love for country. Many Jews of the present generation, especially in New York, wish they could lose all feeling of Jewish cohesion.

If Jews were Jew subjects of a Jewish State . . . not professing to be Germans today, Englishmen tomorrow, Hungarians the next day, Austrians the day after that, and then Poles or Americans, wherever their temporary haven be, the problem would be simple.

179

Like the chameleon, as they change their haven of financial security they take on the color of their surroundings, but it is not a true or permanent color. . . .

That Jews are Germans, or Frenchmen, Englishmen or Poles, Russians or Americans, is largely fictitious. They are in all countries closely welded communities of Jews working first and foremost for the Jewish cause—and the Jewish cause knows no real nationality or boundary; the Jews are true internationalists in thought and deed. . . .

When the Jews become powerful they practice race discrimination without limitation, particularly as they consolidate their positions in one trade after another—in one profession after another—squeezing out the Gentiles as they grow.

Race antagonism began not with the Gentiles but with the Jews—their religion is based on it. The racial discrimination that the Jews of New York and enlightened Americans and English are yelling about and detesting in the Germans has possessed the Jews for thousands of years.

I like many Jews as individuals, but I know that they are instinctively hostile to me. Latent hostility to Gentiles is their basic religion. And that is why they cannot, and do not, assimilate. . . .

There are two schools of Jewish thought on the subject of assimilation, both bitterly antagonistic; one for, and one against.

If you have a young and sturdy race and keep the number of Jews allowed to filter in fairly low, assimilation will work out—it works well in Serbia. The Serbs were too virile for the Jews to reach disproportionate influence amongst them. In Serbia they could not steal the show or the business, and drive the Christians out. There were not enough of them.

The other school of Jewish thought, those against assimilation, are for the setting up of a national Jewish state somewhere on the face of the globe where all the Jews would be subjects of a Jewish state, for the Jews, by the Jews and of the Jews. Undoubtedly that would be an ideal solution for many of the ills that have beset them in the past. But unless some way of assuring smaller nations a greater guarantee for national safety than has been possible in the past is found, such a solution would undoubtedly end disastrously, should a Jewish nation become affluent.

I have always favored the school which advocates the setting up of a Jewish state, perhaps the decadence in me would welcome it; for such a state should end the one-sided economic strife between the devitalized Christian traders and the economically hardy Jews. And for the Jews it would be a relief from purges, pogroms and what have you. No longer would the Jew constantly, like the Gypsy, have to be on the move; no longer would he be forced to stealthily steal across frontiers with his family in the dead of night to escape political persecution; no longer would he have to change his name, his language, his nationality, and his professed allegiance from day to day. No longer would he, fleeing one country, find it necessary to work like a beaver to stir up the new country of his adoption to war against the anti-Semitic state he has just left behind him.

Thanks to the superb Jewish Relief societies and their grapevine systems, the Jews driven from country to country do not have to start from scratch. They are protected and helped by their own. They always band together, while the Christians invariably pull apart. . . .

Now you may ask: How can the Jews who love money so much be for Communism (and 95% of the Communists in New York are Jews)? Well, the answer: There is always money at the top, and if they can overthrow the government there will be money there at the top—witness Stalin at the top of the U. S. S. R.

And at the top, better even than money, there will be power, and power to the Jew is greater even than money. Overthrow the government, deny the right to private property, rule America, put the Christians into subjection. That is the aim of the present generation of idle Jewish youth—or Jews who for some flaw have failed to make the economic grade and is scorned by his fellow Jews except for his intellectual powers.

For a moment I will return to this war and then I will be off to a discussion of lawyers, bankers, politicians and women (mistresses and wives) God bless them! and God damn them!

I believe the state should exist for human beings; not human beings for the state.

Society and the state grow out of human beings and when human beings decay—when their morale is wrecked—when they cannot find a means of livelihood—when they are in desperate want—they turn to dictators; and then war.

I hope we can keep out of this war, but I feel the President will do everything he can to get us into it. It would make a third term easy for him and give him a larger niche in our history books. War with its false prosperity might forestall an economic collapse. But if we are drawn in, the present liberty that you so glibly spurn would be suspended—win or lose, the cost would be so great if we became involved that capitalism would be unable to pay off and would perish in America. Now the thought of that eventuality would please you, but when capitalism dies, according to the precedent of Russia, freedom dies too.

Capitalism may be doomed anyway, as you seem to think, but if so, that is to be lamented, because only under capitalism with all its faults have the working majority people anywhere in the world the freedom, the rights, the comforts and the happiness which to Americans are as natural as the breath of life itself.

Remember, complete freedom of speech, religion and the press, and many other luxuries of civilization known nowhere else in the world, are preserved in peacefulness at least only in capitalistic countries.

I know that it is your theoretical contention that some day it will be no longer necessary to rule by dictatorship in Russia, but after all you must face facts. After 23 years the Russian dictatorship is more ferocious than ever. One man rules millions with a ruthlessness that is appalling. To doubt him, to question him, to fail to please his slightest whim, is to be decapitated forthwith.

The Communists have a song of derision about capitalism and religion: "Work and pray, live on hay; you have pie in the sky when you die."

What I would like to know is anybody having pie in Russia after 23 years of Communism. Russia fares worse today than under the hideous brutality of the Czar.

Why the hell, when we have 3000 miles across of nice deep turbulent salt water between us and Europe as a first line of defense, should we be drawn into a European conflict against the warnings of our forefathers and founders, just to please Franklin Delano Roosevelt?

Ever since Europe has had any history at all, it has been a history marked by continual disputes culminating at intervals in bloody and ruinous wars. As the drama continues its long run, the villains change, the heroes change—sometimes with bewildering rapidity, as witness Soviet Russia, but the plot remains essentially the same.

Speeches and arguments used against Kaiser Wilhelm and Napoleon could serve almost unchanged as propaganda against Hitler, and no going in of ours will ever change this.

I am now, and have always been, for a United States of Europe, in fact I would go farther, as stated in my editorial in *Nomad* in 1931 and in the Farm Christmas Booklet at Melvale in 1934. "We have always been an advocate of an international court supported by an international army and navy, to enforce the edicts of the court and do the necessary policing."

I will try in the pages to come to tell you of the meeting with Melba, of my first dinner with her at the Lafayette; of our love-life together in the studio on Washington Square South. . . .

I will tell you of the Lowden candidacy and the Hoover campaign in 1928, and of Melba's visit and mine to the Republican Convention at Kansas City and the Democratic Convention in Houston. Of my trip west with her. Of my summer in California, and our trips together through the National Parks.

I will tell you about my public speaking at Democratic rallies where I told of the virtues of Alfred E. Smith, denounced the religious bigotry of Mr. Hoover's campaign and stated, in concluding, that as a Republican I would vote the straight Republican ticket.

I will tell you of the parties Melba and I had in the Washington Square studio before we were married; of Florence M's attempted suicide when Tommy Brodix in a drunken moment tipped her off to the fact that I was living with somebody else.

I will tell you how Melba and I were married in Santa Fe—the first who were ever joined in holy wedlock in the old Governor's Mansion on the Square. . . .

I will tell you of Mr. Melsing's death and the extraordinary conduct of Mrs. Melsing thereafter. . . .

I will tell you of our honeymoon trip to Hawaii, Japan, Korea, Manchuria, north and south China, the Philippine Islands, the Malay Peninsula, India, the Himalayas, Ceylon, North Africa, Sicily, Italy, Germany, Holland, Belgium, Paris and England. I will tell you of our return to California, our sojourn in Las Vegas, Nevada, in the middle of the summer for over a month (temperature never below 110) with Melba's children along, as I looked into Neil Vanderbilt's proposal for the purchasing and publishing of the local paper.

I will tell you of our trip across Death Valley and our trek to Santa Fe, New Mexico, and then to Durango, old Mexico, where I had an iron ore mine. I will tell you of the accident when an old army nag up there in the rebel-infested mountains of Durango got the best of me and I came off with a punctured pelvis and nearly died of peritonitis.

I will tell you of the whore houses in Las Vegas; of the gambling joints and the drinking emporiums where alcoholic stimulant was so freely dispensed in that very dry state.

I will tell you about the lesbian places that used to abound in Greenwich Village, as well as about the lesbian and the homo joints in Berlin.

I will tell you of my organization of the Amateur Cinema League of Montreal; of our friendship with the Episcopal Padre there.

There will be much to tell you about the articles I wrote in those days for Movie Makers and local papers in California, and of my connection with the *Nomad* Magazine—first selling advertising space for them, then directing their Camera Department, then as advertising manager and business manager. And why Melba was editor of *Nomad*.

I will tell you of the camera contests in the magazine; the effect the nudist articles had on the circulation of *Nomad;* and of Tommy Brodix's affair with Verna Salmoniski, the leading woman architect of America, and how liquor was his downfall.

I will tell you of my purchase of *Nomad* and the demise of *Nomad*.

I will tell you blackmail a la rape and my interest in air conditioning, and the organization of the Airecooling Corporation.

I will tell you of the inspiration and inception of Hendrik Van Loon's *Geography*.

I will tell you of our trip to California on the first all-air airplane scheduled passenger flight.

I will tell you of our trip to Dallas, Texas, our Thanksgiving at McNary, Arizona, and the smash-up just outside of Globe on the Arizona Desert, when I broke my right arm, shoulderblade and collarbone.

I will tell you how I got stuck in the tub at the Blackstone Hotel and couldn't get out.

I will tell you of the Carnival at New Orleans; of life at the St. Regis in New York; of the yacht *Sydney* (eleven men in crew); of the Chicago World's Fair; of Claire T. and Jarmila M.; of my office at 1 Wall Street; of my trip to Vancouver and through the Canadian Rockies; of my stock market speculations.

I will tell you about the trip we took to Europe in 1933, going first to England and then to France—flying a good part of the way— then to Germany in search of special processes for bringing out a new and better *Nomad* (of our observations of Hitler's first year); then to Czechoslovakia, Austria, Italy, Spain, and back to France.

184

I will tell you of the building of Melvale, of the origin of the Melvale Annual Farm Booklets.

I will tell you of the farm problems; of my bankruptcy; of my mother's death, of the lumber business.

I will tell you of the heartaches of tilling the soil, planting the crops, harvesting the crops and marketing the crops.

I will tell you of the fire at Melvale and our return to New York, and the reasons therefor.

I will tell you about La Guardia and the members of his administration.

I will tell you about the Citizen's Power Plant Committee which I headed in support of Mayor La Guardia's plan for a Municipal Power Authority for yardstick purposes.

I will tell you about Bob Ripley; about my bus trip to California; about the Borah campaign out there.

I will tell you of my visit with Hearst at San Simeon.

I will tell you of a Chicago primary fight.

I will tell you of my return to New York, to find my apartment vacated and to learn of Melba's determination to get a divorce—at the time contending she suspected me of having had an affair with Mary Pickford while in Hollywood.

I will tell you of the Republican Convention in Cleveland, of my joining up with the Whit Publicity organization; of my going into business for myself, of the accounts I got and the accounts I sought. About the parties at 904 Park Avenue; of the proceedings in the divorce from Melba; of the girls I knew in betwixt and between.

I will tell you of having my teeth pulled and false ones made—of celebrating the occasion by getting high and attempting to regulate the New York Police force only to face a disorderly conduct charge, which I beat.

I will tell you of my involvement with a dame from Odessa; of the Trailer Show and the Provident Loan account; of my sojourn at the Ritz and my campaign for Councilman; of my life on 37th Street before I met Eve, and then I will tell you of that happy event and of our trip to Elkton, and something of the complications that ensued, and what I learned of and about the garment business.

And then I will lay down my pen and say adieu.

I laid down my pen, although but temporarily, sooner than I had anticipated—not to say adieu. The forces of distraction were too great —the turmoil and the strife the world over, so stirring since Sept. 3,

1939, that I could not find the time nor had I the taste for glueing my ass to my chair for this purpose.

In the interim, there were many months spent in raising hundreds of thousands for the Dutch (Holland) refugees—a thankless, useless job.

Nearly two years of concentrated effort in the hope of increasing the production of tung oil for defense, a hectic presidential campaign—Roosevelt versus Willkie—followed by a municipal fray—La Guardia for mayor. Then the acquisition of a farm in North Florida to be watched over. Most of this you know about—at least the high spots; the intimacies may be lacking, but then you have your own now.

As an indication of my feeling I want, before returning to pick up where I left off at the end of the first episode, to quote from the little prayer of grace which I offered on Thanksgiving Day, 1941: "In the ninth year of the reign of "Franklin the First," with poverty abolished and the more abundant life; in the land of the new deal and the home of the brave, let us give thanks that we can still laugh (not too loudly), cry, sing and eat (33⅓ less), read, listen, swear and say (with limitations) what we please; let us pray that next Thanksgiving we can do the same if our asses have not been entirely bared for the Russian Bear; God bless our home—our relatives—our friends. Amen." . . .

For a moment, forget the rest of the world and look into our own mirror. When the war is over, not only will millions be thrown out of work, but there will have to be jobs for the men from our disbanded armies.

Production and consumption will decline enormously.

We will be faced with colossal debt. Taxes will be eating out our hearts, our sustenance and our morale. We will be faced with a peace panic. The longer the war lasts, the worst the post-war slump will be. That is not a pretty picture.

Changing the pace, and referring to your personal case which is the thing that must be and is consuming you now—As my friend, Tommy Brodix has so aptly written me, all that counts is what kind of children Eloise [my wife, whom I married in 1942] can give you, and whether she will allow you full freedom for your career. It is something that you had done all yourself from start to finish, as he puts it. She is a little nugget you dug up in the bushes of North Carolina while on manoeuvers—you can always change later if you find that the glitter was not true gold.

186

I was definitely opposed to our involvement in the present entanglement.

I was opposed to our becoming a part of the last great catastrophe.

I approved of the cash-and-carry neutrality act.

Up to this time, Switzerland, Sweden and Ireland have been successful in maintaining their position. Our policy should have been to spend everything necessary for defense, for two-ocean air and surface navies and land-based air forces greater than any combination on both the Atlantic or Pacific.

Now that we are in it up to our necks, there is no alternative but to see it through as rapidly as possible. Then the people must decide whether or not they want to pay the price of ruling the world. . . .

When the morale of human beings is wrecked, when they cannot find the means of livelihood, when they are in desperate want, they turn to dictatorship or to dictators. That has been the history of the oppressed peoples everywhere and so I look, as an aftermath of the war, to more dictatorship than the war emergency has created.

The one constant balancing factor in the human life seems to be the conservative farmer—unwilling to accept any sudden changes since nature, with whom he deals all his day, is the great conservative— his land his own proud possession.

While the merchant, the trader, guards his wealth, it is the "have-nothings," those who are without, who are forever after the assets of those that have; and usually, by the simplest, by the easiest and most direct route.

An eccentricity of the American people is the short life of their heroes—Dewey of Manila fame fell from grace because of a perfectly proper transaction involving a home for his wife. We inspire heroes and then kill them off. A great ball pitcher or a football player is a hero when he is winning, and five minutes later, when he is losing, is hissed and soon forgotten. The same may be true with our dictators. We are a mediocre people, intolerant of the great spirits that fertilize our destinies.

Gresham's law laid down for Queen Elizabeth is not merely restricted to money, but holds good for all other commodities—both of a material or spiritual nature. A bad theatre drives out a good theatre. Bad music drives out good music. Cheap literature will destroy good literature. Bad manners will drive out good manners. Bad government will drive out good government. Bad men drive out good men. The white man drove off the Indian, for better or for worse. Now the black man in many sections of this country is driving out the white man. The Jew, through circumstances forced upon him, has driven the gentile from occupations and from living quarters in many sections of our land. Today the greatest city in our country is ruled by a half-Jew. The Empire State of the nation is governed by a Jew, and our national government in Washington is administered of the Jews, by the Jews and for the Jews. Because of religious prejudice, Mr. Roosevelt was elected Governor of the State of New York. Solely because of the prejudice of the upstate rural vote a Jew for governor on the Republican ticket was defeated by an upstate Protestant, Franklin D. Roosevelt, and by a small vote. Al Smith, a Catholic, had prevailed upon Roosevelt, a Protestant, to run on the ticket to pick up Protestant upstate votes that Al, as a Catholic, might lose, and Lehman was run for Governor to offset the Republican Jew. That election started Roosevelt off to Washington, at the expense of a Jew, where he has been the idol of Jewry the world over, ever since.

Never make the mistake of thinking that our forebearers handed a true democracy down to us. As Noah Webster pointed out, democracy is a form of government in which the supreme power is retained by the people and is exercised directly or indirectly through a system of representatives and delegates, periodically renewed. Even in the most primitive forms, such as the Athenians, where the governing powers were directly exercised by the assembled people, all women and children were excluded.

Money means power and it will continue to until we shall find a moral substitute for this material factor. As you know, and as Mr. William James pointed out, the history of so-called democracy has been in fact an eternal quest for a moral substitute. Ours is purely a constitutional form of government and later I shall go into that with greater detail, because there is every reason to believe that our form of government is on the skids.

As I write this, you have determined to be married, despite the fact that your mother and her parents, for reasons of their own, largely due to social complexes, do not approve. I feel your mother's position was poorly taken—because I know more of her antecedents and early surroundings than is acknowledged by the Page family, and further because I believe that stubborn opposition usually defeats itself. That sort of opposition is extremely harmful in the formative age—it may even promote an irreparable inferiority complex. In this case, Eloise may be sufferer.

Every man should have his woman—men want sympathy and

above all else, an understanding in the accomplishments they have wrought. The important thing is that Eloise be the more interested in the man than in herself. Then the venture is apt to be successful. Some women love their husbands and their families, but their sex passions rule supreme—in that case, the result is usually disastrous.

The mutual and social relationship of husband and wife were considered of the highest importance thousands of years before Christ, and that may be what confuses your mother. Always remember that the truly superior man is not elevated by prosperity nor oppressed by adversity. He is above circumstances—and is naturally adjustable to any situation in which he finds himself.

[There is no transition here in the typescript.]

John B. and I at all of Neile's [Cornelius Vanderbilt's] parties— when we got a girl in a corner would get a "hard" on the minute we kissed them—it seemed to work like a charm. As we hugged and kissed, then we would open our pants quickly and gently steer their hands against our penises. That usually did it—I even get a "hard" on as I write this and think about those days, and that's something at my age. Usually the girls had come to the parties hoping subconsciously to be laid by Mr. Vanderbilt. He couldn't have even if he had made love to them, for he would always come in his pants before he could get his cock out—it was a weakness or something—a great disappointment to all the females who had come hoping to be screwed by Neile.

On the rebound we would get them at the 34th Street house. We sometimes didn't wait for that—we caught the likeliest on the way in, in the hallway. It would be a race between John and myself to see who could fuck the most girls. John would screw six or seven girls a day without coming—he made it a point only to come when he thought it was to be the last lay of the day. I had as good an average and some-times better, but I always "came"—sometimes it took longer than others, depending upon the excitement the girl aroused.

The atmosphere of Neile's was fornicatious—we would read dirty books to the girls, liquor them up, and show them our cocks. Screwing was the principle subject and thought—that's what we concentrated on. . . .

Edith M., a colorful divorcee, being kept in fine style in an attractive apartment on Park Avenue, was most appealing to me. A touch hard to make, but soon rumor had it that we were both a bit smitten. One night at a wild party given by the Francis Gallatins a row insued, some gent contending I had said his girl was a Lesbian (she had been down on another girl in the bedroom and I had seen

it, but Tommy B. was the one who had made the observation—
nevertheless I accepted the challenge) suggested that we go below and
fight it out on the Sidewalks of New York (Park Avenue) so as not
to sully the Gallatin's apartment. At the last moment the "blout"
reneged and Edith gave me the key to her apartment. She arrived
shortly after I got there—we had a few drinks. Then Morris V. and
Edith's cute little house guests arrived and gummed up the works.
Nevertheless Edith put on a negligee, and as Morris and the gal
embraced, fooling with one another, I found my way to Edith's
boudoir. I was hot and so was she—I loved her from head to foot,
running my tongue over her eyes, her tits, her toes, her thighs, her
ears, and in between her rosy lips. I stripped her negligee, took down
my pants and mounted her. Morris, suspecting and loving to view such
sights, had come in with the girl following him. When she saw us,
she in a sex rage coveting Edith, too, screamed: "don't let Ward Smith
make a whore out of you!" I was indignant and immediately dismounted in my drunken protestation. "I had never made a whore out
of any fair maid"—"that had always been done for me." I dressed and
still trying to preserve my dignity, departed, taking Morris with me.
An hour later Edith was removed to a hospital—a ruptured appendix
—a close call for your old man, for if we had continued with the orgy
no one knows what might have happened. In this screwing business,
anything can be in store for you—you never know when it will meet
up with you.

One night at Joe Galleti's Tommy and I met a woman. She
showed us her cunt right there in the dining room. She sat between
us and talked about tools, fucking and sucking, while playing with
our cocks under the table—she was having the time of her life! She
was stinking drunk—the perverted mistress of some fellow with a lot
of dough—we took her to the 34th St. apartment, where her lover
called for her. En route, as we crossed 42nd St. and Seventh Ave.
she opened the door of the cab, called the traffic officer over, pulled
up her skirt and showed him her cunt. Why he didn't pinch us all as
the cab hurriedly started off, I will never know. The taxi driver was
white with fright—the cop too surprised to do anything about it. She
had been showing herself, her tits and cuzzie to the driver whenever
he stopped with the traffic light and could look. At the house on 34th
St. Lillian C.'s police dog (we were looking after him for her that
evening—we had always suspected that Lillian had that dog for
several purposes) when the whore laid back on the chair, opened her

190

legs and called him to her stinking wet hole—lapped it with relish. (Then we knew for sure why Lillian was so fond of that dog.) About that time the whore's lover appeared. Witnessing the performance, he got hot as hell and proceeded—after putting the dog in the bedroom—to lay his mistress right there on the living room floor. He would screw her, beat her and screw her until they both were limp.

It always has intrigued me to find that you could give way to sexual excesses and think just as clearly afterwards about the business of the day as before. It's largely a state of mind to which idleness is conducive. Physical labor is not a deterent—in fact, it increases the desire—nothing else to think about—mental concentration decreases the urge. I have always had too much idle time on my hands—not enough for my mind to be occupied 100%.

Lillian C., a divorcee—friend of Neile's and John Brodix's, they had met her in Miami—had a flair for interior decorating and parties in her Greenwich Village Studio. Neile, John, Tommy, Morris and yours truly all laid Lillian, but at various times.

Lillian favored "tongue-lapping"—she always wanted it kissed. Her police dog was adroit at it—she came to most of our parties and apparently was always faithful to the inner circle and her dog.

Kay Cr. would occasionally slip into the Jane St. apartment and always delighted in a fuck between her tits—a trick I learned from a Broadway whore when I was a kid. It works fairly well with a little vaseline and is fairly safe from venereal disease. . . .

1927 was quite a year all by itself—I moved into the Jane Street Apartment which was a very large room two stories high with a beautiful garden, a great big fireplace and the windows were from the ground floor to the ceiling. You entered at the upper floor and came down a long winding stairway to the living room—it was a duplex. Off the living room was a kitchenette. Upstairs at the head of the stairway back of a balcony was a bedroom and bath. It was most conducive to elaborate and interesting parties. Kay Cr. and her girl friend, who was a dope fiend, were frequent visitors. The parties were wild, furious and varied from the time I took possession. . . .

The Jane Street house was very attractive—it was at #32, about a block and a half south of 14th Street. I got out a little map of that part of the town with the help of Kay Cr. It was called "Removal Notice" and was marked "after June 10th, 32 Jane Street, ring Dudley's bell twice"—"friends, midnight till morn—enemies, to hell." This was signed "Wardie." It was printed in black on red paper and mailed in a green envelope. . . .

The divorce between your Mother and myself became final on the 27th day of August, 1927. From that date until the day after Thanksgiving of the same year, I was a free man. After that I was involved again, because I fell into the clutches of the beautiful Melba.

At the instigation of Captain Lucey, the latter part of July 1927, I sent a wire to all of the Hoover people—that is the old Herbert Hoover admirers throughout the country, whom I had contacted in 1920. My wire read: "SHOULD PRESIDENT COOLIDGE RE-FUSE TO BE DRAFTED FOR THE REPUBLICAN NOMINA-TION WOULD YOU FAVOR HOOVER FOR PRESIDENT? AS I RECALL YOU DID IN 1920. DO THE PEOPLE IN YOUR SECTION WANT HOOVER? I WOULD APPRECIATE RE-CEIVING AN EXPRESSION FROM YOU. PLEASE TREAT THIS WIRE CONFIDENTIALLY." With the replies that I received, I prepared a memorandum which I gave to Jim Haggerty, Sr. on *The New York Times,* and Charlie White of the New York *Herald Tribune.* Before giving this memorandum, however, to either Charlie White or Haggerty, I submitted same to George Barr Baker, Hoover's personal public relations advisor—also to Captain Lucey, Hoover's business associate. On Sunday, August 21, 1927, *The New York Times* headlined: "Says Hoover alone can swing South." "W. Ward Smith gives him nine states if New York governor is Democratic candidate. Ready to boom Secretary of Commerce—His reports from solid South and border states show sentiment for cabinet member."

"Belief that Secretary Hoover if nominated for President by the Republican Party would carry many states in the South, particularly if Governor Smith should be the Democratic nominee, was expressed yesterday by W. Ward Smith, former Secretary to Governor Nathan L. Miller, and an active worker for the nomination of Mr. Hoover in 1920." "Mr. Smith said he based his assertion on personal observations and talks with Hoover supporters in a recent trip to the Middle West when he went as far as Kansas City, and on the exchange of hundreds of letters and telegrams with former supporters of Hoover whom he addressed, with the view of enlisting them in another Hoover move-ment, and with new friends whom the Secretary of Commerce had gained largely by his work in connection with the Mississippi floods." . . .

The New York *Herald Tribune,* on that same day on the front page, carried this headline: "HOOVER DRIVE AWAITS ONLY HIS CONSENT."

"W. Ward Smith heading group urging an open campaign to

endorse Secretary for President." "Says he will split South if Smith runs." "Replies to inquiries show Cabinet member has many supporters here." "An attempt will be made this week to induce Herbert Hoover, Secretary of Commerce, to permit the formal launching of a boom for him for President it was learned yesterday."

"The admission was made by W. Ward Smith, one of the leading Hoover supporters in 1920, and later Secretary to Governor Nathan L. Miller."

"Mr. Smith, acting on his own initiative, and without informing Mr. Hoover of his intentions, early this month began sounding out sentiment throughout the South and Southwest, and in some sections of the East and West."

After your mother and I were separated and had started divorce proceedings, I was listed in the *Social Register* with my mother and father at the Hotel Seville on West 58th Street.

It rather upset father that Hoover was able to reach me at his house. He was concerned for fear that there would be a good deal of publicity attached to my statements and that it would be brought out that I was living with him after separating from Ellen. The result was, though mother afterwards violently denied it, that they wrote to the *Social Register* and requested that they no longer list me at their address, and that was that.

These preceding statements were the opening shots in Hoover's second campaign for President.

I did nothing more about it very much except hear the reactions of some disgruntled Hoover admirers who regretted that they hadn't beaten me to the gun.

After the announcement in *The New York Times* and *Herald Tribune* in August 1927 regarding what an excellent candidate Mr. Hoover would make, he requested us to mark time because he said it placed him in a rather embarrassing position. He didn't feel that a campaign should be started until such time as President Coolidge definitely indicated to him whether or not he would look kindly on a candidate remaining in his cabinet. Well, he never gave that indication and Hoover continued to remain in the cabinet, but he couldn't stem the tide which was started by those two articles. Of course, it is perfectly ridiculous to ever suppose that any boom for Mr. Hoover was ever distasteful or embarrassing to him. . . .

In the year 1927, I had a rather unsatisfactory Thanksgiving— unsatisfactory because somewhere way down deep there had been instilled in early childhood a deep appreciation of holiday occasions.

193

As I look back that was for me a barren Thanksgiving Day. I was living at the Lafayette Hotel, where I had been for some time enjoying to the full the truly French custom applicable to the rent arrangement and especially advantageous to a practicing bachelor. I had a minimum weekly rate, with additions from time to time in the way of a double charge whenever one of the fair sex preferred to remain the night through, rather than be returned to her own quarters or abode, in the wee small hours of the morning.

The afternoon of the Friday following Thanksgiving, I started off intending to get tickets for *The Ladder*—admission gratis. Somewhere between Sixth & Seventh Avenue I encountered a girl who had been living at the Commodore Hotel during the days of the Actors Fund Campaign. (She was having an affair with a soda dispenser there then. Gardner, one of my assistants, and I had taken her out on several occasions, once to dinner at the Claremont—in her youth unsullied—her body had been luscious.) I told her where I was living— I invited her to call the next evening, Saturday and then proceeded on my way. Heading down Seventh Avenue, my attention was caught by a very pretty female who was hurrying north in a purposeful manner. She apparently, or at least I thought so then, was more than conscious of my presence. I immediately turned and followed her, catching up at the curb and assisting her across—with trivial conversation about the ornament on her chapeau and the loveliness of her eyes. She was en route to the office of Chamberlain Brown, an actor's agent, to get an appointment for a job as a night club performer. I took her to the door of Brown's office. I asked her for her name, but didn't get it— neither would she give me her telephone number or address. I invited her to dinner with me the coming Sunday at the Lafayette. She stated she thought she'd come, but would let me know Sunday morning— because she might go out of town to fulfill an engagement. I stole a kiss in the doorway and departed.

Saturday night the girl from the Commodore and Tommy Brodix also dropped in, which was alright as the Commodore girl had brought a friend. We drank a good deal and the party gradually assumed the usual pattern. In the typical French custom, the bathroom was across the hall—which was in perfect keeping with the dirty old lace curtains on the windows. Tommy and the other girl worked out their salvation on the can across the hall: the girl from the Commodore and myself using the facilities of my room to the full. When that fairly uninspiring incident was at an end I was so bored that I feigned intoxication. The result—the girls went home alone. . . .

I prompted the telephone operator to be sure to get the name of anyone who phoned me Sunday and to repeat it to me carefully before completing the connection. Lo and behold—much to my amazement and greatly to my pleasure, and a definite salve to my conceit—the Seventh Avenue pick-up phoned around noon and confirmed the dinner date.

That afternoon I wore my cutaway, went to the office, became engrossed in work and when I returned she was waiting, bedecked in a blue lace (but unbecoming) dress. We proceeded to the dining room immediately where a sumptuous repast with sufficient alcoholic stimulant was laid before my beauteous guest. She had a ticket with her—as a first line of defense—for a performance of Cornelia Otis Skinner. I still have the ticket which you will find among my papers.

My beautiful and voluptuous guest of the evening was Melba M., mother of two lovely children, Diane and Melsing, wife of Charles M. (an interlocutory decree just having been granted in California, with a year to run before becoming final)—daughter of Olive and Gustav M. of Los Angeles, California.

And then!—

And then;—

Prohibition, alcoholic was still the law. The delectable meal finished wherein we had explored the mental depths of each other's sex desires interspersed with scintillating rare bits on the theater, and sundry topics that lept to mind. We prepared—having consumed the bottle by our side (on the floor)—to my room for an absinthe frappe and pictures of my son to see.

Melba was a neat morsel, vivacious, with sparkling eyes. Her eyes intrigued—she was well proportioned—we sat on the edge of the bed looking at baby pictures, hers and mine, and sipping our frappe.

I had had a "hard" on all thru dinner. I had kept my legs close to hers as we ate and talked—I had kissed her at the table—and I was hot as hell.

Soon I began kissing her eyes, fondling her. My lips were burning; so were hers—I gently laid her back on the bed, ran my hand up her dress until I felt her hot wet coozie. I took my cock out—it was big and hard—I was proud of that instrument, I have always been proud of it, although I have had no comparison from which to judge its worth.

After taking my cock out, I slowly removed her dress, taking off some of my own things. I kissed her thighs, then her wet hairy box—finally she was stripped. Then I started running my tongue from her

195

forehead over her eyes, her ears, her mouth, nipples on her breasts—she was wild with passion, rolling and tossing. Slowly my hot burning tongue crept downward over the navel, along her thighs, legs, toes, back again to that most cherished of all spots, the most coveted place in the world, the lips of the female uterus.

Then I mounted her, slowly but surely, and inserted the rod gently. She was tight as a drum, she had not been screwed, finger-fucked, or had she masturbated since her last menstruation.

The night before, I had given myself quite a work-out on a girl from the Commodore that I had known there during the Actor's Fund Drive—so with that behind me but a few hours and the liquor I had aboard, I had no desire to come right away, which greatly added to Melba's joy and prolonged the ecstacy for both. When we came, we came in perfect unison, and did we flood that cavity to overflowing.

We kept at it most of the night—each successive fray the longer delayed, the greater the joy. She sucked me off at dawn—then we slept. At noon we were at it again. That night she pissed in my mouth when I was down on her—that was new and hot.

We never got out of bed for days, and we laid there for three weeks without leaving the hotel—all our meals were brought to us. Tommy came to see us, Clarence Schmelzel, and Mary Alice. Mary Alice spent the night once when high, slept with us in bed, went down on Melba, as I fucked her from the rear.

Tommy B. was the first to call attention to Melba's well formed pretty legs—though not to me seductive.

I had been so fascinated with her eyes and cunt that I had not noticed much else about my lass. After the loan from Chambers we took an apartment. During the prolonged orgy I noticed a bankbook in her pocket-book, the balance was just $23 bucks.

At Christmas time, her father sent $100 and $75 every two weeks. I had money deposited with Florence which I drew on at the rate of $50 a week, plus the thousand loaned from Chambers.

When we moved from the studio, we photographed one another nude and in every pose, with my cock always erect. We bought a mirrored screen and kept it near the bed, the better to see ourselves perform. For days, we screwed and screwed and screwed—sometimes I would come 12 or 14 times in 24 hours around the clock.

For several days we never got out of bed at all, and did the laundryman complain—he said he wouldn't take such sheets—we would be sick from liquor and lie on in all the mess.

196

It was filthy but nice and wonderful while it lasted. After six weeks of constant screwing, I became worried—I feared I would fuck myself out, so I went to see a doctor. He told me not to be concerned—"Practice makes perfect."

One night Mary Alice spent half the night loving Melba in our big bed—then she came into the guest room and fucked me. Melba never seemed to mind.

Erin M. wore black satin a great deal—which always got me. She came to a cocktail party at the Washington Square Studio. While ostensibly telephoning in the guest room, I laid her. She kissed better than fucked—she was a disappointment from the screwing angle, but I was always very fond of her. . . .

Melba loved intercourse, sexual or social. She was sentimental, vivacious or depressed, gay or gloomy—she lived always for today, with never a thought for tomorrow.

Mary Alice, while playing around with Jerry G. had Diane at the tender age of three staying with her. They slept in bed together, and when Jerry spent the night, they had Diane between them—and screwed with the baby in the bed all the time admiring the child's tiny parts and caressing them. Mary Alice confessed all this to Melba —after she and Jerry married they named their first child, a girl, after Diane. They have had several children since and have settled down to a staid domestic existence.

After you have run the gauntlet with a woman every day, it is but a repetition of the previous with slight variations—unless you add new personalities.

Melba was flowing, unwell, menstruating when we were at the President Hotel. Mary Alice was there—she was unwell at the same time. I laid Melba on the bed—blood was everywhere—and I laid Mary Alice in the bathtub. Just before we put Melba on the train the payoff was when they gobbled one another as a parting gesture. Earlier in the day I had whipped them both with my belt—Melba to give her some welts to take with her on the trip and remember me by. She wiggled and squirmed as Mary Alice held her—of course, she came in a great flood of joy.

Lowden having been knocked out early at Kansas City, I had a lot of time to devote to Melba. She had gone to a great deal of trouble over her wardrobe—she looked especially lovely in a sky-blue traveling suit in which she arrived at the Kansas City station. We remained in our hotel late each day, paying more attention to fucking and sucking than to the Republican Convention. Melba's forte was her versatility in bed. She was a good lay and she loved it—she never tired of co-habitation.

Seeing anyone else fucking or sucking, particularly Lesbians or homos, excites me terribly, and I have to fuck. From the time I met Melba with the exception of the Mary Alice party when she was present and participated, I had remained true to the vampire of the West Coast for nearly three years, in mind, in thought, and in deed.

On our trip to the Yosemite in the summer of 1928, the Red Trees, the notification ceremonies at Palo Alto, we went to Del Monte, where we took a hotel cottage atop a high cliff overlooking the Pacific —it was here that Aimee Semple McPherson had gone with her radio man to work on her tubes. We literally screwed to the rhythm of the waves beating on the rocks beneath our cottage—the beauties and the ruggedness of the place plus the stimulation of the invigorating air, inspired us to great heights of connubial bliss. In memory I hold a pleasant co-mingling sensation of the rare charm of that place and Melba's seductive responsiveness to the lovely surroundings.

Melba Dorothy was born a courtesan of no mean proportions.

For years after Melba was born, Mrs. M. never let her husband touch her—he had to content himself with sitting beside her on the bed and masturbating.

She said his cock was too big for her cunt—that her cunt was too small and she couldn't stand it. Having had a child her contention was ill-taken, but he loved her and babied her and sat on the edge of the bed and masturbated instead. I don't think it hurt him, but it did leave a mark on Mrs. M.'s high strung nature—it produced abnormal mental reactions to the commonplaces of life.

In December, after Melba and I had been living together for three or four weeks, she sent her family a telegram announcing her infatuation of the moment, telling them she expected to marry me when her interlocutory degree was finished. I can remember that after-noon very well. We had been riding on a Fifth Avenue bus—it had been snowing heavily and we stepped into the Western Union office on 23rd Street or 22nd St. to send the wire. The reason we had gone out at all was in order to get Melba's guitar—up to that time I hadn't even known that she played the guitar. A few days later we went out again just before Christmas up to R. H. Macy, to buy a lot of toys for Diane and Melsing for Christmas—we bought them candy canes and other little items. We got a package all together and took it down to

198

the postoffice—the main postoffice then, at City Hall—in order to expedite its journey to California and get the package there in time for Christmas.

After a month at the Lafayette Hotel together Melba and I took a skylight apartment, or terrace studio, on Washington Square South. It was furnished—had a piano, living room, bedroom, bath and kitchenette—and that was something. . . .

From the Albert we moved to the President Hotel—somehow or other I was able to conceal Melba's presence there.

During our stay at the Washington Square place we entertained there Mary Alice Gendron, Erin M., Konrad Berkovici, Felix Rosen the violinist, Mendall who built the London Terrace, and the Vendome on 57th St., Hendrik Willem van Loon—in fact the Van Loon situation was quite a situation, van Loon having been a friend of Melba's. At the President Hotel before Melba departed we had several very interesting parties.

On March 12th, 1928 Melba took the Crescent Limited to New Orleans and left from there for Los Angeles. Walter P. and Elt Brock met her at New Orleans as she passed through—I had sent them the money to entertain her. Needless to say my existence was somewhat altered after her departure—I moved back to the Lafayette and my old room, also maintaining a separate establishment in 11th Street in a rooming house in order to fool Florence. Florence kept things stepping pretty lively then—I was rather afraid of serious complications most any day. Eventually she quieted—I told her very little of anything about Melba, neither admitted nor denied that I was very much involved. The first 48 hours after Melba left I sent her three Air Mail letters and sixteen wires and I received two letters from the train and six wires keeping me informed as to her progress. . . .

1928-1929

In February 1928 I attended Sam Koenig's annual ball in search of votes for Governor Lowden. . . .

The Lowden campaign took on the air of a great deal of activity.

That year I travelled through the State of New York in behalf of Governor Lowden's candidacy, went to Washington and to Chicago. Stayed in Chicago after Melba went to California for the months of April and May, coming back only to pick up the New York Delegations' Special at Buffalo and ride on it out to Kansas City. At the Convention, Clarence Buck was in charge of the organization assisted by Mrs. Ruth Hannah McCormick, who for years had been very much in love with Clarence, but too strong a personality for him. Alice Longworth was also a member of the Lowden organization as were Francis Littleton, Arthur Little, Len Small. Much against her father's wishes, Melba returned from California to join me in Kansas City. We had an apartment well out of town, although I had an official room in one of the downtown hotels. That was to give the thing some sort of an appearance or whatever you may wish to call it. . . .

The so-called Lowden coalition was shot to pieces on Monday, the first day of the Convention, when Andrew Mellon, that foremost financier who had been likened to Alexander Hamilton, admittedly broke faith. Mr. Mellon had agreed with Mr. Hillies and Mr. Butler and with Senator Buck, Governor Lowden's manager, to have his delegation vote for Coolidge, Senator Reed of Pennsylvania, or for himself for at least four ballots in order to give the allies an opportunity to solidify their forces in the drive on Hoover and to prevent Hoover's nomination on the early ballot.

If the Pennsylvania delegation had stuck with us, Lowden would have been nominated, but there was a deal.

Mellon was really for Lowden, but Vare [the Pennsylvania Senator-elect] was afraid he would not be seated in the Senate, so he made a deal to deliver his part of the Pennsylvania delegation to Hoover with the understanding that if Hoover were nominated and elected, he would stand back of Vare and see that he was seated. The sad part of that story is—as is always the case in politics—Vare delivered and Hoover didn't.

An interesting incident which may amuse you and which is illustrative of how the political mind works, is the fact that I was talking with Senator Curtis on the telephone 24 hours before he was nominated for vice-president, and told him that I thought he ought to be the party's next candidate for vice-president and he replied that under no circumstances would he accept that honor. This reminded me of the time when Nathan Miller told me he would not accept the nomination for Governor of the State of New York and within 48 hours of that time, the Convention nominated him for Governor.

In thinking of the Kansas City convention I cannot help but compare the Kansas City convention of 1928 with the Republican Convention in Chicago in 1920. The enthusiasm and applause of those two conventions was rather interesting to note. In Chicago in 1920 when Governor Miller placed Mr. Hoover in nomination the delegates sat silent and the galleries cheered for Hoover for almost one solid hour and would have continued longer if it had not been for a woman rushing to the platform to second Hoover's nomination. In Kansas City the cheering was largely among the delegates. It did not last for more than 18 minutes, but of course, the result was considerably different than the result in Chicago, which goes to prove that it doesn't make a damn bit of difference how the individual voter votes in a given State or where the enthusiasm is for the candidate—it is the way the organization thinks, works and plans and manoeuvres in the convention that counts.

In Kansas City the galleries were not wholly disposed to Hoover. The highbrows everywhere wanted him, but the working man, the farmer were in many instances, violently opposed. The farmers paraded through the streets behind bands playing the funeral march, but it got them nowhere. . . .

I had a pretty good time in Kansas City. Of course I was nuts about Melba and spent as much time with her as possible. . . .

[The effort to secure the nomination for Lowden] was a long shot and if it had worked out as it seemed it might, the first day of the convention, it would have been a very interesting story. . . .

[*My father and Melba traveled to California soon after the Republican convention, stopping along the way to sound out sentiment for Al Smith for President. Everywhere they found bitter anti-Catholic prejudice. In Los Angeles they met Melba's parents, Mr. and Mrs. Gustav M. My father describes Mr. M. as "a large, good-natured, honest, pleasant sort of fellow." He had accumulated enough money to buy land in strategic areas of Los Angeles and his investments in land had made him prosperous if not rich.*

Mrs. M. was, again in my father's words, "a nice woman, but full of complexes—complexes that her father had driven in at the end of a whip when she was a mere child."

The M.s were plainly uneasy about my father's relationship with Melba. He and Melba, for their part, spent "a very wonderful summer" visiting the Southern California beaches, attending concerts at Hollywood Bowl and meeting some of the luminaries of the film world.]

The M.s had an apartment of their own and a very attractive and expensive one. While out in California I organized the Melba Company, the purpose of which was to make records for advertisers and ship them all around the country—Melba doing the singing, accompanying herself on her own guitar, while I announced the advertising plug.

I moved to an apartment—furnished—not very far from Melba's house.

Mr. M. was terribly interested in politics. He had been brought up south of Market Street, San Francisco, having been born at the head of a shaft in Gold Hill, Nevada, and was really quite a character.

A great friend of Giannini, a high Mason, an Elk, he had been a baker, a streetcar conductor, a butcher, and everything but a candlestick maker. When he first came to Los Angeles, he worked as an investigator for the lighting company on all accident claims, etc. He went out and made investigations and recommendations as to the settlements that should be made.

Melba's grandfather—Terril B.—was a miser. He made and lost two or three fortunes in California. He came of very fine old New England stock, Bostonian, graduated from Harvard, the blacksheep of the family. He had been in the wholesale grocery business in San Francisco—had married the talented young Annie M., the beautiful opera singer of San Francisco. He was many years her senior, but very wealthy.

After he went broke in one of the early panics, he moved to Los Angeles, establishing himself there in the second-hand furniture business, clothes, harness, horses, etc. There he accumulated another fortune; having lost his money in banks, he never kept any gold there thereafter. Instead he buried it around in little tin cans in the ground.

Early he was separated from his wife and was broken up by it. He kept the child, Olive B., and treated her pretty badly. He never forgave his wife—she had run away with the Mayor of San Francisco, whom she afterwards married. . . .

She was a gay girl and became infected from an unfortunate abortion operation—cause presumed to have been one of the trustees of Grace Church—and died in the prime of her career.

Shrewdly, because Los Angeles has no natural borders, he bought property in the center of the town and then in the North end of it, the South end of it, the East and the West End—the four points of the compass, and they all considerably increased in value. When he died he left close to half a million dollars, mostly in gold, some of it in real estate. I suppose a hundred thousand dollars in real estate. He left it all to Melba—"The Little Girl"—he was annoyed with his son-in-law and his daughter at the time. He thought they were plotting to kill him. On the advice of LeRoy Edwards, Mr. M.'s gas company pal and lawyer, they destroyed or never found the will (leaving everything he had to Melba) whom he called "the little girl." Mr. M. made that admission to me on his deathbed. Also in a moment of alcoholic inebriation he told Charles M. who was Melba's first husband (Melba being his second wife) the same story.

Melba and I had a very wonderful summer that year in California. We visited the many beaches—we spent a great deal of time listening to the rehearsals and also to the concerts themselves in the Hollywood Bowl. I know of nothing more enthralling than the rehearsals in the broad hot sun of the forenoon of the day and the finished performance directed by the baton of distinguished conductors in the Bowl under the stars that same night.

I met Mary Wilshire, the psychologist, a woman of means who spent much time in trying to iron out the cross purposes of the lesbians and the homos.

I talked at many Democratic rallies in Southern California that year and had my first experience in delivering a speech over the radio. In those days they also experimented with loudspeakers which were rather annoying, to the speaker and to the audience. In speaking at public meetings, I always like to be able to look into the faces of my audience and to pick out some sympathetic soul to whom I can address the major portion of my remarks.

During that summer we took a trip up through Yosemite. As a matter of fact we went there after we left Palo Alto. This was all very shocking to Melba's family. . . .

All through the summer of 1928, Melba's father was ailing. His wife didn't seem particularly sympathetic. Apparently there had not been much love on her side for many years. She was a strange female of the species, very jealous of the charm and success of her own daughter, her only child, as a musician, a singer and an entertainer on the stage and in the night clubs. Melba had all the comforts that anyone might ask for, a lovely home, servants and an adequate income to maintain same. Nevertheless, she sought to earn her way for herself, independent of her parents.

Old man M. was very fond of bringing presents to his grandchildren. He had special little German bakery shops that he always patronized and every other day or two he would come usually without his wife, who didn't approve of such visitations—and bring special cookies made in strange and odd shapes much to the delight of the children. He really was a sweet dispositioned, nice old fellow, but Mrs. M. could be put down in the category, as far as her treatment of Mr. M. was concerned in latter years, as a plain ordinary every-day bitch. She really was cruel to the poor old man. In early October of that year he was put to bed where he stayed and never recovered.

He died in my arms the last of October.

Then what a procedure took place. It seemed to release something from Mrs. M. The first thing she thought of was getting her hands on her own money. We suggested that it would be well for her to go to their safe deposit box, if they had one in a joint name which she said they did. She said that she had jewelry there that belonged to her, also money and securities. . . .

Melba's divorce from Charles became final the last of November 1928 and we immediately set forth with Mrs. M. to Santa Fe for the purpose of having our illicit affair legalized. We drove there in Mrs. M.'s car, chauffeured by a negro who had formerly worked for Senator Borah.

En route we stopped for luncheon with James McNary at Mc-Nary, Arizona, where he and Louis Stoddard were conducting a large timber operation on government land. After luncheon we continued with Jim McNary to Santa Fe.

When I visited Santa Fe in 1920 in behalf of the candidacy of Herbert Hoover, I had fallen in love with that old Spanish-Indian town and vowed that if I ever set forth on another matrimonial venture I would have the bonds of holy matrimony joined there.

Jim wanted to know were we were going to be married and I told him we expected that duty to be performed by the Clerk of the Court. He was very enthusiastic about Melba and prevailed upon her and Mrs. M. to have the wedding in the old Spanish Governor's Palace—then and now a museum. He said no one had been married there since the Spaniards had moved out. I told him that I felt sure that an Episcopal minister could not marry us because we had both been divorced. Suffergan Bishop Herbert Shipman of the Episcopal Church (he had married Elise and Eddy Hurd and was a great friend of mine) had explained to me sometime before that an Episcopal Clergyman could marry the innocent party to a divorce action, but the guilty party only when the Bishop of the Diocese was convinced that it was to the best interests of all concerned—morally speaking—and so certified to the officiating cleric—That did not perturb Jim, so he dug up a Presbyterian domine.

204

We planned itineraries and made reservations for Mrs. M. to accompany us on a world tour.

When Mrs. M. created her life trust she impressed upon Judge Ryan and Mr. Kane of the National City that she wished an irrevocable trust so that it would not be possible for some young man to influence her into investing her principal in questionable ventures. At that time she also expected that she would remarry and she wanted to make sure that if she did marry again, it would be only for her and her income— and not for her principal.

I told Nicholas Murray Butler, President of Columbia University, of my proposed world tour and he gave me letters to rather interesting people the world over, including such personages as our American Ambassador to Paris Myron Herrick, His Excellency Tong Shao Yi, the grand old man of China and former Premier under the Ming dynasty, Mr. Miyako, General Consul to the NYK Line in Japan, also Japanese member of the Carnegie Peace Foundation.

I had letters from Congressman Robert L. Bacon of the First District of New York, Senator James E. Watson of Indiana, Senator Guy Goff of West Virginia, Governor Frank O. Lowden of Illinois, Congressman Fred M. Davenport, 33rd District New York, Congressman Hamilton Fish, 26th District of New York and many others. . . .

The wedding flowers had been sent on from Los Angeles by air mail.

McNary persuaded the museum authorities to open the old Governor's Palace for the wedding. This naturally caused a commotion—in fact sufficient to create a wire story.

We received a great deal of publicity in papers all over the country. Henry Roemke collected the clippings for us but when putting them together in a bound volume, lost them.

Upon our return from the wedding, Melba put her Hauser Blvd. home up for auction—sold the house and lot and all the furniture and fixings.

While squandering money on Florence M.—mink coats, Packard cars, diamond rings, innumerable trips hither, thither and yon, theatre parties, night clubs, buying her business for her—I ear-marked a sufficient amount of the cash that I lavished upon her for myself. It was not much, in the neighborhood of four or five thousand dollars, but enough to hold me together on an economical basis for several years.

I continued to dabble in real estate transactions and to speculate on the New York stock exchange. The Wall Street boom was then on in full sway: "two chickens in every pot," "two cars in every garage."

Melba's house and furnishings brought over eleven thousand dollars in auction and the money I had made and accumulated, through real estate deals and through stock manipulations, a trifle more. Together we had about 25,000 dollars in cash at the end of 1928 or within the month after we were married in the old Governor's Palace in Santa Fe.

Christmas 1928—I bought you the power house for your Lionel railroad set—I sent live turkeys and crates of grapefruit and oranges and boxes of California glace fruits and candies to my father and mother, to the Hurds, to my mother's sister (Lucy), Judge Robert McCurdy Marsh (my attorney) and my godmother (Abbie Burt).

Melba's children, Diane and Melsing, had been sent up to their father, Charles M. at Santa Barbara. He was directing the Little Theatre there, and living in an attractive cottage with his third legal wife (Jewel)—(there has always been some question about this marriage having been legal), and her son by another marriage.

We engaged three cottages at Santa Barbara Biltmore for the holiday. One for Melba's mother; one for Melba and myself, and one for Melba's children and nurse.

That was the Christmas that I started Melsing's electric train for him which finally accumulated in the expansive outlay that took two Lionel experts a full day to set up in our living room in the St. Regis Hotel, Christmas 1933. We all dined together on the lawn in front of the hotel overlooking the Pacific. The weather was mild—and it was a bit strange without the usual brisk tinge in the air that one ordinarily feels at Yuletide in the east—it was my first Christmas away from New York and the California Christmas decorations were a little odd to an Easterner. . . .

At that Christmas board was Mrs. M., Melba, Jewel, Charles M., Diane, Melsing, Jewel's little boy, and the children's governess (see pictures). . . .

[Before their marriage Melba and my father had decided to take a honeymoon trip around the world.]

Melba and I made a compact when we started on our world-wide tour—we agreed we would have a sexual intercourse in every hotel we visited and on every boat we traveled and on every train we spent the night. We adhered strictly to that agreement with all the essential variations helpful and conducive to connubial bliss. . . .

At 12 noon on January 14th, 1929, after a hectic morning of last-minute preparations for our trip and after a frantic call to the

206

steamship company by my secretary, arranging for the sailing to be postponed until our arrival, we hurriedly crossed the gangplank of the Nipon Yusen Kaisha S.S. *Siberia Maru*. (They had waited 30 minutes while we were getting documents signed and put in a safe deposit box.)

A moment later the whistle shrilled, the band played and the crowd on the pier cheered and shouted the bon voyages, while the passengers threw highly colored serpentine and confetti, as the hawser was cast ashore. . . .

[My father, it seems to me, had a real gift as a travel writer. He obviously loved traveling (while I dislike it and much prefer to cower at home) and was a keen observer of exotic places and people. His accounts of his global excursions make interesting and informative reading. Unfortunately they are much too extensive to include in this volume. What follow are excerpts from a very voluminous report covering several hundred pages of the original letter.]

Soon we were passing through the Golden Gate. What a gorgeous view that was from Fort Scott West to Fort Riley and south to Fort Funston—a distance of over eight miles—a line of cliffs, seals, rocks and beach—that is the ocean front of San Francisco.

Rapidly we left behind the city of contradictions—the most intensely American, yet the most cosmopolitan community on the continent with aspects as variable as the medley of alien tongues heard in its streets.

On this bobbing cork, the *Siberia Maru,* we steamed out over the ocean blue, the Pacific—but not so Pacific that day as its name might imply, for the waves were breaking very high. The ship rolled and tossed—there were few aboard the decks that day and the dining room was deserted. The ship's doctor—the little man that he was—was hopping about from one stateroom to another, administering little pills with that inevitable smile and chuckle—you never know whether they are laughing with you or at you. Even our beloved President, Franklin I in the 9th year of his reign was deluded so he contends by that smile and chuckle. All the time he thought the little Jap Ambassadors were laughing with him when in fact they apparently were laughing at him.

These little men were and are most efficient—never let anybody fool you on that score. The menu, the ship's directory and the daily news and announcements were all printed in English, although but with two or three exceptions, the passengers were all Japanese. The explanation, a desire to cater to American trade and if possible, wean it away from British and American bottoms.

As we climbed into bed the first night out, huge waves burst over the ship smashing in our window and deluged our cabin sending our luggage floating all about. Our room rapidly took on the aspect for all the world of a dramatic moment in the movies when the ship is sinking and the heroine is standing knee-deep in water hanging on to the inevitable hero.

I had been working very hard, driving myself very fast—I was very tense with nervous energy and had not relaxed. The net result— I was desperately sick—so sick that I didn't give a damn whether we weathered the storm or not.

The little Japanese raced about the cabin rearranging baggage, mopping up with pails, trying to get things under control. The little doctor administered hopefully, but not very effectively to the overpowering nausea.

The Japanese are a strange people—they speak backwards, read backwards, and even if you were to learn the words of their vocabulary, it would not help you to make yourself clear unless you had acquired the knack of thinking backwards, upside down and inside out.

One of the first things that impressed me about the ship, its crew, its passengers, its manners and its habits—was the attendance at the bar. In those days in America, the mere whispered indication of the direction of a speakeasy and the entire male, yes even a goodly portion of the female population—would rush forth to partake of the forbidden fire-water of dubious concoction.

On that little ship where man was free to drink as and when and what he chose—where wines and hard liquors could be lawfully had but for the mere asking at a small sum—the bar was as empty as the most shunned of deserts.

There were sports, tournaments, etc. Under the heading of indoor sports, there was bridge, draughts, gomoku shogi. Under outdoor sports, they had peg-quoits, rotation-quoits and deck-quoits, deck tennis, ping-pong, shuffle board and deck golf. This last was a favorite sport of the tiny Japanese captain of the ship and one could always tell if all at sea was calm and the ship was proceeding on her journey well, by noting if the captain was golfing or not.

Japanese in this depressing city of Tokio are admirable. A sensitive, exclusive, martial people, with a highly developed degree of courtesy and honor. Everywhere, there is evidence of their fixed customs of adopting foreign institutions, ideas and devices to the use of Japan. For example, nearly every house in the land, be it in the remotest or poorest section of the country, is electrically lighted and

208

equipped with telephone and the well-to-do are rapidly abandoning the hibachis or charcoal bowl of heat, for the electric heater. Still they cling to their papier mache houses of bamboo which while attractive are bitterly cold in winter and perfect breeders of flu. The wonder is that the flu, rather than the earthquakes, hasn't wrought greater havoc with the nation. . . .

[The next stop on the world tour was Peking. From there to Shanghai, my father and Melba rode on the famous Shanghai Express.]

Dan Frohman used to say that the theatrical or dramatic falsification of facts was necessary for good entertainment—he pointed out that the people would not be amused by and would not enjoy the truth. They prefer the glorification of fact or, as he put it, they only want to see a picture or a play depicting a situation or a condition that they hoped existed, rather than the one which they knew to be the true state.

In Marlene Dietrich's picture *The Shanghai Gesture,* we saw a train porter or room boy, dressed immaculately in white, bringing in a hot face towel from time to time—I never saw a porter in anything but a filthy white robe. I never had a steaming hot face towel, but that it was as dirty and yellow as the Gobi sand, and caked my face. The little detail of crossing the Yangtze River from Pukow to Nanking was entirely left out and one was led to believe that one could ride a deluxe train, beautifully appointed, from Peking to Shanghai without changing. . . .

A horror of the East—a Gobi sand blizzard—when it blows, how it blows! Sand in the eyes, sand in the nose, yellow sand, sand in the throat, sand in the clothes, yellow sand in the food, sand in the berths—yellow, yellow sand, here and there and everywhere—sandsweepers cleaning away violently at the switches with stiff brooms, sand in the engine gear boxes that blocks the road of progress while we suffer on—sand across the face of the sun at high noon, giving that old orb the yellow appearance for all the world like that of an incandescent lamp in one of New York's Ghetto clothing shops. Dust so thick that vision is completely obscured 5 ft. distant from one's person—dust, dust, dust—ashes of yellow ancestors all over the place, blending perfectly with the horrible filth of the moderns, an experience not soon to be forgot. Sand in the typewriter, sand in your camera and sand on the little towels they gave you to wash the sand off your face and out of your eyes—sand in your shoes, sand down your neck, sand in your pants (every half hour or so on a Chinese train the porter, filthy from head to foot with sand himself, appears in the doorway with a hot towel so that you may bathe and wash the dust from your face).

209

The only difficulty is that this wash rag is usually dirtier than the face it is supposed to wipe and clean, altho the warm water is expected to have a soothing effect of some sort.

In discussing China, one cannot fail to mention that the family comes before the state as a political unit, for the rule of the Village elder remains. It is a most fundamental and important factor in Chinese Government and has been less modified than any other feature of the old Imperial Regime and is the real political hope of the future. Western civilization assumes a very great responsibility if it attempts to break down this family system, for governments come and governments go, but the Chinese family goes on forever.

Despite the uproar, the confusion, the marching and counter-marching of military organizations, the influence and control of the Nationalist Party in China was recognized and effective only in a few provinces in the total of 22 provinces and territories when we were in China in 1929. The Government then influenced directly about 127 million people out of a total population of 425 million people—in area of 300,000 miles out of a total area of about 4,300,000 square miles. The Nationalist Party was just scratching the surface.

Much of the difficulty at that time could be attributed to the failure of the Nationalists to distribute enough of the "squeeze" to the military leaders on the Yangtze at Hankow. They had kept too much of the money collected by devious means in their own pockets at Nanking—rather than distributing it fairly with the generals up the river. As usual, money—filthy lucre—is at the bottom of this strife.

The National Party had bills posted in every available spot on the public buildings in the provinces which it controlled with such interesting slogans as these: "Down with Imperialism"—"Cancellation of unequal treaties"—"Declaration for the Autonomy of Customs Tariff"—"Rule the Country by the National Party"—"Abolish extra-territoriality"—"Obey the Three Principles"—"Don't forget the 21 demands by the Japanese"—"To do good things, follow the will of the people"—"Sacrifice Life for Right." Such was their propaganda.

But that the Oriental was evolving slowly but surely was obvious. The day of the pigtail and the tiny deformed feet in Eastern China had disappeared.

The day did not seem far distant then when the foreign powers would be forced by their own people with a sense of international justice to give the Chinese a place in the sun of international parity.

Speaking of extraterritoriality and treaties, in 1929 the brain in China was mightier than the brawn. Today, it may be different.

210

I said then that the unequal treaties would have to be abolished. Aside from and perhaps next to the internal strife in China at that time in importance, was the burning question of extraterritorialities. The exemption of farmers from the jurisdiction of Chinese laws, which exemptions had in years past been granted either by treaties to the point of a foreign bayonet by usage, or by sheer usurpment, and caused primarily by differences in the laws, customs and social habits of the Occidental from the Oriental nature. The Chinese justly argued that the much abused extraterritorial rights constituted a gross infringement on Chinese sovereignty.

Extraterritorialities granted to foreign traders, advantages which the Chinese did not possess, the foreign consular jurisdiction, put an intolerable burden upon the Chinese plaintiffs—that consular jurisdiction in treaty ports serves all too often to protect the criminal and the vicious circles of vice. The Chinese often declared that until extraterritorialities were abolished, they would not open up to trade any more of the interior, as any such action on their part would, under those conditions, be but a further limitation of Chinese sovereignties, so foreign residence in the interior was then forbidden.

Extraterritoriality is now to be a thing of the past—nevertheless, I wanted to record here for your information the situation as it then appeared to me when passing through.

The foreigners opposed that Chinese stand and were like many of the present affluent Chinamen, living securely within the barrage range of the gunboats guarding the extraterritorialities, they felt safe and secure from the clutches of the Chinese law.

To the foreigners railing against the injustices of the antiquated Chinese codes, the forms of punishment and filthy jails, the Chinese report that extraterritorial rights have frequently been used as a lock to protect vice or crime for which that den of iniquity, Shanghai, is a shining example. Even the records of the U. S. Courts in Shanghai have been polluted by crooked judges, agents, lawyers, District Attorneys, etc. who have besmirched the fair name of their country by their unsavory acts in accepting large bribes in opium and criminal cases. It is easy to understand why Occidentals and other foreigners do not care to place themselves under the legal jurisdiction of the Oriental judicial processes, but then if you must go to China, and live in China, you should be willing to do as China wants you to do—or feels you should do—for after all, you are but a guest in her house.

Everywhere else under the sun, the foreign nationals conform to the "law of the land" in which they find themselves, but in China they felt they should carry their native laws with them, with total disregard of the Chinese sovereignty.

California, for example, would not have been willing to grant extraterritorial rights to the Chinese or the Japanese, therefore, why should China receive treatment from us which we in those days were not willing to give the Chinese in this country. From the Chinese point of view, our laws and customs are just as strange and unjust as we think theirs are.

I said then and pointed out in the articles I sent back, that if American business wished to court Chinese goodwill, then the industrial friends of Mr. Hoover should have prevailed upon him to bring about the immediate abolition of extraterritoriality. And that if that provision were delayed until it was forced upon him—Chinese goodwill would be lost. Quick action would obtain the friendship of these people, so necessary for the proper business development and avoid any possible necessity for the use of arms or the possibility of another war.

Well, America and Great Britain are now acting—but it took Pearl Harbor to force the issue and Mr. Roosevelt's policy of cooperating with the Chinese, siding with the Chinese in the Chinese-Japanese war, to bring this about. In other words, it was not until the Japanese had captured a large portion of the seaboard provinces or the most important seaboard provinces from the Chinese that we all got together and made what is at the moment, really an empty gesture; granting extraterritoriality to the Chinese may point up goodwill on our part for the future, but certainly it does mean much when the Japanese are in complete control of all the former treaty ports and have been for some years past. . . .

As for Shanghai, the sixth city and the third port of the world— a den of iniquity—dope, prostitution and gambling rampant! Much like the rest of the universe—only open and more sordid—where men love to die.

A city of romance, of bubbling activity everywhere—where one comes but for a day and sometimes stays forever. Here are shops in this metropolis of the East, rich beyond a miser's dream. The silks, the jades, the ivories, the carved silver and the Mandarin's coats of rich heavy silk, truly an intriguing city—cosmopolitan community. Bad men, bad women, derelicts from all over the world—seeking a haven to live out their lives with their ill-gotten gains. . . .

Looking back on China as we sail out to sea through the Laimoon Pass there are many things that come to mind other than the salient political, economic problems, monuments, the Great Wall, works of art of the Ching Ling dynasty, and the stress of trade and commerce. There are the many Chinese characteristics which remain most vivid; for example, their disregard of time, their disregard of accuracy, their extreme politeness, their courtesy and hospitality, their talent for misunderstanding, their talent for indirection, the inflexibility of mind in one section of this vast country, and flexibility in the other. The linguists in the North are in direct contrast to the Canton Liberals in the South, who disdain all foreign tongues—their apparent absence of nerves, the Cantonese contempt for foreigners, the intellectual turbity, the absence of public spirit, the indifference to comfort and convenience, the physical vitality, the patience and perseverance, the contentment and cheerfulness in the face of famine and filth, the mutual suspicion and absence of sincerity, the unmisdirected intellect, their cunning, their mercenary piety, their lack of human justice and their passion for squeeze—all these, and many other characteristics are most remarkably displayed in these extraordinary people.

Perhaps it ill behooves an Occidental to become critical of the Oriental when one considers the problems that confront this ancient conglomeration of people for, as Oliver Wendell Holmes has said: "The scientific study of man is the most difficult of all branches of knowledge." . . .

Once the Chinese Government proves to the world at large its ability and permanency, China's domestic and foreign trade growth should be rapid.

The problems of China, its people and its physical background, its institutions, its labor problems, its social background and its philosophy and religions, its contacts with the West, its Government, Christianity and the missionary work, modern education and the student movement were truly a Chinese puzzle, particularly when you were from the outside looking in.

What is China? is the real question. What were her beginnings? What is her family life? What is the status of the women in China, and most important of all, how about the foreigners? What about the village republics, the cities, the craftsmen, the guilds, the calendar and its festivals? What about Confucius, his teachings and his philosophy, and what about Chinese Buddhism and the attitude toward militarism. The openings of the Gates of China, the early foreign intercourses, the setting up of the republics, the struggle for democracy, the foreign trade and the Chinese literature were all spheres of interest I tried to cover. . . .

* * *

As we steamed our way through the Straits of Malacca to Penang and thence on into the Bay of Bengal and the Gulf of Martabs to Elehantca Point and Rangoon, we passed on the east to Gypsy Islands —the pirates paradise—and on the west the Andaman Islands—the English death-house, the wall-less prison in the jungles for the incarceration of Britannia's lifers, where the only compensation for escape in this haven of dark-skinned man eaters—is the cannibal devourer.

After a trip through China where all was poverty, the display of Chinese wealth and affluence in Singapore and Penang, as evidenced by the gorgeous Chinese abodes which abounded in those Strait cities, was startling to say the least, and emphasized the precariousness of the life in China. Such a display in China would mean an immediate levy from the Government or some hungry general or bandit. Two-thirds of the population of the Straits Settlement were Chinese—they did the work while the natives loafed.

Legend has it in the Straits that the native women mistresses up in the jungle hold the white men by the subtle administration of their love potion. It is said that they take menstruation flow, let it dry to a powder, mix it with native 'erbs, brew as a broth and serve the master as a delectable soup. Taken often enough the male becomes so enamored of the female that even if he travel half way 'round the world he can never withstand the urge to return to his native woman and her love potions. . . .

In India and all through the Orient, the British have failed to realize that the energetic American earns his success because of a superior vitality and aggressive intellect born of intermingling of races on the North American continent.

It was obvious in the British settlements that the Englishman felt himself slipping—he was no longer the dominant descendant of the Norman Conqueror. The English failure to absorb the blood of her conquered peoples was slowly but surely making of the British nation a nation decadent.

A visit to the Orient, to Hongkong, to Singapore, to Calcutta, to Rangoon, to Malay and to Penang, to the Straits Settlements on land or at sea, is forcibly convincing to friendly Americans of the English colonists' active antagonism to all things American—while we in the U. S. A. are seldom aware of the active existence of Great Britain or of our own great potential commercial strength. Our successful and rapid marketing in recent years of Quaker Oats, Sun Maid Raisins, Del Monte Fruits, Borden's and Horlick's Milk, Flit, Remington and Underwood typewriters, Ford cars, Waterman Fountain Pens, East-

214

man Kodaks, Phoenix and Interwoven hosiery, Radios, Victor Talking Machines and records, B.V.D.'s, Wrigley's Spearmint Gum, Holly- wood Pictures, Dollar Line tourists and Freight, National City Bank branches and American Express transactions in the Far East, made the arrogant British colonizers envious and disdainful—for they all openly resented the very presence of any American in their midst. Our successful saunterings about the Globe in those days, they at- tributed to our "ungodly profits" from the needs of and necessities of other nations. In this feeling, of course, they were unmindful of their own flagrant cases—all too many to recount—of their exploitation of small, helpless nations at the point of a British bayonet. . . .

India: As we sped onward to Bombay, innumerable irrigation ditches and filthy black witches were producing the crops of Mother India. The ramways which harnessed bullocks tread up and down, drawing water from the wells to fill the ditches, dot the fields of India in limitless number as the ancestral graves drown China's countryside —China might well follow India's irrigation example and put her ancestral mounds to work.

Next Bombay, the gateway to India—on a peninsula projected into the Arabian Sea—where Western British influence is more pro- nounced than elsewhere in this polluted and polluting land—where the Hindu holds sway in dark decay, where the Parsi is ubiquitous in his new found wealth and affluence, where the human corpse is offered up to the carrion while not yet cold, where the Towers of Silence are atop the city's reservoirs—the final act in the Parsi funeral rite, since to these people earth, fire and water are too holy to be contaminated by human remains. The vultures must completely destroy the corpse of man.

The Towers of Silence out on the hill above the city behind the reservoir really left a deep impression upon me. The largest of these Towers of Silence is 276 feet in circumference and 25 feet high. Within there was a platform with depressions for receiving the bodies which were immediately stripped of flesh by the flock of vultures always waiting on the neighboring trees. The depressions were three different sizes. On the outer rim were the larger receptacles for the men then the next circle of smaller receptacles for the women's bodies and then a circle of still smaller grooves near the center of the vat for the young children and babies.

After the vultures have finished their work, the bones are moved to a pit in the center of the tower where they soon disintegrate.

The towers were surrounded with a beautiful garden in which

there was a chapel for meditation and prayer. Many of the finest homes of Bombay were built on that hillside, and the inhabitants were not the least bit awed or sickened when finding pieces of the human carcass about their grounds—choice bits the vultures failed to devour before being scared away.

Twice a day, in the morning and in the afternoon, the Parsees bring their dead to the Towers of Silence. The towers were all painted white on the outside, with what we would call whitewash. The Parsee pallbearers were all dressed in white—and the caskets or coffins were also in white. After services they lay all the nude bodies in the various receptacles to await the descent of the vultures. . . .

Soon the Orient was to be well out of sight. What to do—What to do? was the question. Should the British continue their half-hearted, insufficient, misshapen rule? Should the Indian have his freedom? Here again the answer seemed to be—the Indian people like the Filipinos are entitled to their independence and the right to liberty and self-government under the sun—but to set them free would mean tribal warfare and the strong men of the North would wipe the Hindus and the Mohammedan and the Parsi, the converted Christian, off the face of the continent of India. Perhaps that is as it should be and as it is meant to be—that the strong only shall survive.

The British alone can not solve this problem—they are not strong enough numerically or physically, theirs is a race decadent.

In 1929 I said that the Japanese would take India before the Indians recaptured it from the British for themselves; who knows? Whatever comes the British rule of India is definitely on the way out. After Britain it will be India for the Indians or India for the Japanese.

India for the Indians would be India for the strong men of the North.

Out on the Indian Ocean, infested with churlish British homeward bound for their biennial leave—ranting, railing against the good old U. S. A.—trying desperately to overcome their inferiority complex, only succeeding in thoroughly disproving the ill-founded notion that the English as a class have good manners, are well bred. A fundamental axiom of common courtesy demands that a host must never embarrass or render uncomfortable a guest or a stranger within his gates—this axiom was violated every day by the mass of British middle-class. They never missed an opportunity to insult Americans within their gates. It must be said, however, that the laboring and upper classes did not display this antagonism openly. Perhaps it was the life in the provinces that made them so intractable—for could anything be more horrible than to live in India, the land of the untouchables, of feminine bondage, of holy prostitutes or priestly harems, of feminine crucifixions, of infantile immorality, of child mothers (eight years old), of suttees (young woman sacrificed alive on burning altars of fiery dung in religious rituals), of young men who have destroyed themselves in youth, of moral depravity, of burning ghats, of babies and elders and goats alike slaughtered alive (that there may be better crops), of cities of half castes, the filthy Hindus, Mohammedans, Parsees, of leprosy, of cholera, of small pox and of syphilis.

Great Britain should have either scoured out this hellhole, this black dirty blotch on her fame, or else have gotten out.

For a true detailed picture of India they say you should read *Mother India* and *The Slaves of the Gods* by Katherine Mayo. Although I never have, I have seen for myself.

As we travelled onward, westward, encircling the globe, the lack of real, fundamental emotional differences in mankind forced itself steadily in upon us. In each country similar groups reacted identically to definite emotional stimulus. In India the British and the natives separate the various levels of human endeavor into castes—and we call them groups rather than castes or classes.

The so-called Four Hundred or upper social group in New York, in London, in Berlin, in Paris, in Shanghai, in Bombay, in Rome, in Madrid, in Tokio, in Buenos Aires, in Chicago, prior to World War No. 2 had similar aims, attitudes and restraints and probably will have the same after the war is over.

The peasants in every field plod on slowly, trudgingly with antiquated methods producing the staff of life.

The laboring group in each country thrills to the blood and thunder movie, the prolonged screen soul kiss—home made or imported from the U. S. A.

While the Liberals the world over seek the odd, the different, the unusual and the reverse of the order of the day—

The middle class or clerking groups were everywhere struggling onward with their sex repressions.

The successful barons of commerce and finance, whether on Wall Street or on the Bund at Shanghai were steeped in a false conservatism as they chafed at the traces.

The statesman, the politician, the warrior, from one end of this amazing world to the other was engrossed in his own Nationalistic egotism and still is, United Nations or no United Nations.

Poetry which has stirred the heart of one nation has generally an echo in that of another.

Catchy rythm on Broadway will appeal in Shanghai, Bombay or Paris.

English was slowly but surely becoming the universal language of the trade routes of the globe, and its use will be greatly hastened by World War No. 2.

The proletariat of both hemispheres seeks universal peace with all their strength while the leaders grapple over technicalities that bring about great wars.

It was true that the customs of dress, transportation, edibles, abodes differed wherever you went, but the contrasts were caused largely by geographic and climatic conditions, or were dictated by religious creeds.

In outward appearances sects differ greatly. Yet, in the last analysis there was little variation in the basic ritual idea of all the faiths the world around. It was simply a matter of form—all doctrines, Christian or non-Christian play upon the credulence of mankind and the everlasting fear of death ingrained from child birth.

"We know not where we came from nor whither we are bound." Which of the wise men's cults with their elaborately concocted creeds will prevail no man can say—faith is the soothing syrup of troubled man the world around. Will Christian or non-Christian survive the test of time?

Today the non-Christian holds overwhelming but disputed sway. God must—paraphrasing Lincoln—have loved the non-Christians, he made so many of them. One billion non-Christians in all, while only five hundred million Christians grace the face of the earth. . . .

From time immemorial the wise men, the upper group, the leaders have played upon the emotions of their peoples, the masses, that they might the more readily keep them in complete subjection and servitude.

As universal man expands and with broadened vision grows he discards the emotional shackles of his religious bonds and finds his peace in the consciousness of his mind, the evolution of his race and the international fellowships of man. That the world is divided into classes rather than races is the conclusion of most nomads who have wandered afar.

A witty Frenchman was once heard to remark: "Le monde est partout comme partout." "The world all over is as the world all over."

For all men, who have very nearly the same feelings and

sympathies, are much less modified than we think by distance and customs.

With the continued modernization of the Far and Near East we will find not only common ideals in every nook and corner of the world with one huge family of nations kept in order by an international air, naval and land police force, adjudicated by a world court—an Utopia not far distant, if the New Dealers have their way.

In 1929 in my California column and again in 1934 in our farm booklet, I advocated an international court supported by an international army and navy to enforce the edicts etc.

At the beginning of the century the late President Theodore Roosevelt advocated the same thing.

The barriers of borders are rapidly disappearing as the similarity of racial interests becomes daily more clearly apparent and will be wiped out altogether if the proper peace is secured at the conclusion of World War No. 2.

We were practically ostracized on the British boat upon which we sailed from Colombo to Suez. Only one individual, a leader of the Boy Scouts in Madras, talked to us on this long voyage to Egypt, although they played Victor Talking Machines and used Underwood Portable Typewriters, ("they" being the passengers, British provincials). . . .

A visit to Mussolini's superbly organized Fascisti nation once known as Italy (for then Mussolini and Italy were synonymous) was a pleasant relief and contrast to the disorder of the Orient.

The wonders of the early Christian era and the beauty spots of that fairyland were visited in peace and quiet, devoid of the vociferous beggars and parasitical guides, thanks to Il Duce, from Southern Sicily to the Northern Italian Alps—he had put the fear of God into the hearts of his countrymen and with it self-respect.

That a man who has had the iron will to bring order out of chaos and ruthlessly and single-handedly to dictate the everyday existence of the humblest citizen should live in daily fear was an amazing study in dual personality—few great men have been so constantly surrounded by such a heavy personal guard—armies of detectives, soldiers, policemen protected him every moment of the day and night—and he appeared most fearful at every public appearance.

For a man to control a nation by a dilation of the eye is indeed remarkable—all his magnetism and control seemed to radiate from the eyeball. . . .

Here if one does not intensively cultivate his property the State condemns his land and sells it to another. The Fascisti is a one-man organization. When the Premier dies, all will be unrest and revolution again. A poor foundation at best. . . .

Just before we left Rome, I wrote a letter to a Monsignor Spellman at the Vatican, enclosing an introduction from Monsignor York of New York.

Monsignor York, a great friend of President Theodore Roosevelt, had been the Catholic lobbyist in Albany. At the bottom of my letter I added a postscript saying that we would consider it a great honor to be presented to His Holiness the Pope, if that could be arranged—on the theory "nothing ventured, nothing gained." Melba always said: "P.S., would like to meet the Pope."

We sent the note by special messenger and then departed for a further sightseeing visit of Rome. On our return to the hotel that evening there was much excitement. The Monsignor had called during our absence and left a note. The note directed that we should be at the Vatican the following morning for a private audience with His Holiness. Thinking that we had better find out something about the procedure other than that Melba was to be covered with the black mantila that the Monsignor had left for her, and that I was to wear full dress and gloves—we put in a phone call for the Monsignor.

We found him at his hotel and he invited us to call that evening. We explained we were dressed for the evening, as we were going out to dinner, but he urged us to come. For some unknown reason, I had expected him to speak Italian, but to my surprise, he spoke a very virile Irish-American lingo.

When we reached his hotel, he proceeded to completely disarm us. He knew the innermost details of my life, private and public—he graciously opened a bottle of wine and we spent a very pleasant hour with this very distinguished and brilliant prelate.

He told us of the arrangements for the following day and suggested that if we wished to have any little trinkets blessed by His Holiness for our friends back home, that we visit a certain store, favored by the Vatican, and purchase such articles there.

We visited the store early the next morning and purchased trinkets which were subsequently blessed, for our friends.

After passing the outer Swiss Guard, we were met near the entrance gate of the Vatican Proper by Monsignor Spellman. From there, we passed down long hallways enroute to His Holiness' quarters. The Swiss Guards in their vari-colored uniforms all snapped to attention as we passed, saluting the Monsignor with their spears. I had no knowledge at that time of Spellman's great importance at the Vatican.

The ceremony was solemn, impressive, imposing. We knelt before His Holiness and kissed his ring—it was their custom—and when in Rome you do as the Roman Catholics do at the Vatican. The Holy See's knowledge of World affairs—international and national—was amazing.

After the presentation, we took the Monsignor to the Grand de Russe for a champagne luncheon. It was a brilliant and scintillating affair—Spellman had a marvelous sense of humor and a keen intellect.

He would not be photographed with Melba, but he took photographs of us dressed in our presentation regalia.

At lunch he told us that he had had a very restless night—he contended that Melba's extreme decollete of the evening before had been the cause.

The Monsignor, I later discovered, was at that time Assistant Secretary of State for the Vatican for North America. He is now Archbishop of the Diocese of New York—and his former boss—the then Secretary of State, is now Pope. . . .

In 1929 Munich still retained the flavor of olden Teutonic days—the famous Hofbrau Haus with its huge "Festsaal" where the world-renowned Munchener beer was still served, exuded a warmth of "comradery" seldom found abroad at that time.

Berlin was then a charming, a modern, a live city bent on rehabilitation—where perversion was rampant with molestation—where feminine men in girlish attire and masculine women in boyish attire disported themselves in the public cafes without interference from the authorities—where societies for the development of the human form were thriving without fear of public intervention. Within the grounds of the beautiful lakeside estates of these fabulous nudist organizations, its members were seen by us in utter nakedness, attending to the chores and pleasures of their every-day existence.

The Kaiser's old palace still stood—a grim reminder of the glory of the Hohenzollerns. It was at the Kaiser's palace that Theodore Roosevelt reviewed the goose-stepping hordes of the old Empire.

The land of Goethe, Schiller, Wagner was still renowned for the creation of perfect lyric ecstasy.

The first day we were in Berlin we went to the Haus Vaterland where there is dining, drinking and entertainment of eight different nations going on simultaneously in one building. It is a huge structure

221

on Potsdammer Platz. We had lunch in the Rhine Room where they had a large panorama or back drop sort of mural—but animated—of the River Rhine with little river boats sailing up and down the river and railroad trains, cars and wagons moving along the roads, through thunderstorm, nightfall, moonlight and sunshine, the weather changes or moods occurring during the orchestration of suitable music. They also had a Wild West room, a London room, a Harlem room—in fact you could dine under almost any kind of local atmosphere you desired.

I learned of the Nude Clubs from a guide at the Adlon Hotel who insisted on offering his services—in despair at his inability to interest me in a sightseeing tour, he finally suggested the Nackt Club. I thought at first he meant Nacht Club and I felt I had no need of a guide in Berlin for night clubs or otherwise because Melba had lived there for several years, but I was wrong, for it was Nackt or "Nude" clubs that he meant. . . .

We spoke to Hooper Trask [a friend in Berlin] about the Nude Clubs and he obtained memberships for us both in a rather nice one.

It was a strange sensation. The place was out in the country, well kept up, beautifully run—lake, playgrounds, tennis courts, golf, etc. The main club house where tea was served had lockers for the members who just came out for the day. The men and women would arrive and disrobing in the same room put their clothes in their lockers, and naked, run out to play or stop for a cup of tea or a biscuit first. It gave you the feeling of seeing Niagara Falls in reverse.

There were many bungalows and quite a few tents for the week-end guests.

The oldest member of the club was a fellow of 84 years. He was an honorary member and on the board of governors—very fond of young girls of slight build. He became excited one day as two passed him on the porch—his prick got hard and stood up and looked at him. The girls reported him to the house committee, for that was a serious infraction of the rules—and in public. After much deliberation and much concern for the honored member, the committee decided it was "love's last blush," and determined to ignore the incident, as they doubted if it could happen again.

We visited the Silhouette in Berlin, a homo nightclub and dance-hall—the fairies had been certified by the health officers and given a permit to dress as women. They were beautifully turned out in exquisite evening clothes which produced a most perfect illusion. My principle sport was to dance with the sons of bitches—being high on scotch I would always have to get a feel in to be sure that they possessed

222

testicles and tools. We threw a champagne party for half a dozen of them and everybody got quite stinko—I still have a rubber tit that I swiped from one of them—he announced that when Jimmy Walker had visited the place the year previous, he'd gone off with the other one. It just so happens that whenever I've seen Jimmy since then, I haven't happened to have the tit with me for comparison's sake—unfortunately. The Silhouette was, of course, extraordinary in itself and I purchased things from the boys, such as erotic sketches and paintings, many of them very cleverly done. The place that was most interesting was a restaurant where homos dined, but did not dress up—there you would see men in their daily business clothes wooing one another across the dinner table—and when I say wooing, I mean that their passionate lovemaking was something to behold—hot stuff. They would dance together, and if some of them didn't come when they were dancing, then their actions belied their acts. My favorite spot, of course, was the lesbian hangout—there were many lesbian places in Berlin, but one in particular was most intriguing. There, too, the girls were quite open in making love to one another across the table and when they danced. The street-walkers were numerous—the whore houses plentiful—in fact every time you left the Adlon there was some male or female eager to remove your penis for a price—or should I say your load. Of course you didn't have to leave the Adlon—the bell-boys could produce and so could the maids—and you didn't have to send for the maids, they were right there in your room waiting.

In Berlin I had a sense of having been there before; whether I got that from my study of German in school or from my German school-master, I don't know—but there was something very familiar about the city. I almost felt as if I had lived there at some time in my life. . . .

I liked Berlin. I liked Munich. I liked the bar at the Adlon Hotel—and particularly the Eden Bar, where they specialized in champagne cocktails—it was smart there. A restaurant on Unter den Linden especially appealed to me as did Femina, a large dance hall. . . .

And so to Paris—the greatest "sell" in all the world—fortunately for the future of the Republic—Paris was not France. . . .

Out of the whirl, the swirl and the froth of gay Paree, the Eiffel Tower rose majestically, mystically yet firmly above the entire city.

The Tomb of Napoleon and the Unknown Soldier were living symbols of the human sacrifices that had been made—maybe in vain.

To the most casual observer, it was self-evident in those days of reparations, uncertainties that Germany was better able to pay than France.

The Parisans had the feel of a whipped people—that was in 1929—the Germans of a determined and successful nation.

Taxes, taxes, taxes everywhere in France—taxes for this, taxes for that, taxes when you sat down, taxes when you stood up—all this was in the land of victory, while in Germany, the land of the vanquished, not a tax raised its head to mar the serenity of the visitors—which spells out clearly for those who choose to look realistically, that the victor many times pays too great a price for the victory—that is something that people and statesmen seldom take into consideration in their emotional upsets following so-called victories after prolonged wars.

France had paid a terrible price for victory and was crushed.

Why Paris? I often wondered. Even the women of the streets were frumpish in appearance, no style, little charm—where were the Parisian creations to be found? Why, on the American women, of course—or the Russians exiled there. American women lead the world for smart clothes—not the girls of France. The Russians next, and the South Americans and mistresses of the Rajahs also come in for a fair amount of style acclaim.

Why do Americans, I wonder, buy American and German-made goods in Paris, when they can get more for their money at home? Fashion, how strange thou art!

Little did I know then that I was destined to learn much about Paris fashions as brought forth by the famous Parisian couturiers and the influence that the Paris silhouette had upon American fashion.

The Folies Bergere—a stiflng, ill-ventilated gilded hall—internationally famous for novelty revues abominably executed, the mecca of American feminine bourgeosie, where the butter and egg boys from across the sea rub elbows with the Babbitts and the elite of Newport and New York.

How pitiful these futile efforts to cast the inhibitions of a lifetime aside—why people accustomed to the best that George White, Flo Ziegfeld and even the Shuberts had to offer, should have wasted their time with these tawdry amusements of Paris is difficult to comprehend.

Did American women relish the insulting admiration forcibly thrust upon them when they venture forth about that renowned city, Paris, by the amorous French gentry? Did American men succumb to the active solicitation of the dowdy French demi-mondaine? I doubt it.

In Berlin vice was genuine—you didn't feel it was a setup for the visitor. What you saw there was the earnest participation of the natives in the excesses and perversities of nature—but Paris—ah! that was different—that was a setup for the tourist trade, the goldbrick for the sucker from Joe Zelli's to the House of All Nations. And as for the Folies Bergere the scenic effects were handled better by Mr. Minsky in his heyday. Joe Zelli gave us the name of several establishments. The first one we visited we didn't care so much about—we then went to Madame Dorione, 122 Rue de Provence. This establishment was most attractive—you were received in style, taken to a large and sump-tuously furnished parlor, champagne was "cracked" and when the girls came in, they were beautifully gowned—were introduced all around, partook of the champagne and then proceeded, somewhat after the fashion of the Japanese dancing girls, to perform in slow motion a strip tease tableau accentuated by varied colored lights thrown upon their nude bodies in different shapes and forms. This performance concluded you then determined the "maidens-fair" you desired for your pleasures of the evening—they had mulatto girls and white girls and girls of varied nationalities—they had oriental girls and Egyptian girls—they had lesbians and girls who went in for flagel-lation. Melba picked the two that appealed to her most—I selected a couple for myself and we first went to the bathing pool which was a mirrored room with inlaid tile, very similar to the chambers in which the Hindus disported themselves in the Indian palaces in the days of yore. There was much affectionate interest and more drinking of champagne as we played about in the pool. We then proceeded to a luxurious chamber where more champagne was consumed and the lesbians made love to Melba—they gave her a strenuous workout. I was not wasting time myself—after I had finished screwing the two girls and Melba was near the point of exhaustion, I got in the last lick with her—I gave her a good juicy fuck. We both rested, bathed and then went up to a tower or a room that had the appearance of a tower where the sadists were awaiting us, gowned as nuns. There they had every form of lash and rod for catering to the most depraved of sadistic impulses—they had a belfry tower wheel to strap the girls to, they had a cross to tie them to and various contraptions to which they could be fastened while being tortured. I didn't suppose that that sort of thing would particularly intrigue or excite me, but it was effective when the girls' robes were removed and I afterward laid them with relish, although one is supposed to get one's satisfaction from beating or being beaten.

I spent more than I had anticipated or contracted for, more than I had intended—because a stiff prick knows no conscience and will carry one away on extravagant ventures. So the madame sent one of the maids with us to the hotel where I dug up the additional francs to discharge an obligation that was well worth every penny—the whole thing was done nicely and, of course, in much better style than they do it on 47th Street, New York, or than Anna Swift ever dished it up in her prime. We visited many of the innumerable night clubs where the girls disported themselves in the nude, but it all was an anti-climax after Berlin, because it was commercial—you never got away from the idea that you were part of a show for profit, and commercialism in prostitution has its cooling effect. . . .

The Frenchman in years gone by had his wife and inevitable mistress—French women do not seem to object to their husbands' girl friends. A wife would raise hell in America if she knew, but in France, it seems to be an accepted fact—perhaps that's why the Frenchman is not so busy running around to the hot spots of his metropolis of an evening, in search of sexual stimulant—the wife and mistresses being sufficient unto the day.

In France you are not considered to have obtained your full manly stature until you have at least two mistresses to your credit, in addition to your wife. The wives frequently entertain and go out with their husbands' mistresses. French wives have been known to boast of the number of mistresses their husbands had. That, I think, explains why most of the houses of prostitution and the nightclubs in the Latin Quarter seem to depend on the tourist trade for their income and not the natives. That's what gives the vice of Paris as the visitor sees it, that hollow, insincere ring. . . .

In London effusive politeness greeted us everywhere—with its "Thank you" for this and "Thank you" for that, "Thank you," "Thank you," "Thank you" until you almost go mad—such a relief from the provincial British of the Orient.

London—brisk, alive, active, smartly clad women (all the frumpish English women must have been exported to the U. S. A.)— well dressed men (carrying umbrellas rather than canes). The weather is a bit muggy at times.

Then there was a parade of the Scotch Guards at Chelsea Barracks in red coats—a dress rehearsal of the Trooping of the Colors of the Horse Guard on the Whitehall parade ground, for the spectacular occasion of the King's birthday then approaching.

And "London Bridge is falling down, my fair lady," The Bloody Tower, Westminster Abbey, The Thames, Limehouse (reformed), Hyde Park (oratory still flowing freely), Picadilly Circus, Trafalgar Square, Charing Cross, Lyons Tea Shops, the Mayfair Hotel, the Kit Kat Club, the Busses (placarded like a truck on election night), the underground trams (entered through the gentlemen's lavatory)—the English must all be afflicted with weak bladders (they go in so for men's rest rooms, and women's, too), Parliament, Buckingham Palace, St. Paul's, The Bank of England, The Bobbies, Pall Mall. Silk Hats, Opera Hats vie with derbies—every shop seems to have a "By appointment" to some king or queen or prince.

Morning coats and social unrest were still astir and the Ascot and the Derby were approaching. Old Bond Street, Grub Street and Fleet Street had their charm—but to Ye Cheshire Cheese you must go and sit in the box where Charles Dickens placed Darnley and Carter in the celebrated scene depicted in Chapter IV of the *Tale of Two Cities*—and to enjoy ye old famous pie, turtle soup, and Devonshire cyder. A real delight after the hurly, burly tossing and battling about on land and sea of a world-encircling venture. . . .

In England, as in France, all wounded veterans seem to be employed as doormen, lift boys, pages—poor reward for giving one's body to one's country—pauperized soldiers, neglected by their countrymen, left to prey upon the sympathies of American tourists—not a pleasant taste. Distinguished service medals must have been passed around freely by Johnny Bull, or else all the Islanders distinguished themselves not less than six times each—for every taxi driver appeared to be an exact replica of old Nat Wells, the famous vaudevillian comedian tramp. . . .

Melba phoned Thelma Furness (then Lady Furness, now Thelma, Lady Furness)—she had known Thelma very well in Hollywood; she first wrote her a letter and then phoned her without success—since then Thelma has had many explanations to make of her failures to see Melba in London, but she was on the crest of the wave at the time. Now, Gloria and Thelma and Melba are inseparable. . . .

At sea we had left behind England, "the old dame, sitting there in the silver seat, the Mighty Mother of us all whimpering to herself —unmindful of everything save her own safety," always looking the Gift Horse in the mouth.

To me, "The Motherland was a sort of regal Mrs. Gump whose cupboards were full of grisly skeletons, abortions and miscarriages and who recognized some legitimate children with difficulty." England was slowly dying of self-absorption. . . .

So to the Statue of Liberty, Bowling Green, and the customs inspectors at the docks.

In reflection at that time, we decided that the world was a big place and a long way round. For civilization—give me London; For efficiency—give me Berlin; For the mystic—give me Peking; For vice —give me Shanghai; For romance—give me Rome; For charm—give me Veere, Holland; For Bohemia—give me Paris; For filth—Benares on the Ganges River; For contentment—New York—it's home. . . .

1929-1931

When we arrived in New York—which we did quietly, incognito, as we didn't want Melba's mother to know we had gotten back, nor to stir up Florence M. Florence had written Judge Marsh asking him to try and prevail upon us when we returned to the United States to do so quietly without publicity or fanfare, so as not to humiliate her with her friends. How it could have bothered her I don't know, inasmuch as all the papers had carried considerable copy on my marriage to Melba in the Governor's Palace at Santa Fe. We were met by mother and father who had never seen Melba before. They were glad I was married again and acted as if they approved, although I doubted it. . . .

I had been so accustomed, when travelling in Europe or in other parts of the world, to tell Melba to direct the cab driver to the destination we desired—she was being a versatile linguist—that when I entered the cab on the French Line Pier in New York, I told her to direct the cab driver to the Savoy Plaza, forgetting for the moment that New York cabbies could understand my English.

We saw something of mother and father for the few days we remained in New York. This was in June of 1929. We didn't remain long, however, and soon set forth for California—on arrival in Los Angeles, we first looked up Mary Alice (G.).

When we arrived at Mary Alice's, Jerry opened the door—it was 2:30 in the morning—we were a little high—we had so many things to tell. Jerry called to Mary but I went upstairs to bring her down in my arms. Mary hearing the racket had awakened, was in the bathroom about to put on her robe—she was stark naked—and that sight after so long an absence, was seductive. I succumbed—of necessity the inevitable was a quickie, on the johnnie. I don't think it occurred to Jerry what we were up to, and I know that Melba was unaware until Mary and I told her some years later.

[From California my father, Melba and her two children, Diane and Melsing, traveled back to Durango. As my father wrote: "My excuse for going to Mexico was to . . . look for mines and timber to develop—way down deep I suspect it was to escape the suits and unpleasantnesses that were piling up—fear of the unknown was always gnawing at me—fear—fear—fear—and the desire for female flesh has had more to do with my failures in life than any other factor except extravagance, and the desire to be liked. I liked women and I felt they liked me."

The trip to Durango was a nightmare. A Mexican pony threw my father and the fall broke his hip. It was improperly set. Peritonitis set in and he almost died from the infection. One leg ended up shorter than the other and my father walked for the rest of his life with a pronounced limp.

From his hospital bed in Durango my father wrote me a revealing letter. I was then twelve. I had met Melba in a brief visit in June, 1929. She seemed to me "common," in no way comparable to my mother and I must have indicated in what I said and in my manner my feelings about her. Apparently at the June meeting in Baltimore I had also expressed resentment over his failure to contribute to our support and his extravagance in taking his world tour.]

Page—the transformation that has come over you since I saw you at school and then at Ruxton in the Station in November of 1927 is indeed remarkable. I can't help but believe that the real Page was— the big manly boy of that November afternoon—and not the self-righteous emotional tear-swept mimic of last June, despite the fact that your present environment is making its impression on you. I shall keep and cherish that November memory of you and Marshall as the real fundamental character of my boys no matter what false exterior has been since placed upon them. That the resentments that

229

the Pages have all had for me long before you were born in fact before I even married your mother, resentment at my daring to call my soul my own and lead my life untrampled, resentment, hatred and bitter antagonisms that finally cumulated in the permanent separation of your mother and myself, should leave its mark upon you is not surprising.

I regret that you so heartily disapproved of my world tour. I could hardly be considered as deserting my boys when I couldn't be with them if I remained at home, because of that horrid divorce paper and other obstacles as we shall soon see. Yet you must have heard of parents, yes even fond mothers deserting their wee babies for pleasure sojourns in Europe, to say nothing of deserted husbands left behind to sweat out the family livelihood while mama cavorts about the continent, just glance about you and you will perhaps find such cases near at hand, they are not uncommon, you know. Perhaps then you will cease to disapprove of your father's pilgrimage. . . .

Your mother expects me to support you all—but she doesn't wish to share my own sons with me or to permit me to have a voice in your education or training—When she is willing to discuss a fifty-fifty sharing of my boys with me, then I will be glad to discuss support and she knows it. I think you both should go to a ranch school in the west for several years and then to some military school like Culver in Indiana, before your college exams. If you plan to go to Princeton, then two years of high, the last two should be spent at Lawrenceville and accordingly any college you plan to enter you should go to their principal preparatory school first. Of course, college is something which must be worked for. . . .

You spoke of the present financial difficulties. It would seem that you all are pretty comfortable. Beautiful Mansion, lovely grounds, gardens, plenty of cows, pigs and chickens, two major cars, horses and lots of servants. Say, young man, for many, many months while you were living down there with all the comforts and warmth I slept in the cheapest of rooming houses with no heat by the day or night in my room, with little cover, and for days on end, and my only meal was a ham or roast beef sandwich and maybe a five cent bar of Hershey's, to keep my body and soul intact. My clothes threadbare and cardboard stuffed in my shoes to keep my feet off the ground. Now, I don't begrudge you and your mother all your comfort, thank God you all have escaped privation and have not known want, hunger and cold, but when I contrast your lot with my own and that of millions of others in the world, I get darn tired of the constant cry of wolf, which you too have apparently taken up. Say, son, you don't know how lucky you all are to have that fine home. Think of the thousands of mothers who have to work in stores, offices, factories, live in cheap furnished rooms and keep their children in charitable institutions or in cheap boarding schools where they can only see their babies occasionally.

I am sorry that your mother seems to find it necessary to sell things for pin money but there is nothing unusual or horrible about that—thousands of splendid women today—many in order to augment their husband's income are engaged in business of every conceivable nature—why, do you know that the 1920 census showed 8,500,000 women engaged in gainful occupation which was 21% of the entire female population over ten years of age, and it's safe to say from the Bureau estimates that the 1930 census will show an increase of 20% over the 1920 figures. Why in the very state you are living in Maryland, there were 127,221 women engaged in gainful occupations in 1920, as against 466,257 men in gainful occupations, so it is not unusual for the women in Maryland to keep occupied, the figures speak clearly. In New York state there were in 1920, 1,137,000 women in gainful occupation, while 3,367,000 men were so occupied. Nothing unusual about women helping themselves in my native state, either in these days of equal rights for women and countless thousands are darn fine mothers too. It may interest you to know while on this subject that in 1920, 12.7% of these women were engaged in agriculture, forest and animal husbandry pursuits, 22.6% were in manufacturing and mechanical industries, 2.5% in transportation, 7.8% in trade, 0.3% in Public Service, 11.9% in professional service, 25.6% in personal service, and 16.7% were engaged in clerical occupations, and a small number in extract and mineral work. Now, as I have often said, I regret that your mother feels it necessary to have her shop. My principal regret, however, is because it seems so distasteful to her, but that it is neither necessary or unusual, I think my figures should convince you that women today, by choice or circumstances, are not idle. I spoke of thousands in the forepart of the paragraph, but there are millions upon millions, so your mother is hardly alone in her activities. So "can" the self-pity, greatly abused stuff, and be grateful and thankful for the many advantages you have over your fellows. By the way, I forgot to mention there were nearly 100,000 women working in Baltimore in 1920. Helen Orrick has worked for years—still works—

Now, as to my present wife, let me say—as you will some day realize—the laws of nature are such that every man needs the companionship and understanding of some woman who loves him—I now have all that with my present wife—She has worked harder and done more to help and comfort me with understanding, than anyone ever has, except my own mother, but then a mother's love is different.

I admire and respect your mother very much. But my son don't get a mother complex. Love her, respect and honor, but don't let the mother complex get you.

As to children. You brought that up too, so let's have it clear on the record. No matter how you may feel about me, my love tie is to you and Marshall first, although complying with your expressed desire—I may never see you again, but I want you both to know that if you are ever in any difficulty, no matter how slight or how great, you can always come to me and I will do everything in my power to help you out of your jam—Let me tell you that I will understand your problem, whether it is illness, wine, women or song—youthful indiscreations—financial difficulties or merely fanciful troubles or wrongs. I have been in or seen every kind of hell there is, and I know the ropes, from the hard school of old man experience. I will help you always with your problems, and I know how to steer you straight. I have no inhibitions, nothing to embarrass me—all of us have grave faults—no man is perfect. Come to me with your confessions and I will help you clear—that is what a father is for, to help you over the hurdles. And remember, come hell or high water, you and Marshall are always first with me, but you must come to me now. I shall never try to hold you, for you must select, choose and live your own lives fighting your way in the world and carving your own names on the rocks of posterity.

My present wife has two children—a boy and a girl—four and six—by a former husand. . . . My wife teaches her children to love and respect their father and yet she has had every provocation to do otherwise, much more so than anyone I know. It is the only decent moral way for people that are incompatible to do in this enlightened age—divorce. We are all very friendly, no matter what we think of one another—It is the only fair deal to the children. We all had Christmas dinner and a tree together last year, all the parents and the respective children, and I thought what a pity you and Marshall and your mother could not have been with us. But then I am not a large money maker, so that wasn't possible. I only regret the lack of wealth, because it keeps my boys from me, but thank God that the almighty gold dollar, filthy lucre, is not my god. I mustn't buy you toys, you say, with the few pennies that I gather. Why! why! I ask you? Is it a fear that my small gifts may hypnotize you? You say send clothes, but when I write to learn your measurements, no one takes the trouble to inform me, and I am not a mind reader, and I will never send cash to your mother until she permits greater freedom and access to you both.

I trust you had a pleasant birthday. I didn't send you a gift because I was too sick, and then if I had been well, there would have been your grateful admonition in the way.

Son, I have said a lot, much perhaps that you may not comprehend the full purport of, but let me tell you that as man matures he expands and discards the emotional scheckles of family childhood hokum tales and religious bonds and finds his peace in the consciousness of his mind and the evolution of his race.

I hope I have discussed all those little perplexities that have been troubling you.

Your devoted father

[Where in Durango my father unearthed his formidable array of statistics concerning the number of women employed in Baltimore, Maryland, in 1928, I can't imagine, but it was somehow characteristic of him. The business that my mother was engaged in and that he alludes to was a shop that produced hand-painted and decorated trays, wastebaskets, matchboxes, screens, et cetera. Although it was certainly true that we lived in relative luxury at my grandparents' ugly but spacious old house, attended by a retinue of servants, it was also true that mother constantly impressed on me and my brother that we— that is to say, she and my brother and I—were poor and dependent and we were in this state primarily because my father was improvident and irresponsible in failing to contribute to our support as the terms of the divorce had stipulated. My grandfather gave my mother a modest monthly allowance which apparently was not enough to pay for our schooling (and more particularly the constant tutoring that was required in order that I should keep up with my schoolmates). My mother thus started her business making gift-shop items to give herself some degree of financial independence and prior to the Depression employed as many as five people. Even during the Depression years she usually grossed in excess of $20,000 a year. She had excellent taste, great energy and considerable managerial skill.]

[From Mexico my father traveled in considerable style to New York, arriving there on the morning of Election Day, November, 1929.]

Mother and father met us at the pier—it was the first time they had seen the children. We went up to the Gotham Hotel, where we stayed while in New York on that particular trip.

The next day I went to see Doctor Whitman—he looked at the

pictures, heard the history of the case and then remarked, "If I had had you in New York, I would have operated and had you strapped up for four or five months, but it is obvious that you heal rapidly and adhesions would have set in and you would have never had the freedom of action or the spread that you now have by virtue of your drunken carryings on when you got up out of bed and walked on it, your travelling around, moving about, falling down, swimming with your wife and having intercourse." He then suggested that I should be in a cold clear climate while the balance of the healing was taking place. He made more pictures and offered to operate and take the broken bones out, but said it wasn't necessary as they had a perfect protective coating, so we left them as they were.

We stayed at the Gotham for about a month in order to be with father and mother.

In the summer of 1929, father collapsed on the sidewalk at 57th St. and 6th Ave. just outside of Acker-Merrill & Conduit, specialty grocers, where he had been making a purchase. Seeing the commotion outside the clerk investigated and discovered father—they all knew him, as he and mother were customers of the store. They phoned mother and she got hold of Dr. Sanford and father was brought right home—they were only living around the corner on 58th St. so they didn't have far to go. Father never completely recovered from that first attack. He lost a good deal of weight, was in bed for a long time and there wasn't much that could be done for him. (It was cancer of the stomach. . . .)

The early part of December we set off, bag and baggage, for Montreal—Dr. Whitman had recommended that I be in a cold dry climate and that I soak my hip every day in hot water. He said I could have the hip baked by lamps, if I wanted to, but he personally didn't think they did much good—more of a psychological help than anything else. He also wanted me to swim every day. . . .

[In Montreal my father took exercises to regain use of his leg, edited the 100,000 feet of film he had taken during the world tour, and started an amateur film society. The children were put to school in a convent of French-speaking nuns and Melba found a job singing and playing her guitar on a radio program sponsored by the Canadian Railway.]

What with the market crash and family adversities, our 1929 had been hectic—our first full year of legally married life.

The bursting of the Wall Street bubble had ruined many—it had hurt us, but the end of the year found us again on the up grade with the promise of better things to come—we had swung the pendulum of joy and anguish and were all together and happy. I had slipped from perfect health and financial security to broken health and empty pockets, but health and wealth were recovering. December 1929—and I was again indulging in sexual excesses.

1930 saw a continuation of our stay in Montreal until Spring, when I returned to New York, still on one crutch, to become advertising manager for *Nomad,* the International Magazine of Travel, which I eventually purchased. . . .

In the Spring—April to be exact . . . I took up my work on *Nomad.* Kenneth Murchison and an architect by the name of Hood, in combination with the National City Company and the Fuller Construction Company, had built a modern studio apartment house on East 44th Street, known as the Beaux Arts. It was designed primarily for artists, writers and sculptors. I went to see Murchison and arranged for an apartment—it was large and attractive—in exchange for an ad in *Nomad.* We put the children in the Conroy School at Ridgefield, Conn. . . .

We fitted out the apartment at the Beaux Arts with our blankets from Mexico, and head gear, and spears, and all manner of trinkets from all over the world. There we entertained the advertising executives in a semi-bohemian atmosphere. Lydia Goedecke dropped in often with the gang from J. Walter Thompson—Frank Bell, advertising manager of the N.Y.K., Harry Millar of Ampro, Malcolm Douglas of the American Express (he had an urge for Melba). We threw a lot of parties and had a lot of fun. I got Niel a large suite on an upper floor where he entertained his friends very lavishly. . . .

[On *Nomad*] there was a good deal of controversy about the art work in the magazine—and girl authors were always offering free ass to Niel, Tommy and myself along with their manuscripts. Sometimes we bought from those with the better tail rather than from those with the better tale. . . .

I inaugurated a world-wide contest for usable pictures on travel, offering $25 each month for the photograph accepted. Thousands and thousands of pictures were sent us—most of them terrible. A few we could use. Men sent in pictures of their girls' legs, leaving little to the imagination—girls sent in pictures of themselves in scanty tight fitting bathing suits or showing much leg and thigh. Many wrote letters and some even sent pictures of themselves in the nude—when they looked very good and sexy, and were in this area, we would have them come in to see us to discuss the matter—or go to see them. I picked up several good lays that way—hot numbers.

One girl was in Philadelphia—I ran her picture, but before doing so, I went to see her and spent the night. She certainly earned her prize money and the publication of the picture.

We had some luscious stenographers, girls Tommy and I had hired. They liked working on a magazine and they loved to screw—some preferred to suck.

Niel when he first started on the magazine, playfully put a condom in the desk draw of every steno in the place. This caused much excitement the next morning—one or two were indignant, but nobody left or sent for the police.

I put *Nomad* on sale in nearly every first class camera store the world round—hundreds and hundreds of them and they sold very well. People from every part of the world subscribed and submitted pictures. . . .

We got out car cards—for the subway, the street cars, the New York Central Railroad, N. Y. N. H. and Hartford, and the Long Islands Railroads, commuting trains—announcing the nudist articles and stories by Van Loon etc. Then when the November issue was published Walter Winchell simply said: "Go to your nearest newsstand and buy the November issue of *Nomad*." In 24 hours the stands from coast to coast were sold out. The magazine went to $5.00 a single copy and subscriptions poured in by the thousands—we naturally got out a reprint of 20,000, but it didn't last long and didn't begin to meet the demand.

The article and the continuance of the series gave the circulation of *Nomad* quite an impetus. It was real honest-to-God circulation—no hocus-pocus. . . .

1930 hadn't been as full as 1929, but it wasn't dull by any means. We were entertained a lot, we entertained a good deal at the Beaux Arts, and dined a good deal in speakeasies. At one time during our ownership of the paper, we made whoopee at the Beaux Arts and lived at the Gladstone Hotel and at Pierre's. We usually did that during Holidays, when the children were in town. We spent Christmas 1930 at the Gladstone and Easter 1931 at Pierre's. But we will come to that later—when we get into the disaster of 1931.

1930 had seen the rise of *Nomad*—1931 was to see its fall, Father's death, the blackmail case that missed fire, and poverty. The

236

chart was rushing downward fast in 1931—in fact so fast I thought I would never recover—but I must get on with my story. . . .

Father died on the 16th of February, 1931—he had been pretty sick for months. I didn't see too much of him, but a great deal more than your Aunt Elise did. In fact she was not with him at the end—only your grandmother Smith, Melba and myself. His last words were (it was mid-afternoon)—"How is the weather out?" I replied that there was a slight flurry of snow. Raising himself slightly he looked toward the window and then turning his head in my direction (I was standing at the foot of his bed) said: "You damn fool, that's not snow." Then he dozed off and never opened his eyes again—a few hours later he had crossed the bar. . . .

Father's death left a strange empty vacuum in my life—one I have never completely gotten over. We fought violently, but I was devoted to him—I really worshipped him—I was proud of his character and his looks. He was a rare man among men. While he was alive I always felt that in any jam he would be there behind me, as firm and strong as the Rock of Gibraltar—ready to brace me up.

Father was keenly interested in American politics and knew many of the important men in the political arena.

I often wondered how I would get on without him standing back there to prop me up—you will never know that loss because I (fortunately for you) have never been a "prop" father. When I married your mother that is what I had hoped for and planned for—that's why I married so young. I wanted my children to be nearer my own age than even I and my father and mother had been (but the best laid plans of mice and men, etc.)—well, anyway I missed him every hour of the day and night—it was as if part of me had died.

For years I dreamt of Father—I don't think it was until I married Eve that I stopped dreaming about him at night. He always had a foremost part in all my thoughts, conscious and subconscious, always the one I turned to, always standing there approving or disapproving—but always ready to help. . . .

Father, as his father before him, left everything to mother—all his interest in his own business, etc. This was fully expected by me—but a great disappointment to his employees who thought they would inherit it.

Mother, to keep herself occupied, went to father's office every day—her entire work consisted largely of addressing circulars, she had no idea of what was going on. She drew $100 per week for this

237

activity—she also had the cash that father left in their joint safe deposit box, plus the securities and outstanding notes receivable. He left no debts. . . .

Appreciating that nothing is certain save death, I have never been much interested in it. Burying Father in the Ward family plot at Trinity was mother's idea—altho there was plenty of room in the Smith plot at Beechwood, New Rochelle. The irony of it—Father and his "in-laws" never got on—he didn't care for them and they were not very fond of him. But there he is, surrounded in death by the Ward girls that he abhorred all his life. It makes little difference I suppose where our remains are laid. Father loved New York—particularly the banks of the Hudson as well as the River—and during the early days of the construction of the George Washington Bridge his favorite pasttime was to hire a car and drive up to see the progress of the work on the Bridge.

He rests in the shadow of the Hudson span on the banks of the river he adored surrounded by the elite of old New York and the Ward sisters—and "may his soul rest in peace—God bless him.". . .

A short time after we opened up on 42nd St. Melba received a visit from a very nervous foreigner—he implied he could tell her much about the Nude Clubs in the United States. Feeling that was a subject with which I was better able to cope she turned the gent over to me. As a matter of fact, a female name at the mast head of a magazine publishing stories on nudism attracted a lot of screwy fan mail for Melba—telling of all and sundry types of sexual perversion as practiced in these United States and in other parts of the world.

The man was a fellow named Herman Soshinski. He was a chauffeur—his wife a cook—they had read our articles. They thought we were sympathetic to their movement—they felt Bernard McFadden was just commercial in his exploitation of nudism, doing it for circulation purposes only. Well, that's what we were also up to but I didn't tell him. Herman was then secretary of a very active club which met weekly in a gymnasium at 96th St. & Broadway.

He didn't tell me this at first—he simply asked me if I would like to attend a meeting of the New York Nude Club. I do not know why I was so dumb as to think it was a business meeting where everyone would be dressed but I did. We arranged to meet at the 96th St. subway entrance on the East Side of the street. He was then to escort me to the club rooms. As usual I was late and I missed him. After waiting around awhile I went my way.

Soshinski came to see me again and we arranged to meet for dinner in a restaurant at 96th St. and Broadway—in the intervening week I received a good deal of mimeographed literature from him, explaining the rules for playing basketball and other games in the nude—also the regulations for water sports.

Again I was late for my engagement and missed the man. However, the literature had created the impression that their meetings might be held in a gymnasium so I went into the corner drugstore and looked in the red book for ads of gyms in the neighborhood that boasted a pool. I found one directly across the street on the northwest corner of 96th Street that filled the bill—it was under the movie house there—I went over; the entrance was down a flight of stairs into a basement. I rang the bell—it was like getting into a speakeasy—they peeked out thru a peep hole. I announced myself, said I had come to attend a meeting at Herman Soshinski's invitation.

They slid back the bars, opened the doors and let me in. Herman came forward and escorted me into the office where I was introduced to the President and the members of the Executive Committee. *They were having a business meeting*—but in the almost-nude, for they wore "little trunks" or "jock straps" covering up the vital organs or spots as it 'twere. In fact I had a fleeting glimpse into the main gym room as I passed and I noticed that the boys and girls all had some sort of covering—scant but sufficient to cover the interesting sex parts.

We talked about *Nomad*—about McFadden (deciding he was a rat and a lousy publisher)—about the movement—about the Berlin Club I belonged to (under an assumed name—but I didn't tell them that). Then a gong rang and they all dropped their trunks and "g" strings—then invited me to come into the gym and address the assembly—that was too much. I got a "hard on"—as usual I was wearing a double-breasted coat. It's against the rules to have a "stiff prick" at a nudist gathering.

I walked into the room and there to my wondrous eyes did appear a semi-circle of nude humans—stark naked—as were the committee members beside me. The men were on one side, the women on the other. Most of the women and girls were well built. The men looked as if they could never get "it" up again. I walked over and stood behind the piano as the President discussed the subjects of the evening and introduced me. I stood behind the piano because I thought it would hide my erection.

Father always told me when I boxed as a kid to watch the white of my opponent's eyes—never watch their hands. Remembering that sage advice in my moment of peril, I lifted my sights (not my cock) and looked only at the whites of eyes—I soon regained my composure and concentrated on what I would say.

When I was finally called upon I was sufficiently under control to talk about the magazine, my injury in Durango, etc. and thus save the fair name of our very ethical publication *Nomad*. It was trying but I got away with it amid much applause—afterward I met many of the boys and girls principally in the swimming pool.

My excuse for not participating in the games of leap frog, basketball, etc. in the gym was the fact that my hip injury wouldn't permit. So the committee returned with me to the office and continued their "talks"—this time they were entirely in the nude and it was a bit distracting to say the least.

At 9:30 another gong sounded and they announced that was for the pool sports. Franklin Roosevelt had made swimming for cripples popular and the water was supposed to be helpful. I had told them about my swimming experiences in Havana—so there was no out for me when they suggested I join the nudists in the pool.

I disrobed as quickly as possible and rushed for the cold shower —enroute I passed the open door of the women's dressing room— that was almost my undoing. They were in all varying degrees of undress and a woman partially dressed is more alluring and exciting to me than a woman entirely nude. Anyway I got by the door without having "it" fly up and knock me down—I turned the cold shower on full blast. If there is anything that I hate more than a cold shower, I don't know what it is—but drastic, yes heroic measures were the order if I wasn't going to give my inner turmoil away to my everlasting disgrace with nudists—this was sex control personified. After a final dose of cold water on the old "boy" himself, which left him bedraggled, in a shamefully shrivelled condition, I hobbled as fast as I could to the pool and jumped in. God what a sight!—particularly the women. Men and women immediately swam over to me—the men introducing their wives, daughters, sweethearts and mothers, women doing likewise with their daughters or girl friends—a veritable reception in the water. All the time their tits were bobbing up and down on top of the water—I was almost nuts trying to keep from getting a "hard" on. One girl especially tantalized me—she never stopped swimming on her back and always kicked out gracefully just as she glided past me, giving me a perfect view of that most heavenly shrine of all mankind, her cuzzy. Finally she got to be too much—she always had some friendly greeting as she slipped by. I tried swimming alone or with some of the men but always she would manage to be nearby. So when I felt the "son" was rising and could no longer be restrained I left the pool on the dead run and rushed back again for the cold, cold shower. I stayed under it until I shivered and shook—then I ran for the committee dressing room; again I had to pass the open door with the girls dressing—some with stockings on and nothing else, some with only their panties on, some with only their brassieres on— at that sight the effect of the cold water was rapidly disappearing, as the most wonderful sensation known to man crept up and down my spine, playing tricks with my mind. Only by the exertion of sheer will- power did I make the dressing room—"it" was hanging "large," but not up "stiff" as yet—I wasted no time drying and getting into my clothes. Hurriedly I said my goodbyes, asking them all to submit manuscripts. That was what they were eager to do—they wanted me to consider publishing a magazine devoted entirely to nudism.

There were several factions within the club, jealous and fighting each other. When I reached the street and the open air it was a great relief. But I was immediately seized with a violent headache—the or- deal had been too much for one who had always been noted for get- ting a "hard" on at the slightest provocation. Melba was waiting for me across the street in a restaurant. I hurried over—I needed hot food and a good screw. I told her of the evening's entertainment—or what a publisher goes thru for material or "circulation."

My headache didn't leave me until I got home and deposited my load well into little Melba—there was no holding back that night, my retailing of the story had stirred her sufficiently so that she came with me. Melba never took very long to get going—some women take much longer than others to get a real release.

I afterwards learned that the beautiful creature with the gorgeous body who was so busy swimming on her back married an officer of the Hamburg-American Line who met her in the pool—she gave him a swell case of the big (venereal) disease (syphilis). He died from it— you never know what lies lurking for you at the head of any cavern (especially female). . . .

1931-1932

On the morning of May 13th, 1931 with the May issue not yet on the stand, altho it had been due there the 25th of April, I informed the Nomad Publications that unless they came to terms by 3:00 PM that Travel Publications would file [bankruptcy] that afternoon. The stupid people thought that I was bluffing. Trying to high-pressure them into giving me better terms.

I was desperate—my publishing castle was crumbling about me. They didn't offer any relief, and that afternoon Travel Publications just before 4:00 o'clock "filed"—and that was the end of our thrilling experiment in the publishing world. *Nomad* had been going for five years—I had been with it for 13 months. . . .

At 5:00 o'clock the afternoon of the 13th we closed the doors, pasted a sign on the doors stating that the corporation was under the jurisdiction of the United States Federal Courts of the Southern District of New York and to apply to them. We never went back there again except to confer with the receivers agents once.

We took a complete file of the magazines during our reign with us—a few pencils, erasers, notebooks and rubber bands—the rest was left just as it was in action, but quite still—for *Nomad* was dead. . . .

We didn't have much cash left out of the wreck—but we were able to stay on at the Beaux Arts because they owed us a good deal for ads that had been already run. . . .

[Soon after the failure of *Nomad* Melba got a job as editor of *This Week on Long Island*.]

Melba's name went to the Mast-head with the second issue, Vol. I, No. II. [She put an ad in the *Times* for a stenographer.]

One girl who replied to her ad . . . with an excellent letter, but whose test did not compare with the work of some of the others, called Melba up a half dozen times pleading with her for another test. Melba finally weakened and told her to come around—she made an appointment for 3:00 PM of the afternoon of the 2nd of June, 1931.

I thought I would never forget that date—but I had to hunt it up to record it here. About a quarter to three, Mr. Garrett called Melba up to come over to the office forthwith—it was a new job so she felt she shouldn't offer excuses. She asked me to give the girl the test (in those days we would dictate from some *Nomad* copy, keep a record of the time it took the girl to take it down and then to transcribe the notes).

Our studio apartment was a large one-room affair on the ground floor—the windows were right on the street, a side door opened on a little setback garden upon which other apartments opened, but all on the street. There was also a rear door to the hotel proper—we had a kitchenette and a bathroom. The apartment adjoining ours was occupied by the bookkeeping department—their door opened right at right angles to ours—they could see into our apartment, we into theirs. An iron grille work covered the windows to protect us from forceful entry from the street—principally kids.

It was a sunshiny June day—our doors were open, our windows open—the bookkeeper had her windows and the door next to ours open. The painter was at the window painting the grillwork. There were doormen or carriagemen dressed as gendarmes on both sides of the street, in fact right outside our door and windows—also taxi drivers on the line awaiting fares.

The girl arrived a few minutes after three. Her real name was Hannah R., but she had given us an assumed name, which slips me at the moment. Her husband's name was Martin. I gave her a notebook and pencil, and dictated. Then when I finished I gave her the paper and set her down to the machine right by the window. The painter almost fell through the grill looking in at her trying to transcribe, which she wasn't doing very successfully. Finally it became so painful that I told her not to bother further, that I would show her work to Mrs. Smith. She hung around the door—said she wanted to talk to me about getting a book of hers published. I said I couldn't talk to her as I was in a hurry to join Mrs. Smith. (We had a tea date with some friends of my mother's at 4:00 on Riverside Drive & 86th St.—some friend who wanted to meet Melba.)

The R. woman then said she would wait and walk out with me. She continued to stand by the door.

The kids were beginning to hang around as they came from school to watch the painter and pass remarks. I was in my shirt sleeves but I slipped into my coat and putting on my hat and picking up my cane set forth. I was quite lame then and walked with a perceptible limp. The bookkeeper greeted me—the doormen, carriage men, painters, taxi drivers all hailed me as I passed. I am a friendly soul —even the cop at the crossing (2nd Ave. & 44th St.) who was there to help the school children across, called to me. R. continued to jabber away about "the best way to get a book published"—how should she go about it, would I give her letters to publishers, did I think she would get the job with Melba. I said I didn't think she would. Would I pay her for coming over from Brooklyn to take the test—she had lost the entire afternoon. I answered all in the negative. It was a slow process because I walked slowly in those days on account of my hip. When we reached Lexington Ave. & 44th Street, to be sure I would get rid of her I asked which way she was going. When she told me, I said I was going in the opposite direction. And that ended that—I took the shuttle and at 3:45 I met Melba at the Times Building. In fact I was there ahead of her.

We took the trolley up to meet Mother—visited with her friends and then we three went to dinner.

We returned home and went to work getting copy ready for Melba's next issue.

I had two phones—a private wire and the house phone. All my friends used the private number and came in the front way. The hotel was supposed to say were were out to anyone trying to reach us on the hotel phone—all the creditors of Travel Publications Inc. were after me.

It was 4:00 AM in the morning—we had been collaborating on a review of Konrad Bercovici's new book. The phone rang violently; for awhile we didn't answer—when it kept up I finally picked up the receiver. The night manager said there was a man in the lobby who wanted to see me—very important. I asked who it was—he pretended not to know. I suggested that he come around to the apartment, but he asked if I would come out, said the man wanted to talk to me there. I replied they would have to come to the door—I went to the door and there were two men. I asked them their business. They said they wanted to talk to me alone—didn't want to disturb my wife.

When I persisted in knowing who they were they showed their badges. Then I insisted that they come in—they were reluctant, said they wanted to discuss a matter I might not want brought up before my wife. I replied I had nothing to hide from my wife or anyone. Then they asked me if I knew a Hannah R. The name was a new one to me—I replied that I did not. They said she had been there that afternoon. I said not while I was there, that the only person there other than myself had been—and I gave the name I had for the lousy bitch. They announced that was the same girl.

Then in a whisper they wanted to know if I had had or had tried to have intercourse with her. If the building had suddenly been swept away to sea, leaving me standing naked atop Turtle Bay Hill, the shock could not have been greater. That question to me spelled ruin —it was a shock I never fully recovered from. From then on for weeks and months I lived a virtual hell.

I told the detectives frankly just what had occurred—just as I have related it here. They walked over to my Mexican holster and I think were disappointed that they were unable to find a revolver in it—they looked the entire place over pretty keenly. I phoned Bob Marsh and Christie Bohnsack (Secretary to the Police Commissioner at the time of Grover Whalen).

Detectives are sly fellows—after their preliminary conversations they announced—especially after I had called the police commissioner's secretary—that they wanted to be helpful, that they knew I was in a tough spot—it would be better if I told them the entire truth, that I could trust them, then they could help me, could tell me what to do. I could only answer that I had told them all there was to tell, that it was a frameup for a shakedown, and that the girl had asked me for money that afternoon and I had refused.

Judge Marsh talked to them—told them that if they arrested me without a warrant they would be liable to a charge for false arrest and possible imprisonment themselves. They had no complaint in writing, not even a warrant. They hinted that the matter might be all fixed up for a little dough to them and to the girl.

Christie Bohnsack told them not to take me down for lineup— not to photograph me and to keep me "out" until just before court.

I tried to get Joe Galletti for some money but he had closed for the night—I had only a few dollars in my pocket. I called Harry Greenberger, Vincent Astor's right-hand man—he said he would bring his brother, a small court lawyer to court for me. Bob Marsh agreed to be present and to represent me. He loaned character to my picture, but he was a Republican and not familiar with the rough-and-tumble Magistrates Court. All agreed the case should go over to enable us to get our witnesses.

While we were waiting around during the early hours of the morning, one of the "dicks" went over to Brooklyn and came back with word that the girl might withdraw her complaint for Five Hundred Cash. Judge Marsh felt that wouldn't do.

After going over to see Joe Galletti at the Italian Cellar Restaurant where they played Bulla (like bowling) we went uptown to a restaurant at 51st Street & Lexington Avenue where the "dicks" had something to eat on me. Then we strolled leisurely to the East 51st Street Station House where I was booked, finger-printed—you have to be finger-printed to get bail—then for more coffee, then up to the Magistrates Court on 57th Street between Lexington & Third, the Fourth District Borough of Manhattan.

The charge was attempted rape. The R. woman claimed I laid her on the couch, took my cock out, pulled her clothes up and asked her to screw me (all in plain view of the painter and the passersby on the street)—that I rubbed my cock against the outer edges of her cunt but did not enter or try to force my way in when she asked me not to (what a gentleman!)—then she said I took my cock and put it in her mouth (THAT IS SODOMY according to the statues of the State of New York)—that I came in her mouth, that she swallowed it, that I went into the bathroom, got a towel, wiped my cock off, followed her back into the bathroom when she went in to pee.

The case was put over and I was held under five thousand dollar bail—Judge Marsh and Greenberger's Brother were prepared for that.

Before my case was called for a period of half an hour while they were drawing up the complaint and getting the crazy cunt to sign it, they put me in a cell with all the bums and drunks. That was even worse than the shock of the charge, the arrest and the finger-printing, and the knowledge that the tabloids would have a front page field day—which they did—at my expense.

The premium for the bail was $500. I called Nathan Hugg and Eddie Hurd on the phone and asked them to get me $1,000 without delay, but not to tell Mother about it. Nevertheless they told her and got the money from her. Teneralli brought it to me (he was Miss Hugg's husband)—I turned it over to Judge Marsh.

Joe Gransky—proprietor of the Ball & Chain, a protege of Charlie Hilles, a secretary (probably steno) at the White House under Bill Taft—suggested that Freddie Pecora, famous Tammany District Attorney would be an excellent man to defend me in court. Freddie was then a member of the firm of Banton Sheridan, Hartman & Pecora or something like that.

Melba never left me for a minute all night except for the half hour I was in the "jug" with the scum from the middle East Side (New York).

While awaiting trial we left the Beaux Arts and went to live at the Picadilly. The torture of the publicity—the humiliation and the fear that I might not beat the rap, that I might have to do a stretch—were ghastly. It was a period of continuous day and night nightmares of the most hideous and terrifying type that could possibly be conjured up. . . .

[Ferdinand Pecora, a famous prosecuting district attorney, was hired to defend my father along with Judge Marsh.]

[A newspaper account of the episode appeared in the New York Daily News, *June 4, 1931, under the headline.]:*

MAD ATTACK BY RICH MAN, WORKING WIFE'S CHARGE

It isn't always so pleasant to work for a wealthy society man as the movies so often suggest. Mrs. Hannah Rentzer, an attractive blonde wife and mother, of 1259 56th St. Brooklyn, found that out Tuesday, when she answered an ad for a secretary, inserted by W. Ward Smith, 37, No. 310 East 44th St.

Smith, former executive secretary to Governor Nathan Miller was held in $5,000 bail in Yorkville Court, Wednesday, as the result of the story that Mrs. Rentzer told police.

"I answered the ad I saw in the paper by writing to the box number. Monday, while I was out, there was a phone call, but I got the message too late. That night I got another call from Mr. Smith and made an appointment to go to his apartment, where he lives with his wife, Mrs. Melba Smith.

"When I got to see him, I was impressed by his good looks and aristocratic manner, and thought that he would be a fine boss, if I could get the job. He dictated several articles to me from travel magazines," Mrs. Rentzer said, "and then told me to transcribe my notes.

"I sat at my desk and started. Suddenly I felt a hand on my shoulder. I looked up into the eyes of a wildman.

"You're going to work for me, aren't you, he muttered, tearing and ripping at my dress and arms," Mrs. Rentzer's voice broke.

"His wife was out. I was at his mercy, the beast! As soon as I could, I fought him off, and rushed into the street. As I neared Lexington Avenue (and you can imagine the condition I was in) Smith overtook me.

"I shuddered as he took my arm again. 'Please don't say anything about this', he pleaded, 'I will do everything I can for you, but promise to say nothing. We want to part friends.'

"I shook him off and staggered to the train. When I got home

I told my husband. We decided that for the sake of other girls who might fall into similar traps, we must make a complaint."

Former Supreme Court Justice Marsh represented Smith in Yorkville Court. Marsh said that the charges brought by Mrs. Rentzer were unsupported.

Smith is a member of a wealthy family. He has been a Member of the Republican County Council for years, deserting it in 1928 to support Governor Smith in the presidential campaign. For a time he acted as general manager of the American-Canadian Lumber & Pulp Co. here, was an associate director of the Savings Division of the United States Treasury, and chairman of the board of directors of the Valley Stream National Bank.

A private detective [was] put on the case by Judge Marsh to find out what he could about the family. Rentzer had a baby, a husband, and a father who worked intermittently. Her sister was in an insane asylum.

Rentzer had framed several small shop owners in Brooklyn. One of them put up a fight and the matter was in court and disposed of while my case was pending. Her racket was to go to some store where she had bought stockings or lingerie and try to return items she had bought and washed and worn. When the salesgirls objected she would then demand to see the owner or manager and blandy announce that unless they exchanged the raiment for new articles, she would run from the store screaming that she had been attacked and call a policeman. In some cases she had gotten away with it—the proprietors or managers giving her the new garments to avoid a scene that might adversely affect their business.

One little Jew wouldn't fall for her line or threats, so she had him arrested—he fought it and beat her.

She had a slimy Jew uncle who was a lawyer and advised her badly.

The painters, the taxi-cab drivers, the policeman on the beat, the doormen at the Beaux-Arts, and the bookkeepers, telephone operators, etc. were all in court to testify for me. When the hearing got under way the Judge told Melba that she could leave and it would not be held against me, that she wasn't by my side—but she elected to remain.

The detective first told of the arrest, and when asked by the D. A., a fellow by the name of Kantor, what I had said, he replied quoting me, "She asked me for money and I refused to give it to her." Then he went on to say that I had denied every bit of her filthy story.

Then the bum herself was put on the stand, with her Yiddish Papa and greasy husband nearby, her Jewish uncle to rave and rant about her chastity.

She burst into a violent tirade when they asked her about her sister in the nut house—at times dribbled like a half-wit herself.

When they got around to her underclothing—what did she have on underneath, did her drawers have a slit in them—she objected with vehemence to that question as being indecent but admitted they didn't have a slit. On direct testimony as led out by the D. A. she had virtually confirmed the contents of the complaint she had signed, written up for her by the cops.

The charge of attempted rape holds good even if you don't partially enter the cunt—rubbing the cock around the outside is all that is necessary to put you in the "jug," provided the dame says she said with violence "no."

They all say "no," even when they most want it. Bobbie R., a cunt from Savannah, Georgia, once said after she had said "no" right up to the last, "It's so wonderful to resist—and so marvelous when you insist."

When they brought up the Brooklyn case, Rentzer tried to squirm out of that—but when faced with the record she nearly collapsed.

Judge Gotlieb, getting tired of Pecora's indifferent cross examination took a hand with the questioning himself. He asked her to open her mouth, to show her teeth, to turn her head, then he wanted to know if what she said was true—if I had put my cock in her mouth and she had sucked and she had not wanted to—why hadn't she turned her head to avoid my penis or closed her mouth tight or bitten my cock when it was in her mouth. She said she was too cowed to resist with the turn of her head or the closing of her teeth and mouth.

They then asked her if she had noticed the painters at the window—she said she had—she had also taken notice of the bookkeeper and admitted that the doors and windows were open, but claimed I had pulled a screen around to the foot of the couch. She admitted the cop was on the corner, that we passed Railway Express guards and other policemen as well as the doormen, that Lexington Avenue was crowded, that she had walked from Second to Lexington with me as

249

I limped along, that her clothes were not disarranged or torn or her hair mussed and that she had made no outcry and had at no time called for help, that she had done some shopping afterwards, had gone home in the subway and made no effort to make a report to the police.

She calmly admitted that it was not until after dinner with the family gathered about that she had discussed the matter with her husband, father and her (lawyer) uncle and that her uncle had advised her to go to the station house (he went with her) and have me arrested. Even then apparently the uncle and the father and husband hadn't been quite sure that was the way. . . .

When the State rested, Judge Marsh made a motion to dismiss and the Court asked for briefs on the subject of corroborating evidence in cases of attempted rape and Sodomy. . . .

[The judge granted a motion to dismiss on June 20, 1931.]

The year 1931 had started out on thin ice and it had ended very close to the poor house—it was tough going.

Nomad had failed, father had died, the rape case had laid me low—what money I could get leaped away from me. . . .

It was my tough year—the end of my 37th and the beginning of my 38th. . . .

We took an apartment at $50 per month at 42 West 52nd Street south side—two rooms, one small one for the children—they slept together—and a large room which served as a livingroom and bedroom for us, a good bathroom, a tiny kitchen—but it had a Parapet for the children to play on.

We organized a group of our friends who were short of cash —we called it The Parapet Club. Each one chipped in a dollar and we bought an awning to cover the Parapet—very colorful—linoleum for the roof floor to resemble brick, flower boxes, a lattice screen to shut out the neighbors and grow vines on. We charged 60¢ for meals prepared by Melba—the girls helped her cook, the men helped me wash the dishes—liquor bootleg was extra. Walter Piel brought real beer from his brewery in payment for his meals—he was that short of cash. Harry Millar kept us supplied with a motion picture projector and we showed pictures of our travels and filthy pictures as well. I got out a typewritten sheet nearly every day called *The Parapet News* with dope about what the neighbors were doing as well as our friends and what we thought of them as well as of the nation and state of the world. We always had at least half a dozen every evening—it was hard work, but it meant meat for the children. 52nd Street was a busy street even then with the best speakeasys in town on it and a number of good eating places. We had a lot of fun —we put on a campaign against the telephone company for its high rates and charges and generally enjoyed ourselves. On Sunday, Mother would drop in and take the children for a walk in the park and during the week, Kaye Lyons would take them out too. The toughest part of the deal was keeping the place clean, scrubbing down the roof on the Parapet—I would get up early every morning with broom and mop and give the place a thorough going over while the sun was on the rise. That helped to dry it off quickly. We grew sweetpeas and sunflowers in the flower boxes and other things in season so that there were always flowers blooming. The children adored morning glories. After dark we hung out Jap lanterns (made of tissue—colored— lighted by candles). The tables were lit by candlelight.

We had drop curtains in the event of rain arranged so that we could enclose the entire porch. . . .

The best way to tell the story of Parapet View is first to set forth "The Whys and Wherefores."

Parapet View was first, last and all the time our home, Melba's and mine and the childrens and we never failed to make that clear to all.

It was also the home of our friends, as my home has always been and will always be, whether it is a palace or a broken down porch—or without porch at all.

The Parapet Forum was developed spontaneously and voluntarily by a little group of understanding friends who in those times, that tried men's souls and women's chastity, realizing that Melba and I were not in a position to carry all the expense of entertaining our friends alone, felt that they could do no less than to pay for the actual cost of their food, iced tea, and incidentals.

We did not run Parapet as a public restaurant—it was a convivial gathering place for our friends and acquaintances who came as paying guests. . . .

A la the Provincial Forties, we gave our guests for 60¢ per head—

Tomato Juice or Fruit Cocktail   or   Soup, hot or cold

*　*　*

Lamb or Pork Chops with Peas and Potatoes or Hamburger Steak Sandwich

		or
Chopped Beef and Fried Potatoes	or	Cold Ham and Potato Salad
	or	
Spanish Rice and Salad	or	Spaghetti and Salami
	or	
Cold Cuts and Potato Salad	or	Eggs, any style
	or	
Waffles and Bacon	or	Griddle Cakes

* * *

Jello or Peaches, or pears or shortcake, or any fruit in season or layer cake, or prunes, or applesauce, or puddings when we had them.

* * *

Tea or coffee—hot or cold.

We charged the guests who brought their own gin—for the mixing ginger ale, etc. 50¢ per mix.

The dues were $1.00 payable in advance.

By that plan we were able to maintain open house all that summer. . . .

We were glad to carry any of our friends on the cuff for a week, but we tried to get settlement on Fridays in order to pay the butcher, the baker and the candlestick maker—Melba put all her enthusiasm, energy and strength into the game and we felt that we should get the money in, so the housekeeping bills could be paid weekly.

We had a lot of trouble getting the guests to put their ashes in the ashtrays and not on the plates.

We charged a 50¢ deposit on any of our ordinary books that were borrowed and a rental of 10¢ a week.

On a special—or obscene book—a deposit of $5.00 was required and a rental charge of 50¢ a night or a dollar a week was made.

We did not serve dinners unless we were notified in advance not later than noon of the day of the reservation.

No cancellations after 12 noon were accepted.

Two helpings were allowed to all 75¢ meals and one helping to the 50¢ and 60¢ meals—additional helpings after the regular allowance one-half the cost of the meal extra.

Van Loon's philosophical leaflets were on sale at 25¢ a copy.

The big excitements of that summer were the B. E. F. [Bonus Expeditionary Force] in Washington, being driven or burned out by MacArthur and Hoover, and the Presidential election.

We felt it was a great political blunder to call out the troops to disperse the recalcitrant members of the B. E. F.

It never helps to call the police to oust an obstreperous or unwelcome guest—it leads to disastrous results.

We agreed that soup is better than tear bombs and that bread is cheaper than bullets.

We were opposed to bonus raids, but we believe it the right of every citizen to petition Congress and in the obligation of the state or nation to care for the needy in their hours of distress.

If the Reconstruction Finance Corporation could dole out eighty million dollars to save Charlie Dawes from the abject poverty, why wasn't it possible for the Hoover administration to barrack the unemployed that came to Washington, whether they were war veterans or not, and ration them on McFadden meals or prison fare.

All that were physically able to labor could have been employed in improving the waste areas in and about Washington at a nominal fee, namely, sufficient to cover the bare cost of the food and a cover for their heads and medical attention.

If a centralized national employment exchange had been set up, as Mr. Hoover advocated before becoming President, it would have been possible to shift those men to places where there would have been work for them.

As it was they were thrown out of Washington and thrust upon other communities. . . .

It did seem as if it were more or less appropriate when cities like Toledo and States like Ohio ran out of funds and ways and means to care for their unemployed, that those men and women should trek their way to the seat of government.

Undoubtedly there are grave abuses in our bonus and pension systems, but some provision should have been made for the poor as well as the rich in those troublesome times.

We wondered then if Jesus of Nazareth would have answered the starving pleas for bread with machine gun bullets, tear gas bombs, drawn sabres and tanks.

It certainly was a great blotch on the fair name of these United States that martial law had to be declared at the seat of our government, particularly when the chief of the district police had the entire situation so well in hand. . . .

The parties were very gay—many times that summer strangers tried to get into Parapet, thought it was a speak or public restaurant. It looked bright and gay from the street.

Bad as Herbert Hoover was, he didn't try to pry into your private life—and we were unmolested by local, federal or state authorities. In fact we were left alone except for gay couples on pleasure bent—there were no questionnaires to fill out, there wasn't any rationing, and we weren't worried about income tax returns. We were poor, but still free men and women. The Jews hadn't taken over to wreck our way of life—women were safe on the sidewalks of New York any hour of the day or night if they went about their business and didn't flirt with pickups. The negroes knew their places and kept them—Eleanor and the New York Jews had not turned the darkies' heads. A man could screw as and when he wanted to without permission of a bureaucrat in Washington.

We were only trying to feed ourselves—we were not bothering too much with feeding or running the rest of the world and they weren't trying to force their political or economic standards on us.

Morris V. always said he didn't have the longest but he had the prettiest tool in the world—he was everlastingly screwing [his wife] Lyle after dinner on our couch for the guests to see or participate in (he only thus indulged when drunk). He invited John M. to watch one time—it was too much for John, he wet his pants.

On one occasion when we all had been drinking and looking at filthy movies, I screwed Lyle in front of Morris on the bed. She sucked my prick first and Melba sucked Morris'—then we both fucked hell out of each others wives—it was hot, as those doubles always are, and the guests enjoyed the picture. Lyle was a "hot" natural—she would rather fuck and suck than eat. She and Melba would have quite a time of it when they would get together. Morris' tool was not long and neither was it thick, but it tickled the girls—he was insane about having it sucked off. I can think of no better method of giving a lucid picture of Parapet than to quote from some of the copies of *The Parapet News* as they appeared at that time. These choice morsels that were pounded out by the old maestro on those hot summer days of 1932, when freedom still rang throughout the land—show you what we were thinking and doing then.

It would be false to say that Lyle didn't get you sexually, no matter how many other women were around—I was always hot about her, but she was a double-crosser with men—and as swell a bitch as ever double-crossed a horney bastard.

During the summer, Lyle decided to take up professional dancing so she could be on her own. . . .

Lyle wanted to buy a dancing costume so I went along—I don't know why except that Melba was taking the children to the Park and thought that I would be of help to Lyle in deciding on her costume, which consisted of black velvet (shorts), trunks and a white silk waist. She made the purchases at Nat Lewis' original place on Broadway between 47th and 48th St. (east side of street). The fitting rooms were in the basement—they didn't have doors, just curtains.

I have always had a weakness for buying women's clothes and watching them dress and undress. Well—that performance made me plenty "hot" as she tried on the different outfits—in fact, the memory of it as I write stirs my blood and makes the old pecker stand up and look me right in the eye.

When Lyle was about to take off the outfit she decided on, she sent the salesman away for a bow. Unable to withstand the pressure, I laid her on the floor of the dressingroom, tiny as it was—she was tiny too, and the mirror on the three sides helped. Fortunately we were through before the salesman returned—screwing women in dressing rooms or bathrooms has always been a passion of mine—maybe that's my perversion.

When Lyle lays you she lays you—that was all there was to it. You never forgot her—there was something very insidious about that child. . . .

Stanley H. was staying at the famous 42nd Street Whore house that summer, the St. Margaret Hotel, fucking his head off. Lyle fell for his prick and the poetry of his soul—Stanley would read his manuscripts to her by the yard, work her up with his poems and a touch of liquor and then take her over to the St. Margaret for an incision of his long episcopal tool. . . .

We opened the Parapet on the 4th of June—we closed it on the 9th of October. Our last week was our biggest—we took in $79.40. Our poorest was our first—$10.25—no sales taxes then. After the third week we kept above $20.00 weekly. The last nine weeks we averaged around $30.00 per week.

The last night was Melba's birthday. The children dressed up for the occasion in paper caps, etc. Diane in her best "bib and tucker" came out on the porch carrying the cake with its candles lighted and singing "Happy Birthday"—a gust of wind caused the candles to ignite her costume. It would have been a horrible mess had not Walter Piel grabbed the cake from the child and John McNeil grabbed her in his arms thereby smothering and extinguishing the flames in a flash.

Melba and Diane and all were pretty well shaken—but the party went on—we had a wonderful evening.

Near the end of the season (the taxi drivers had always been friendly) we noticed a taxi driver waving to us from across the street. He beckoned us to come down—at the door he said the Federal men were in the street to raid the speakeasies. They were on the roofs, and he had seen some of them in the empty apartment in the house next to ours. He said he didn't know whether I had any liquor or not, but he thought he had better warn me.

Under the children's bed we had champagne, real beer, gin, and bootleg rye. I thought I better act fast (to prevent any nonsense in our place) so I called police headquarters (they answered the phone quicker then—LaGuardia wasn't Mayor) and reported thieves on the roofs and in the apartment next to ours. They sent out a riot call, closed 52nd Street at both ends—trained searchlights on the buildings and turned dozens of cops and plainclothesmen loose in the street, through the buildings and on the roofs. To the chagrin of all the cops, they only uncovered undercover prohibition agents—but we saved ourselves and the other speakeasies on the block. . . .

One night when Harry and Frenchie were at Parapet, Walter P. was also around. The discussion turned, rather extraordinarily to sexual intercourse. Melba got on the subject of married virgins and Frenchie agreed with her premise—Walter came up for air. When Frenchie complained that so few American men understood the fine art of preliminary stimulation, how necessary it was for the female and how "cunt-lapping" helped, Walter was horrified. Frenchie reiterated that unless a man kissed a woman's cunt and caressed the lips of her "pussy," as well as the lips of her mouth, he couldn't expect the female to experience real joy.

The more versatile the tongue the greater the joy. We trapped Walter on the discussion by asking him if a cunt tasted salty—he fumbled that one (I hope you know it does—if it is ripe).

Walter said he had never "gone down" on a woman and wouldn't —little Wally contended that a woman's cunt was filthy and that it was revolting to him even to think about it. I commented that for years I had been under the impression that he was a finished swordsman—and that he had his "Union Card" for sexual intercourse, and I asked with surprise, "Why Walter, haven't you even caressed a female asshole with your tongue?"

We accused him of being selfish, thinking only of himself and not of his girl's pleasure—we told him that he could never hold a

Some Women
in Ward Smith's Life

woman that way, that they would try him once and then let him go if they could get anything better.

When he reiterated that cuzzies were filthy, I asked him if his mother's had been dirty, too (the one he had come out of)—that got him.

We all agreed that the female slit was the holy of holies, sacred to most men—and to be loved, admired, caressed and worshiped.

Walter thought it was all right to have a girl "suck him off" and to come in a girl's mouth—but he didn't want to go down on the girls.

He and a friend, while in their cups, had taken two girls to Sophia's for a night—they started playing around and the dames agreed to go down on the boys and suck them off if the boys in turn would go down on them.

The deal was made and they took their girls into the bedrooms. After Walter's girl had sucked him off, Walter refused to go down on her thereby breaking the bargain—that infuriated Walter's girl so that in her drunken rage, she raised merry hell, throwing the furniture around and smashing the bric-a-brac.

It took all Walter and his boy friend could do to hold her down and get her out—she didn't want money, she wanted to be sucked off. When it looked as if the police would have to be called, the other fellow, to quiet the jane, went down on her—which made Walter very sick.

After that we all started riding Wally—telling everyone that he had not won his "Union Card" as a fornicater. This upset him a great deal.

During that period they often had parties—beefsteak parties at the P. Brewery. We went to one such—the entire P. family and their close friends were there—there was much beer drinking and the steaks were "rare"—it was a great feast with much singing.

It was at one such party that Walter met a girl he especially liked. He invited her to take a trip to Bermuda with him—she agreed, then a few days before the trip she spent the night with him at Sophia's and the next day called the trip off. He decided then and there that he hadn't been able to satisfy her because he hadn't gone down on her. Personally I thought it was a combination of an inadequate prick and tongue—he didn't love her properly to begin with, did nothing to stir her—even animals sniff around their girl friends with their snoots—and then when she wanted more rope, he didn't have any to give. . . .

In October 1932 we rented an apartment at 2 Horatio Street. It was new and very attractive—high up—overlooked the entire City —a big fireplace graced one side of a dropped living room. Modern bath, kitchen etc. completed the picture. . . .

Our credit situation was so tough that we rented the Horatio place under my pen name of "Dudley Brooks."

Chelsea moved us and we left 42 West 52nd in a battle over abuses we felt we suffered from the landlord—and owing a month's rent. We sold the awning to the woman next door and that was the end of Parapet View.

We fixed the Horatio place up attractively with our Mexican things, but much to our dismay discovered that the couch which we slept on had bed bugs—it was a box spring on legs and difficult to clean.

During this period I had a mail address with a Miss Holzer at 11 East 42nd Street—telephone messages etc.—cost $1.50 per month.

One morning shortly after our arrival at Horatio Street I went out to phone the office (our phone had not been installed yet). I only had a nickel with me (you could get a loaf of bread at that time for a nickel)—if I was to phone and get the loaf of bread without sacrificing one for the other, I would have to beat the phone company. I felt that they could stand it so I dropped my lonely only coin in the slot, called the operator and explained I had received the wrong number—she returned my coin, I got my number and my loaf of bread.

Miss Holzer informed me that she had a red star telegram for me. She was excited—said that that meant it was very important, like a death or accident or something special. I had her open it and it was a wire from Charles M. in Dallas stating that Melba's mother was dead. She had been run down while crossing Hollywood Blvd. en route home from the movies alone. The driver of the car had been window shopping and had not seen her at the crossing where she had the right of way—for the green light was with her.

Charles' brother had seen a small notice of the accident in the newspaper and had wired Charles and me and Judge Marsh.

I returned immediately to Melba who was still in bed trying to sleep in the day time when bed bugs don't come out and bite—if you keep a bright light on at night it has a tendency to distract them. I gave her the glad sad tidings.

Melba was greatly excited. I went to Paul Alaimo's stationery store at 11th and Greenwich and phoned from there on the cuff to mother and Bob Marsh. We went down to see Marsh and to map a campaign. Melba knew that her mother kept large sums of cash around the house hidden all over the place, and she was afraid her Aunt Dora would swoop down and grab all. It was decided that Melba would have to get a California lawyer right away to protect her interests. I called George Barr Baker for suggestions and he recommended Joseph Scott (Scott had put Hoover in nomination at Chicago in 1932) who was an outstanding lawyer and the leading lay Catholic of the West. Melba remembered that she had gone to school with a daughter of Scott's so we went to "Honey's," mother's, and Melba called Scott on the phone. I did the preliminary talking and then she chatted with him. He agreed to take the case, learn the details about the accident, get in touch with Edwards, Mrs. M.'s lawyer, and see to it that nothing was touched.

As Melba was talking to Scott, Dora was racing down to San Francisco with her daughter Alfreda, having sent Melba a delayed wire in care of Judge Marsh as she departed. She got into the apartment ahead of Scott, but he made her put up elsewhere. We wired everyone we would leave for the coast at once.

In order to give Marsh and Scott time to prepare their side of the picture we decided to fly instead of going by train. Scott made all funeral arrangements etc.—in fact attended to everything—undertaker, services and cremation.

Melba had to get mourning clothes—anyway her wardrobe was badly depleted—I needed a presentable suit. Mother advanced us a thousand dollars.

We engaged air transportation to the coast—in those days they were flying part air and then going by part rail—you flew during the day (clear weather) and rode on the train at night (or bad weather).

Melba's mother died on the 29th of October. We set forth from Newark for Glendale the night of the 5th of November. It was the first scheduled flight—all air 28 hour service—from coast to coast.

Walter Winchell's daughter broke a bottle of champagne over the nose of the ship. Slim Lindbergh was there. It was quite an occasion. Mother and her sister, my aunt Lucy, rode out in a hired limousine to see us off—the news photographers and reporters were all present. We had not been aware that it was to be an inaugural trip.

Scott, Judge Marsh and mother knew how we were going out but no one else did. They all thought we were coming out by train. We had excess baggage and had to pay extra for that ($45.00).

Camden was our first stop—we arrived there to the blare of a band and the greeting of the Mayor and the inevitable press. After the ceremonies we were told to disembark, that the ceiling over the Alleghenies was too low and we would be taken to Pittsburgh by train. Cabs were waiting and we were bundled off to the Broad Street Station of the P.R.R. They gave us a drawing room and we slept quietly into Pittsburgh.

When we reached Port Columbus, Ohio (after having travelled all but 90 miles of the coast-to-coast-all-air-route so far by train) we were advised that we would be laid over in Kansas City all night. That meant that we would be not the fourteen hours we were then behind at Port Columbus, but 24 hours late coming into Los Angeles.

[The passengers protested and TWA flew them to Glendale, California, by substituting air mail pilots and division superintendents for the commercial passenger pilots.]

What a trip that was, especially from Albuquerque into Glendale—bump, bump, bump over air pockets as we crossed the desert and hedgehopping—there was hardly a second when the plane wasn't bouncing and banging all over the air. I thought my guts would come right up through my mouth—I hadn't been so sick since the *Siberia Maru*.

The so-called meals aboard were a snare and a delusion—the picnic boxes served in flight were appetizing but hardly would constitute a meal. We had none served us on the ground—we had to buy those ourselves and it would have helped to have met up with just a hamburger cart or a hot dog stand or a soft drink cooler or a newspaper or candy stand at any of the airline stations. . . .

The fiasco of that first trip had but one redeeming feature—it avoided publicity on our arrival in Los Angeles. If we had flown straight through our arrival would have been spread all over the papers as the first "coast-to-coast-all-air" passengers.

We went straight to the Hotel Biltmore as soon as we arrived—we were so shaken from the trip that we had to go to bed for several hours after bathing, in order to settle our stomachs, rest and hear normally.

Then we met Scott [the lawyer]. After that we met Dora and her daughter and the other members of the family, then we went out to Mrs. M.'s apartment. Before Scott had gotten there, someone had looted the place of all the cash and some of the clothes.

Mrs. M. was cremated and her ashes put in the urn with her father and her husband. At the services in the Memorial Chapel in Hollywood's great showplace, Joe Scott sat with Melba and myself in the first pew—Dora, in the next pew, the culprit, the scavenger,

260

the abused one, the boot licker, became hysterical—and her only interest in "Teetie" had been to get what she could out of her. . . .

Mrs. M. had left a will leaving all the property in the original trust set up for the children which she had attacked and broken—in trust, by will, for them just as she had had it in the trust that she spent so much money breaking. Such are the ways of women—emotional not logical.

The lawyer disclosed that it would be necessary to get Charles M., the father of Diane and Melsing, out of the picture in order to expedite the settlement of the affairs. He wanted Melba appointed sole guardian of the children.

Scott felt that that should be done at once. We discovered that it would take longer to go by train than to motor to Dallas, so we bought a second-hand Packard phaeton for $1,000. . . .

We set forth for Dallas driving night and day. We took Mrs. M.'s chauffeur with us. He rode on the back seat during the day and at night up front with me—while Melba dozed in the rear. The nigger worked the radio—going through mountain passes you keep losing your station unless you change your dialing or volume. That may not be true today but it was then. The radio tended to keep me awake.

We made that trip in forty hours.

We register at the Adolphus. The papers had arrived by Air Mail for Charles to execute.

We had a nice time with the children and Charles signed all the papers consenting to Melba being guardian in California. And the papers Mark sent on making her guardian for them in the State of New York. We had sent Bob certificates of death etc.

In Dallas I bought the chauffeur Lee a heavy coat for motoring in the North.

Our job completed in Dallas we started back to Los Angeles—driving leisurely taking it easy now that we had Charles signed up and the guardianship matter safely tucked behind us.

Melba bought the children new clothes and gave Charles spending money for them. . . .

[On the way back from Dallas, Lee, the black chauffeur, complained that my father had done all the driving. In response, my father turned the driving over to Lee. Lee went to sleep at the wheel, the car turned over and my father's shoulder and collar bone were crushed. No one else was hurt but he spent several weeks in the hospital at Globe, Arizona. The following article appeared in the Globe newspaper.]

261

VISITOR HERE ENJOYS WESTERN HOSPITALITY ON FORCED STAY.

"Though I had visited most countries of the world, seeing all kinds and conditions of people, I have never been treated with more consideration, thoughtfulness for my comfort and with the true hospitality than I have right here in Globe during the past 10 days."

That was the statement made last evening by W. Ward Smith, wealthy publisher of New York City as he lay in his room of the Dominion Hotel swathed in bandages as a result of an automobile accident south east of Globe November 25th when he suffered a broken right arm, a broken shoulder and various other injuries.

CAR OVERTURNS.

Mr. Smith accompanied by Mrs. Smith and their chauffeur was enroute to Los Angeles when the accident occurred. The chauffeur was driving. The car, a big Packard, turned over one and a half times. Mrs. Smith suffered bruises to her head and body. The chauffeur escaped with but minor hurts. . . .

"My friends brought me bass from San Carlos Lake, turkey, chicken, duck and other fancy foods which I enjoyed to the utmost. I shall long retain a memory of my enforced visit in Globe. Usually we drive right through these mountain towns and never know just what they are like. It has certainly been a revelation to me and Mrs. Smith."

During the past couple of days Mr. Smith had been in a wheel chair and was noticed by many residents of Globe while being pushed up and down Broad Street. He talked to New York by telephone from one to seven times a day to keep in close touch with his business affairs there. He kept the telegraph wires hot between here and the eastern metropolis.

Mr. and Mrs. Smith had left New York on November 5th in the inaugural of the 28-hour schedule of the Trans-continental Western Airways, arriving in Los Angeles Nov. 6th. After a week there they motored to Dallas, Texas to visit with their children and were on the reutrn trip to the coast from where they had intended taking a boat through the canal to New York when the accident happened.

LEAVE FOR NEW YORK

They left this morning over the Southern Pacific for New York.

Mr. Smith was executive secretary to Nathan Miller, governor of New York, in 1921 and 1922. He came west in that year to organize Hoover-for-president clubs, being a great admirer of the president at that time.

While in California in 1928 he met and married Mrs. Smith.

Besides publishing a high class travel Magazine, "Nomad" Mr.

Smith engages in banking and lumber business in New York City. While he was here James A. McNary, head of the Cady Lumber Co. of McNary was a visitor.

In a radio broadcast from New York shortly after Mr. Smith was hurt, Hendrick Willem Van Loon, noted author, and Heywood Broun famed columnist gave Globe some advertising by mentioning that their friend Mr. Smith was a temporary resident of the City.

The chauffeur was sent to Los Angeles to buy a new car and take personal affects of the couple on to their home in New York.

While still in Globe, I wired the Gotham and the St. Regis for rates and then made a reservation in both hotels from Chicago. There was little to choose between the room rates—the St. Regis had the advantage for me, of having the barber there (Frank Fisher) who had cut my hair and shaved me on and off since my days of Berkeley School. Fisher was the manager, in fact, he owned the barber shop at the St. Regis, and the accommodations there were nicer as were the manicurists.

The New York Central people were as thoughtful and considerate of my comfort as the Southern Pacific people were, and I went thru the performances of being looked after by station masters, division superintendents and pullman representatives from Chicago to New York.

We sent Charles M. the money to bring himself and his fourth wife to New York for Christmas.

In order to cut down expenses we took a large suite at the Gotham with a big, high-ceiling living room, a room to be fixed up as an office for me, and a double bedroom, also a room for the children, a room for their Governess and a room at our expense for Charles and his wife all on the same floor, connecting with our suite.

We had bought the Christmas tree and were at the Gotham arranging to have it set up—all the furniture removed from the living room—when the management of the St. Regis got hold of me and breathlessly offered me the same accommodations in their hotel, at the same rate that the Gotham was charging me, which was as I recall it $150.00 a week.

I paid the Gotham for one day's occupancy—they had gone to a great deal of trouble to fix up the suite for us—and remained at the St. Regis.

The tree that was set up in our St. Regis living room was a large one that reached from the floor to the ceiling. My breaks were still tender and I was not able to personally set up the Christmas display for the children.

The Lionel people sent two men up to the St. Regis after I had had the tree brought back from the Gotham.

It took the two Lionel men nearly all afternoon and evening to get the tracks laid and trains working after the tree had been set up—they had a great deal of difficulty with short circuits. There was an outer track of standard gauge (large size) that circumvented the extreme outside borders of the room—went through tunnels and across bridges, criss-crossed with crossovers, in the center of the room and then came back to have two inner circles, all of which was connected up with a roundhouse and additional side tracks.

There were three standard passenger trains and one long freight train; signal towers flashed the all-clear and danger signals as the trains raced by switching from one track to the other and passing one another in their headlong electrical rush.

There were signal lights and crossing gates and signal bells that indicated the approach of the various trains. One train of cars could not enter a block until the other train had cleared it.

From a central switchhouse, it was possible to throw the switches by remote control—the switches were marked by conventional red and green lights (in miniature). In addition to the roundhouse and freight stations, there was a passenger station with miniature passengers, porters and baggagemen—around the base of the tree was still another setup, that was a narrow gauge track—and a small passenger train just circled around the tree in and out of tunnels constantly. Melsing also had a sleigh and some other toys such as soldiers, a fort, etc.

For Diane we bought a large doll's house completely outfitted from cellar to garret with miniature furniture and dolls. She also was given a complete set of *The Children's Encyclopedia,* a small writing desk, and a complete and workable electric stove and oven. For her dolls, she had a three-tiered baby basket with all the little accessories that one would have for a real baby, only they were for her dolls.

A Santa Claus was placed near the tree and the management of the hotel hung a very beautiful silver-tinseled drape on the wall as a backdrop which set the tree off in stunning fashion.

Melsing was thrilled with his Christmas—Diane seemed disappointed and morose. She sulked and was quite unpleasant—she has never been able to explain her Christmas attitude as a child. She always appeared disappointed with her Christmas (altho she now says she wasn't) no matter how much she was given. She contended that it was a mixture of shyness and jealousy of Melsing and his Christmas gifts, altho we always struggled to make sure that she received more than he got, because she was older.

Due to Diane's manner on this annual festive occasion, Melba usually flew into a rage at what she considered Diane's ingratitude and then there would be tears and the little girl would go to her room in great distress. I don't suppose that she ever really had a spontaneously happy Christmas the whole time I knew them—her reactions were always the same, whether we were in a railroad flat in Montreal, a tenant in New York, a house on the grounds of the Santa Barbara Biltmore, or a lavish suite at the St. Regis. . . .

Hendrik van Loon sketched an Xmas card for us that year to send out in addition to the books we distributed. It was about seven by ten and showed what purported to be catastrophic world with the deluge about to encompass all, to which we added in Melba's scrawl "The world is a bit shaky, but nevertheless, Merry Christmas, Ward & Melba." . . .

1933

The ushering in of 1933 was more auspicious than the ushering in of 1932—it promised much but hardly held its own—1932 had actually been a year which had started with rags and ended in for us, riches.

1933 was to see the closing of the banks, the beginning of the reign of Franklin the First, a hilarious visit to the Mardi Gras at New Orleans, Palm Beach in season at the Breakers for the first time, the World's Fair in Chicago, Jarmila M.'s visit to the United States, an affair with her and Claire T., a trip through the Canadian Rockies, a visit to Victoria, a trip to Europe with the children, and the purchase of Melvale, a tax fight in the State of California and a Federal Suit with United States Government Department of Internal Revenue over the Melsing estate, as life went marching on—and not the least,

September 24th, 1933 was to see my 40th birthday when life is reputed to begin. . . .

At the St. Regis suite, we occupied at Xmas while Charles and Margaret were with us, including rooms 809, 808, 807, 806, all with baths—living room 805, dining room 804, bedroom 803, 802, 801, 835 and 834—all with baths and better than half a floor of the old building 55th Street & Fifth Avenue side all for $150 per week.

That December 1932—while lavishing presents upon Diane and Melsing—I had not neglected you or your brother, as your "thank you" notes and your beloved mother's acrimonious communications attest.

I sent you sleighs, toboggans, skates, skiis, boats, soldiers and other things—perhaps not many in quantity but high in quality— Alex Taylor's best. Clothes would also have been forthcoming had it not been for your Mother's constant wrangling—the record speaks for itself. On the exchange of letters between your Mother and myself you can judge the motives involved. It was a sort of tug of war— you were the prize—and she had possession and possession is nine-tenths of the law. . . .

Following my letter to my Mother you will find a letter I wrote you from the Hospital in Globe, Arizona—it was the philosophical outburst of a man in great physical pain marooned in a desert town.

My letter to you is followed by a note to your Mother which I wrote her on the Twentieth Century Ltd. enroute to New York, December 9th, 1932, asking her to let you and your brother stop over in New York for a few days with your Grandmother Smith or anyone else your Mother might choose—also inquiring as to what clothes you might need for Christmas along with your toys, etc.

Then comes the correspondence about the things I sent you for Christmas—your Mother seemed to feel they were too lavish and was constrained to question my good faith and taste—but that was her wont, whether intentional or not. Attorneys who read them professionally felt they were shallow and condescending.

With this correspondence, you will find the letters about the tuition for the McDonough School—as you will note, I felt your Mother had her figures a bit confused. The school's statements are here for you to judge for yourself.

I have steadfastly refused to permit myself to gauge your Mother by the rigid standards I apply to most—either in my discussions with you or with others—primarily because Ellen West Page Smith was the Mother of my sons, for better or worse, and because I was aware of the provincial environment of the old conservative South that had produced her.

That correspondence ushered out the old year 1932 and in the New Year, 1933. . . .

Melba and I bought a specially built Lincoln convertible—the body was designed and built by Broun of Buffalo. There were only three others like it and they weren't finished in the same way. Ours was black and silver and the leather was of an almost white color, probably beige. Tommy Manville, Edsel Ford and the Shah of Persia had similar cars with different color combinations. The job cost between $5,000 and $6,000 delivered New York—I turned in the Packard limousine as a down payment arranging to turn over the wrecked Packard Phaeton at the time of the Lincoln delivery, along with the balance in cash. They allowed me $2,000 for the two cars.

The Lincoln was not to be ready for delivery until May. In the meantime I used a rented Rolls-Royce with chauffeur.

In February we cut down the number of rooms that we were using to four (809-810-811-812). They charged us $90.00 a week for them. However, our rooms, meals, telephone calls, laundry, valet, newsstand, theatre tickets, motor hire, beauty parlor and barber shop charges, postage, telegrams, florist, drugs, totalled approximately $1,000 a week. . . .

All during our stay at the St. Regis we maintained the apartment on Horatio Street for midnight parties—we kept a Jap there on full time so that we could drop in whenever we liked for food, alcoholic stimulations or love. . . .

[My father and Melba decided to go to New Orleans for Mardi Gras. The letter includes a lengthy description of the social events surrounding the Mardi Gras and the pageant itself.]

On our way home [from the Mardi Gras] the morning of March 2nd, we bought one of the Extras from the newsboy announcing that Huey Long, as he boarded the Crescent Limited en route to Washington to attend the Inaugural of Franklin Delano Roosevelt, had announced his proclamation closing all the banks in Louisiana.

New Orleans is on Central time, an hour later than New York. We did not go to bed—we took baths, ordered breakfast, and at 7:00 o'clock New Orleans time, 8 o'clock New York time, I telephoned my mother and urged her to draw enough cash out of the bank to take care of her incidental expenses for a month or two. She was then living at the La Salle Hotel and didn't need much cash—I told her what had happened in Louisiana, and warned her that more than likely the New York banks would be next, and in fact the entire nation would have to follow suit.

A few minutes before 8, which was just before 9 New York time, I got Arthur Bowen of the Corn Exchange Bank, Grand Central Branch, New York, on the phone and instructed him to wire me fifteen hundred dollars by postal telegraph and fifteen hundred dollars by Western Union, and to do it immediately, before the telegraph services shut off funds in New Orleans. I also told him to send me $2000 in cash by Air Mail registered to the Breakers Hotel in Palm Beach and to send it in $20.00 bills.

At 8:30 the Postal informed me that they had the wire and a few minutes later similar words came from Western Union. It caused great consternation in both offices but I didn't give them time to catch their breath. I was at the Postal almost as soon as the wire got there and before they opened their safe—they paid me out in cash. The Western Union gave me half cash and the balance in their own $50.00 checks —which I proceeded to cash whenever I could at Western Union offices all the way from New Orleans to Palm Beach. . . .

On with the Melba trip—we rode bicycles, we rode in chair cycles, had our favorite pushmobile boy and the bicycle man who always produced the bike that he said was Grover Whalen's favorite. We enjoyed the swimming, the massages, and the night life at Miami. Clark Davis was in business then in Miami and we went the rounds with him to the hot spots and the track.

The one and most emotional experience that lingers with me is the recollection that I'm not particularly proud of. One evening—it was moonlight—the night of Franklin Delano Roosevelt's first fireside chat. He had closed all the banks throughout the country—the nation was jumpy, starvation seemed just around the corner, even in Palm Beach. We went out for a spin in the car. It was a heavenly night out there under the stars. The radio was on and we had just been listening to a program—the Consolidated Gas, a plain steal of Stanley Howe's "Musical Epic of American History." It was coming to us way down there clear as a bell from a New York station—right out of the dashboard, as if we were sitting in a New York studio witnessing the show.

At the conclusion we were taken to the White House to hear the president. We left the damn thing on—why? Curious I guess. That

268

address will always go down in my mind as the best and most inspiring F. D. R. ever made—or has made to this writing. All his others have been an anticlimax. It stirred me to my very depths—it brought the tears, the thrills and ripples—it moved Melba too. We were for Roosevelt that night if we never had been before—whole heartedly—and never were again. He stood before us that night out there under the blanket of stars, as a true savior—a knight errant—a real leader of his people, guiding them out of the wilderness into the light.

There were quite a few of the top-flight Jews—the big money gents—at the Breakers. That month the late Adolph Ochs then owner of *The New York Times,* with Mama Ochs, tottering along behind him, and Adolph Lewishon, were among the shylocks present.

The Breakers that season perhaps more than at any other time because of the depression and the stock market debacle that had cleaned out so much of the youth of the nation, had a preponderance of distorted, dried up, wizened beauties—parading about in beautiful feathers and startling bathing suits in a useless attempt to appear thirty or forty—when they were in fact between sixty and seventy.

At times the old dames would even spoil the natural beauty of that charming citadel—which was the personification of resort luxury.

The housemaids, waitresses and masseurs were the sole attraction—sexually speaking—in 1933. . . .

I never forgot the gypsy at West Palm Beach—like most wenches of her tribe she sat by her tent letting her tits show. In passing she called to me—my cock got hard and I went in. She professed to read my palm—it was during the hell that reigned following the bursting of the Florida bubble. Altho I took my prick out and covered her with semen as I came, she continued to read my palm, as her baby crawled around beneath the table we sat at—nothing perturbed her. She told me that I was not a lawyer, but that for many years I would have much to do with the law. She explained it would be litigation over civil actions in equity—I thought then, and I still think (when I am rational) that that was a natural conclusion to reach regarding anyone who was in Florida at the time doing business in that panic. Yet, every time anyone has ever threatened to sue me, or sued me, or I have been in a tight place financially, I have thought of her predictions and like a dope wondered. I know that nothing in my hand has had anything to do with my life—it was just an obvious conclusion to come to at that time, and sufficient—with the sex by-play—for me to cross her palms with silver.

In Baltimore there was a friend of your mother's—in fact of the

269

entire Page family—some old crackpot who reading my palm before we were married, predicted that we would live in a small unpretentious Harlem flat (only niggers there now). That prediction like the one of the old roadside gypsy haunted me from time to time, especially during reverses—I never thought of them when I was on the top of the wave.

Ethel Barrymore once told me that an old witch had predicted she would die in poverty—an inmate of the old "Actors Home"—and she freely admitted that she was fearful that she might spend her last days there. John died broke—their recent years particularly hers have been tough—and would have been tougher if it had not been for her brother Lionel.

I don't take any stock in the palm reading. I have known many who have told me of their tricks—how they get people to tell them things and then turn around and tell it back as part of their wisdom—they go by appearances also. Astrology is just as bad. The trouble with all those things is the fact that (if your mind isn't strong enough to throw them off) the power of suggestion is so great that by thinking the thoughts that the witch has imparted, you bring about the actuality of the prediction—and it is seldom the actuality of the pleasanter things or the things you think you would like to have happen—but usually the things you don't want to have come about—the things that you wish to avoid.

Nothing upsets me more than shortage of funds, threatened lawsuits or lawsuits, yet I have been everlastingly involved all my life in litigation—principally from over-extending myself in moments of affluence. . . .

I suppose I would have enjoyed greater substantial and permanent success in life if I had not been such a rolling stone—primarily interested in women—suffering acutely from an inferiority complex. Shyness and the fear of being rebuffed held me back in my youth—but in maturity, lack of fervent partisanship, the ability to see both sides to every argument, did much to deter me. Then, too, I always relied on memory rather than an accurate record to keep track of important contacts—and I failed to keep up with friends. I could do for others and push others, but found it hard to push myself. My mind was never nimble enough in emergencies—I could think clearly before or after but never during. Pop a question to me in any gathering or on a witness stand and I would draw a blank—pop it at someone else and I could always give the other fellow the answer. It was a form of what some people call "stage fright." Telling friends off that displeased me or who tried to cheat me, either face to face, violently, or through the medium of the pungent pen, never helped me—in the long run it hurt, especially at crucial times when those friendships would have been helpful. . . .

I took a very nice office on Liberty Street for the Airecooling Corporation which I organized, and which I owned. It was fitted up as a work shop for Mr. Anderson to continue his developing and improving on both the Airecooler and the Electric Ice Box. . . .

[In March] I drove down to Baltimore, and by arrangement with your mother, took you and your brother to Annapolis for the afternoon. . . . In the gymnasium we all had a try at the Circular Track. We did the old Navy yard from one end to the other. It was a very delightful afternoon and we took a lot of pictures both still and movie. As we drove down past Carvel Hall a very gorgeous young vision appeared on the stoop. As I remember she had on a white Leghorn hat. You couldn't take your eyes off the vision, and when I chided you with "what are you looking at son" your rejoiner was "The same thing you are Dad."

We were a little late getting back to Ruxton, and I gave your mother $50.00 for a Junior Membership for you in the Ruxton Country Club.

[A flurry of letters and gifts followed the Annapolis trip.]

It has always been my wont to write letters. If the art of letter writing had only not been lost it might have been profitable for me. When I say lost, I mean not only the art of writing but of appreciation as well—letters.

The letters will all have to speak for themselves.

7 East 42nd Street
New York, N.Y.
March 20, 1933.

Mr. Charles Page Smith,
Ruxton, Md.
Dear Page—

I cannot begin to tell you how much I enjoyed seeing you and your brother and your mother the other day.

I was especially glad of an opportunity to see you in your uniform and then to see my very much grown-up son starting off in his dinner coat.

Of course, what interested me most were the very excellent drawings that you gave me to show Mr. Van Loon and I also liked your poetry and was much impressed by the modeling you had done. I think it all most excellent and I think you should continue to keep up your interest.

I notice that many of the sketches were done in 1929 and 1930 and that apparently you have not been drawing much lately and I wonder why?—I would hate to see you give up when you have displayed such real talent for depicting life in a satirical mood as well as being able to do the more serious things.

I hope now that we have succeeded in breaking the ice that it will be possible for us to see one another more often and that our visits will be more frequent than they have been in the past. I feel that perhaps your mother and I are approaching a more agreeable understanding than has been possible in years past. . . .

I appreciate having been to your school—now—I realize the great distance that you have to travel each day, I am amazed that you are able to find time to write at all. . . .

As I told you, I gave the woman at the candy store a dollar for you and a dollar for your brother for you to buy ice cream and candy with. I will write you more in a day or two, but I am very busy catching up with a lot of work that accumulated during my absence. . . .

Your devoted father

7 East 42nd Street
New York, N.Y.
April 6, 1933

Dear Ellen:

I have been so busy since I returned to New York that I have not had time to write and thank you for your consideration the other day when we passed through Baltimore and dropped in to see the boys.

I hope from now on that you and the boys and our side of the house can meet together from time to time in the same amicable manner.

The financial situation is such that it isn't possible for me to be of any assistance at the moment, but I feel that within the course of the next two or three months that we should be able to sit down and work out some way of alleviating part of the burden that you have been carrying so bravely.

It was nice to be able to talk to you without acrimony and I am sure you must appreciate how much it meant to me to see the boys and to talk to them, and to learn about their work. I think Page's drawings, many of which he apparently executed between 11 and 12, are excellent and certainly his modelling shows great promise. He looked very well in his military uniform and exceptionally attractive in his dinner coat.

They must indeed be a great comfort and joy to you. . . .

I have already set to work to find something for Page on one of the trans-Atlantic liners, but before discussing it further with him I should like to talk to you more about it, and also to have a frank talk with you about a lot of problems with which Page is bound to be confronted.

I am rather glad that you and Melba met the other day. Melba for her part found you very attractive and a surprisingly nice person —which of course does not speak well for me—but then I have always been aware of your attributes while unable at times to reconcile myself to some of your ideas and theories. . . .

This communication is a sort of preliminary word to let you know I have not forgotten the boys and that they figure very much in my plans for the future. I sincerely hope that we can work together agreeably for their best interests. It was nice to see you and the boys, and Melba joins in sending best wishes and the hope that we may be able to repeat the pleasant meeting in the not too distant future.

Sincerely,
Ward

Wednesday April 15th 1933

Dear Father;—

Thank you a lot for the pralines they were very good and we all enjoyed them very much. I hope you are having a good time in Miami. Poor brother has had the chicken-pox and on top of that Dr. Dabney had to operate on him for two awful abscesses on his arm. He is very brave about it. I have taken up clay modeling a little and have done two statues. Mr. Van Loon has been so nice to autograph all those books that I thought I would write him a short letter. I do not know his address. I am enclosing it and I hope you will either mail it for me or give it to him. I am on the debating society at school and just finished the hockey season on the second line (varsity ice hockey I played right wing). We have started a paper in Ruxton and I am the Editor (just we boys) I write the stuff and they typeright it out. We are running a serial in it called "Red Vengence" by me. Hoping you enjoy yourself

I remain
very Sincerely your Son.
Page Smith

[My father, armed with his new wealth, gave every indication that he intended to decide where and how my brother and I were to be educated. My mother, of course, was equally determined to rebuff his erratic interpositions. She explained to him that my whole academic career had been precarious in the extreme and that only the interest and help of the Gilman teachers and Mr. Pickett, at whose

tutoring school my academic deficiencies were repaired each summer, had enabled me to avoid expulsion for bad grades. As she wrote my father, "Mr. Pickett has agreed . . . to tutor Page in two subjects at no extra cost. He and Mrs. Pickett are devoted to Page and anxious to get him back to Gilman. He says that the teachers (at the camp) who are all Gilman masters, can decide after working with Page, whether he can make the grade or not."

My father, after having promised my brother and me that he would put up the money to send us to camp had then stipulated that if he were to pay he must name the camp. My mother was furious. My brother, as she wrote, asked every day when he returned from school "Has my father sent the money for me to go to camp? I don't mind Page's being disappointed nearly as much for he is never as keen about anything as poor John is, and being older has more philosophy or resignation or whatever you care to call it . . . John has come in at the small end of things always. Everything that I have had to spend has gone on Page. Not only because he was older but he seemed to be more of a problem and to need things more. Johnny is so fine and manly and I have been able to do so little for him. I have never seen anyone with a nobler or finer character . . . You made a promise to the child and I will have one more big score against you if you disappoint him or keep the matter dragging on any longer."

My father replied: "This will acknowledge your dictatorial communication of recent date. It both amused and interested me—I had hoped that you had outgrown those tirades of rhetoric—they are so futile—however your imperious letter would have done the Gazi Mustafa Kemal Pasa proud." My father then went on to reiterate that if he was to pay for camp and school he must have the last word on where we were to go. Culver Military Academy in Indiana was his choice, for summer as well as winter. I should take Naval Studies at the Culver Summer Camp in preparation for Annapolis—which I hadn't the slightest interest in attending—and my brother should take woodcraft. We could both attend the Chicago World's Fair on the way.

My mother, knowing a lost cause when she saw one, left it to me to reply to my father's letter. I wrote: "Dear Father, . . . Neither Johnny nor I have ever wished to go to the World's Fair and Mr. Pickett's camp was the choice of both of us. If you are interested in sending us to any camp you could not find a better one than Mr. Pickett's. We have always been very happy there. . . . The things *you wrote about Mother hurt my feelings terribly. When I am older I will express my opinion. I only know that mother has worked hard for years to help grandfather take care of us, and we have had no help from you since you left us all in Morristown. Thanks for the fireworks, we all enjoyed them very much. Yours truly, Page."*

To which my father replied:]

If your last letter had been read to me aloud, I would have been sure that it was your Mother's composition and phraseology. At that, even your hand-writing is quite unlike your normal script as I know it, and I can appreciate that you were forced into taking the position and writing such a letter which you couldn't help but be contrary to the true feeling of you and your brother.

I am glad the responsibility is not mine of having robbed you both of a most interesting experience of a lifetime, to-wit, a visit to the Century of Progress Exposition at Chicago and a summer in the finest Boy's Camp in the United States, particularly adapted to you, if you . . . plan to go to Annapolis.

The letter was not a bit your style or like your real, true self.

If your mother prefers to play the role of the harassed, the abused and the martyr there is little I can do, but regret her stand for ultimately you both will be the real sufferers.

Of course getting around as little as you all do, you do not have the opportunity to see and understand and appreciate what is going on in the rest of the world and how other people live and do things. . . .

You are quite right, when you are older you will see and understand all in its true light, for I hope as you grow older that in spite of the circumstances in which you now find yourself and the narrow confines of your present environment, that you will be able to see things in their true perspective.

If your Mother steadfastly refuses to accept the assistance which I can arrange for you both, or to accept tuition for you in good schools simply because of a desire to wreak an inverted passion upon me, I can do little at the present moment to stop her.

As far as the so-called sacrifices she feels she has made in order to look after you both I doubt if she would ever have had to make them if she had been civil to me and my family, but her arrogant manner was not conducive to eliciting sympathy, particularly when she has so consistently refused to cooperate or to compromise in regard to you and your brother, your education and making it possible for me to see you from time to time, or have you see your grand-parents, or your cousins. . . .

At times I wonder if she and her family are not suffering from a violent inferiority complex and if that is not the real cause of most of the difficulty. . . .

When the time comes, when you are old enough, if you are interested, I shall tell you or I shall have some unprejudiced, disinterested party tell you the truth of the whole situation. It's a long story, and I shan't set it forth now, or for some time to come. For the present, let me say, the impartial persons have been amazed at your Mother's letters and have all felt that in view of her attitude, my communications have been considerably moderate.

I am sorry to have to write you this way and I am sorry that your mother will not let you go to Culver or to the World's Fair or to the type of school that would best fit you for Annapolis or that she won't let you see your grandmother who has been ill for so long and so anxious to see you. I am sorry that she won't make it possible for you to meet and know men and the wisdom of them, of the type of Hendrik van Loon, Carveth Wells and others. . . .

I am glad that you and Marshall enjoyed the firecrackers. There would be a good deal in the world for you to enjoy, if your Mother didn't so consistently and deliberately stand in the way.

As ever, your devoted father

[This letter marked the virtual end of any exchange between the Northern and Southern divisions of the family. I did not see, or so far as I can recall, correspond with him until I went to college, four years later.]

And so, we slothfully wended our way through April—a bit dull, but busy with plans for the new office, Airecooling, *Nomad,* Ampro Distribution, Harry Millar's new corporation, and a multitude of other schemes were brewing all around as we approached the Merry, Merry month of May.

I rented a beautifully panelled office (old Colonial Style) high up on the 39th floor of One Wall Street—the entire floor. It had a magnificent view of the Bay, the East River and the Hudson. As far as the eye could see, North, South, East and West, the Metropolitan area was spread out below me. It was truly Manhattan's inspirational point.

Watterson Lowe did the entire decorating—a friend of Hamilton P.'s by the name of Howley sold me the furniture—both charged me well. I had a big open fireplace in my private office with a colonial mantle. On one side of my desk was a stock ticker and a news ticker —on another side a small board, upon which the stocks I traded in were listed with the purchase price and the high and low changes as the market fluctuated.

276

My brokers were Baar Cohen & Co., and Satchkin & Pell (this latter firm I always suspected of being a bucket shop and my only reason for doing business with them was because of my friendship for Hamilton P.). I had two private secretaries, a Miss McClean and a Miss Murray—I dropped Miss Hendricks after my return from Florida.

My luncheons were brought in every day from the Savarin Restaurant—I seldom went out but often had business appointments for luncheon in my own office. Melba had a desk but she rarely occupied it. A ship's clock that she had purchased from Abercrombie & Fitch for $150.00 graced the mantle, and my most precious autographed photographs hung on the walls, and my Governor's chair was in place behind my desk. The office was air-cooled, the rent $250.00 a month.

When I say the office was air-cooled and conditioned I mean by my own apparatus in the single cabinet, which Anderson had made for me and which you will see in the pictures—the first of its kind patented in the world. . . .

After Diane and Melsing had finished their schooling at Peekskill—St. Mary's Episcopal School for Girls, and the Peekskill Military Academy for Boys, Melba took the children out to Chicago to see the World's Fair.

We had had word from Kauder that Claire T. was coming on to see her mother-in-law and to settle up her husband's estate. We telephoned her step-father's parish house at Islip and learned that the Reverend Mr. Garth and Mrs. Garth were at Keene Valley. We phoned there and Claire got to New York just before Melba left for Chicago, with the children. I had developed quite an urge for Claire in Berlin in 1929, and was thrilled with the prospect of seeing her again.

She arrived in the morning and came straight to the St. Regis— we got her a suite adjoining ours, connecting rooms. We all had lunch together, mother coming over to bid the children good-bye had lunch with us on the roof, and then mother, Claire and I went to the station to put them all on the train.

Mother didn't think well of my having to remain behind on business—she thought Claire attractive and suspected the worst of me —and Melba was sure. As we parted at the station mother warned me to watch my step, which I had no intention of doing, in the direction I intended to go.

That evening I took Claire to dinner—(she had arranged to take over the representation of *Variety* in Berlin, one of the jobs her husband had had before he died, while here she was writing for some German papers of a similar type). She was very eager to see our burlesque shows which had had a revival and were then in full bloom and assiduously patronized by me—I bought through the broker in the hotel, tickets for the leading one on 42nd Street, and also a Box for the one on Irving Place. We dressed for the evening and after dinner we went to the 42nd Street show for the first half. Still high we took in the Irving Place show for the second half. That night we used the Rolls-Royce, so we were really cutting quite a figure. When we got to the Irving Place theatre we found some people in our box and had to have them put out. As was my custom I offered a prize of $10.00 for what I considered the best strip-tease—that is the most complete, and a second prize of $5.00. . . .

From Minsky's Irving Place Theatre we drove down to my office at 1 Wall Street where, from the 39th floor we scanned the city in its fairylike glory of dazzling lights—before the days of blackouts, New York ,always reminded me of an over-lighted Christmas tree prone on the ground.

Claire was intrigued by the office and the view. From Wall Street we went up to my studio on Horatio Street. The purpose of that visit was to show her the film negative taken of herself and Melba in the nude when we all visited the Nudist Club in Berlin in 1929. By the time I located the roll, we were both pretty tired and so we returned to the St. Regis—all had been most circumspect. We sat up for a while, in the living room of my suite—purpose a night cap. She told me then that her husband always contended that if anything ever happened to him, she would within a fortnight have an affair with some other man, probably one of his best friends—and under the emotional stress and strain of the accident, she had done just that— "Bundy" M., Jarmila's husband, had been the lucky man.

The next morning, James [Taylor], finding the door unlocked between our suites, felt certain, I am sure, that we had had an affair but such was not the case.

After breakfast we set out for Sadie Weiss'—Claire wanted to outfit herself with a new wardrobe before returning home. Dressing the female carcass has always been a weakness of mine and, as usual, was my downfall then—the whole performance was too much for me to stand.

I had subconsciously coveted Claire for years. Alone with her in

278

the dressing room as she fitted one costume after the other my excitement grew to uncontrollable proportions. My cock was hard—I showed it to her—she felt it—I caressed her, got my hand down on her box—she had a lovely garden. I nearly came I was so hot.

The wardrobe complete, we returned to the hotel for luncheon.

I was taking the Century for Chicago to rejoin Melba and the children there at the Fair—the time was short. We sent James off to the kitchen for a sumptuous repast. I could hold back no longer and she seemed eager too so there and then I laid her—for the first time.

Claire was something to conjure with, she knew every trick in the trade and what a "Dutch" girl does not know about sexual intercourse or the ways of a maid with a man are not worth knowing. By luncheon we had completely satiated ourselves and had agreed that she would return to town from Keene Valley on receipt of a wire from me.

The plan—I would return a day ahead of Melba and the children and that 24 hours we would spend together at the studio—the surroundings there were more conducive to unlimited sexual consummation.

After lunch I caught the train for Chicago and Claire took the train north to rejoin her in-laws in the Adirondacks.

When I reached the Blackstone Hotel, Melba lit into me. It was the first time I had seen a flash of jealousy from that quarter since we had been married—but she was hell bent for election then. She accused me of having stayed over for the sole purpose of fornication—I frankly admitted the allegation but only as it developed the second day. There was no sense of making any bones about it because she knew I had an unquenchable urge for Claire.

As a matter of fact she really was sore because she was not in on the show too. After the first excitement blew over, we took the children and visited the General Motors Exhibit which was the most complete of all. There they not only assembled the motor but they built bodies on the endless chain production plan and turned out cars for immediate delivery as they came off the line.

The Transportation Exhibit showed aeroplanes, the latest in Pullman cars, special freight cars for carrying shells for the Navy, the famous London, Midland and Scottish train "The Royal Scot." They had been big advertisers with us in our *Nomad* days. The Chrysler Exhibit was in a modernistic building but did not approach the General Motors Show. There were wild west shows for the children, Pony Expresses, American Indian villages, a midway with all types of side shows and an enchanted island for children with a mechanical dinosaur and other prehistoric animals, a replica of Fort Dearborn and of Abraham Lincoln's Birthplace attracted the elders more than the kids.

The Hall of Science and the electrical exhibits fascinated the children—a transparent man, a model of the human body which when illuminated by trick lighting, clearly showed skeletal, vascular, respiratory, digestive and muscular systems which excited the kids no end.

Hundreds of young college boys dressed like the State Troopers pushed the customers around in wheel chairs for 50¢ or 75¢ an hour. College athletes, many from good families, were the ricksha boys. They had a radio and communication building containing a complete international telephone system in active operation. They had home planning exhibits, agricultural exhibits, dairy exhibits.

The Firestone people made tires while you waited and watched.

The Sky Ride was an attraction difficult to get the children away from.

In the lagoon was Admiral Byrd's polar ship, the one he used on his trip to the South Pole.

Innumerable restaurants dotted every part of the Fair.

Mammoth Greyhound busses, built like railroad observation cars at the New London and Hudson River boat races—Harvard and Yale or Poughkeepsie—went from one end of the Fair to the other passing thru the midway at a maximum charge of 10¢ per entire ride.

After several days of this exhausting performance, I returned to New York 24 hours ahead of Melba after wiring Claire.

My train arrived ahead of hers the next morning and I met her at the station. We went immediately to the studio where we freshened up as the Jap prepared a delicious luncheon. Luncheon over, having consumed a moderate proportion of alcoholic stimulant so as not to adversely affect our sexual desires, we sent the Jap on his way.

Claire had a passion for playing with assholes. She would put her finger up mine and I'd put mine up hers. I even tried to get my cock up her rear end. We sucked one another off at first—and then we played with our tails until we both came again. Eventually we both shit the bed—it was too much and my first active encounter with that performance—manipulating assholes—an old German custom.

Claire liked to ride on top—in fact she had great joy no matter what the position. We never got out of bed until the next morning— we both came at least once every hour—we didn't sleep all night. Sometimes in the early stage we came more often—we drank just enough to keep us going. She was a seductress of no mean proportions.

The next morning Melba arrived in town with the children.

Claire and I met her at the train and we all returned to the St. Regis together—we had luncheon on the roof with mother and Mrs. Van Loon. That night Claire returned to Keene Valley—we had hoped to meet her that summer in Germany but her boat did not arrive until the day ours was leaving so we missed her by 24 hours. I did not see Claire again although we corresponded frequently until after Melba and I were divorced and I had remarried for the third time "legally." . . .

At one time we contemplated chartering Roy Howard's houseboat but it wasn't in particularly good repair and so we passed that by. There were also some other hitches which I do not recall at this time.

We looked at boats from $1,000 a season to $1,500 a week and we finally fell for the S. S. *Sydney,* owned by Sydney E. Hutchinson, a brother-in-law of Mr. Stotesbury in Philadelphia. The Latter part of June I chartered her for $1,000 a week. It cost me another $1,000 per week for fuel and food. The charter ran from the 23d of June, 1933 to the 7th of September, 1933.

At Melba's special request we put our own little upright studio piano on board. The *Sydney* was a twin screw motor houseboat 100' overall in length. The crew consisted of 11 men and from time to time as we gave parties, I increased the number of cooks and stewards. In order to fly the Seawanhaka-Corinthian flag, it was necessary for me to charter this boat with Rayford Alley, who was a member of the Club (and my attorney for the aircooling corporation).

My personal insignia or private flag was the *Nomad* "trademark" —a Nomad riding across the desert on his horse, gun held aloft in black and white.

One of our most successful parties was considerably photographed, both stills and movies. Among the guests were Mr. and Mrs. William O'Donnell Iselin, the Sterling Ivisons, Major Stanley Howe, the Howard Chandler Christys, the Seton Lindsays, the Ongs, Freddie Davenport, the Hamilton Pells, the Mulhollands, the Clay Morgans Lyle Volck, Eddie Ballou, the George Genungs and a hundred or so others whose names for the moment slip me.

Our bedroom was attractively decorated—it contained two single beds and two comfortably upholstered chairs, a writing desk, a vanity table and a dresser. Our bathroom contained a full size tub, dresser, shower, etc.

The dining room was beautifully appointed, large enough to seat 12 or 14 comfortably.

The living room, as you will see from the photographs was also quite sumptuous. There were 4 guest staterooms on board, each with a private bath.

In addition to the well-furnished quarters for the children and their French governess there was an aft deck below the main deck for them where they could disport themselves undisturbed by the rompings of their elders.

A charming sun parlor completed the main deck before coming out on to the main aft deck.

The galley crew quarters and engineer's were forward.

In addition to the three lifeboats, wc had a fast motor boat which was used primarily between the *Sydney* and shore. The top deck amply accommodated a good many guests.

The bridge was my favorite spot especially when we were under way. . . .

We did most of our cruising on the Long Island Sound, around Oyster Bay, Shelter Island and Lloyds Neck. . . .

Coming out of Greenport or Shelter Island, we ran into quite a storm (thru Plum Gut). We had to lash down the piano and the furniture. The old *Sydney* rolled and tossed but we came through without any great difficulty. That trip was reminiscent of the days when I used to sail through Plum Gut with father on his racing sloop, the *Syce*—we had no motors then—the wind was all we had to propel us against tides and seas.

We set off several hundred dollars worth of firecrackers for the children along the shore of Port Washington Harbor the morning of July 4th; we arrived there the night before during a beautiful sunset and anchored.

At noon of the 4th, we weighed anchor and proceeded to Oyster Bay where at night fall on the signal of a flare from the *Sydney,* over a $1,000 worth of firecrackers which I had donated for the occasion, were set off on the lawn of the Seawanhaka Club. At one time it looked as if that display would not take place because rainy weather temporarily settled in. After the firework display we went to Piping Rock Club for supper and dancing. . . .

Wherever we went by water the Lincoln followed by land and was always awaiting our arrival. . . .

At the Piping Rock Club I met a luscious young thing. I got hot and so did she—we left the dance floor and took to the private hedge. Although in evening dress she first sucked me and then laid me there in the bushes to the beat of the dance orchestra. . . .

I had one of the aircooling apparatuses in my stateroom for

282

demonstration purposes and Anderson, the inventor was frequently aboard. James (Taylor) was always along as valet. . . .

As I had said I had chartered the *Sydney* from the 23d of June, until the 7th of Sept., and when I tried to extend the Charter to cover the week of the boat races at New London, the owner tripled the charter rate for that occasion. This made me so mad that I *cancelled* the charter and returned the *Sydney* to her owner on the 7th of July. . . .

On our return to New York we went to the St. Regis for a day or so and then down to the Essex and Sussex from where I commuted by motor daily between New York and Spring Lake.

As an item of interest, I am including herewith our hotel bill from the second of July to the eighth of July, 1933. This was in addition, of course, to our expenses aboard the yacht *Sydney*. It shows a total of approximately $1,900 for the week and that, of course, does not include cash gratuities although many of my tips were included on my checks.

We found mother and the children enjoying themselves immensely at Spring Lake. Mother said they had behaved very well during our absence, that Charles M., their father, had been down to see them with his new wife Margaret and that they had both spent the night as our guests. The children had been given swimming lessons in the Club pool to the tune of $50 apiece and had progressed very well.

[In the fall of 1933 my father, Melba, Diane and Melsing took a European tour. The trip started in England. From there they went to France, Germany, Spain, Switzerland, Austria and Italy. The descriptions of Germany where Hitler had recently come to power are the most interesting of my father's characteristically voluminous travel accounts.]

[From France the party went on to Germany.] The Germans were marching and counter-marching all day long and well into the night. Hitler had wiped out homosexuality and scattered the lesbians far and wide closing all of their notorious joints or assembly centers— even the street walkers were few and far between and the Jews had lost their arrogance and become servile again. . . .

Our last night in Berlin, we went out with Knickerbocker, Carl Dickey and John Gunther. Knickerbocker's mistress, whom he afterwards married, also came along. In the party was a very beautiful lesbian who in the days prior to Hitler had been the proprietor of the most notorious lesbian restaurant in Berlin. A Black Shirt was very much in love with her which gave us the entree to several night clubs that presumably were being run very much on the Q.T. and underground. That evening we had quite a night of it; along with us on the party was a German College Professor who also was smitten with the lesbian. It was a gay night, Hitler or no Hitler.

I had letters of introduction from the head of the German tourist Bureau in New York to Propaganda Minister, Dr. Goebbels.

I didn't meet Goebbels, he was in Nürnberg at the time in charge of the festivities that were taking place there, but he had left word that Melba and I were to be provided with transportation and accommodations if we wished to attend that all important celebration, when hundreds of thousands of Germans descended upon that famous historical city.

We wanted to go very much and we always regretted that we didn't, but we had the children with us and we couldn't take them to any such shindig, and we feared to leave them behind.

Instead of going to Nürnberg, we hired a limousine and drove to Vienna by the way of Dresden and Prague. We stopped for lunch in Dresden—it was a most attractive City and the German Troopers, Brown Shirts, Black Shirts, war veterans, local Guard and village burgers were marching and counter-marching all over the City to the beat of drums and the blare of trumpets. The Germans were again holding their heads high—they were no longer a beaten or oppressed people hanging their heads in shame. Even passing through you got the thrill of it, a thrill that Americans have not yet experienced in this present war—it was a martial thrill, an inspirational thrill—although you were no part of it, it made you tingle all over as you witnessed the preparation for the onslaught to come. It was the spirit of their enthusiasm that was infectious—the spirit of a people who had found themselves again, who had thrown off the yoke of semitism. . . .

On the way back [to the United States], as on the way over, I talked constantly with my brokers in New York, and traded over the ship-to-shore long distance telephone—I talked to New York at least once or twice a day every day while I was in Europe, carrying on my business and giving my purchase and sale orders.

Mother was at the pier to greet us—James Taylor, my valet at the St. Regis, the St. Regis porter, with his truck—Henry the chauffeur was there with the car. Madamoiselle was also on hand to take over the care of the children. . . .

* * *

The fornicating manicurists at the St. Regis were ready to take up or off where they had left off—they were beautiful girls who loved to screw (for money) and they knew their business. I always had two come up at a time to manicure me—Melba's masseuse had an electric vibrator that they used to stir me up with. Then when she had me hot they would fuck the guts out of me while Melba watched and played with herself.

Immediately on my return, I continued negotiations with Anderson and concluded an arrangement with him in September, between the Airecooling Corporation, Anderson and his partner, whereby they granted the corporation an option to acquire from them all their rights and interests in certain Airecooling patents and Ice making patents for a period of two years for a consideration of $8,000.00. . . .

As soon as we returned to the United States we set to work looking for a farm. Somehow or other I had the feeling that a place in the country would be an anchor to windward, come a war or any other national or international devastating catastrophe.

In October I paid the St. Regis $500.00 a month for rooms 805-806. . . .

I was keenly interested in Fiorello's campaign for Mayor—I had always been one of his staunch supporters. I had hardly returned to New York when I started handing out free advice to the Little Flower and his campaign manager—Stanley Howe and George Bell were both active in that fight. . . .

When the Mayor considered having a big rally at Madison Square Garden, I suggested to the Campaign managers that they have a series of torchlight parades converging on the Garden that night from all parts of the City. The suggestion met with approval and the parade end of the rally was worked out in my apartment at the St. Regis, and although I did not publicly take the lead I planned it and directed it. They marched up from the lower East Side—they marched up from the lower West Side—they marched down from the upper West Side— they marched down from the upper East Side, and they marched across 59th Street from Queens, carrying their "transparencies." Most of these units were composed largely of the active members of the various political clubs. It did not begin to reach the proportions of the Torchlight Parade that Karl Behr and I had put on for the candidacy of John Purroy Mitchel when he was running for Mayor. Nevertheless, it was a good turn out. . . .

During the campaign I gave a cocktail party for the Mayor, Stanley Howe, Heywood Broun and Theodore Dreiser. When they first arrived none of them would take a drink—La Guardia was very much on the defensive. He had a terrific inferiority complex when it came to men of letters. As time went on they all broke down and proceeded to do a bit of light drinking, which was a great relief to James, who having prepared for a sumptuous alcoholic repast was fearful at first that his efforts had all been in vain.

Dreiser contended that no man was ever completely honest even with himself—to say nothing of being honest in dealings with his fellow man.

He accused La Guardia of harboring, perhaps subconsciously, an ambition to be Governor of the State of New York and then President of the United States. La Guardia replied, without a moment's hesitation, that he had no such ambition in the first place and in the second place there were too many vowels in his name.

Following that up, Dreiser then said, "Mayor, have you ever spent a night in a hotel with a woman other than your wife?" This question was prompted by the fact that a short while previous (when investigating the so-called ruthlessness of coal operators in a Pennsylvania mining town, where Dreiser had really gone to lend a hand to the striking miners under the guise of a writer) he had been arrested on the ground of moral turpitude by the local authorities. The charge —he had had a woman in his bedroom all night. The evidence—when he entered the room with a woman, the hotel management and local authorities at the instigation of the operators and their private police, had placed toothpicks outside Mr. Dreiser's door. In the morning when they entered the toothpicks had not been moved, which proved conclusively to the authorities' satisfaction that the young lady had not left the room during the night. To Mr. Dreiser's query of the Mayor regarding his personal morals, the Little Flower snapped, "Mr. Dreiser, if I have ever spent the night with a young lady in a hotel room, other than my wife, or if I ever do, I have always made sure, and shall always make doubly sure, that all the toothpicks have been removed from the premises before I retire." The Mayor was tickled to death with his quick rejoinder and promptly repeated the episode to his wife and the intimate members of his campaign management.

As our guests became alcoholically stimulated the conversation became more and more scintillating with the little Mayor on the defensive most of the time.

Theodore Dreiser engaged Melba in a discussion of the virtues of black flesh. He having had a negro mistress was a great advocate of the cross-breeding of the races—Melba did not agree with him.

It was Dreiser's contention at that gathering that anyone could start a revolution in the United States at that time because of the dire poverty of the unemployed, by simply crossing the country, holding aloft a red banner. To the contrary, Heywood Broun contended—and I agreed with Broun—that such a movement would get nowhere outside the industrial centers, where the foreign-born predominate. Broun was emphatic in stating that the American farmer, the American landowner, the American suburbanite would not participate but would in fact oppose any such revolutionary uprising. Fiorello didn't get into this discussion too deeply, but he inclined to the Broun theory. Broun had a great respect at that time for the rural backbone of the nation.

During the arguments, Dreiser sat on the livingroom floor—he seemed to find that more to his liking than the chairs or the couches. Like many of his statements, it was but a pose to get him attention.

After the party was over, I took La Guardia into the bedroom and there I gave him $250.00 in cash for campaign expenses. In doing so, I told him that I knew that there were many expenses in an election campaign that could not be included in the returns to the Secretary of State, and that I did not wish any favors in return.

All fall, I was busy visiting various parts of the country looking for a farm—a farm that could be a subsistence farm in the case of dire need—and a commercially operated proposition under fairly normal conditions. I felt strongly that war in the Pacific was in the offing. In those days it seemed to me that we would do battle in the Far East before we went to war again in Europe. From World War I, I had learned the importance of agriculture. We scoured the Virginia countryside; the Maryland countryside; the Delaware countryside; going down the Peninsula of the Eastern Shore of Maryland to Cape Charles, Va. and back. We looked at property in Pennsylvania, in Connecticut, in Massachusetts and all over New York State. . . .

Election Day I went down to La Guardia's headquarters at the Astor Hotel and in the presence of Rosalie Love Whitney, I gave La Guardia my final contribution. . . .

One day, while driving thru Columbia County, New York, we came upon an old house, 150 years old—about half a mile in from the highway at North Chatham, New York. We were taken with the place and the rolling country around it; it afforded a great deal of privacy and was just what we were looking for. The real estate agent took us to the village, and I made the owner and his wife—the place had been in her family ever since it had been built—an offer of

$4500.00. There were 112 acres in the place. They went into a huddle and decided to accept the offer, so I made a deposit of $50 or $100, subject to the search of the title and the closing. The deal was also contingent on their ability to persuade a neighbor owning 12 unproductive acres of knoll overlooking the house, to sell same to us for a couple hundred dollars. We then returned to New York and I engaged John Crandall, the Republican County Chairman of Columbia County, a former County Judge, to look after my interests in connection with the transaction.

The place was devoid of electric lights; there were no telephone or electric lines from the highway to the house, the only toilet facilities was a two-holer in the backyard—the water was from a well not too far from the two-holer. The fireplaces were in great need of repair, and the only thing about it that really intrigued us was the lay of the land, and the age of the hand-hewn timbers that were the frame of the house. But we will return to that later. . . .

We were enthusiastic about the place at North Chatham—I had a corporation set up to buy the property—we called it "Melvale Inc." after Melba. We decided to call the place Melvale Farm. While the title was being searched and the purchase negotiations completed we made many trips to North Chatham, meeting with carpenters, plumbers, electricians, plasterers, painters, and the like, getting bids on the work we wanted done, and done in a hurry. . . .

We took deed to the property in the name of the Corporation on the 8th of December and on the 23rd of December, we moved in. . . .

Ninety acres were tillable and the rest of the farm was in woodland, meadow and marsh—the soil was rich black loam on flat limestone top mixture and the place entirely fenced by wire, much of it erected by me.

It was a truly lovely location, nestled away in the foothills of the Berkshires.

Hank Van Loon, Hendrik's son, who had been an architect of considerable ability, came over from Dorset and gave us pointers, particularly on the importance of timing the work so that it would run along properly synchronized, in other words, the plumbers and the electricians would get their work done before the plasterers, the carpenters preceding most of the gang, and then would come the painters, etc.

We started our construction work on the 9th of December and we literally tore out the entire inside. We removed the back stairs—we built on an extension with two rooms and a bath for the servants—

we turned three rooms on the ground floor into one living room, and then we made closets out of a single room and a bedroom and dining room out of four other small rooms. To boot we added a bathroom— Crane's most modernistic—the tub, the longest they had, black of course, a black toilet bowl and wash basin, and the whole thing finished off in black and white tile with curtains to match, and a black Medicine Chest. We built a new main staircase.

We sank two great big highway tiles down over the spring, which was about 100 feet from the house—this gave us an unlimited supply of drinking water which never dried up. On the upper floor we also constructed two guest rooms with connecting baths and fixed up two adorable rooms for the children with a balcony overlooking the living room so that we could keep an eye on them. The Balcony served as a play room.

There was an ice house on the place, carriage house, tool house, a farm office, a sheep barn with 70 ton storage capacity, a cow barn with 20 stanchions, concrete floor, newly shingled, a manure runway and a spring and milk cooling shed. The horse barn was of 4-horse capacity—the poultry houses took care of 100 hens—there was a silo.

I had the stables, the barns, the garage (which was big enough for two cars), the farm office and milk house electrically wired.

I installed an electric pump to pump the spring water to the house and I cleaned up the well back of the house—the water for the barns was supplied from springs that never dried. When I bought the house there was a hot-air furnace in the cellar which heated the center of the house downstairs—but I changed that, altho I kept the hot air, I installed steam heat.

Being fearful of fire, I had all the chimneys torn out, three in number, and had new ones built from field stone which we gathered on the place. It was quite a proposition. We papered the bedrooms and the dining room—the living room we left bare with rough plaster between the hand-hewn timbers. We bought old wrought iron fixtures. The living room fireplace was large enough for a man to sleep in.

During the construction work we had over 60 men employed on the place at one time—to add to our troubles we had to go thru a snowstorm right in the middle of the work.

Not only did we have to sink the caissons around the spring but we had to pipe the water to the house, and in addition we had to run drain pipes to take the water out of the kitchen and away from the bathrooms, and not only was it necessary to lay the drain pipes, but we had to construct a cesspool and in addition I put in a septic tank—

289

I directed the entire work myself, letting the contract for the plastering, the plumbing and electrical work, as well as the papering. I coordinated the entire job as well as planning and designing the work.

During this time I rented a room from the Village Parson, but spent a good deal of time commuting between New York and the farm by motor—I was invariably too tired to drive myself so would have Henry drive me.

Van Loon agreed as usual to make up our Christmas cards for us and also design a letterhead for the farm.

But that promise was never fulfilled—the correspondence relating to it follows and tells a more eloquent story then any I could set forth as to just what occurred.

As so often happens in such matters, Hendrik's failure irked me to no end—and on the last day of the year I wrote him a letter which terminated our intimate friendship, and altho years later there was a reapproachment, we were never really close again.

He showed my letter to many, and I distributed copies far and wide—many people who knew him delighted in my vitriolic tirade—it was probably a mistake to have ended a friendship with such an illustrious one, but I doubt if it was ever much of a loss to either of us.

I am including that famous letter of December 31st here, altho you yourself may have seen a copy of it before this—I thought then that Van Loon had it coming to him, and I still think he had it coming to him. A re-reading of that letter today, almost ten years later, convinces me that everything I said was substantially correct.

Dear Hendrik:
. . . Apparently you have found the post of glorified Lecturer, Barker, Ticket Seller, and Professional Host for the Cunard Line preferable to carrying out agreements to speak before distinguished audiences. Despite all the ballyhoo, on a reservation basis, the excursion is not such a howling success. There have been bigger and better trips without you as the drawing card—it disgusts me every time I think of you having sunk to the level of the moronic creatures directing—as Host or Hostesses, according to their perversions—the lectures and the tourists on various excursion steamships cruises. . . .

Although a great literary genius, you are still but a human being who has prostituted his Art to Commercialism and therefore no longer entitled to abuse the rights of others, in a world where a lot of people have to live together.

I am sorry that I have been forced to write you as frankly as I have, but then I had to do it, because of your lack of appreciation of true friendship and common ordinary decent conduct. The real fault perhaps lies with your friends who, because of their admiration and devotion to you, have gone on overlooking your bad manners and insolent ways. . . .

I hope you had a miserable Christmas, for that might in some small way have atoned for the shabby treatment you have accorded others for years. . . .

Sincerely,
[Signed]

While the construction work was going forth furiously at Melvale, Jarmila M. took the train to Poughkeepsie one morning and I met her at the station. Henry drove me down from the farm and I dropped him off at a gas station with his transportation back to New York, while I took the car over—met Jarmila and went to the Nelson House for lunch. It was a beautiful day and we were able to drive with the top down—altho winter was about to descend upon us it was more like Fall. From the Nelson House we crossed the River and drove down the West side to West Point, where we stopped at the Thayer Hotel. Returning to New York, I left her off at her hotel where she proceeded to freshen up a bit and then she joined Melba and myself at the St. Regis for a late dinner.

We drank a lot and after dinner we undressed and the three of us went to bed together. She loved Melba, sucking hell out of her cunt —while I fucked Jarmila from the rear. Then to top it off, Melba sucked my cock off while I ravaged Jarmila's lovely cuzzy with my hot tongue, until she came with spasmodic burst of love flow. Those two girls—the one blonde and slender, the other jet black and buxom, both with beautiful bodies—were red hot with passion—when I had had enough I left them to their own devices for the balance of the night, while I retired to the guest room to recuperate. Jarmila was really hot about us both—she always contended that she was torn between Melba and myself—she never could quite make up her mind which of us she loved most. She was an ethereal creature heavenly to look at and wonderful to screw. . . .

We were having a dinner party the night she sailed, but I left the party long enough to give her a farewell suck in my study, and then screwed her on the way to the pier in Brooklyn.

On the 23rd of December, the vans from the Chelsea Storage arrived with all our belongings. The chimneys had been built, the plumbing installed, the bathrooms were in working order, the lights on, the house was heated, the spring water was running, the telephone was connected, and the painters were putting on the finishing touches.

We were in for Christmas—a white Christmas on our own farm. Melsing and I set forth with the chief handy man (Hoagle) the afternoon of Christmas Eve for our own woods, where we found the ideal pine tree, which we cut down, brought back to the house and set up in the living room—it reached from the floor to the topmost rafter—it had been a struggle, but we made it.

Melvale was 128 miles from New York, and with the roads a good deal narrower in those days than they are today, and traffic much heavier, and parkways but for a short 30 miles of the trip, it took us on the average of 2½ to 2¾ hours from the St. Regis to the farm or vice versa. . . .

1933 had certainly been a full and vigorous year—it started out with the trip to New Orleans—it wound up with the farm at Melvale. In between had been the House Boat *Sydney,* the World's Fair at Chicago, the trip to Europe, the affairs with Claire and Jarmila, the La Guardia campaign, the falling out with Van Loon, stock market manipulations and trading, the passing away of our dough with easy living and sex orgies.

1934

The transition from 1933 to 1934 was rapid and marked a definite turn in my life—a life full of twists and turns that had now turned rural with a vengeance—and a frantic almost panicky effort on our part to save a little of the thousands that we had scattered to the four winds. . . .

We had spent Christmas at the farm but the bright lights of the big city were irresistible for the New Year's celebration.

We still kept a suite at the St. Regis—we owed them so much. Hamilton Pell threw a party atop the Hotel Delmonico—Freddie Davenport and Jarmila were there—it was festive but not rural— Melba especially was finding the change over from fast-moving urban life to slow-tempoed country, irksome.

When Hendrik failed to do our letterhead which we were going to use as a Christmas card, we decided to get out a mimeographed sheet to send to our friends in lieu of a Christmas card, telling them all about the pleasures and hardships of life in Columbia County— or the "Trials and Tribulations of Country Life in America—" . . .

Everyone thought we were "lousy" with dough—we were such free spenders—Mother thought so too—when as a matter of fact we were but two jumps ahead of the sheriff most of the time. I was trading heavily in my Wall Street Office, but my gains were small.

The wallop I received the previous summer when Ham Pell bought instead of selling liquor stocks, in violation of orders given him on long distance from the West Coast and then got the money out of my account from Bowen of the Corn Exchange without authority from Miss Murray or myself to the tune of $10,000, had been a blow hard to recoup on a sluggish market.

The office eventually grew to be a place to go to receive summonses, in suits from creditors to collect large sums. In fact at the end that was its principal activity.

We paid $1.40 for two lamb chops at the St. Regis in those days, but up in the country we could buy two whole live lambs for that amount.

It was bitterly cold that winter (1934) at Melvale—we kept the Lincoln at Nassau, 8 miles away, or in Albany—using the station wagon or the cutter (sleigh) to get in and out. The drifts of snow would be ten to twenty feet deep in the cuts along our drive-way into the place and the highway ploughs couldn't get in for days—we only kept the road partially open by the utmost diligence, and that took the constant effort of six men daily. Even then it was closed completely on many days. . . .

Chickens and cows were scarce—the State discouraged breeding in single lots—they wanted you to do it wholesale or not at all—and the Federal Government was out to make it as hard as possible to raise anything. The State said the local people shouldn't keep single milk cows—they wanted the ruralites to buy their milk, cream and butter from the big distributors—more sanitary said they, more dough to the milk barons we said—and so it was.

When we first arrived at Melvale, the local telephone company wasn't able to put in a private wire—didn't have the copper and the entire community would listen to our long distance calls.

I suspected a Mrs. Magill of being the worst offender—so with the aid of Hank Van Loon I framed her.

One night after the usual conversation with Hank I asked him if he had heard that Mrs. Magill (the treasurer of the Sewing Guild of the local church) had stolen the church money in her care. Our last words were hardly out when a shrill excited voice (Mrs. Magill's) shrieked over the wire, disclosing her tuning-in presence, "No such a thing—it's a lie, it's a lie—" and then bang went the receiver.

Altho the local telephone company was very independent and we had lots of trouble with them, they finally strung the private line out to the house—that helped some but the operators in the country exchange always listened to our choicest bits—they got much more fun out of tuning in on our wire than tuning in to their radios.

The great question that January was whether life was really beginning for the Squire at age forty.

I had always lived the usual high pressure life of New York, nothing but rush and bustle—accomplishing little or nothing—on the island my ancestors had settled—now I was to see what farm tempo would do for me.

I felt we were living too fast in the machine age—in olden times men built for permanency, homes were handed down from generation to generation. Today nothing is permanent—new buildings have a life in peace time of but 15 or 20 years—men lose their homes, their savings of a lifetime overnight. In the twinkling of an eye all is swept away by the shifting quicksands of our ever-rapidly changing economic modern way of life in America. Just when men feel they have achieved the success they have always desired, when they believe themselves on the firmest ground obtainable, all about them crumbles and is laid waste. That was true in 1933–1934 when we bought Melvale and it is truer today than ever—only today, thanks to the global war, it is worldwide. The monuments that men have erected over the ages are destroyed in the flash of a second by steel hurtling downward from the skies—such are the ravages of the machine age. It's all so in vain —it always has been so and it always will be so, peace movements to the contrary not withstanding. . . .

We found that the farmer was more regulated and dictated to by the State than the city dweller. The Farmer is told how to farm his farm, how to raise his cattle, what he can raise and what he mustn't breed or grow, what to sell his milk for, and is taxed for this, that and the other thing—he cannot even have a gun or a dog to protect his home without permission from the state—and his cider must not get hard, for that is a crime too.

In February one very stormy night, we returned from New York

—it was fifteen below—the wind howled and the snow had drifted high.

We drove out from Albany in a cab—the driver left us at the entrance gate on the main highway. It didn't look so bad at first but the cut was impassable—so we started across the fields. We had wired the farm superintendent to have the cutter at the gate but we were late—we had dillied in the Falcon Room at the Ten Eyck for a nip. It being bitterly cold, he had returned to the house when his fire died out—our men were always so considerate of our horses. It was tough going—time after time we were in the snow drifts up to our middle with hardly the strength to drag ourselves up and out and on—poor Melba dropped exhausted twice.

That quarter of a mile was the longest quarter of a mile I have ever travelled—it took us nearly an hour and a half to make the house. Calling was useless—no one could hear—more than once it looked like the end was going to be right there in Columbia County. . . .

The servant problem became quite a problem at Melvale—urban maids didn't go for the hardships of the country and the country people were not cut out for waiting on city folk. . . .

Mother hung on thru February—sinking faster and faster. On the 9th of March she passed away at Elise's. The day before she died I went into personal Bankruptcy—she never knew, she and father were spared that humiliation. I did it quietly, using my first name William and my middle initial. My schedule was something to behold —I failed for over a quarter of a million.

At Melvale it was always a great relief to learn that our innumerable callers were frigidaire salesmen, horse and cattle dealers, automobile salesmen, fertilizer salesmen, feed salesmen, tree salesmen, furniture salesmen, etc. and not process servers. We had a hard time getting accustomed to country solicitation. From our city experiences, we always suspected the worst of strangers—and awaited the inevitable presentation of that slip of white paper (known as a summons and complaint) with palpitating suspense.

We were happier in Columbia County than we could have been in New York—Columbia County was opposed to reform and progress, and while we inwardly admit that both are essential, if the animal is to survive, we, in our old age, are satisfied to let things be as "they be" and watch governors come and governors go while the State goes on forever, as the younger generation sweats and fumes and chafes at the bit.

By the last of February, the financial pressure had become quite unbearable—there wasn't any light. I engaged Sam Falk to take me thru bankruptcy—not a pleasant performance at best—it's a job that requires some one with skilled training, with a particular aptitude for such work in order to assure a safe journey without complications, avoiding the pitfalls that might cause difficultes with the Federal Government. . . .

In February 1934 I predicted that the New Deal Administration would eventually fail and in the long run we would all return to that time-honored game of dog eat dog and the survival of the fittest, to solve our problems in the trenches, in the air and on the high seas. And that's exactly what happened. I also said in that issue of the Booklet—*Moo*—the question was simple—either the machine would have to be destroyed and the race returned to manpower or man would destroy himself, and destroying himself is what he has been doing these last three years.

It is interesting to note our political dogma or private views on public matters in that year 1934, and I think I shall set them down now before continuing with the retailing of the bankruptcy proceedings. . . .

> We are rapidly racing into a governmental paternalism that may eventually so weaken us as to destroy the nation. The day of strong men and hearty individualism has gone. But all the king's horses and all the king's men, all the Hoover Committee, and all the Roosevelt alphabets with their artificial panaceas cannot defy the time-old economic law of supply and demand. Water will not run up hill, and until man can harness and control the elements, political jugglers cannot reestablish the national or international equilibrium by artificial stimulation.

> The virtues of the modern machine age have proven a boomerang and are destroying western civilization. The saturation point of production can be reached so much faster than man can consume, the world over. In other words, the machine in the home, on the farm, in industry and in business has brought about a vast over-population in this age of mediocrity. . . .

Foreseeing the bankruptcy—and knowing that bankruptcy only clears you of the indebtedness already incurred, especially under a rental lease, and does not relieve you of the contractual obligation extending on and passed beyond the filing of the petition—in bankruptcy, I decided that it was important to get myself clear of my Wall Street office liability. . . .

As to the St. Regis, I had quite a bill there running into $6,000.00

or $7,000.00. It had been my home for some time and while I lived there I had paid from $50,000 to $60,000 for rents and extras.

I didn't want any difficulty under the Innkeepers' Statutes with the St. Regis and while they couldn't have gotten anywhere, they might have made it unpleasant and caused disagreeable publicity. I went to them and gave them a series of notes to cover my obligations. I paid the first two that came due in order to confirm the transaction. That left their attorney without a case. It wasn't pleasant, but there was no other way out. One has to think of one's own skin in such an emergency—and they had made plenty out of me.

Maybe I am a dead-beat—I can't judge myself—but whenever I have the money I pay in full. In fact, I get a thrill out of drawing cheques to pay off my bills, if I have the money in the bank. The hell commences when you haven't got the dough and can't pay. . . .

The services for my mother were held in Elise's home in Red Bank. Mother was buried next to Father in the Ward plot in Trinity Cemetery, New York City.

She hadn't changed the will that she had written in the Roosevelt Hospital the year previous, so Elise fell heir to all the stock in father's lumber companies. At that time, I could have inherited it direct without danger of creditor attacks, but she couldn't have known of that. Elise received the cash and securities in her safe deposit boxes and the cash in her different savings banks accounts. She had around $10,000 or $12,000 in her savings accounts and about $6,000 or $7,000 in cash in her safe deposit box, and there were approximately $7,000 or $8,000 worth of other securities besides the company's stock. All of this went to Elise. She and I were executors without bonds. . . .

I am sorry to have to admit it but I fought with both my Mother and Father constantly and violently.

The rows with Mother were especially bitter during the first year or so after father's death, when Melba and I were very short of cash. I never got over mother's avowed partiality to your Aunt Elise, altho she always denied it. Mother was warped on the social angle— Elise had made an effort to maintain the position into which she had been born.

After your mother and I were divorced, I failed to keep up with my family or strictly social connections—my friendships took on a distinctly democratic hue—cosmopolites appealed to me more than social gad-abouts. My mother, your Aunt Elise and your Mother never could gracefully accept such within their circle—so the strife was bitter. Maybe it was jealousy—Elise and I never liked the same people. She lived an indolent wasteful luxurious existence—I wanted only to know and be with people who were vital and doing things in the world, affecting the daily lives of others for better or for worse. Mother was interested in national and international affairs, well versed in them—but her main concern was Elise's social success and her children. Both the Hurds (Eddie's father and mother) and my father and mother supported them in their extravagant mode of life. . . .

The farm intrigued me more than the business did, and I was harassed in my efforts to get the land broken, fertilized, planted and cultivated. I had to have it ploughed and harrowed and at the same time it was necessary to keep right behind the Lumber Company business. The shavings and the sawdust!

On the 23rd of April, a little more than a month after mother died, I purchased over $300.00 worth of seed from the Cooperative Kinderhook Pomological Association. . . .

I borrowed a thousand dollars from your Aunt Elise in April— it was quite a job getting it out of her—for the purpose of buying draft horses for the farm. We worked three teams there constantly.

I did a good deal of the ploughing, the harrowing and the planting myself.

I conducted a lot of the business of the Lumber Company over the Long Distance telephone—I had a secretary at the farm.

I fired all the girls in the Lumber Company office as soon as Nathan left and started the New York office off with a new crew— the Lumber Company was a great help to us that spring and summer and kept us going until the crops came in and some of the California money loosened up. . . .

Personal bankruptcy is not a very pleasant thing—the supplementary proceedings—when a bunch of small-minded small-income dopes gape in amazement and try to prove legitimate expenditures were for the illegitimate purpose of concealing assets.

A recap for the bankruptcy showed that we spent on our personal activities in January 1933 $1,118.50; February 1933 $8,619.01; March 1933 $1,809.92; April $3,205.98; May $8,918.59; June $11,621.92; July $9,342.82; August $7,425.37; September $2,-125.54; October 1933 $2,505.35; November $1,209.46; December $1,505.31.

Our European trip in 1933 cost $9,421.10, according to the vouchers I retained, but it probably cost two or three thousand more.

We had spent nearly $75,000 in one year for living expenses which was not high for the life we were leading.

298

From December 1932 to January 1934 we spent $49,000 at the Hotel St. Regis. . . .

Between my Bankruptcy, which was an aftermath of the collapse of the Florida boom, Mother's death, the Lumber companies to run, the Airecooling Company, Harry Millar's business, the Stock Market, and the planting on the farm, I was as busy and harassed as a one-arm paper hanger—and as disconnected as this tale of those hectic activities.

On the 31st day of May 1934, I was discharged from bankruptcy by Federal Judge Robert P. Patterson, which discharge was attested by my old friend Captain Charles Weiser (a fine cocksman) clerk of the Federal Court, District Court of the United States for the Southern Distrct of New York.

As it always happens, the unimportant creditors—the small ones —howled the loudest but it got them nowhere. It was their nagging that forced me to bail out of my financial difficulties (through the bankruptcy courts). For 8 years I had tried to weather the storm kicked up by the Florida collapse, but it was a losing fight, the handicap was too great—I never recovered from that mess—that was the beginning of my downgrade march financially. I had gotten in so deep that only large sums could get me out—Melba had been no party to that (it all happened before she came into my life), and there was no reason for her being penalized for my past mistakes or transgressions.

The bankruptcy stigma attached was never to be lived down and so when the mechanics of that performance were completed under the adroit guidance of Sam Falk, I returned to Melvale—a new life to lead, I hoped. . . .

In twelve months at the farm, we had fourteen couples in the house. If the men were good farmers the women were terrible cooks and housecleaners. If the women were excellent cooks and efficient in household duties, the men were impossible. . . .

Government paternalism has done more to spoil good honest labor in this country and reduce the produce for feeding the people than any other factor (before the war, labor wanted to be paid for idling—and much labor is still paid for the same purpose).

War or no war until the Franklin Roosevelt labor gangster, labor racketeer and labor murderer coddling policy—

We first planned a subsistence farm. There was much to be done —the place had not been worked in ages—the house was a hundred and fifty years old, and looked it. There was no one to turn to for advice and guidance. The only publications available on agriculture were years old and were designed primarily for the farmer with a lifetime of experience in agricultural pursuits. There were no primers for the beginner. The local people, the farmer neighbors, the Cornell graduates, the agricultural experts were all lacking in practical, authoritative information or ability to guide or explain or suggest as to the proper treatment of the soil, the proper crops to sow, the preparation of crops for market, the best markets, where to purchase seed, fertilizer, bags, baskets, crates, what crops were plentiful, what were short.

They did not know that a lot of Baldwin apple trees and peach trees in the Hudson Valley had been killed by the previous bad winter —so as a guide to all and sundry on our list of friends, acquaintances and enemies, we have set forth in an appendix some facts gleaned from our first year at Melvale as a contribution to a much needed Farm Primer.

When we first took up farming, the lack of knowledge generally as to the breeding cycles of the live stock was so amazing that we decided to gather together the information which we picked up by experience and set forth such breeding, gestation, and sexual maturity data as we had learned at Melvale. . . .

Some of rural enigmas at Melvale were:

Why it costs more for potato seed than you can get for the potatoes, assuming you can get ten bushels for every bushel planted. Maybe Franklin can answer that one.

Why the N. Y. Department of Agriculture was never able to locate a farmer's almanac, when thousands are published annually? And even Woolworth sells them.

Why no two agricultural authorities agree on any given subject.

In June, 1934, horse feed cost $1.45 a hundred; in August, 1934 it was $2.45 a hundred. That's how the farmer wins. Chicken feed, cow feed, horse feed, pig feed—all going up. The price of farm produce going down. Why?

We spent part of the winter 1933–34—the part when we could get through the snow—pruning our apple trees and then spraying them, only to learn as summer came on, that the trees we took such care of, the trees we had pruned and sprayed and fertilized, would give us fewer apples than the big old trees we neglected. . . .

We planted 100,000 cabbages on our hands and knees— 50,000 grew big (300,000 lbs.) but the hell of it was that by the time they were ready for market, there wasn't any market for them.

300

The following were some of our rural observations that year—

We called on a man about a cow. He wanted to sell the cow to buy cement. It was a grade cow. He had paid $90 for the cow but the market value of the cow was only $35 fall, 1934. Nevertheless, the cement that he had to buy for the farm with the proceeds from the sale of the cow cost him just double what it cost when he bought the cow for $90. That's what the N.R.A. and the A.A.A. and Franklin Roosevelt and the Brain Bust have done for the long-suffering farmer.

An acre—the amount of ground a yoke of oxen can plow in a day.

The farmer gets too little, and the consumer pays too much for produce. . . .

Seasons come and seasons go—farm life goes on forever.

First we were the cherry man, then the strawberry man, the cabbage man, the corn man, the onion man, the celery man, the lettuce man, the broccoli man, the tomato man, the pea man, the bean man, the melon man, the potato man, the apple man, the cauliflower man, the pumpkin man, the cider man, the veal man, the pig man, the turkey man, the goose man, according to the seasonal loads we brought to market. . . .

The farmer has no conception of the urban problems and the urbanite has no conception of the farmer's problems.

Newspaper wrappers never removed, mail never opened on a farm. You're too busy during the day keeping ahead of Dame Nature —and too tired at night.

A farmer cannot be successful unless he has a number of sons to work for him as farm hands in place of hired help. Then he has no cash outlay to make—merely the teeth to feed. . . .

Thirty-five percent of the farms in the United States produce 80 percent of all the farm income—65 percent of the farms produce only 20 percent of the farm income.

The 35 percent have an average income of approximately $2,500 annually, while the 65 percent have an annual income of approximately $250.

The big money in truck gardening is in out of season produce. That's what makes farming profitable in Florida, California and Texas, when the land is purchased right. . . .

The rural routine at Melvale would go something like this most any day—the Daily Dozen—

One of the mares is calling for attention. Attention she craves can be obtained for $15 from excellent stallion.

One thousand strawberry plants have arrived and will have to be set out immediately.

Twenty-five thousand cabbage plants are at the Boston & Albany station. They also crave attention.

Standard Oil man phoned and said he could not furnish drum and pump under N.R.A. code. Buying gas for farms saves from $2.00 to $2.50 on fifty-gallon lots.

Electricity went off during thunderstorm. Oil burners and pails of hot water were immediately put in chicken house as substitute for electric brooders. Quite a few baby chicks lost—seventy-five in all.

Montgomery Ward phoned and said 300 rods barbed wire fencing were not obtainable at Albany, but could be gotten from Baltimore, but this would cost $30 more.

Seed has arrived from Peter Henderson and is at Post Office. Must have attention.

Sows and boar arrived from Bethesda, and craving food and water.

Nursery, in filling order, was compelled to put in fifty first-grade and fifty medium-grade trees on account of bad winter—crave fertilizer.

Plumber held up on account of delay in delivery of his pipe valves, elbows, hydrants, etc.

Peter Henderson shipped plants from Red Bank, N. J. They may arrive Sunday.

The cow came round but we were too busy, so she'll have to wait until next month.

The spring dries up and the cattle cant: "How Dry I Am!" while we fetch and carry water by the gallon to assuage their thirst.

By God, how the cattle eat!—and drink!

Ho hum—nothing to do until tomorrow.

We had 100 hens and raised 400 broilers from little chicks. Our eggs at some seasons cost us nearly fifty cents apiece and the broilers —those not eaten in the house or by the farm hands were sold at a terrific loss.

In the summer of 1934 we planted twenty bushels of Dibble Russet Potatoes certified, at $4.50 per bushel. Total, $90.

We received from the ground, thanks to heavy cultivation, commercial fertilizer and hard labor, 100 bushels, which we sold at "prevailing market price" for approximately 20 cents per bushel. Total return, $20.

From that 20 cents you must deduct the price of the basket or container in which the potatoes are taken to market and sold. Total loss, not counting containers, labor, market expenses, transportation, etc., $70.

We planted about 100,000 cabbages, from which approximately 50,000 survived the woodchucks, the deer, the pheasants, the rabbits, the worms and the drought.

100,000 cabbage plants cost	$200.00
To set them out	150.00
The plowing, the harrowing, fertilizer and lime, preparation, spraying and cultivation of the soil	400.00
Harvesting of the crop, packing in barrels and bags	200.00
Barrels and baskets for shipping	200.00
Expense of marketing, transportation	200.00
	$1,350.00
The cabbages brought us one cent apiece	500.00
Loss on this operation	$850.00

which hasn't taken into consideration the feed for the horses, or any allowance for our time and labor or the grub for the men on the place. But we still have the land, which is probably more than we would have had if we had stayed in the stock market.

Further evidence of what the N.R.A. and the A.A.A. have done for the farmer. All this is on land so rich that the quack grows almost as rapidly as the crop.

"Cider apples" brought 75 cents per hundred. Windfalls $1.25 per bushel, but we only had one-twentieth of a normal crop, and the total income from the apples and cider wasn't enough to cover the cost of spraying, to say nothing of the pruning of the trees.

Cauliflower. We set out 30,000 plants. We ploughed the field, we harrowed the field, we fertilized the field. In addition, we gave each plant a shot of nitrate of soda to speed the growing along. Total cost, without labor, $205; 240 crates cost another $30. Total $235. 2,880 plants matured, were brought to market and sold for $1 a crate of a dozen heads. Total income $240—$5 profit, if you do not charge any labor, transportation, gasoline or packing charges against the crop—the balance of the plants that were doing nicely, thank you, were destroyed by a freeze, a thaw and a freeze.

We sold 4,500 gallons of cider in the Albany area in one month at a profit gross of 2 cents a gallon, but it did not cover the handling costs, the breakage, and the loss when sweet cider turned hard—it hardly paid for the labels and the cleaning of the bottles required by law—oh, well, we had lots of fun selling it—we guess.

In fall of 1934 general retail prices advanced 2.7 while the price to the farmer went down.

The great trouble with the price of farm produce in this country is the fact, whether Franklin likes it or not, that the buyers simply haven't got the money. In 1933, when potatoes were scarce they didn't bring a good price because the people couldn't afford to buy potatoes as scarce as they were at the prices demanded for them, and the prices fell off, so whereas the farmers with the shorter crop should have had the benefit of higher prices, they were unable to get the proper price for their produce.

Mr. President: The farmers in New York State got much less for their potatoes, sweet corn and cabbages in 1934 than in 1933, before the Supreme Court socked you in the eye. Now answer that. . . .

Agriculture is as precarious an occupation as municipal, state and federal office-holding.

We trust this recital of how truck farming pays will serve to encourage you to follow the President's advice and become another one of our competitors, thereby further depreciating the price of farm produce.

Ah! Hell—anyway, we had a lot of fun delivering produce to the garbage entrance of the Ten Eyck and drinking it up in the Falcon Room.

Life on a farm is one continual round of fighting blights, bugs, frosts, droughts, grubs, wet seasons, groundhogs, pheasants, woodchucks, deer, rabbits and other pestilences that infest the crops. It's either the weeds or the bugs or the weather that are struggling to get ahead of or destroy that which man has planted for the benefit of the race and neither the New Dealers nor Franklin D. have ever been able to do anything about it.

We never understood why the American farmer remains so docile in view of the discriminations against him. All winter long he has to hibernate within his farmhouse shell surviving the rigors of the winter as best he can. When spring comes he must till his soil, cultivate it, fertilize it, and plant it. During the growing season when he is harassed by weather conditions beyond man's control, drought or an overabundance of rain, or blights of various kinds, he must cultivate and weed and keep clean his crops. When the crop matures it must be harvested, made ready for market, packed in bags, in baskets, in

304

crates, or in barrels and then trucked to the nearest market place—sometimes that is 100 to 200 miles from the farm. On the market place the produce, the results of his toil, his labor and the sweat of his brow, will bring him anywhere from 400 to 500 percent less than the ultimate consumer pays for his green groceries.

The Scottsboro decision by the U. S. Supreme Court should tend eventually to stamp out that famous old Southern custom of white men raping colored women with impunity—for too long it has been a heinous crime for a black boy to cohabit with a white woman, while white men from the time of Georgie Washington have gayly enjoyed their dark meat—with negroes on juries in the South perhaps the gallants of Southern aristocracy will no longer go scot free when caught forcing their favors upon the black lassies. Let the whites and blacks keep to their own.

The time has not yet arrived for a racial comingling—until it comes let each race respect the other.

How much of the American foreign policy the world over is dictated by the Standard Oil interests? That's a question we would like to have the State Department answer.

The only people that we have found the world over worth a second thought were the sophisticated bellyrubbers who acknowledged that this was a ballbearing universe, revolving every twenty-four hours on a phallic axis, and once having conceded that, forgot it.

Vice by itself is drab and dull. Nevertheless, we are opposed to reformers of all kinds, sorts and descriptions when it comes to the sex life of the people. We are for snappy shows, snappy movies, snappy burlesques and snappy literature—for adults. . . .

Every time we witness a May Day parade of socialists and communists in New York, we realize how far apart and how fundamentally opposed are the rural and urban radicals. Theoretically, they have much in common, but as individuals and types little if anything. A great many of them in the cities would be happier, we believe, if furnished free transportation to Stalin-land.

Great country America—the aristocrats struggle to be common people—the common people struggle to become aristocrats. Think we'll go back. . . .

Chickens, chinamen and New Yorkers have one thing in common—they love to cross the road directly in front of fast-moving vehicles.

It was gruelling hard work at Melvale—hard in the kitchen,

hard out on the farm, it was work, work, work morning, noon and night.

The interludes of getting to Albany were few that summer except to attend to the lumber company's business—and to New York fewer, except to attend to Mother's estate, etc.—we tried to sublet her apartment but without success.

The children when they were home from school loved Melvale. I liked it—it suited me I thought, although most everyone else felt it was incongruous. I liked farm work—I liked going to market—I liked the local people—I liked drinking with the politicos and the newspapermen in the Falcon room of the Ten Eyck.

Bringing your produce into the garbage entrance of the Ten Eyck and going upstairs to drink up the proceeds with judges of the Court of Appeals (the highest court in the state), had its points—if you had my type of mentality. . . .

We left Melvale, I regret to say, before my nature series was complete. To compensate in part for the lack of graphic illustrations, and as a guide to friends who might desire to follow in my footsteps, I prepared a breeding table for all and sundry. There is such a lack of authentic knowledge on the subject in most rural and urban communities.

Speaking of the rural urge to reproduce—while living at Melvale I had the urge to screw one of the sub-normal country maids, the real peasant type, strong in body and muscle but low in mentality, and observe the type of progeny that combination would produce. Somehow or other the consciousness of the complications involved deterred me. I always regretted the opportunity I threw over my shoulder at Melvale for that genetic experiment.

There are so many mental and physical malformations in the country—whether it's the result of the hard life, the incest that is rampant in small places, venereal disease, perversion, over sex-stimulation or what, I wouldn't know.

Farm life is hard—to save fuel and effort, large families, even of long-line Americans, live in squallor all huddled in one large room shut off from the rest of the house, where the cooking, the sleeping, the sitting, the fucking and even the shitting, is done. It's horrible but true—and sometimes they have the stock in with them—that condiion is prevalent all over the country U. S. A. . . . .

What the New Deal economic dreamers never have understood is that farming is a most senseless pursuit, for you sow that you may reap, and then you reap that you may sow—and let no New Dealer

306

for one instant believe that farming is governed by good judgment and labor, even if you had an abundance of both, but by the most uncertain things—winds and tempests, rains and drought—and above all, as Edward Gibbon once said, let all farmers beware for "all taxes at last fall upon agriculture." And never forget that while the farmer fattens most when famine reigns, he is lean most of the time.

In cultivating any place and producing from the soil you must always remember that constant tillage will exhaust any field.

I liked to plough—I liked to cultivate—I enjoyed cutting the hay—I enjoyed raking the hay—I enjoyed putting the hay in the loft, filling the silos with corn and then as our crops matured, taking them to the City market and to the farmers market at Menands. Some of our produce was so fine that the local hotels displayed it in their windows. The Ten Eyck specialized in Melvale Melons—paid us $8.00 per barrel of eight—but they were all the same size and shape, every day.

The De Witt Clinton and other hotels and restaurants plugged our produce and put it on display. . . .

From July on, we were on our market stand most every day but Sundays—it was a lot of fun, but little money. We had planted many of our crops such as cabbages and cauliflower on our hands and knees—some of the plants we had put in with a horse drawn planting machine borrowed from a neighbor. . . .

I cannot repeat too often the dilemma in which the farmers find themselves—he seldom turns his investment over more than once a year—he must plough his field, harrow it, fertilize it, plant it, and cultivate it—he must fight against insects, groundhogs, moles, rabbits, drought, and in the case of cauliflower he has to take the leaves of each plant and bind them over the tops of the cauliflower with rubber bands in order to prevent the sun from scorching the white heads as they mature.

The animals of the forest will make a good farm their haven unless they are driven away. It's hard going, noon and night and then you have to buy your boxes or your baskets, and after harvesting or picking your crop, get it to market as quickly as you can—if possible, before the market becomes deluged with a seasonable crop. More often than not the poor farmer goes thru all this work only to take his crop to market and find all his neighbors there with tomatoes or corn like his or what have you, with little to choose between his produce and theirs and no buyers.

The tomatoes and the corn are a glut on the market that day—

307

his sales are few—so he is left with most of his load to take back home with no alternative but to feed it to the pigs (if the Roosevelt administration let him have any). It's a disgusting heart-breaking life. Even if the farmer is able to sell his load to advantage, get his crop in ahead of his neighbor, just enough out of season to get the top price, he then returns home with his cash without any prospect of turning it over again until the following year.

A commission broker on the other hand can theoretically turn his capital over every twenty-four hours for approximately 300 days out of the year and a retail produce man can do likewise—but not so the poor farmer.

We tried to protect ourselves against the weak cabbage market by digging ditches in the ground 4 to 5 feet deep and storing the cabbages in the ditches to be brought out in the winter when the price was higher.

It was a good gamble because that year the Texas winter crop was very short—but as luck would have it, the local farmers, feeling that they knew more about it than the city slicker, during our absence while we were on the market, dug the ditches only 2 and 3 feet deep —the result, a hard and heavy freeze completely ruined the tons upon tons that we had buried away, and spoiled our only chance of recovering our cabbage losses. . . .

For a moment this hot June day (1943), I will interlope with a few current observations. . . .

Looking at the war situation objectively I am forced to concede that Herr Hitler is a true German patriot seeking only what he considers to be best for his people—Benito Mussolini likewise is a true Italian patriot, in search of greater territory and riches for his people. The Emperor of Japan is currently engaged in increasing the wealth and territory of his people. Churchill and Stalin are largely and exclusively concerned with the nationalistic interests of their own people —whilst Franklin Delano Roosevelt has devoted his entire time since being elected in a partially successful attempt to destroy the true concepts upon which our Government was founded by the founding fathers—not content with that traitorous behavior, he determined upon a foreign policy of sharing our resources with the rest of the world, lowering our standard of living while raising theirs.

If he can succeed in completely destroying our economic system and reducing the nation to abject poverty with his grandiose globular scheme of sharing everything we have with the rest of the world, he will then have succeeded with his "Franklinstein" cunning to ruin and destroy the land of the free and the home of the once brave—Benedict Arnold was a piker compared to Franklin Roosevelt. . . .

We were at Melvale at the height of the depression, yet with all the unemployment and all of the people out of work and going hungry or selling apples on street corners, it was most difficult to get good every-day farm labor. The New Deal had already inculcated the vicious idea that the laboring class should not have to work—particularly the foreign born or those who had been here for one or two generations. Mr. and Mrs. Roosevelt and the New Deal semites had given these people the impression that they were entitled to something for nothing—they were all looking for government handouts. Government paternalism was their watchword—they wanted the government to buy them farms and to stock the farms for them and to give them the machinery for their farms and guarantee them a livelihood without any effort on their part regardless of the success of their crops.

A nation of non-workers is doomed to destroy itself—only by hard work can a people survive—most morons or mediocrities or mass thinkers never realize that the Government is but a creature of the people, that it gets its support and maintenance solely from the sweat of the people, that when the people do not produce, the Government loses its ability to collect taxes and the entire system collapses. Governments are only as wealthy as the ability of their people to develop their natural resources. When the people stop producing, stop growing, and only take from their government, the whole crashes by its own weight—for without production there is no wealth. . . .

That Fall after Mother's lease ran out, I stayed at the McAlpin whenever in town.

On one of my visits, Ruth R. and I got very tight over luncheon at the McAlpin and we went up to my room. The McAlpin management was very strict so I had George Brelsford stand guard in the hall outside my door—he had had his stenographic agency there since the beginning of the building and knew everyone, housemaids, floor clerks, managers and all.

Ruth was a hot piece of tail very passionate—a wonderful fuck —contrary to Eddie Ballou, who always contended she preferred sucking to screwing.

Ruth was living at the Saint Moritz at the time in a room on the 17th Floor. Late one fall afternoon we were hot at it, shaking the bed to pieces when a rap came on the door. We ceased firing with paralizing shock—there was no way out but thru the door or out the window—we both were sure it was Bob (Ripley). The knock was not repeated—so after a long pause of intent listening and waiting, I withdrew my limp cock from her cooling pussy and dismounted. There shoved under the door was a telephone message, put there by a page boy who had knocked (hoping for a tip), announcing that "Believe It Or Not" would be around shortly. That was enough—I dried my penis while she washed out her cunt. Then we both dressed hurriedly and I left by the service elevator—much pleasanter than a fistic encounter with Bob or a 17 story jump to the "terra firma" below.

I was very fond of Ruth—she had a lovely body, a good mind and knew how to love—she was a Jewess—afterwards she took an apartment at the Navarro on Central Park South and I often fucked her there in her seductive surroundings. . . .

The second Christmas at Melvale was a tough one financially—we were in a hole, we had just had a fire, and the fantasy of Santa Claus had flown out the window.

The fire was a determining factor with us—after surveying our situation very carefully we decided to close the farm shortly after the New Year and return to the City. The struggle with nature had been tough—the fire, the blights, the pests, and the lack of market for our produce had all conspired against us.

The cabbages which we had stored for the winter in beds of corn-stalks in scientifically constructed pits (but not deep enough as I have mentioned before) for sale and for our own table were frozen and of no use.

A stupid lug of a farmhand had left the cellar door open one very cold night and our potatoes were frost bitten.

Another farm boy had failed to put leaves in the beet barrels and besides he had dumped the beets in when they were wet, so most of them had rotted.

The only thing that had survived were the turnips—and we didn't like turnips!

The canned goods that we so carefully laid up for the winter with malice aforethought were fermenting in their jars—others had a lovely green mould over the top, and those that looked all right had a peculiar taste, or too much spice or too little seasoning. In other words, the entire canning project had been a dismal failure, and we hadn't laid in any Del Monte canned goods from the local store, and the heavy weather had already set in. We had ripped the rear end

310

out of the station wagon trying to buck one of the early storms—a week before the fire we had spent two or three days with Dandy and the sleigh, and the Packard, with all hands at the shovels and on the ploughs working constantly day and night to get the road open.

All of this contributed to our decision to return to the great metropolis.

1934 had surely been a strenuous year and I learned many a lesson from nature that had not been imbued in me during our summers at Oyster Bay when I was a youngster or on my visits to Purebred Stock Farms thruout the East in the search of orders for our Sanitary Bedding—baled shavings and sawdust. . . .

Farming in the East on the small truck farms is a hard, unremunerative grind—morning, noon and night—it would have been a complete nightmare had it not been for the interlude in the drinking room of the Ten Eyck with the newspapermen and the politicos. We also enjoyed having our friends come out from New York for a weekend or for visits of a longer duration. Like my father I have always preferred to be visited and to entertain than to visit and be entertained. . . .

The end of 1934 found us considerably in debt with prospects pretty dim. I was in a constant state of trying to get in money to deposit in order to cover checks already given or predated; often I had to resort to sheer kiting between New York, Oyster Bay, Kinderhook and Albany—having my usual substantial hotel credit was a help at the Ten Eyck and also of assistance at the McAlpin in New York.

At the Ten Eyck I would cash checks on the Oyster Bay Bank and deposit the proceeds left over from drinking in the Kinderhook Bank the same or the following day. At the McAlpin I would cash checks on the Kinderhook Bank, or the Oyster Bay Bank and deposit the money in Kinderhook, etc. It was a merry whirl while it lasted. . . .

We had learned a lot about the land, hard labor and laborers— that was our sole asset at the end of the year.

[Before they left Melvale, my father and Melba devised the two "job wanted" ads. That they were ever actually used I doubt.]

JOB WANTED—MALE

Executive, experienced, wholesale lumber, coal, hay, real estate, air-conditioning, banking and brokerage businesses, printing advertising, publishing, editing, commentating. Knowledge farming, politics, photography (16 mm and still cameras); organized and successfully managed national banks, export and import companies, 150 commercial, industrial and professional groups for government loans; established 50,000 sales agencies for government securities, organized state-wide political clubs in forty states of the Union. Executive secretary to Governor Miller of New York State; former Associate Director Loan Division of Treasury; published *Nomad* Magazine; manager of Advertising Campaigns and Solicitations; have raised millions of dollars for charitable purposes; written monographs on economics of railroad freight transportation; and many other subjects, such as banking, travel, politics and agriculture; world-wide travel experience. Advertising or publishing business preferred, but any job from office boy to lobbyist acceptable.

Address W. Ward Smith, Melvale Farms, North Chatham, N. Y.

JOB WANTED—FEMALE

Executive, experienced, editorial, musical. Trained concert and radio singer, widely traveled. Extensive European education with leading masters, unique repertoire international folk songs in Spanish, French, Hungarian, Italian, German and English. Programs on WOR, KFI, KNX, KHJ, KFWB, CNR, and on coast-to-coast hook-ups. Former editor world-wide magazine. Complete knowledge magazine make-up, lay-out, caption and copy. Conducted fashion, social, theatrical, motion picture and musical review, columns. Farming, domestic science, editorial or broadcasting work preferred, but will accept anything from musical instructor or copywriter to milkmaid.

Address Melba Smith, Melvale Farms, North Chatham, N. Y.

1935

1935 was to see our return to New York—first to the Mansfield Hotel and then to a sublet apartment at 2 Beekman Place which we subsequently furnished when we took over the lease in October 1935. 1935 was to witness the inception of another burning affair of the heart with complications and ramifications—semitic, but true.

It was the 10th of April 1935 that I first met Ruth G. and succumbed.

In 1935 I headed the Citizens Power Plant Committee—supporting Mayor La Guardia in his campaign for a public Power Plant Authority as a yardstick for determining the proper rates for electrical current in the Greater City.

I had my row with the police over the pushcart peddlers that year which made local history in the inner municipal circle.

I published *Moo*—the second booklet about Melvale our farm—and continued the battle for the reduction of Federal taxes on the Melsing Estate.

On the side I sold printing and managed to keep the O'Connell Press from losing their annual contract for publishing the Fatal Statistical Indices of the City of New York.

In the Spring of 1935 Melba started a regular weekly broadcast on WNYC and an affair with one of the young announcers.

All this I shall tell you about in some detail.

It was not a productive year. It was another struggle—it had its public aspects, but it was not of financial profit. . . .

At the end of January, we packed everything of value to us and sent it back to storage and hied ourselves back to our beloved Metropolis, which we probably never should have left in the first place.

Before our departure we came to New York and canvassed the hotel situation. We first thought of the Iroquois on 44th Street near the Algonquin—but down the street further, near Fifth Avenue, we came across the Mansfield. It was inexpensive, $17.50 a week for a livingroom large enough to park the children when they were in town, and bedroom and bath—the furnishings were not so hot but it was a parking place. . . .

We reached the Mansfield about midnight, unloaded our baggage and boxes and selves, and after tucking the kids in bed, the cars in a nearby garage and ourselves in the bar below, wondered where the next dough would come from. But all hands were glad to be back—for to me, New York has always been home—my roots for too many generations have been too firmly planted here for it to be anywhere else.

We left a couple behind to care for the place, look after the stock and keep the pipes from freezing. They were an indolent pair, but recently married—and consuming one another with screwing—in other words, they were fucking themselves into a decline.

They spent all the money I sent them for the feed, care of the dogs and stock, on alcohol and entertainment in the hot spots in Albany—they busted the station wagon and let everything go to hell.

We stayed at the Mansfield for a month while we searched for a furnished apartment. . . .

We had a lot of fun carousing in the bar at the Mansfield and there, Melba renewed theatrical contacts and got herself a boyfriend.

I busied myself keeping under cover from the farm creditors and trying to get something to do.

We found a furnished apartment at 2 Beekman Place, overlooking the river at an angle east—and the servants quarters of the swanky #1 Beekman Place cooperative.

Directly opposite from our apartment (we had a bedroom, living-room, bath and kitchenette) was the bedroom of a lovely little girl—a cook who cooked in her shorts and entertained her boyfriends between courses. She seldom pulled down the shades that warm spring—even when cooking a big dinner, she would leave the kitchen for a caress—on more than one occasion she was "laid" between courses. She seemed to like it that way best—there were four or five servants in that particular retinue, including a butler, but nobody interrupted. I would get as hot as hell watching them—Melba was out a lot singing and I would come as I watched the cook fucking.

One evening in May she caught on to my interest—saw me watching then after dinner she stripped for my benefit. I, too, took everything off and she would watch me jerk off as she fucked.

Often when her boyfriend was not around she would lay on her bed completely nude and play with herself as she watched me jerk off. I never met her, but that performance went on for several months until the apartment at 1 Beekman was closed for the summer.

In the fall when they returned, it started up again. Why we weren't caught, or the police complained to, I never will know—perhaps if anyone saw us they might have liked the show too much to complain. . . .

All through my life I have always had a feeling of unreality—as if I was bluffing my way through. I have always felt that I was in-efficient at whatever I was attempting—that even goes for sex. I have always had a notion that I was an inadequate lover—that my prick wasn't big enough or my tongue wasn't long enough—women have raved about my rod and in my youth my caresses, but I had the idea that it was just insincere flattery, for what it was worth—like the barber who always greets you with "I was just thinking about you yesterday and talking to Miss Brown (the manicurist) about you." You like it but you know it's the bunk—so when a dame tells you what a wonderful cock you have, you always feel she wants it harder or bigger or a fur coat.

Much of what I have revealed here to you about my life I have wondered whether it were fiction or fact—or just an old man's flight of fancy, especially when telling stories to others, and I have told many of them to all and sundry within the sphere of my acquaintance. When I have verified my recollections with some of the personalities involved or from documentary evidence still in my possession, I have been amazed to find that my memory has not played me tricks.

In my youth my sex interests and behaviour were matters to hide from view—as I grew older I grew bolder.

As a youngster, I thought my varied sex interests, the departures from the straight and basic incision of my sword into the scabbard of the female, was an abnormality peculiar to me, that my sex reaction to lewd pictures, that the thrill of exposing myself to the opposite sex and the reading of obscene literature, was peculiar to me. It never occurred to me that other men and women got hot and came when indulging in such pursuits.

Talking to girls on the phone, getting hot during the off-color or passionate conversation, local or long distance and "coming" while I did so—and my addiction to the practices of the masseuse—I felt set me apart from other men as something strange and peculiar.

While in fact a great lover of my own home and an avid accumulator of personalia I was considered a gay blade with a way with women—a sort of wolf without the "sheeps clothing." How I acquired such a reputation I do not know—perhaps it was largely because I wasn't two-faced about my various affairs, or surreptitious.

Most of the men that I came to know well in all walks of life were doing about as I was doing—and the more successful they were the busier they were at it—but discreetly and under-cover. Most of my friends were busier screwing everything in sight than I was—getting more involved than I was—yet I got the name while they had the game. . . .

[In 1934 my father met Ruth G. and began an affair that lasted some four years. An account of his first meeting follows.]

I didn't take to the idea of dining in Jewish homes on the West Side—I begrudged the taxi fare across town—in fact none of it appealed to me. At the very entrance to the apartment house I balked—Melba protested and urged it would be good liquor and good food without cost, a dividend on the crumbs we had scattered far and wide, so we went in.

That fatal decision was to usher in another burning desire—an unquenchable thirst for an insatiable female.

There were about fifty guests for dinner and we were seated at tables of four or six.

Melba was at a table with Harry Hertz, the wayward husband of the guest of Honor. The guest of Honor and her amour and a Mrs. Benjamin (Ruth) G. were seated at the table I was placed at. Nearly every one there but Harry and Dorothy Hertz were strangers to me. There wasn't a gentile in the place but Melba and your Pa. Some of the others we had met casually from time to time at Dorothy's—such as Mrs. Baron, the Hostess, and Mrs. Goodney (so she claimed) but not impressively enough for me to even remember meeting them.

It was a shock to my staid quakerish background to find that Arthur Kramer, Dorothy's lover, was at her table celebrating her birthday within her husband's very presence—

The cocktails before dinner were potent, and as the meal progressed the liquor flowed freely. Everyone was gay, and the Jews revelled in filthy stories—men would come over to our table to felicitate Dorothy and drink to her health—and use the occasion as an excuse to drop a dirty one or two—some were clever, others just "stank." The women who came to the table would do likewise and would all but open your pants and take your cock out. Their yarns were good and dirty—nothing but sex.

Ruth (Mrs. G.) and I got along fairly well until I caught her switching scotch and rye on me and that annoyed me. I was good and tight—she was lewd to the point of being neurotic—she got me hot as hell and I felt her all over—she fondled my cock under the table as my hand caressed her cunt. I was good and drunk. In my annoyance over her switching the drinks I proceeded to say what I thought of the Jews, making it very clear to Dorothy, Arthur and Ruth and anyone who might be standing by that the yiddish termites had ruined the beloved, fair City of my aryan ancestors—Holland (dutch) and English who had settled here and done so much to found and build up the town only to have it pass into the hands of the Jews—the miserable lice that they were and are the most hated and contemptible peoples on the face of the globe—a people, truly without a country because no one wants them.

I denounced them for their crooked financial practices. Nothing that I said seemed to faze them in the least—I finally reached the

316

stage where I could hardly stagger to the bathroom to piss—about then the party broke up.

Ruth had given me her private telephone number before I got too drunk. Her husband strangely enough had been at the table with Melba and Harry Hertz as had the Hostess.

On the way out I was still boisterous and "horney" and denouncing the Jews, declaring to all that I hadn't wanted to come anyway.

Ruth G. was living at the Majestic Apartments, on the spot where the famous old Majestic Hotel had stood, the corner of 72nd Street and Central Park West—higher type than West End Avenue but still 100% Jewish. It was an attractive apartment with terrace and plenty of room, furnished conservatively and in good taste. . . .

To get on with this (tail) tale—about ten PM that Friday a collect call came in from Cornwall-on-the-Hudson where Melsing was attending New York Military Academy.

I accepted the call altho they had called for Melba—Melsing had been stricken with double mastoid, had been rushed to the local hospital and placed under the care of Dr. Stillman (brother of James Stillman of the National City Bank—Flo Leeds of Indian Guide fame). He was an excellent doctor—his wife and your mother had been good Junior League friends in their youth. The School principal wanted authority to have Melsing operated on at once. There was no way of getting up there at that hour or of getting hold of Melba. I had no idea when she might get home—she had acquired the habit that spring of staying out late upon one excuse or the other—and usually returning home in the wee small hours of the morning with that innocent look in her eyes "having went." The attention that Freddie Davenport showered upon her the previous Thanksgiving and subsequently had gone to her head. She had been having affairs with Davenport, the boy at the WNYC radio station, Oscar Cooper, "Beau of Imogene Snowden," Eddie Ballou, T. R. Smith, Harry Millar, Renato Bellini, Joe Lilly, Charlie Bayer and Henry Clive and maybe others that I hadn't caught on to. So I told them to go ahead and operate—before doing so, however, I talked with the doctor up there and doctors in New York and all agreed that it was the thing to do and do quickly.

Melba did not arrive home until after midnight, full of phony alibis. I told her the story and she phoned the school and arranged to go up on the first morning train—she was hysterical and terribly upset that she had not been home when the call came in.

I had to remain in town in order to raise the dough for the operation.

En route to the train Melba phoned Ruth and told her what had happened. Ruth insisted that I come to dinner anyway—that was a mistake for all hands.

At noon I learned that Melsing had come thru the operation all right and so I went to Ruth's for dinner. It was a large party and I sat on Ruth's right—which marked me as a new something or other.

The dinner went off well enough—much conversation about Melsing, etc. After the meal was over in true semitic fashion the card tables were brought out—not playing cards, I was an odd fellow in more ways than one (I do not play cards—I don't know how—I am not interested). . . .

Ruth and I spent a great deal of time out on her terrace that evening and we took a lot of kidding from everyone whenever we came in.

Her husband, Ben, made a point of commenting after one of our terrace sojourns that Ruth was fickle—that no matter how much she philandered, she always returned to him. In fact he told me that I was just another passing fancy.

That night we agreed that on my return from Cornwall the following day we would meet for tea at the Plaza. God what hot pants I had for Ruth—I could hardly contain myself—but I was devoted to Melsing and I determined to visit him in the hospital the next day. So Ruth would have to wait until evening.

I took the early train up to Cornwall and spent the day there, leaving early enough to get back in time to keep my date with Ruth.

I felt sure that Melba saw thru my subterfuges when I didn't stay the entire afternoon at Cornwall. But Melsing was doing well and I was on the hunt, my blood was tingling and I was almost on my prey.

I arrived on time but didn't stay at the Plaza too long, just long enough to acquire an edge—drinking out in the open was still a novelty in those days.

On some flimsy pretext we went to my apartment at 2 Beekman Place. My real reason was that Melba was to call me there about Melsing and it was a good place to screw. There I fucked little Ruth for the first time less than a week after we had met at the birthday party.

She was a hot primitive number and gave me one hell of a work-out. We kept at it all evening until we were both exhausted.

When it was all over she left but forgot to take her gloves which Melba discovered on her return from Cornwall. . . .

Having tasted of that luscious cunt with my cock and tongue, I craved for more. Ruth was brazen, cruel, neurotic, erotic, imbued with certain sadistic tendencies—mental rather than physical.

Ruth had been born in Odessa and brought here as a child. Much of her early life was spent at Sea Gate—almost 100% Jewish—low type. Sea Gate was the once lovely haven at the entrance to New York Bay of well-to-do "micks" (Irish Catholics).

Ruth spoke fairly well—dyed her hair blonde (on her head)—and was an inveterate reader. She had drive and a great deal of force and singleness of purpose. She was anything but a beauty—very Jewish in physical construction. With the characteristic hump on her back, well developed tits and small hips.

Ruth had wandered astray from Ben on another occasion—an affair that had lasted for several years and then blown up and she had returned to her husband's bed.

Ruth had a daughter about 9 years old to whom she professed great devotion—she was a nice child, very quiet, a definite Jewish type. Ruth kept her mother hidden from me—she was orthodox. Her brother had been mixed up in some shady business, he could not practice dentistry under his own name, and he and his mother lived in a house Ruth provided for them at Sea Gate. . . .

Her friends always contended that the money was hers—at one time I think Ben had been connected with a shady bucket shop but Ruth always denied it. Her maiden name was very Yiddish—that was the English translation of the Russian—I have forgotten what her first name in Russian was—I liked it better than Ruth but couldn't pronounce it. She always contended that the money was Ben's that he had made it.

Two Jews publishing a couple of men's furnishing trade papers for wholesalers to advertise to the retail trade stores the styles in men's clothes, decided to get out a men's furnishing general magazine to help the retailers educate men to changing clothes and fashion in men's gear.

They (Dave Smart and William "Bill" Weintraub) called the magazine *Esquire*—it didn't go over well at first with anyone but the "fags"—then women bought it but the advertising was for men. The circulation was special and limited and the sources of advertising revenue scarce. The publishers—whoremasters at heart—were in deep water financially. Bill Weintraub knew Ruth and Ben—he was of their smart Jewish social set—first generation immigrants in the United States.

Smart and Weintraub (the publishers) were desperate—they had to get money to keep going. They took their troubles to their affluent friends Ruth and Ben, who by then had moved out of the Coney Island Ghetto (Sea Gate) to New York's smart middle class Jewish apartment, the Majestic. The Jews migrate from one Jewish neighborhood to the other as their fortunes increase—their financial affluence is all they have in life. They have to climb always upward until they reach the heights of an exclusive Christian community, which they buy into over the misfortunes of some broken down aristocrat—and then they take over, destroying the entire section for anyone but Jews—when the Jews have ruined a place then the niggers move in and that puts on the finishing touch—but I have been over all that in detail before.

Well, Ruth loaned Bill the money to keep *Esquire* going. Weintraub wanted to give them stock but they wouldn't take it—Ben said that if the paper were saved Bill could pay back the loan at six per cent—if it failed he could forget it. Well, that dough was just enough to keep them going until the repeal of prohibition when the big, new (previously unheard of) Jewish liquor companies (which had been speedily organized after the repeal of prohibition) seeking a truly man's organ as an advertising media that was read largely by women—slightly on the risque side—found in *Esquire* their perfect medium—and Weintraub & Smart turned the corner, out of the red into the blue. . . .

I developed the habit at first of dropping in on Ruth of an afternoon for a drink and a bit of wooing. Much of my preliminary courting all my life has been done on the phone—that is usually my approach, lengthy talks—it's cheaper and stalls off complications. You can talk to a girl on the phone for an hour for 60¢ and it appears extravagant, but to take her out will cost from $1.50 minimum to five or ten dollars an hour depending where you go for liquor or food or whether it be peace or war time—and an evening out may run up to a hundred bucks and during the speak easy era the sky was the limit.

Shortly after Melba returned (from nursing Melsing back to health) she attended a luncheon that Dorothy Hertz gave at the Sherry-Netherland. Ruth was there and trying to be vivacious, blandly announced that she was pregnant, whereupon the scintillating Melba never at loss for words on any occasion, quick as a flash facetiously shot at Ruth, "You must have found Ward a pretty good lay." Ruth was speechless—she never forgave Melba—but she had brought it on herself, she had given Melba a perfect opening. Ruth was a flop at repartee—she had no fast come back. Melba had scored—a ruthless jab as she invariably did whenever their paths crossed which was

320

seldom after that. This had much to do with Ruth's hate of Melba—she was no match for the firebrand from the Sunset State in a wordy battle—but between the sheets that was different. Ruth had ways of her own and her tormenting preludes to sexual intercourse were irresistible to one of my temperment, who always sought to conquer.

I would rather argue my way to bed than caress my way to the best lay in the world—the more violent the mental abuse the greater the pleasure of the eventual conquest. Ruth knew this by instinct or design and played upon that weakness of mine masterfully.

She would invariably hang up the phone whenever I called her—that is as soon as she knew who it was. After you persisted with frequent calls—during which attempts she would even leave the receiver off the hook for varying periods of time—she would condescend to talk. At first the conversation would be devoted almost entirely to her annoyance at my persistence—then she would be argumentative about some picayune thing and declare that she would never see me again, that there was no need of my calling—she wouldn't, simply wouldn't talk to me that she was fed up with me etc. This would go on for an hour or so and wind up by my coming up there to her apartment, meeting her for lunch or dinner or cocktails and screwing hell out of her—she loved her "nookey."

Her friends and Melba thought she was kidding when she announced she was pregnant but she was with child—I had knocked her up.

Melba became very suspicious the first evening I returned home late for dinner after that with a sun burned face (gotten on Ruth's roof) and I suppose some rouge that wouldn't come off—plus the gloves, plus a tip from Dorothy Hertz that Ruth had been singing my praises far and wide. I passed the sun burn off with the statement that I had been sitting on a park bench writing copy for *Moo* and hadn't noticed the sun beating down upon me.

I was very frank with Ruth about my finances—I told her right off the bat that there wasn't any money to play around with—that's why that April, May and June I saw much of her daytimes (her daughter was at School), in her home, on her roof, and on her liquor—frequently lunching with her in her own apartment.

Ruth spent a great deal of money on clothes—and her lace negligees were numerous and seductive, designed to give her height and take the Jewish hump out of her back.

Her maid was aware of what was going on for I mauled her in her living room, on the terrace, in her dining room, in her bedroom—

and fucked her all over the place, usually departing before her daughter arrived home from her school and playtime activities.

Once a week she had her Mother and brother to dinner—once a week she had dinner with them at Sea Gate—once a week she had dinner with Ben's family in her own home or theirs. On Monday nights Ben didn't come home for dinner but was usually home by ten-thirty. Sometimes she didn't go with Ben to his family. Sunday Ben played golf all day. Saturday night they always entertained or were entertained.

When I first saw her ice box and cupboard I was shocked—plenty of liquor supplies but no food to speak of in the ice box or on the shelves or the pantry. She ordered from day to day from an expensive chain grocer, Gristede's and never had anything over—this horrified me because a full larder has always been the pride and joy of my life. . . .

One evening (a Monday night) in early June I met her down stairs in front of her apartment—we were to go for a ride in her car (a big Cadillac). She thought it safer to go out in her car than in ours—she was afraid of Melba. As she stepped across the doorway she called my attention to a twenty dollar bill on the sidewalk. I told her to pick it up it was good luck. As she did so she announced that since we had found it we should spend it.

So we decided to go to dinner and hit upon a Japanese place between eighth and ninth Avenues on West 58th Street. I had gone there with Henry Clive and Melba and Sonea and had liked it and Ruth loved oriental food—Chinese or Japanese. It was called Miyako —afterwards it was moved to 20 West 56th Street and for a while after Pearl Harbor was closed—but then it was opened again.

The House of Chan when it was on Broadway between 56th and 57th Street was a favorite of the Jewish clique—it was Chinese.

But back to the Miyako. We got very drunk from drinking and very hot from ????—excitement, first fighting then caressing, then she had to pee. The Miyako was in an old fashioned brown stone house —high stoop, the dining room on the first or parlor floor, the privy on the floor above.

It had been the master's bath in days of yore—the tub had never been removed. I stumbled up the stairs after her—my ever present weakness to be in the can with a female getting the best of me—and we went into the toilet together. This seemed to excite the Japanese no end—or on-end for they jabbered excitedly like a lot of monkeys.

We were so drunk and hot that we fucked on the can—being in

the "little girls room" with a female has always made me hot as hell. As we stumbled out dishevelled and unkempt, we fell over a Jap who had been at the keyhole—the little yellow bastard had been peeking and jerking off as he watched—in my drunkenness I showed him Ruth's cunt and this excited us all over again and I laid her out on the top of the stairs in the hall outside the can and gave her another shot— as the son of nippon spilt his load all over the carpet. The proprietor and his wife or some Japanese female belonging to the joint came running up the stairs and got us straightened out and back down stairs —fortunately for all concerned we were the last in the place. With another drink we paid the cheque and departed. Ruth drove the car— why or how we got over to Park Avenue I will never know, but there we were going up the Avenue. Twice she drove up on to the Center garden plot right up over the curbing. I had come twice in the restaurant but my cock was still hard—I had it out of my pants—she was drunk and trying to drive and feel my cock as I in my cups played with her pussy—she loved to play with me and be played with in the car.

Ruth liked to fuck in the car—she missed a couple of lamp posts by inches.

We crossed the park at 72nd Street and at the half way loop or parking space overlooking the 72nd Street Lake, we parked and got out. We wandered up a knoll there and I laid her on the grass behind a bench and some bushes.

Everyone was doing something at that late hour—boys were finger-fucking their girls on park benches and fucking and sucking them off in the bushes, or on their ass in the grass—fairies were picking one another up or making new conquests or converts—masturbators were jerking off as they watched boys and girls together, or fairies or lesbians doing their stuff—cock sucking and buggering were rampant —blackmailers and petty thieves were doing their prowling—some just came out to walk their dogs for a pee or crap before turning in for the night.

It was dangerous, exciting and conducive to fornication in its many varieties and perversities. It had always been a favorite haunt of mine since early childhood—for finger-fucking, straight diddling, cunt-lapping or masturbation—and on occasion I have sat on a bench in the park and jerked off as some fellow fucked his girl—and at other times I have pulled my pudding as some other guy on the same bench pulled his and while some fellow across the pad put in his rod, or a dame went down on her boy friend—it was hot stuff—it saved room rent etc. In the warm weather the cops were few and far between and walked with heavy tread on the pavement—the place was poorly lighted in those days and the benches were always in the shadows.

The risk with Ruth was twofold—blackmail if followed home or robbery if her jewels shone too brightly—she always wore row upon row of glistening diamonds—all over her wrists were big wide bracelets, typically Jewish, worth a small fortune.

In addition there were her priceless rings—diamonds, diamonds everywhere.

Ruth liked it on her ass on the grass or anywhere for that matter —those that had autos did their fucking mostly in their parked cars. In the parked cars in Central Park, the favorite practice was for the girls to suck the men off.

That night in the park after we found the twenty dollars (I always thought she planted that dough as a face-saving for me—a way of having a night out on her own money), the night of the Miyako incident, I fucked her three times on that hill and then I went down on her and as I sucked off the load she fainted. It was the first and only time she had ever passed out on me—but we were pretty drunk—too much liquor and too much fucking had been too much for her.

It took her some time to come around—and it scared the piss out of me. I didn't want a dead woman and married at that on my hands in Central Park. I was always in mortal terror that we would be held up and she would be robbed by some bum or thief in the park. If that had ever happened everyone would have said I had a hand in it— instead of my cock.

When Ruth finally came to I got her to the car and got her home. The ground had been damp—it had rained during the evening while we were at Miyako's getting drunk—and we both were pretty messy sights, covered with dirt and mud and grass stained and human semen —our clothes all askew.

On the hilltop between fucks we had quarreled—and slapped and clawed at one another until we were both bleeding from the scratches on our faces made by our respective nails. She was so intense in her love making quarrels that she often clawed and clawed deep and I retaliated.

It must have been something for the doorman to write home about—how she covered up with Ben, I don't know. She instructed the doorman to send the car to the garage and then kissing me good-night she slapped my face as a parting gesture and went on up to her husband, as I grabbed a taxi and slunk home to Melba. But Melba wasn't home so I removed my clothes, cleaned them as best I could,

324

doctored my face, pissed, washed my cock and then the body and went to bed—a bit more sober than when I had left the Miyako.

The next day we drove out to Jones Beach. She brought along the liquor and the picnic lunch and the balance left over from the "twenty" paid the entrance fee, the parking charge and the bath house fee—she had her own towels.

We spent the day there—she loved the beach—many women do. I got a burn not only on my face, but on my entire body, altho we didn't go near the water. She wasn't much on the swimming end—we read and talked and made love—it was Tuesday and there weren't many there.

When I got home what a time I had trying to hide the body sun-burn from Melba. We never wore any night covering or clothing when we slept, summer or winter. I guess she noticed but kept mum because I had so much on her.

At the Hamilton P.s that year Melba got out of hand at their annual cocktail party—so I left around nine and she remained behind. Melba never wanted to leave a party—I went home and after talking to Ruth on the phone went to bed. Melba arrived about 2:30 AM.

Much to my annoyance she and Eddie Ballou parked in front of the apartment for over an hour and they weren't talking. If they wanted to do that sort of thing it was my contention that they should have parked elsewhere and not in front of the very apartment in which she was living with her husband (still) and children—and I told her so in no uncertain terms.

Most of my friends coveted Melba—many of them made her—all of them thought she would have gone to bed with them had they been willing to betray a friend (me). . . .

A brief interlude—a jump from 1935 to 1943—pardon the inter-ruption.

5:04 PM Sunday the 25th of July 1943 at Smiths Folly on the River—East—in our V for Vanity Garden. Eve in her bathing suit sits across from me in a porch chair—your father is in his shorts only—the fountain is playing in the center of the garden. Convoys are passing by up and down the river—operatic recordings are on the air from New York City on Station WNYC—flash-flash-flash—the music has abruptly stopped and Tommy Crown is announcing that Mussolini has been dismissed—King Victor Emanuel has assumed command of the Italian Army. As the music is resumed we hasten to phone *The New York Times* for verification. Eve remarks, "All worldwide dramatic news seems to happen on Sunday—Pearl Harbor, etc.—England goes to war"—I phoned Elise—she was lying in bed at Chestertown resting from her arduous farm labors, worrying about her men in the armed services—Especially Russell [her son] with Montgomery unheard from for three months.

She was incredulous—she said she would stay glued to her radio —while talking, further details came over the radio. I placed the telephone transmitter near our radio so your Aunt Elise could get the story from our own municipal station which had scored a beat.

Hardly had I gotten settled back to normal to go on with my own little inconsequential yarn and sex revelations than Elise phoned back to say nobody down there had heard the great news—the real beginning of the end. I assured her all the New York stations had verified it—the House of Savoy was saving the seat of Christendom from the ravages of the semitic maniacs ruling the destinies of America and attempting to gain control of the world—but more about that in reflection when I come to it. Man will do well if he does not destroy himself completely.

Maybe the wops are just big talkers and little doers when it comes to physical encounter—they just don't fight, no matter what side they are on (and what a false alarm that turned out to be).

I was wondering what you were doing when the dramatic news broke—

Well, back to the letter and the year 1935—and Ruth and the Barbizon Plaza.

I was getting in deep with Ruth—too deep—I had no intention of marrying her—I was ashamed to be seen in public by anyone I knew while with her, except her own friends, Jewish. . . .

I liked Ruth and enjoyed her society but I did not want to be seen in public with her. She wanted to go to all the leading restricted hostelries in the east as Mrs. W. Ward Smith—and that was not for me—I didn't care how much dough she had, or what fabulous jewelry. Later she told me she had taken all her property, stock and bonds and cash over into her own name and to her own physical possession for the purpose of living with me, marrying me, and keeping me while I got on my feet.

That break didn't end our meetings, although I had to make amends by much extra screwing and wooing.

During all this period Melba and I both went in for massages— she for reducing her bodily flesh and some of the personal pleasure

326

from the caressing manipulation of her cuzzy, and I for the reduction of the extended main organ by proper stroking. . . .

During August I spent most of my time, when not out with Ruth, down at the O'Connell press supervising the makeup of *Moo,* reading and correcting proof and I am a hell of a proof reader of my own copy. . . .

Strange but true—I would not cross a "T" or dot an "I" today of my "Topsy Turvey" platform as set forth in *Moo* in 1935—nine long years ago, and years before there was a second World War.

And here it is for re-reading—

OUR TOPSY-TURVY PLATFORM

We advocate a National Central Banking System.

We are for Federal and State ownership of telephone, telegraph, radio and electric utilities. The Federal ownership of all the coal, oil and timber resources of the nation.

We are for the abolition of credit bankers; partial payment loans on household goods, automobiles, real estate, by private corporations. We propose the substitution of a Federal credit corporation in the place of the present money leeches.

We are for Federal maintenance of toll highways and supervision of all forms of transportation, air, rail, water and automotive.

We are for the development of centralized market places, for the exchange of goods and produce rather than credits.

We would keep the church and the state entirely separate and prohibit all prelates from preaching or discussing political or governmental subjects of a controversial nature.

We believe that voluntary segregation of creeds, cults, and races should be respected. We believe our gates should be closed and our births controlled until all but a normal and seasonal ratio of unemployment has been eliminated, then the gates to be opened gradually and the population increased by a rising birth rate until all the virgin lands within our borders are under cultivation and production.

We are for centralized taxation by the Federal Government, with distribution back to the states, and counties and cities and villages under National Government supervision.

We are for Government lotteries, the parimutuels and for Government-owned and controlled gambling.

We are for the destruction of privately operated policy rackets.

We oppose corporations issuing stock representing anything but cash contributions to their capital structure.

We would eliminate all private utility advertising from newspapers and non-fiction publications.

We believe that not more than one-fourth of the legislators in any law-making body should be lawyers.

We would make public hearings on all legislation, municipal, state or national, mandatory before the legislating as well as the executive branches of the government. We would exclude professional lobbyists from such hearings.

We would pay U. S. Senators $15,000 a year, Representaives $10,000 and prohibit their being engaged in any other activity whatsoever. We would pay N. Y. State legislators; Senators $10,000 Assemblymen $7,500.

We are opposed to crop control, destruction and processing taxes.

We are for a quicker, cheaper and more economical distribution between the producer and the consumer.

We would have the Federal Government allot $2,500,000 to each national party polling over a million votes in a presidential year for campagin expenses. No other contributions permitted.

We would have the state and municipal governments appropriate money for local campaigns to local parties.

We would have the state, local and federal chairmen of the respective parties salaried men paid by their party treasurers.

Political leaders under a statute making it a misdemeanor would be prohibited from discussing legislation with any elected officials.

Moneys should be loaned to farmers with less red tape regardless of their financial condition for periods of thirty-three years or more, at ½ of 1 percent for the purpose of permitting them to discharge their present obligations and to refinance their farms. A tax moratorium of five years should be declared on farm properties.

We are opposed to the squandering of millions to clear up congested areas in metropolitan centers so that modern abodes may be erected for the foreign-born, while not a cent is being spent to rehabilitate and modernize the dilapidated farm homes of millions of Americans.

We are for federal hock shops.

We are for a union of all nations, with legislative, executive and judicial branches, regulating the international affairs of the world, supported by an international air, naval and land police.

The new domestic was Graham De Ryder—photographed one early August afternoon across from the then still-existing Central Park Casino and what a luscious lay she was then and for some years thereafter.

To our Topsy-Turvy Platform as contained in *Moo* we would add a six-year term for President of the United States—nonsucceedable, subject to impeachment, and Congressmen for terms of three years each, but not to exceed two successive terms—Senators not more than two successive terms of six years each. . . .

In the Fall the fellow I sublet the apartment from at 2 Beekman Place moved out and we rented direct from the owner, bringing some of our things in from storage.

Nearly every Monday night Ruth and I went out on a tear on her money—after the stall of finding the first twenty dollars on the street she had no hesitation in offering me the difference between a meal for two at Childs and a meal for two at El Morocco.

She was a peculiar woman—whenever Melba and I would run across her at a night club, and she was always with her husband, she would immediately depart. I never understood why—she would tell her friends that she was afraid I would do something rash—what, I don't know. On several occasions we took a suite at that "creep" hotel, the Coolidge, across from the St. Margaret. One night we drove up in evening clothes, quite tight, bought a bottle, ordered some chinese food and fucked like fools. About two in the morning, still high, we dressed, checked out, drove around the corner to the Metropole and ate roast beef sandwiches with french fried potatoes at 15¢ a plate plus a nickel beer and pickles—then I took her home and crawled back to Beekman Place myself—Ruth didn't like the St. Margaret for sexual intercourse. . . .

The following was released for the Sunday Morning papers of October 6th, 1935—

CONSUMERS PUBLIC POWER PLANT COMMITTEE
299 Broadway
Tel. Barclay 7-1566
FOR RELEASE IN SUNDAY PAPERS

The Consumers Public Power Plant Committee announced yesterday (Saturday) that it had appointed Mr. W. Ward Smith as manager of the campaign it is conducting in behalf of Mayor La Guardia's proposed "Yardstick" Public Power Plant. The Committee is proceeding with the organization of its campaign pending the decision by the Court of Appeals on the application of the Consolidated Gas Co. to prevent a referendum vote upon the proposal at the elections, November 5th. The Consolidated Gas Co. is trying to prevent the referendum on technical legal grounds, but if the company is successful the Committee will carry the fight to the Legislature.

   Mr. Smith, who has been identified with conservative financial interests, accepted the task of managing the campaign and threw himself into the fight despite the fact that his family has been connected with the utility companies and the Consolidated Gas in this city, in high executive capacities, for four generations. The Committee regarded his acceptance as highly gratifying, since Mr. Smith has managed successfully a number of important patriotic, civic, and political campaigns during the last fifteen years. . . .

   [My father directed the campaign for a consumer-owned utility with typical energy. La Guardia, having used the threat of a city-owned plant to force down Consolidated Edison's rate and calculating the political pluses and minuses, lost interest in the issue and the plan was abandoned much to my father's disgust.]

1936

   1935 hadn't been much of a year—Ruth was a liability, the power plant campaign had fizzled, our money was dwindling as was our interest in one another.

   1936 was to offer still less.

   The thirst for wealth, filthy lucre, money, or the possession of worldly goods in excess of one's fellow man has so often been the root of much evil in the world—and that goes not only for evil in the dealings between men but between communities, between states and between nations—perhaps it would be better to define it as greed, insatiable greed.

   Listening to tales of the vagaries of some mortals—tales that were told almost at first hand—jolted me into a realization that before there can be justice and understanding in dealings between nations, there must be a higher standard of ethics in the transactions between men in all walks of life.

   We in this country as a whole are much too tolerant of the

pettifoggery of men in public and private life. Even grand larceny seems to be condoned by the populace at times—and so being condoned is widely practiced. . . .

The New Year, 1936, didn't begin auspiciously and wound up poorly—that year saw the breakup—permanent—of the Melba interlude. I went West to look after the property in her estate and also to further the candidacy of William E. Borah for the Republican presidential nomination—I visited Mr. Hearst as his guest at San Simeon—I made whoopee in a bungalow in the Hollywood hills—I had a violent affair via the U.S. mails with Mary Dunn of Abilene, Texas. I met Frank Knox, then publisher of the *Chicago News* and a potential candidate for President, which eventually materialized into the vice-presidency under Landon—I met Marion Davies and became enamoured of Mary Pickford.

I returned to New York to live for a while in a hall room in Watterson Lowe's tenement apartment—I then moved to the St. Margaret for several months, and eventually took the apartment at 904 Park Avenue, which you visited at Thanksgiving time when you came down from Dartmouth. . . .

In the summer of 1936, I became associated as an Account Executive with the Lawrence B. Whit organization, a publicity outfit, and prepared a plan for publishing an American edition of the Illustrations published by the Holy See. I prepared a plan to publicize Robert Ripley "Believe It Or Not"—and to steer the Provident Loan Society thru troublesome waters.

I travelled the width and breadth of the country, from New York to California by bus. It was an experience, especially that part of the journey when I tried to sleep in a berth at night between St. Louis and Los Angeles—the bunk wasn't long enough and there wasn't any head room to speak of, so you couldn't double up very well.

In the following pages I will try to make 1936 as brief as possible and hurry on to 1937, 1938 and 1939. . . .

At 2 Beekman Place I evolved the scheme for economy's sake of serving small very thin slices of Hormel Ham out of a can on thin slices of French bread with a thin slice of butter for hors d'oeuvres, and a rum cocktail consisting of cheap light rum, gin, orange juice, lemon juice, grapefruit juice, sugar, and ginger ale. It was inexpensive—and you could give a party for 100 people on that diet and with a "chink" to serve it, it would run around $18.00 for everything.

We became known for our Rum and Ham parties.

We also had potato chips delivered from the wholesale dealers that we had dealt with on 52nd Street, during the Parapet days—we served them in the big cans they came in.

The French bread we purchased from a bakery around the corner on First Avenue, the Betsy Ross, run by a funny skinny Frenchman and his buxom wife—the poor bastard had worn himself out knocking his woman up, and baking his cakes and pies and breads.

In the old days before prohibition was repealed, when I first met Melba, I served tuna fish on crackers for parties.

Before I left for the coast, Alma Phipps—her husband was a partner of Harry Hertz—had a birthday party at the Vanderbilt Hotel—liquor flowed freely and the conquests were many and easy that night. The party was downstairs but the Phipps had a suite upstairs for their guests to repair to or straighten out their hair or their cocks or their cunts—and it was a "friggen" swell party of the Englewood in-betweeners. Twenty-four hours later I was on my way West.

A Mrs. Francis H. of Lydecker Street, Englewood, N.J.—a friend of Alma's—was the best tail there—three times we went upstairs and fucked in the bathroom. She had a great deal of money and a jealous husband—I never saw her again.

Before running off into that story which was a hot one, I want to refer a moment to the stupendous rally that they gave Bill Borah in Brooklyn on the night of January 28th.

The Hall was packed—the press pit was overflowing—klieg lights or flood lights for the movie cameramen were all over the place —hundreds and hundreds of stills were flashed of the colorful old warrior from Idaho, that great individualist in domestic and international politics, undependable, unpredictable, an erratic genius, swordsman extraordinary, that silver-tongued orator, that lovable old potato—did a swell job of it thru nigger heckling and all. It was his opening gun in his campaign for the Republican nomination for president, an honor he was never to attain. Few could have been worthier—I did not always agree with the grand old man, but I did admire his brilliance of mind and tool—intestinal fortitude—it was an inspiring occasion. . . .

William Randolph Hearst, the publisher, with his string of dailies from coast-to-coast and his magazines, was supporting for President an unheard of, unknown and untried Governor of Kansas by the name of Alf Landon—a good man, but a colorless one—more of that later on.

332

It was Sunday night, February 2nd, 1936, or rather 2:00 o'clock Monday morning, following a Sunday morning hangover after Alma Phipps' liquid birthday party, Saturday night at the Vanderbilt.

Fortified with the best sirloin steak the Divan Parisien could boast that night at dinner, I was setting forth on my first transcontinental modern motorized stage coach jaunt en route to Los Angeles.

A week before at the same Divan Parisien, Melba and I had awaited Gloria (Mrs. R. Vanderbilt). She was late—she had had a date with her lover, Blumenthal, husband of the Lesbian Peggy F. At that date they had broken off—"Blumey," as she called him was flitting around with the season's debs, forsaking Peggy and Gloria— he found the new crop of fresh young things more to his jaded tastes.

We had a sumptuous repast that can best be purchased at the Divan within reason.

Gloria was full of her former Yiddish lover and how he had let her down. During dinner, among the many anecdotes which she related about herself, Peggy Fears and Blumey and their cunt-lapping, fucking performances, was a story about her sister, Thelma, Lady F. For years, Douglas Fairbanks had fenced around and around, sparring for an opportune opening with Thelma.

Finally, one night while they were still living at the Sherry-Netherland—before they moved to the house on 72nd Street—Fairbanks, Sr. took Thelma to dinner and the theatre and for a nite-cap afterwards to a nightclub. Long after midnight they returned to the Sherry-Netherland and Thelma invited him in for a brandy—and then it happened—the Great Fairbanks laid the former mistress of the King of England.

Fairbanks was all hot and bothered—so hot that he stuck it into Thelma and before he could give her any kind of a workout or preliminary love-making, he shot his load—he just couldn't hold back —and those sisters were accustomed to workouts with finesse.

Fairbanks was chagrined at his own lack of control and flop as a lover—the next day he sent Thelma two dozen American beauty roses with his abject apology.

The trip to the coast was for the purpose of getting an honest lawyer—if such did really exist—one free from the taint of the Barbary Coast days.

Lured by full page bus advertisements in the daily press and in the leading periodicals of the country, claiming that the busses equalled the time of the 20th Century Limited and the Santa Fe Chief at one-half the railroad fare, I set forth on my journey.

There were no sleeping or night coaches out of New York—the tunnels and bridges between the great metropolis of the East and Kansas City did not permit the passage of such super-coaches in those days.

The drivers of those up-to-date chariots on North American highways resembled in looks, youth and physique and vitality and self-assuredness, the pilots of the pioneer airways, the mounted constabulary of the various states, or the North Western Mounted Police —they were God's gift to womenkind.

At that season of the year (mid-winter) sleet, wind, rain and snowstorms blocked the highways and it was sub-zero weather. Few women were being lured forth even by these Adonises for long journeys.

In New York I purchased my ticket thru to the Coast and paid $1.50 to have a reservation made on the night coach out of Kansas City for Los Angeles. The reservation was confirmed and the ticket was bought on the assurance that all connections would be held for this extra express service, which called for a schedule of exactly four days (96 hours) from coast to coast.

On board the bus, I purchased a soft pillow thru to St. Louis for 25¢ and checked my baggage thru to the coast free except for a valuation insurance charge.

I was no sooner comfortably ensconced in my reclining chair than at the very first stop—all seats out of New York are sold by seat numbers and you are assigned your seat before you leave—a bride and groom entered and lowered their seats in front of mine to a reclining position. That was my first discomfort. Being long-legged it bothered my knees, but I twisted and turned until I had assumed a fairly comfortable position, when at the next stop a perfect replica of negro fighter Jack Johnson seated himself plumb beside me and sprawled his legs in the aisle—for the first time I realized my error in having bought a window seat. By this time it being cold outside— 5 above—the heaters were on full blast and the mingled body odors of those who had not bathed recently were becoming unmistakably noticeable—the lights had been dimmed and some snored and some talked.

Every two hours we stopped and a handful of the most venturesome would dismount to partake of a Coke or a hot dog or a ham-

334

burger or the pleasures of the unsanitary comfort stations. And so on thru the night, down thru Somerville (for comfort); Allentown (for breakfast); Harrisburg (for comfort); Lewiston (for lunch); Duncansville (for comfort); and points West. With the dawn came the cold white beautiful snow as we climbed thru the rugged Alleghanies on and on—15 minutes here, ten minutes there for comfort—one half hour for breakfast at a nondescript joint, one half hour for lunch.

During the bleak snowy afternoon a couple of show girls in the rear came up for air—they were just recovering from a hangover of the night before—and proceeded to entertain with dances to amuse the driver, or thrill him. How he kept his eyes on the road and not glued to the mirror no one will ever know. One of the dear things sat down directly behind the young and virile pilot of our caboose and proceeded to rest her charming ankles on each shoulder, much to the edification and joy of those on the front seat—oh yes, I had moved forward as the crowd shifted during the day, the better to afford my legs a place to stretch—and never did I relinquish that point of vantage again—seat #3 to the coast and back.

The other dame, not to be outdone, proceeded to kick the rear view mirror on the ceiling of the bus for a pint of rye—this was too much for our driver. He had to stop the bus for a better view of this stunt, or to be frank, the dame's cunt—especially since the charming girls had no panties on at all. Maybe the males on board should have written New York Police Commissioner Valentine and thanked him for the entertainment—it was the night of the big New York raid on apartments of questionable fame—or was it the night they removed the dance studio signs from the Ripping Seventies? And the whores were leaving New York like rats skipping a scuttled ship on every available bus and train.

At Blairsville, the youthful steward was so overcome with the free display of feminine pulchritude that he couldn't help the passengers on and off with their baggage—he was busy fucking one of the bitches prone on the back seat.

Oh well—the party was fun while it lasted, even if the bus never did quite get going again on the even tenor of its usual way—rye was cheap in Pennsylvania, and it was the reward I offered for the best female high kicker. Nearly every guy on the bus, including the driver who screwed one of the girls in the rear of a comfort station, had a "hard" on—one of the lovelies jerked me off on a back seat as I fondled her cunt before we reached Pittsburgh. . . .

All manner and types of people were travelling. There was a

soldier returning to his post; he was bound for foreign shores. A boy and girl going back to college—women joining their husbands on business trips—drunks returning from a funeral—a farmer going to town—trained nurses out for a spree. There was a girl making whoopee with everybody on the bus, and trying to date the bus driver up at El Paso for the night before she reached her prospective groom, whom she was to marry within the next day or two—and then there was the salesman who travelled the bus, but charged the railroad fare up in his expense account.

Some folks never entered into the festivities—others kept up the fun-making all the time.

When I reached Los Angeles at the end of the delayed cross-continental trip, it was with great relief that I registered at the Biltmore for a comfortable bed and bath.

Bus-riding kinda gets you—it's damned uncomfortable at first, pillow or no—but after a while you get the hang of it and sleep well sitting up, provided the driver isn't a city traffic expert out on the open road, for the city drivers are hell on the nerves.

You get interested in their working hours, the personalities of the different division heads, their families, the pension system, the advantages of the Santa Fe Railways over the Greyhound, and vice versa, the salaries, the mileage they make, the experiences they have in fighting the elements, what they do to keep awake, etc.

The fastest run was from Tulsa to Kansas City—310 miles, 40 stops, 20 minutes for comfort, 65 passengers and their baggage on and off, the aisles frequently filled, 7 hours flat for the entire trip. The Eastern drivers say that people in the East have no respect for the buses or drivers, but in the West it's different and I guess they're right.

One of the drivers stopped suddenly, rolling a pair of fucking lovers off the back seat onto the floor—they didn't know he could see them in the mirror—it was dark, but they forgot the small light burning overhead. I thought that one hell of a trick until at the next stop he turned off all the lights and told them they would have a half hour to themselves unmolested, thereby redeeming himself for his earlier prank.

The segregation of the colored folk in the South and the whites who refuse to ride sitting beside them preferring to wait hours for another bus, was difficult, but necessary.

In the big open spaces, the buses are as fast if not faster than the fastest train and just as comfortable as any plane. Many older men

336

of moderate means spend their winters riding thru the warmer climes, calling on relatives and friends, travelling seven or eight hours a day by daylight, sleeping with friends or in inexpensive hotels at night. They say they see the country that way and learn more about the customs than any other way they could travel, except to drive themselves.

Bus-riding is a trifle hard on the system, but then any form of travel is. The big railroads were gradually buying up all the bus lines and with the aid of the Interstate Commerce Commission, will gradually combine them into a few big systems. Then progress in improvements will start to decline after competition is brought under control.

Romance is always sprouting on the bus runs—sometimes it is only a quickie on the back seat, sometimes it is good for an over night stop at some small local hotel away from the home town, sometimes the spell lasts longer, sometimes it endures for life—but that's the way with man and maid most anywhere, that cocks and cunts find themselves together.

[My father, writing of his trip to California, six years earlier, was distracted by wartime convoys passing up and down the East River.]

The flaw—and most distracting day after day, hour after hour, almost minute after minute—passes a convoy bound in from the sea or bound out to the sea—the procession was continuous.

During the writing of this page alone, four ships raced in on the tide—empty—their gay crews cheering and calling to the nursemaids and mothers and juveniles along the river walk—the channel was but a hundred feet off shore at this point. Most of the boats were flying the stars and stripes, a few the British "Jack," an occasional tri-color, and once in a while the Russian Scythe and Sickle. Now and then a neutral ship would glide by—another has just passed (as I write this) going out—she was heavy, moving slow against the tide, like she didn't want to leave—tanks, trucks and all manner of cases lashed on her decks. She was heavy to her water's edge—now a loaded tanker follows.

All fly the gaily colored international code flags for their clearance or their entry. Those flags even give the somber outward bound ships a festive air, which the demeanor of their silent crews belie—no waving to the girls along the walk, they are sailing out to meet the enemy slinking beneath the sea, to send them sprawling to Davy Jones locker. The toll is great—each man knows the danger that lurks without the harbour gate.

A Carrier has just slipped by, graceful and swift. Her commander's orders over the loud-speakers clearly audible ashore. P.T. boats on active duty, Navy, Coast Guard roar up and down on important business bent—landing barges struggle against the fast-racing tide thru Hell Gate in practice runs for the crews and trial runs for the machinery. A Destroyer has just moved past—as I write and glance up, it looks for all the world like a stage set. They all move by so smoothly they look as if they were being pulled across a stage. Smoke pours from the funnels of the busy puffing snorting little tugs—alongside those that don't handle well in fast tides. The whistles blast and blast and blast day and night. Thick heavy soot lays down upon the garden tables, furniture and plants, thick dust hourly pours thru the screened windows and the poor flowers and plants have to be washed like ourselves—to keep their pores from choking up.

A hospital ship, all in white, is moving by—there are recuperating sailors and soldiers on her decks—they call to the girls along the shore as an airplane roars overhead—one of the penalties of war, the maimed and wounded returning from the field of battle. Some will recover whole, others will never be the same—some will always be charges on their families, their state or federal government for the remainder of their helpless lives—worse off than the comrades left so gloriously or solemnly on the field of battle.

This is August 1943.

And before I return to the tale of 1936—I will interlope here a thought often expressed by me in conversation and written word—

There will always be wars as long as man is man—there can never be a permanent peace. Man cannot defy the economic law and succeed—he cannot make water move up hill without artificial aid—man-made aid. Men quarrel amongst themselves—men are always seeking the greener grass on the other side of the fence—man always desires to expand. Just as the jew thrives on misery and the ill-fortune of his fellowman, the Aryan thrives on success and expansion—the Aryan is the pioneer seeking new fields to conquer regardless of the physical price; the Semite seeks to exploit the established, to chisel in—the Aryan builds for the Semitic to destroy.

New devices—the manual saving machines—over populates the land. Then man must destroy the machine or be destroyed—and when

338

man continues to improve the machine, to perfect the machine, he is in effect perfecting and hastening his own destruction from the face of the earth.

Wars are economic—rudimentally they arise from man's inborn urge to improve his lot in life whether on the Yangtze or the Hudson.

When men are crowded into small areas they crave to expand to break their bounds. The British did it—the Germans have been striving likewise and valiantly—and in fact superbly when resources and manpower are considered—the Japs are having their try at it— the Dutch, the French, the Spanish all took their turns. Just as long as nature implants the basic urge of progeneration—or procreation— in man, so long will there be wars.

Now what are the results of all this fighting and wasting and destroying of men and materials?

Let's look at nature. In plant life—let's take the Tung tree— you plant a tree, you nurse it along, you fertilize and cultivate it. After a number of years the tree begins to bear.

And after it arrives at a normal bearing prolific state, what happens? One year you have ten bushels of fruit, then the next year there may be an unexpected late frost or an early frost and it is just too bad—or it may be heavy rains—but frost is the most damaging. Your orchard may be on the best land for soil and water and air drainage, but the frost gets the tree and you lose most of the crop.

The tree's development has been arrested—the crop will only be a bushel—but the next year it will come back to ten or more or nature may intercede again. The third year the crop will be the biggest yet— then there will be a setback, a recuperation and a surge ahead and then another setback. Nature never permits the trees to race ahead beyond their strength, to give greater and greater bumper crops each year—she always retards, levels off.

Now for war—man races ahead, gets beyond himself, life becomes too easy—there are too many for work and not enough work to do. So come the wars, the normal fatalities around the world from disease, natural causes, normal accidents, disasters—hasn't been fast enough—war steps that up.

In some cases it took the best men, the top cream and destroyed them—that was nature's way of destroying the ruling class and revitalizing by letting the lower order develop and come to the top— birthrates fall in peace time, but are sharply accentuated in war.

One man said, "In peace time there are more men than women. That is not good—there can be little selectivity of females by the males in such a society, so the race is weakened." After wars there are more women then men—a man can be more selective.

My observation, however, is that man is seldom more selective—a stiff prick arises out of other considerations that have little connection with the male's mature consideration of the type of offspring to be produced by a union.

Seldom does a healthy boy stop to consider the eugenics of a union—hot pants give little thought to the type of brat a fuck will produce if the gal gets caught. . . .

Well, war—in modern warfare, as in days of yore, old cities are destroyed, antiquities are gone forever—that enriches those that are left. New cities will have to be built—out of this conflict as out of the last will come newer and more radical advances in machinery on land, in the air, on the sea and under it. Transportation, communication, television, improvements in the home, in the office, great strides in commercial and personal aviation, household appliances, the automobile, even agriculture and foodstuffs will be improved if the present Secretary of Agriculture doesn't destroy the American farms with his socialism.

Novel and alluring edibles as well as advances in personal adornments, habitats, clothing, etc.—ultra modernistic homes will arise the world over. We will lag behind Britain, Germany, China, Japan (if we ever get to the mainland of the Rising Sun), because so much of their old has been destroyed. In defeat, Germany will gain.

The air raid blitzes over London were good for London—it has revived that tottering, rotting, decaying capital on the Thames.

Much in New York could have been destroyed to the betterment of the metropolis—as young as she is and prone to tear down and rebuild without the stimulant of destruction by war or fire or quake, it would have been well for us.

New cities rising on the ashes of the old are always better cities—that's progress. It would have been well if Rome and Paris had not been declared open cities—they will have to be destroyed sooner or later to make way for the modern advance of man.

No, we remain alone untouched, except for an upset in our ideologies—our ancestors came here to get away from European methods, old world superstitions, restrictions, jealousies, nationalism, bigotry, corruption and poverty. This war is bringing us closer than the last to a revolution that will return us to the old countries' ways—for the scum of Europe will be in the saddle, in charge of the new order which will be but an embracement of the old countries' discredited ways. Freedom of speech, of worship, the right to work where and when one chooses and to live one's own life is vanishing before our very eyes—in fact, has almost vanished.

No longer do we enoy or will this generation enjoy or many generations to come enjoy the right to work harder than the neighbor next door, and have a better home because of that harder work.

No longer will one man excel another at his trade.

No longer are we to have the right to enjoy that which we have worked so hard for.

No longer are we to have the right to secure for our children better opportunities than we had.

No longer are we to have the right to enjoy the freedom of initiative and individual enterprise.

No longer are we to have the right to be a Horatio Alger.

No longer are we to have the right to rise from rags to riches.

No longer are we to have the right to rise from newsboy to the White House.

For the future—and even now—we must submit to the dictation of the European minorities—walk alike, eat alike, dress alike, talk alike, worship alike (new Gods—not the old) and fuck alike, as ordered by the state, complete and total regimentation—that is what we are winning out of this war and that is to be our fate until another war or complete economic collapse wipes out the European ruling minorities, and a new regime and form of regulation comes up in their stead.

As we grow older we like to reminisce over the homes we liked to visit, the old plays, the old songs that brought us joy in our jaded youth. We call those the "good old days" that are gone forever—and they were good to us, even better in retrospect than they were at the time. Age tints our glasses—they were nice times—the people we knew then behaved as we were brought up to behave—that was the era of civility in human relations. Altho you were robbing your best friend in business, you were what was called courteous about it. The ruling classes enjoyed innumerable servants to assure them the comforts and case of life—comforts that the mechanical age strives to afford the ruling classes now on their way into power—none of what the former generations knew as the niceties, the beauties of life are to remain.

Taste in food, eating habits, have all become regimented, have been revolutionized—inevitable with the migrations from the rural to the urban and industrial area.

The family group living together in the home, eating together

341

good well-cooked wholesome food, has given way to mass eating palaces where thousands are fed daily at a fraction of the cost of home cooking—and at much less the wear and tear on the housewife, who now takes her place beside her mate in the commercial and industrial life of the country, reluctantly taking time out for child delivery—and menstruation is a bore—nursing babies is also passe, and so it goes. The last war developed, or at least brought out into the open, large crops of lesbians and homos to further complete the natural scheme of recreation.

To those who knew the old, were reared in it, this all seems a sacrilege, as they moan the passing of the past they knew and loved— their Santa Claus of life has vanished, and so will the generations to come look back upon the glory of their youth and wonder and worry and fret about the changes that have taken place about them and are taking place about them as they mature and ripen into old age.

Just as men and women lose their teeth, their hair, so their eyesight dims, their zest for screwing wanes, and so will they always long for the days when—nature is that way, always changing, never stagnate —life is change, change is life, life is perpetual motion from the womb to the grave, forever tearing down the old, building the new. Wars are great contributors to the process—just as fire, and water and pestilence and volcanic eruptions play their part.

Wars hasten the improvement and progress of life—wars are great levelers, one of nature's compensations for the human race. In present life, war takes up part of the slack created by the machine age, and man will fight until he has exterminated himself, for man is a self-destroying creature at best.

A submarine has just sleeked past, long and narrow and trim— a thing of beauty—her crew on deck, almost awash as she skimmed thru the narrow channel without a sound. She had been preceded by a large tanker, name unknown—PIII was all she had upon her bow. Our flag was at her mast—she was swift too.

But the submarine—the serpentine of the sea—my! that was something to see. It was the first time either Eve or I had seen one under way, down the river or up the bay.

Above me, upstairs in an apartment overhead, a little girl prepares her way—she plays her scales all thru the day—she never stops to see a ship and only ceases when she has to take her pip to pee.

Just above us is a man, crippled—sans furniture sans bed sans light—a candle seems to suffice, and old papers cover the floor for his bed.

342

His girl friend paid the rent—$1,600.00—in advance. He is a menace to health and a fire hazard of no small proportion. So much for the present.

And so I will slip back into the past again—as Roosevelt blasts drooling words from Ottawa to help Churchill help MacKenzie King, the Canadian Prime Minister, hold his job—and we nominate candidates for Lieut. Gov. that may well or well not seal the early fate of the nation and affect the lives of others outside our borders—because it is on trifles that great issues are made.

And Sidney Hillman decides to implement the newly formed but struggling labor party by taxing all union members for its maintenance. . . .

Yes! Times have changed—an American fast Scout ship roared by a British K and neither dipped their flags in mutual salute, recognition, courtesy, or respect—no greeting. Yes, that is a change too, just like the evolution of the military uniforms. They will get the seamen yet—aboard ship the changes have been slow, too much real tradition still there.

Sometimes I wonder—perhaps it's old age creeping up—if there is not a place for tradition and the lessons of the past. Is there not something in the best of what there was that might not well be preserved as a sacred heritage in the ever-changing scheme of things— might not there be just something a bit worthwhile preserving, something that would be of value and of guidance, something that might be a yardstick for the future generations yet to come. Or should there be no guide posts on the road of life?

On with the yarn. At the Los Angeles Biltmore on the Square, Grimsted the credit manager of the 1931 days was still on hand to welcome me with ample credit and good service—too much credit and too little cash has always been my downfall. . . .

It was a Sunday afternoon. I had been writing to Joe L. and several others—I dictated the letter to my secretary Frieda S. direct to the typewriter as I always prefer to do anyway. In that letter to Lilly as I went along I expounded on Frieda's charms and my attraction to her and my urge for her. Business was dull that afternoon—I had made my interest and eagerness clear in my letter to Lilly—so when I suggested that she close early, she acquiesced, and we went out to dinner and did quite a bit of drinking.

After dinner we strolled over to her apartment. She invited me in for a night cap—we were both pretty high by then. All thru dinner

I had been making love to her and dancing with her between courses —I had had a perpetual hard on while dancing and talking to her and she naturally felt my hard prick up against her as we danced—we were both damn hot by the time we reached her apartment.

We had only been in the apartment a few minutes—hardly finished a drink—when while loving her on the sofa, I unleashed the old boy and stuck him in. She took it like a tigress grabs a raw piece of meat—how she loved it. I pulled my pants off—her drawers were already down and off—and we had the next one on the floor—as I came the next time, she pissed all over me and herself—hot pee—that was a real sensation.

Her cunt had been very wet from the first time I put my finger on it, as I fondled it and played with it and as I kissed her, caressed her bubbies and made love to her until I shoved my cock up into her— but the piss when it came was like the rush of the Niagara River over the Horseshoe Falls. It drove me nuts—she must have been holding it back for a long time.

She had to take everything off then and so did I—we were both too drunk to clean up much, so I spent the night there with her.

Somehow or other every time we fucked that night and she came, she peed on me too.

Well, it got me down—the next day and for days after that she would come to my room in the Hotel, ostensibly for dictation—she she would strip and we would fuck—God, she was a find. She had me almost out of my mind for a while.

I grew so fond of her—wanted her so much—that I started to think of her seriously, about living with her—but circumstances in my turbulent life prevented, altered that course for me, so to speak.

The necessity for my going out to Ken Johnson's house did much to break it up. She came out there several times, but she couldn't take my fear complex spasms, my hysteria—as she discovered I was in hot water financially, her interest waned and I found new and better tail on the sides of the Hollywood hills that was ever ready and willing and no marital complications. Yes, she was a Jewess, too—in fact that seemed to be my Jewish sex cycle about that time.

I have always remembered Frieda and her piss—if I found myself in her vicinity even today I suppose I would hunt her up to see if she pees as well now as she did eight years ago—and she probably wouldn't.

I have always wanted to write, to express myself with my pen or

344

typewriter, but I have never been able to do it well. In the first place, I cannot spell—of grammar or English composition I know next to nothing—I do not know a split infinitive from an adverb and my writing isn't legible, my vocabulary small, too small for writing and my pronouncing vocabulary much smaller. There are so many words I know but cannot pronounce correctly—because of my deficiencies, the writing of this letter is a slow struggle.

Hotels always make me hot and bothered—the maids, no matter how old or young always stir me up and I am constantly bothered by a stiff prick when in them.

In Los Angeles, they had several get-together agencies or matrimonial agencies or outfits that purported to bring lonely girls and boys together, of all ages and all types. I got in touch with several, paid one of them five dollars down, more to come—fucked the woman who ran the other, and started out on a cheap evening's adventure, selecting gals from the files that were willing to stay at home.

Most of the girls were of moderate means, working, nice girls but not follies beauties. I laid them all. The approach was usually a bit difficult—they were invariably the bashful type, a little stiff at first—but once thru the ice they were damn good lays and hot as hell. They had really joined for scratching—they lacked the personality to attract men and didn't have the chance of meeting them. Some had come to Hollywood for the movies—others were just off balance—most of them wanted to hold on once they got a grip on you. They were great letter writers—one learned of my name and hotel and she became quite a pest writing, phoning and following me around. . . .

The Burlesque Houses on Spring Street were a favorite haunt of mine, where I jerked off during the strip tease acts as they stripped off. Nearly half the customers openly played with themselves in and out of their pants—some fellows were too bashful to take their cocks out and come outside, so they came in their pants—others just shot their loads on the seats in front of them.

At night they had dance halls in the tougher sections. There you danced with a girl for a dime and a drink—if you bought her a round of beers she would fool around with your cock under the table and would give you a look at her cunt—for half a buck you could go in the can with her and she would jerk you off—for a silver dollar she would fuck or suck you off if you preferred.

L. A. also had the shows like they had in Chicago where you

paid a quarter each time to see a little more—until at the end you got a look at a cuzy after you had shot a couple of bucks in quarters and a load in your pants. . . .

The urge to take one's life, particularly in periods of adversity, is very great—it doesn't make much difference whether one is drunk or sober. Frequently, the desire is greater during the height of a mental depression as one comes out of a hangover. . . .

Macy and the Borah people in Washington felt that while I was out on the Coast I should contact William Randolph Hearst. The great question came of the best way to reach him. . . .

About the middle of February, the *Los Angeles Examiner* had carried a full page editorial lauding Senator Borah's Washington Birthday speech to the skies and Macy and Thomas and I figured that old man Hearst might be in a receptive mood to consider Borah as his second choice if he couldn't put Landon across. . . .

In one of Melba's letters she suggested "the California situation is simply an episode, a stepping stone to other and better things." And in the same communicaton—"We need *plenty* in order to live up to our standard, and I propose we shall have it," and then she concluded with "You seem to have drifted very far away from me lately and I can't see why because I certainly have been with you mentally all the time—I have given our matters a great deal of consideration and have even refused several invitations to parties—which you know I love— to stand by and write to you and get your letters and messages and do everything in my power to lend my moral support."

I got involved in two situations—one was that I told the newspapermen in Los Angeles that I was leaving on a tour of the West Coast States in behalf of Senator Borah's candidacy; in addition, several females were a little too eagerly persistent so I had my name taken off the rack, as checked out, but I continued to stay at the hotel until the 1st of March when I moved out. . . .

[Melba, in New York, exhorted my father to greater efforts in settling her financial affairs.]

For God's sake, don't go hay-wire now—unless of course you want to chuck the whole thing between us and go separate ways.

I know we get just about what we deserve in the scheme of things, and when the big things don't come, it's because we have closed down on our capacity to let in the big thoughts—You and I have come through a period of some pretty small, mean, miserly thoughts, and it's high time for expansion.

When you first went out there, you started out doing things—I don't mean extravagantly—but in a big way—and now you lose your grip—Why?—You certainly have more requisites than anyone I have ever known—brains, looks, ability, intelligence, shrewdness, blood and *guts*—I hope! . . .

As for the future, if it doesn't scare me I don't see why you should be quaking in your boots. All I ask is to have my immediate obligations cleared and the next few months taken care of, my health and the future to look forward to. I'd like your cooperation but even that I can do without if you want to stop and lie in the gutter. Let's not be noble any more, let's just work and stop thinking about how much you can or can't get until you start getting something, even if you only support yourself that's something and the little the children get will help with them. Who in Hell knows what the future holds for anyone much less just us—certainly the world is never going back to the old standards—a whole new scheme of things and different sense of values is being ushered in and I for one think it's all swell and healthy and I want to keep up with it and if our hard luck is forcing us to keep up with it while we still have our youth & health I say HOORAY for the hard luck. . . .

I certainly DO read your letters very thoroughly but perhaps you do not realize how vague and scattered you have been. Why not take stock of yourself about now—politics, sex, women, drink are only temporary escapes, you still have yourself with you and our relationship, which seems to have some importance to you. Your self-styled hermitage would seem a good place for that but perhaps the desert would be better as an expansive locale. . . .

Lovingly, Melba

Aimee Semple McPherson—the red-headed rip snorting high powered evangelist with "it"—that had the City of the Angels by the ear and the nation all atwitter, was still packing them in when I was on the Coast in 1936. She put on a great show of ranting and raving and threw the sex all over the place.

Judge Carlos Hardy, an old friend of Celeste Ryus, was her attorney—he offered to introduce me to the firebrand of feminine sex unleashed. I chose the hard way—it was safer—I went to one of her Sunday night revival meetings where converts threw themselves at her feet. Out there on the stage in her flowing robes accentuating every line of her body she was something as she exhorted her followers and the shekels poured in.

I waited until after the show was over and stood in line to shake her "mit" and a better close up look-see. Sitting in the balcony as she carried on, I got an urge, slight, but an urge. I thought I might try a piece of it—it looked like good tail—in fact the idea was taking root until standing almost at the end of a line that must have had a thousand souls on it—mostly eager admirers eager to touch her hand, her gown, and get a thrill—my turn came to shake the hand of the Los Angeles Goddess come to earth. She was older, close to than her picture showed or klieg lights showed—she was worn and a bit haggard, exhausted from the night's effort and her long hand-shaking performance. Her hand clasp was limp like a wet cloth or dishrag—her appearance and handshake knocked all sex urge sky high—killed it there and then. Perhaps it was just as well—but she attracted thousands of men and women the country over.

I think that oftentimes we are attracted—I know I am—to some feminine personage, usually of the stage—not for what they are but for what their buildup or publicity has made you believe them to be. And so it had been for me with Aimee—the reality was a cold awakening. . . .

On the 3rd of March, Kendrick Johnson, who was head of the Borah-for-President Club in Hollywood, drove me out to the Warner's lot to keep an appointment with Mr. Randolph Hearst, that had been made for me by wire and telephone through the Editor of the local *Los Angeles Examiner*.

Cosmopolitan Pictures—a Hearst Organization producing Marion Davies pictures—was sharing part of the Warner lot—there was some tie-in between the two organizations.

Marion's bungalow was in a corner near one of the entrance gates —it was a palatial two-story affair that would have been a most comfortable mansion on any country estate.

I sent my name in at the gate and was ushered to the bungalow where a woman in the garb or dress of a trained nurse greeted me and ushered me into a large and beautifully decorated living room. A few minutes later, Mr. Hearst made his appearance. He escorted me into a large room he uses as a sort of combination office and study. He has a capacity for great cordiality along with his gracious dignity, which puts you immediately at your ease.

Marion's bungalow was very beautifully decorated—it was a two-story affair. After seven years, my vision of it is somewhat dim, but I was impressed.

In Mr. Hearst's study, on the ground floor, we sat informally and discussed the National political situation, as well as many of his employees. One thing that did impress me was the fact that he seemed to feel much closer to Henry Clive than he did to Howard Chandler Christy. He looked upon Clive as sort of an incorrigible boy.

During the course of our talk the trained nurse came in to tell him that Governor Landon was on the long distance phone—Landon was Hearst's candidate for the Republican presidential nomination. When I heard this I suggested that I should leave the room, as I did not think I should be in on the conversation between Mr. Hearst and his candidate—Hearst protested that that wasn't necessary but nevertheless I went outside until he finished with the call.

The purpose of my visit was very largely to get the famous publisher to commit himself on Borah for a second choice.

Kendrick Johnson, the local Hollywood Borah leader, drove me out the Warner Bros. lot and waited for me—

The old man was easy to get on with—showed a great fondness for Borah, but unquestionably felt that if he could put Landon across, he would have a more amenable men in the White House than the unpredictable Borah.

Marion's little dachshund was all over the place and Mr. Hearst exhibited a great fondness for the little dog—the glamorous Marion herself did not put in an appearance. . . .

I found Hearst at that meeting in Marion Davies' bungalow on the Warner lot exceedingly charming and delightful. The whole meeting was very cordial and very friendly—you would have thought we had known one another for years. We covered quite a range of subjects—different things we were both interested in. He agreed with me entirely regarding Fiorello—he thought the "Wop" had handled the Building Employee's strike in N.Y. very badly, although he mentioned that it hadn't affected any of his property. It was Mr. Hearst's observation at the time that F. H. was prone to lose his head at critical moments. . . .

I moved out to Kendrick Johnson's bungalow at 6225 Winans Drive, in the Hollywood Hills. It was the type of shack that one finds very largely in the Philippine Islands—there was a living room, fairly large, a good size bedroom and bath, also a large kitchen, and a screened veranda where one could work or meditate and look off over the valley of Los Angeles County for what that was worth, day or night. I gave a cocktail party there—was visited daily by Kendrick Johnson—had several girls working for me part time—and had a lot of fun keeping house. The rent was free, the only thing I had to pay for was the telephone, the electric light, the ice and the food. . . .

One of the great past-times in California at that time was the interviewing of beautiful damsels that came to Los Angeles in search of movie stardom. They came in droves, yes, in fact by the thousands—they came with parents, they came alone, they came by train, they came by plane, they came by boat, they motored West, they came by bus, and they hitch-hiked.

Grimstead, the Credit Manager of the Biltmore, had told me of the practice some fellows made of coming in and renting a minimum room, and advertising for photographic models or for girls to "cast." Such advertisements in the local Los Angeles paper always brought a deluge of replies from the hopeful. The girls never seemed to be able to differentiate between the legitimate "calls" and the illegitimate snares. The Management objected seriously when the advertising was done by a guest with a minimum who did not patronize the hotel facilities. If a guest had a sitting room, bedroom and bath, and was a good spender, they let him have his fun. While I was out on Winans Drive Ken and I thought it would be a lot of fun to put such an ad in for material, so, we agreed upon a time for interviewing—an afternoon when he could get away from his girl friend, and I put an ad in with the telephone number and without the name in the local Hearst paper. The replies were numerous, appointments were made and Ken came over all ready for the prey. When he discovered the ad had been run in the Hearst paper, he became panicky. It seemed his girl friend had a hobby or made a hobby of reading the Want Ads in the Hearst paper—so, in his confusion he called her up, told her he had changed his plans for the afternoon and took her driving. I kept my local secretary, a skinny gal, Katherine Neuworth of 5946 Sunset Blvd., around for a cover, and what an afternoon and evening I had. Some of them came alone, some of them with their boy friends some with their mothers, etc. They brought numerous pictures of themselves in all degrees of dress and undress.

The parents or friends usually waited outside in their cars, while the young lovelies entered the den of iniquity. The procedure: they would come in, give their names, addresses and telephone numbers, show photographs of themselves, and then walk back and forth across the floor in order to give an idea of their carriage and demeanor. After that they would, without hesitation, display a full view of their limbs and at the first suggestion would disrobe and pose in the nude on a slightly raised platform, which I had provided for the purpose. After

350

With unidentified companion, Durango, Mexico, 1929

With Melba, before leaving on honeymoon, Los Angeles, 1929

With Melba, world tour, 1929

Egypt, 1929

With Melba, flanked by the Gilbert Whites, Shanghai, 1929

With Diane, Melba, Melsing, and Page, 1931

Cornelius Vanderbilt, 1932

Melba, with guitar; Lady Furness, far right; Melsing, second from right; Diane, facing Melba; Gloria Vanderbilt, foreground; others unidentified, 1932

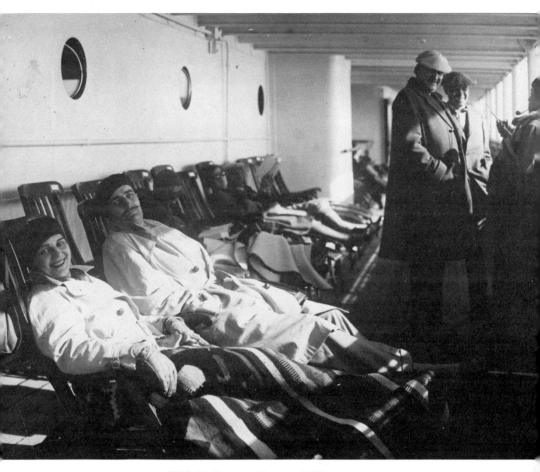

With Melba, world tour, 1933

China, 1933

With Melba, in Florida, 1933

Melvale, 1933

Melvale, to market, 1933

1936

With Page, 1938

With Eve, Palm Beach, 1939

With Eloise and Page on the day
of their wedding, July 11, 1942

Stowe, Vermont, c. 1948

With a photographer's model, 1948

Eve, 1949

With Eve, c. 1955

passing upon their lovely forms, with a feigned professional eye, I would then take measurements of the various parts of their anatomy, beginning at the ankle or the wrist and working up or down. There was a set professional procedure for this, and you not only took their measurements from their shoulders to their wrists, but from their armpits to their wrists, and from their hips to their ankles and from their crotch to their ankles.

Naturally I would get hot and especially excited when I measured their tits, or from their hairy cunts to their ankles—some of them, in fact many of them had their hair shaved off their "pussies." Howard Christy always deplored that practice—women all over the country are forever sending him pictures of themselves in the nude, with cunts shaved—and he contends it annoys him for they lose all their personality and look for all the world like "navel oranges."

My stiff prick would not be refused, and before more than one measuring job was completed I was laying my rod in up to the "hilt." Variety is the spice of life, and I fucked nine different girls that afternoon—they were young and luscious, beautiful creatures, all eager to please—women were legion in Hollywood then and jobs few. It was ideal for free tail—and I made the most of every piece of lovely ass that came my way. You didn't have to urge—the slightest suggestion was readily understood and they would roll over on their backs before you could get your pants unbuttoned. It was wonderful fucking—a perfect bliss—"Hide," "Hide," "Hide," how heavenly it was.

It is difficult at times, when I reflect, to recall the exact details of all that took place during the periods about which I am writing—especially things that I feel would be of interest to you. So often, in fact most of the time, I am only aware of what others do to me, and not what I do or say to others, and likewise I find that others are able to vividly recall what I have said to them or what they have seen me do, but are not able to remember what they said or did. In retrospect it is difficult without keeping a diary to have even a fairly impartial or unbiased picture of past events.

We always remember things we want to remember, both pleasant and unpleasant—and perhaps not always as they really were or as the other fellow saw them.

I have assiduously tried to hew to the facts as closely as I could, and a perusal here and there of old files and correspondence in order to check my recollection, has more often than not confirmed the correctness of my memory.

* * *

Things were getting pretty hot from a financial standpoint—trying to maintain Melba in New York and myself in California was difficult.

Between looking after Melba's property and trying to keep the Borah crowd in Washington from consenting to Campbell's plan for Borah to enter the California Primary, and take care of the lovely ladies at the same time, I was kept pretty damn busy. . . .

[The project to visit San Simeon was revived.]

[Hearst] invited me to come up to San Simeon for a further talk before I returned East. This I agreed to do—he then suggested that I come up the next evening, but I told him that I had just met a very beautiful girl at a cocktail party who was coming to have dinner with me that night—and he said that he understood my feelings and that he didn't blame me in the least for wanting to keep that date. So it was agreed that I come up on the day following.

I had always been eager to visit Mr. Hearst's palace, high up in the California Hills, along the shores of the Pacific, about half way between Los Angeles and San Francisco. Had I been sober I probably would have accepted immediately and cancelled the dinner engagement with the beautiful buyer from Bullocks-Wilshire, who I had met thru Celeste Ryus at a cocktail party given by an old Dowerager—a friend of hers—Mrs. Grace G. of North Beverly Drive.

My staying over afforded me one of those rare thrills that only come once in a lifetime, as I shall now relate.

Grace G., an old girl with dough and a big house at North Beverly Drive in Beverly Hills—a friend of Celeste—was giving her annual cocktail shin-dig. She invited me at Celeste's suggestion. So I took Celeste in her Ford.

Altho I took Celeste out to dinner from time to time, it was more to have a male escort than to return my hospitality that she took me about.

It was a large party—the Hamilton P.s were there and many attractive people—but one woman in particular stood out. She was lovely to behold—prematurely gray—she was the belle of the ball. I didn't have any money, but I had a lot of nerve. The Mayor of the town and all the bigwigs and little ones, were laying siege to the lovely creature—she was a vision, and one I never forgot.

Well, your old man plunged in where angels were fearing to tread—and lo and behold, he made it—the grade, I mean. I couldn't take her anywhere and I was going home with Celeste in her car—so I tried it and it worked—I invited her to the Hermitage for a home-cooked meal by the maestro, with the stipulation that she cook the dinner. I built it up and sold her a bill of goods—she accepted and I was thrilled.

Thereafter, at the party I had a hell of a time, dividing my time between her and Celeste. She was a widow, Mrs. Harriet Gardnier by name, of South Palma, supporting her two children.

That was the date I had when Hearst asked me to come to San Simeon. That's why I delayed my visit to the publishing Tycoon—I have seldom seen a girl as popular at any party as she was.

Well, I was living on air—I worked myself into a frenzy preparing for the event. She told me what to get and I borrowed the money from Kendrick to get the food and liquor. He was as excited as I was. She was by far the most attractive girl I had seen in California. It was to be my day of days. I was to have her—the loveliest of them all—up there in the Hermitage all alone.

She too seemed eager when I talked with her over the phone.

Slowly the day crept by. She had arranged for her children to visit friends that evening while she philandered.

It was dusk and I was waiting. It was still up there in the hills—the lights were beginning to twinkle in the valley below, the lights of that palpitating, fornicating town. Soon she would be there within the very portals of my shack—my cock was big and hard in eager anticipation.

Then the silence was suddenly broken by the ever-omnipresence of the instrument of mental torture—the tingle of the phone bell. I hesitated to answer—I didn't want intrusion, a conflict of foreign thoughts and ideas forced in upon me. I wanted only to contemplate the heavenly vision that was due to arrive any moment.

The ring was persistent—as if the caller were sure I were there or long distance trying to get thru.

Reluctantly I lifted the phone and there were sobs coming from the other end—it was my gorgeous guest of the evening. Haltingly she cried—a wire had just reached her that her mother had been scalded—she was on her way out the door to me when the boy gave her the message. Rushing back into the house, she phoned her mother's home in Detroit—she had been boiling beets and had pulled the pot off the stove and badly scalded herself. The doctors thought she at her age had scant chance of recovery. She phoned a brother in Texas—she was home alone—she asked me to come right over. She was going to fly to Texas on the first plane to Detroit—now that poised a question.

I said I would come at once—but she was way across the city

in the Beverly Hills section—the taxi fare would have been several bucks. I consoled her as best I could—I was brokenhearted—my night of nights was shattered. I phoned Ken Johnson, told him my plight, pointed out the only salvage would be for me to get to her while she was still in a highly emotional state—and before the friends came in to console her. There was a chance, just a chance I might be able to break thru and give her what it takes to calm a female in a highly wrought-up condition. He agreed, conferred on the subject with his lady love, and rushed over in her car, driving me across the city to Harriet's apartment.

She was still very emotional when I arrived—I had gotten there before her children had been reached or friends had come to help her get away.

Ken departed and left me to my own devices. She was more delectable, more tempting than ever—my urge surged within me at the very sight of her. I took her in my arms to comfort her—I started to get a drink to steady her nerves, and we went to the pantry together. It was the first time I had been in her home—she seemed as distressed about the spoiled evening as the contemplated demise of her mother.

Before a drop of liquor was poured, she was again in my arms in another spasm of crying—I didn't wait, I don't think I gave much thought to what I was doing or where I was, but I was hot as hell and she was quivering. Then and there it happened, as I soothed her, stroking every part of her lovely body in passionate embraces—right in the pantry, with couches and beds all over the place, we fucked and fucked and fucked right on the pantry floor in one mad passionate orgasm after the other.

I never had the like before—I have never had quite the same since. When we were completely exhausted we slowly came to our senses. We both wondered why it had been the pantry floor that we had honored.

We hardly had time to adjust ourselves, our clothes etc. when the bell rang and the consolers started coming in to comfort her, and to help her pack. By the time the children arrived home she was quite the perfect mistress of herself. I didn't stay late—I had a long journey of crosstown on busses to get home to Winans Drive.

She was all I had expected and more—but it was all over too soon. As wonderful as it was, maybe she wouldn't have been as exciting or responsive if nothing had happened and she had been able to keep her date at the Hermitage.

354

She told me on the pantry floor that she had been hoping that I would love her at the Hermitage, that she too had had a great urge for me from the time she met me and had trouble sleeping the nights in the interim.

I heard from her from Detroit and wrote her for a while but left Los Angeles before she returned. We never met East, if she ever came here. Her mother died and I never saw her again—I have never forgotten her or her fornicating ability and capacity under stress and strain—she was wonderful, wonderful, wonderful. It was a passing fuck in the night, but one of those never-to-be-forgotten—the best pieces of tail are that way. A crowning thrill and then each on his and her way—never again to meet and if you were to meet, you would be unable to repeat.

It's the inspirational emotion of the moment that makes for the best in sexual intercourse—and accounts for bastards (born out of wedlock the result of a passing fuck under great emotional stress) being such unusual specimens—frequently superior mentally as well as physically.

Naturally I have often wondered about her, wondered what she is like now—then I was lean and just past forty.

I had had my clothes pressed and dry cleaned and my laundry all done for the occasion. . . . Although we started late—6:55 instead of 6:45 from Glendale—the Sunset Limited reached its destination San Luis Obispo on time at 1:00 A.M.—and whereas I had left Glendale well fortified with the alcoholic snifters and in fact well heeled, when the journey started, I was cold sober when I got off the train and was met by one of William Randolph Hearst's secretaries who had one of Mr. Hearst's cars at the station to drive me the intervening fifty miles along the Coast to the Hearst Hacienda.

I think perhaps that here is a good place to insert the letter that I wrote Melba on my return from San Simeon—it was fresh then in my memory—and whereas I glossed over certain facts in order not to arouse her suspicions as to my amorous conduct, the letter in the main is largely correct, and so here it is:

Los Angeles, Calif.
March 31st, 1936

Dear Melba:

To San Simeon—took the 6:45 P.M.—the Sunset Ltd. from Glendale. Ken Johnson drove me over to the train—had my clothes

355

pressed and dry-cleaned and my laundry done especially for the occasion—Before leaving fortified myself with a few snifters and was well heeled when the journey started—reached the San Luis Obispo Railroad Station at 1 A.M.—Was met by a Hearst motor car and driven the intervening fifty miles along the coast to the Hearst hacienda—it was a beautiful drive even at night—for miles and miles we could see the castle brilliantly lighted awaiting our arrival—the climb up the mountainside after we left the main highway and passed the Hearst flying field with its twinkling varicolored lights—the house is 1800 feet above sea level—reminded me of the winding roads up the Himalayas on the way to Darjeeling.

The first gate one comes to at the bottom of the hill is guarded by an attendant who takes your pass and then after unlocking the gate releases a secret spring so that the gate moves upward and aside in ghostlike fashion like a modern drawbridge—As we passed thru the attendant telephoned word of our arrival up the hill.

After that, we had to open and shut our own gates—formerly you had to pull a rope to do this, and on rainy days the water would run down your sleeve, but nowadays there are trippers, and when you ride over them, after going through the gate, the gate closes automatically behind you. In the enclosed fields, along the road approaching the castle, are white deer, llamas, ordinary deer, and in fact all manner and description of animals.

When we reached the castle we were met by a guard and a valet and I was escorted to the "Hero Room." I later told Mr. Hearst that I suspected I was assigned to that room with malice aforethought because of my worship of contemporary political heroes.

The room had a huge fireplace of ancient design and above the mantel carved into the granite block was the figure of the Madonna and Child. The ceilings and walls were paneled and beamed, with heroic figures of the ancients painted between the beams with Latin inscriptions in gold lettering below each figure, fully describing same.

The bed was a beautifully carved high posted affair—fit for a king or queen—in spite of my long legs I had to step up on a stool to climb into it. There was a large comfortable couch and several small benches before the fireplace—electric heaters in the wall were the only modern touch—the bureau was outfitted with a toilet set that would have made your eyes bulge.

There were big closets and a private bath finished in marble from ceiling to floor with a sunken tub and up to date glass-enclosed shower—the essentials for either male or female or both—with or without luggage—were at hand—There was a private entrance hall and a private exit—the windows had shutters that were in fact huge panels—they closed you in completely if you so desired—the Pacific ocean lay below and the flying field with its sparkling lights contradicted the medieval character of the room—a beautiful clock ticked the time away noiselessly.

The household had retired by the time I arrived—2:30 A.M., so I took to bed. Thinking of dear Diane and how she would have gloried in it all.

I did not awaken until 10:00 and then I wasn't called—I up and dressed and strolled around the grounds—a beautiful amphitheatre embraces a lovely outdoor pool that the ancient Easterners might well have envied. The indoor pool is even more beautiful—the finest in the world.

As you enter the castle there is a tremendous baronial fireplace and a room that must be nearly 200 feet wide and looks out over the mountains on one side and down over the Pacific ocean on the other—back of this big room is the dining hall, about 150 feet long —it is narrow, and at one end is another huge fireplace protected by glass screens—of course the fires were burning brightly in all the fireplaces—baronial banners hang along each side of the dining hall and the light comes in from small windows near the top—the tapestries are exquisite and the silver service is simply massive—the whole room smacks of a set prepared for the days of King Arthur.

One long table runs the full length of the room and is laden with fruit and every kind of preserve and cheese—there isn't just one centerpiece of fruit but there is fruit from one end of the table to the other—Yesterday was an off day—there were only thirty of us at the table for dinner and the room seemed empty.

There is another livingroom to the rear of the dining hall, not quite as large, but extremely attractive. It too has a fireplace. Off this room are innumerable little dressing rooms for men and women. Then there is a large pool room also on this floor and a sumptuous and beautifully decorated theatre with the most comfortable chairs in the world—one could curl up and go to sleep in them without any trouble.

It was apparent that it was the custom of the house to wander at will into the feast hall uninvited and unannounced—and so I entered and partook of a sumptuous repast (breakfast)—others were doing likewise—strange men and women—people I had never seen before in my life—were constantly drifting in and out, sitting beside me or across from me at the table, indulging in small nothings of conversation—no one being introduced; it seems that Mr. Hearst likes people to get acquainted without knowing the background or anything about one another at first.

After breakfast, I explored again—the Hearst home is a cross between the completed Taj Mahal in India and the uncompleted

357

Cathedral of St. John the Divine on Morningside Heights; the real difference being that the Hearst castle is occupied and a center of great activity and industry.

In every nook and corner of the house and all about the grounds there are telephones galore—little boxes hidden in the trees, at various corners of the swimming pool and along the paths and the highways and the byways—on the tennis court there are two and the damn things are ringing all the time—in fact, there are phones everywhere except on the tennis balls, and when they are not ringing, the valet is bringing memoranda and messages which Mr. Hearst replies to pronto on scribbled memorandum sheets.

There is a large office staff ensconced in a sort of temporary field shack at the west driveway entrance that has every appearance of the headquarters of a military organization in the field, or the engineering shack of a subway construction gang.

There is a menagerie, but before you get to the menagerie you pass dog kennels where there are dozens of every breed of dog, all barking and howling; in the zoo there are bears and lions and tigers, panthers, monkeys, everything imaginable—bigger and better than the biggest circus—it would put Billy Rose's *Jumbo* Menagerie to shame.

When I returned to the castle I read the news bulletin in the large hall. They come in on a teletype machine just as they come into the newspaper offices.

The radio did not work so well despite the fortune that has been spent on it. For quite a time there was a great deal of static and interference from the ships still using the old spark set as they steam up and down the coast.

And so the time crept by till lunch—about 2 o'clock—Marion Davies stepped out of a panel in the wall of the large livingroom—the entrance, altho in the height of simplicity was most effective. She was greeted cordially by several friends nearby and went directly to the dining hall. Shortly thereafter the gong rang and everyone wandered in for a sumptuous buffet luncheon. Miss Davies sat down next to me and after a very respectable period had elasped, turned and introduced herself and was very cordial from then on.

I told Marion about Gloria Vanderbilt's grandfather, General Kilpatrick—How he married a little native girl while he was Ambassador to Chile—and insisted that the trustees of the Smithsonian Institute in Washington allow her tiny shoe to be displayed with his Civil War boots, saber and saddle—or else "no accoutrements" of his preserved for future posterity—And how Mrs. Commodore (Neil's grandmother) Vanderbilt was on the Mayor's reception committee that went down to the battery to receive the Ambassador-General's remains when they were brought back from Chile under naval escort. It seems that those within earshot were enchanted with the tale.

When lunch was about over, just as everyone was ready to leave the table, Mr. Hearst entered—his first appearance of the day—He espied me and greeted me most graciously and then proceeded to walk around the whole length of the table from one end to the other in order to arrive at my chair where he shook hands with me most cordially and was very friendly—the perfect host.

He then returned to the buffet table and helped himself to a heaping plate of lunch—after which he came back and sat across from me; at Marion's suggestion the others all left—except Dr. Barnham, who is a partner of Mr. Hearst in the publishing of the *Herald Express*—who remained for a few minutes—when he noticed the turn the conversation was taking, he left—He has a very nice blonde wife, a woman of about 40 or 42, who felt a little out of it because her square diamond ring was only 10 carats while Marion's was 16—wives are like that when their husbands are in business together.

On the way up to the ranch the driver said Mr. Hearst was famous for inviting people up and keeping them waiting days to talk to him—this was confirmed by one of the RKO executives present and several of Mr. Hearst's secretaries—so I was quite surprised and particularly pleased when Mr. Hearst launched forth immediately into the subject of my visit—we covered all that I had in my mind and from my standpoint it was a highly successful conference.

After lunch we continued the discussion interposed with political gossip and reminiscences—in talking with Mr. Hearst, he bemoaned the fact that there were so few men who could write politics or understood anything about them, in the newspaper field.

After our talk we watched Marion and her friends play Monopoly—tuned in on Bob Ripley's "Believe It Or Not" Hour and then to the tennis courts where Mr. Hearst played doubles with his sons, Jack and George and with Marion—while the others played the other courts. . . .

Mrs. John Hearst—or Jack Hearst—is a very attractive girl. Her first name is Gretchen—and they have the most adorable child I think I have ever seen outside of Melsing, Page and Marshall. At the age of two and a half hc is a dead ringer for Charles Augustus Lindbergh, Jr.—makes a great fuss over his grandfather and his grandfather makes a great fuss over him—

Hearst does everything very easily, one never gets the impression that one might be intruding or interfering in any way with his comfort, his pleasure or his business.

Despite all of the conversation about rules for guests I did not see any, nor was I admonished not to mention death in the great publisher's presence. I suspect that this is all hokum.

The safety match covers bore Mr. Hearst's initials and the slogan "Buy American."

Tell Henry Clive that Marion's little dog Gandi was everywhere.

There was a Mr. and Mrs. Harry Joe Brown. Mr. Brown is the production executive at Warner's Bros.—Someone said that he had at one time been Lew Cody's valet—His wife, I do not know her professional name, played with Eddie Cantor in *Strike Me Pink*.

There was a countess who affected the pose of Helen Wills Moody on the tennis court and the screen manners of Greta Garbo in the dining hall of the castle.

Also a seventeen year old girl who expected to marry a man by the name of Eddie Kane, but he died just three days before that and Marion Davies had invited her up to help ease her grief—the death was sudden—too much Scotch I take it. . . .

There were quite a few single girls, ever hopeful of movie careers with their mamas to chaperone them. . . .

We finally got around to dinner and was that something. The place cards indicated it was not to be a help-yourself affair. While no one dressed, the women did change from sport clothes to tea gowns, and Mr. Hearst put on a dark suit. I found myself one seat from the squire's right and next to Mrs. Jack Hearst. Hearst and Marion Davies sat in the centre of a large table opposite one another. Miss Davies seems to be a kind person, a devout Roman Catholic, who does a world of good to people in trouble. She is charming, attractive, and intelligent. Ham Fish, I understand, gave her quite a rush on his visit to Mr. Hearst's other mountain ranch.

The chair between the squire and yours truly at dinner was at first vacant—to my mind most of the women there, in fact all of them, had nothing to offer and were most uninteresting to talk to and not particularly attractive to look at—

At the dinner table there appeared to be a great deal of excitement about some girl who was to sit between Mr. Hearst and myself, whose name it seems was Mary, but it meant nothing in my life, and so I continued to talk about farms and children with Mrs. Jack Hearst —you remember David Cowles told me Jack Hearst was looking for a farm.

Just about then there was a considerable flutter and all the males arose from the table, and Marion Davies got up to greet the late arrival who came over and sat down between Mr. Hearst and myself —while I had no idea who she was, I must admit that for the first time that day I was tremendously attracted, and while I realized that

Mr. Hearst was her host, and entitled to all prior rights, I determined to let the very sweet and interesting creature know that I was on her right.

When the dinner was about over, I stole a glance at her place card and much to my amazement the letters on the same spelled Mary Pickford—and was I thrilled. Of course I had nothing in common to talk about as far as her interests and friends were concerned, but I quickly discovered that she knew a great deal about politics and was quite well aware of what was going on in the world outside of her own activities—She had been to Hong Kong and Shanghai and had an excellent suggestion for La Guardia, with the cooperation of John D. Rockefeller Jr., for improving the condition of the dwellers in the New York tenements—To me who was never over enthusiastic for her on the screen, she seemed most lovely. She appeared a bit depressed over the loss of Doug Fairbanks—She was still carrying the torch.

I had only two hours and a half to go before I had to leave for my train, and most of that would have to be spent in a movie, worse luck—nevertheless we chatted together after dinner while Mr. Hearst went off to his office, and when he returned we went to the movies.

On the front row most of the women were seated with Marion, and Marion had saved one place for Mary—but Mary said she preferred to sit in the back—that she did not think it was fair to leave the men alone, and so with a grand fanfare she refused Marion's proffered seat and entered a vacant row. We curled up in the big comfy chairs and I completely ignored the picture, directing my entire attention to the charming young lady beside me. But of course the hands of the clock moved surely around and eventually the major domo arrived to announce that it was time to go and so I had to leave the lovely creature.

Miss Pickford told me that her secretary, a Mrs. Lewis, had some strange phenomena about her. She said she had bought her dozens of watches but that whenever she puts on a watch or winds a clock it stopped and refused to go. It will go for anyone else but not for Mrs. Lewis. It seems this condition has existed all of Mrs. Lewis' life. Mary thought Robert Ripley might be interested. You might mention it to him, or Ruth Ross when you see them, and if Bob wants to write to Mary or to Mrs. Lewis they will furnish him all the data. I wish he would write her anyway because I told her I would tell him all about it. It sounds like a real "Believe It or Not."

In my enthusiasm over Mary Pickford, I forgot to mention that we had oodles of champagne for dinner and a perfectly gorgeous meal—more God damn fresh vegetables than I ever saw at this season of the year in my life—farmer that I am. It was novel being in an American household where the servants were American.

Riding in the same motor with me on the way back to the station down the hill, through the wild animal enclosures and thru the gates, were Lloyd Pantages and Mr. and Mrs. Harry Joe Brown and a bottle of Scotch. In the second motor for the train were four or five women.

When we arrived at the station, I discovered that Mr. Hearst had arranged for pullman transportation for all with his compliments. The couples had drawing rooms and the singles had compartments. . . .

That was a week-end visit to write home about—Hearst had crate upon crate of priceless art treasures piled high all around the place—never opened—things he had picked up in his travels and for which place had not been found—he told me that the steps approaching his castle were not in proper proportion to the building and altho they were stone blocks imported from abroad at great cost, he planned to rip them up and erect a larger stairway. . . .

Devotedly, Ward

The creditors were crowding in on me—milkmen, stenos, models, icemen, bakers, cleaners, grocerymen, etc.

I hocked my camera and borrowed a few bucks from Johnson. . . .

After a last visit to burlesque houses and clips joints—I boarded a bus for Mecca—heading back East with my tail behind my legs like a licked dog and leaving a trail of bad cheques and unpaid bills behind me. . . .

It was a long hard ride—with the usual merriment of the loose women that boarded between terminals to ride with their bus driver boy friends free, or to see what could be picked up—at a buck a fuck.

One thing that Melba wrote that stuck for a long time—she said if I would only be myself instead of trying to be someone else I would really amount to something—I wonder who I was trying to be then and why I wasn't being myself. Was I just cunt struck—could that have been my trouble I wonder—I often felt it was. When coming to that conclusion I would rationalize that many of our leading citizens (our most successful men in all fields of endeavor) were cunt struck. That they fucked and chased to excess—and that that was true of brilliant and successful gifted women as well. Perhaps I lacked the essential gift of brilliance of mind to offset my preponderant sex urges

362

and uncontrolable cravings—who knows—who will ever know. From Dallas I went by bus to Chicago.

[In Chicago] I was very short of cash—so I had to pull a stroke. I had the Blackstone Hotel porter get me a lower to New York—and a railroad ticket for same.

The charge for the tickets was put on my bill. When checking out, I gave my cheque for the room, restaurant, stenographer, barber, telephone and tickets—to say nothing of room service. Then I drove to the station, cancelled the reservation, turned in the tickets for cash and went down the street and boarded a bus for Washington, D. C.

That ride was boring and uneventful—but I wanted to meet Borah. . . .

I had a very pleasant visit with Senator Borah (the old firebrand of the Senate)—gave him a full report of the West and my talk with Hearst. He was pleased to learn Hearst was so friendly. . . .

I took a bus for New York—the end of my journey—I had been gone almost three months.

When I arrived at the bus terminal I phoned 2 Beekman Place. I had wired the time of my arrival to Melba—but there was no Melba to meet me which was unusual—the phone had been disconnected— I had tried to reach her by phone from Washington, but the phone never answered.

Finally I got hold of the apartment superintendent and he told me that Melba had moved out that very day bag and baggage and furniture—I was disconsolate—I phoned Joe Lilly and told him. He suggested sending her a wire with a request for a delivery report— this he did for me over his phone. Then I called up my old standby when in trouble, Jane H., and went down and spent the night with her—I would have stayed longer but she had a big black cat and I don't like cats—altho I liked screwing Jane. Joe had given her a rush and a bit of screwing while I was away.

All night the telegraph company tried to deliver the message— finally in the early hours of the morning they reported that they had delivered the message to Melba at the Sutton Hotel, a cheap joint on East 56th Street.

That had been one hell of a night—with me in a nervous uproar. I don't know how I ever got in hand enough to screw Jane, but I did.

The next day I got together with Joe and learned all he had to offer and then I phoned Ruth and imparted the glad tidings to her.

363

She was jubilant—at last I was free, for her alone—but I wasn't. It was a great shock, a blow to my vanity—I had Ruth—she was a sex delight but I was devoted to Melba and the children.

I couldn't get Melba on the phone or get her to agree to see me or answer my wires.

I got in touch with Watterson Lowe and rented his hall room for $3.00 a week (in his tenement apartment at the corner of 41st and Second Avenue)—he was away at sea most of the time so I had the apartment with its kitchen, largely to myself. The only annoyance was the few days a month when he was home—then he would have his boy friends—lovers—in to spend the night—black or white—and I was always nervous about running into them and interrupting their pleasures. . . .

Some days after I wrote Melba on the 24th—she agreed thru Joe Lilly to meet me in Central Park. . . .

Melba said that she was wasting her talents with me—that she had as much as the twins [Gloria Vanderbilt and Thelma Furness] and that she was going to marry a man with lots of money to take care of her and her harassment over finances. Freddie Davenport had been very attentive to her during my absence—it had turned her head a bit. Joe Lilly and Charles Bayer, my newspaper friends, according to Tommy Smith, had also been smelling around.

Well, we decided to do the thing quietly without rancor and without publicity. Freddie Davenport's firm, Chadbourne Stanchfield and Levy, had been advising her thru a stooge named McGrath—a guy who did the dirty work for them.

It was decided that she sue me under the name of William W. Smith and bring the action in Westchester.

I agreed to give her the phoney evidence thru one of my friends. First of all I talked it over with Morris Maltzer, whose office I used for certain mail and phone calls (Watterson Lowe didn't have a phone) —but I decided that Morris was not the man for the job so I took it up with Julius Hallheimer—this was all in the way of stalling—it seemed to throw our friends and the lawyers for as much of a loss as it did me.

Everyone seemed fond of us both and felt badly that we had come to the parting of the ways.

I was torn between two emotions—my devotion to Melba and the children and my relief at being a free agent and clear of the responsibility and burden of supporting the entire family. I have never been a steady provider and the fear of want of tomorrow has always harassed me to death—so it was a relief.

As to Ruth, I had no intention of getting hooked to that Semite —I would have cringed in shame to have been caught out in any Christian Assemblage with her.

Well—I stalled along hoping for some solution that would mean a solution of our marital rift. . . .

Joe Lilly and Gene Early tried to get me the job of Secretary of the Midtown Tunnel Commission—building the tubes to Queens under the East River—but it went elsewhere. . . .

One night after my return from the West I asked Melba to have a steak dinner with me at "Rudy's" Second Avenue Rail—a place famous for its beer and the multitude of free lunch of all kinds of sliced meats, pickles, bread and butter, cheese and crackers, etc. and beer only 5¢—hot dogs were on the house.

While we were dining there, Tommy B. entered with Betty Campbell and a new girl, a nurse he had picked up in a Third Avenue Bar a few days previous when he had first gotten his Army bonus money (from World War I), and started drinking it up as fast as he could.

Her name was Mary—she was a beauty with a very lovely body —as I was to afterward to learn.

Mary was a nurse at the Ruptured and Crippled Hospital and a bit fond of drinking herself—in fact I think she preferred drinking to screwing.

Tommy showed me his wallet which for him was bulging with dough—he bought everybody drinks and then we pretended we were going out to piss. We went across the street to another bar where Tommy told me all about Mary and his bonus money and his desire to ditch Betty, while in the gin mill several English beauties leeched on to us to our delight and theirs, at Tommy's expense.

Finally we got away from them—returned to Rudy's and drank until closing time. We insulted Betty and she went home, so we got a bottle from Rudy, and Melba and Tommy and Mary went to Watterson's with me—he being away on a ship.

We were all pretty drunk—the girls stripped and so did we. Melba went after Mary like a house on fire and Mary came right back at her.

Melba certainly loved to love girls—any hot number would do

her—it finally got too much for me so I had to give her some of my rod. God, how she fucked me that night—while I was screwing Melba, I was sucking Mary—poor old Tommy was very drunk and confused and tried to get his pecker up for Mary to suck, but he had no luck. Finally in despair, he went down on Melba—after I had left her with my load.

At dawn I took Melba to the Sutton and her children—it had been quite a night. I returned to Watt's.

Later in the morning, Tommy, wanting beer, went out for a few bottles. I was in the tub soaping myself—the bathroom door opened onto Watterson's bedroom—Mary was lying nude on the bed reading Casanova. It was too much for me—I got up out of the bath, soap suds all over my cock (erect) and gave Mary one of the best fucks I ever had out of her—returning to the tub as soon as we had both come.

Tommy came back shortly thereafter. Noticing the wet trail of my footmarks and the wet bed, he accused us—but we denied the allegation with a flimsy alibi.

I don't think Tommy believed us, for the next morning before daybreak, he got Mary up and out of there before I was awake— he couldn't do much for her with his cock, but he was determined that I was not to reap the benefit of his filling her with liquor at his expense.

After that I went to Cleveland for the Republican convention by bus. I stayed at a very cheap hotel with some farmers. I saw a good deal of King Macy—he was busy doing what he could for Borah but it was by then a lost cause. Landon had it in the bag. . . .

The most interesting event of the convention was a press interview—mass interview that Borah gave during the first day of the Convention—It was the greatest intellectual treat of a free-for-all give-and-take I ever saw, Borah matching wits with the ablest political correspondents of the nation. He never appeared to side-track or dodge—he stated his position on the platform and what he proposed to have in it. He was fighting to the end but while he got his way as to platform planks he wanted he didn't get the nomination —and he knew he was too old to try again.

I visited Hoover in his hotel room after he had delivered his oration to the convention—a speech which he had hoped would sweep the crowd off their feet, and cause the convention to nominate him by acclaim. It missed the mark—it fizzled out—Hoover was a sad sight that night, dejected, forlorn and neglected. . . .

I was with Borah during the balloting—he too was alone in his room with but his secretary, Cora Rubin standing by. She was depressed and weeping—they both knew that the Senator's last chance to be President of the United States had come and gone. He would be too old to try again—he died before the next one.

American crowds are wonderful—when they think a man may be a winner they crowd around to get on the band wagon—they push and fight and jam to get near him—but when the tide turns and he is thru or licked, they desert him like rats deserting a sinking ship. Then he is left severely alone by all, to commune with himself and contemplate the hollowness of his fellowman. He hasn't changed—he is the same fellow, with the same ability and charm—but the crowd has changed, they have raced off to idealize another hero newly made—and so it goes. . . .

I returned from the Cleveland convention of 1936 to start working for the Lawrence Whit Public Relations Organization on a commission basis. . . .

I got a room and bath at the Hotel St. Margaret for $7.00 per week to be paid for as I could. I moved myself and papers—they were voluminous—things Melba had turned over to me.

It was a creep house where men took rooms and Dave C. the night manager sent them girls to assuage their sexual appetites—and some brought their own women—it was cheap. Stanley H. had lived there in a drunken stupor for several years before La Guardia gave him a job as a Deputy Commissioner of Welfare and then made him "Secretary to the Mayor."

[I remember the St. Margaret and Dave C. very well. My father took me there, introduced me to Mr. C. and told him to get me a woman whenever I wanted one and charge it to him along with the room rent.]

Ruth came there once or twice—on several occasions when we got real tight we stayed at the Coolidge Hotel across the street from the St. Margaret for hours at a time and had chinese food sent in with liquor while we screwed hell out of one another often rowing, beating, scratching and biting in our blind passion.

Melba came to the St. Margaret several times to be fucked. Sometimes I never left the Hotel from one day to the other just laying there fucking my head off.

I picked up a waitress in the Savarin—a hostess. She lived in Brooklyn but came up occasionally for a matinee. She was Alva H.

who lived at the Montague Hotel—103 Montague Street, Brooklyn.

One night during the Olympics which were being held in Berlin, Joe L., a Tax Commissioner afterwards president of the Board, and Stanley H. (the Mayor's Secretary) came up to see my dirty movies and get fucked. Dave C. got us three lovely girls—when the pictures started running the boys got hot. Stanley H. wasn't drinking although a bottle was at his elbow—he ignored it, but Joe made up for that— as they got hot they started to work on the girls. In no time at all the dames were stripped and the boys had their cocks out—the girls licked them and one another—soon they were in keen competition with the movies. I have trouble getting an erection with professional "whores" —my prick wouldn't rise. They all worked on me but I left the fucking to my illustrious guests—Stanley between long distance calls to the Olympic officials in Berlin tore off two pieces while Joe got in three— Joe had to try each girl. After the girls departed Joe became remorse- ful—raving about his lovely wife and adorable child and worrying about getting a dose of clap or syphilis. He was so worried he washed his cock in piss, cold water and soap and then took three prophylactics —Sanatubes. After Joe's cleansing outburst we went to dinner at the Brass Rail and Joe swore that never, never, never again would he be untrue to his wife—he was worried to death—he was always that way after every promiscuous fuck. After dinner we went back to the St. Margaret—Joe wanted to take another prophylactic. In the lobby was a pretty prostitute—a blonde. Joe got "het-up" all over again— when we got up to my room he had me phone Dave for the girl—he wanted to talk to her about her life. She came right up and in no time he forgot all about her life's story and was fucking her on my bed— five dollars' worth. When she departed he started to rave and cry about his wife and child as he administered another sanatube—it's guys like Joe who enrich the Sanatube Company.

Across the Street in the Coolidge, on the floor level with my room, were two girls, sisters, with a man who was the husband of one of them. I often saw them having a three cornered workout— it would get me so hot that I would jerk off watching them. One night when I had the light on they noticed me playing with myself —the next day when the husband was out they ran around nude near the window waving to me and playing with their pussies—as I jerked off. After several days of this monkey business I signaled one of them to come over, it was right after supper. The girl had no sooner reached the hotel and gotten up to my room than Melba arrived with some papers for me—but really for a fuck. I hurriedly placed the girl—she

368

spoke only French—in the room next to mine occupied by a Spaniard antique wood worker named Mario and I asked him to look after her until I could get Melba satisfied and out of the way—this he did with Dave standing guard to protect my interests until Melba left. Then I took on Frenchy. She couldn't understand English and I couldn't understand French but we both knew how to screw. All this took place after Melba had sued me for her divorce on the grounds of adultery—and that adultery if there had ever been any real adultery that she knew about and disapproved of she was condoning by her very acts at the St. Margaret. . . .

One time when Melba came to the St. Margaret to be fucked, I tied her hands over her head to the bed posts and her feet to the foot boards or iron, then with my belt I beat or lashed hell out of her until I drew great welts and blood in some places. She loved to have her cunt lashed and slapped, it excited her terrifically and me likewise and then we went to it.

On this last occasion Melba begged me never to use her weakness against her in fighting the divorce. (Whenever a wife has intercourse with her husband regardless of the marital status, in the eyes of the law she has condoned all of the previous acts which she has claimed to disapprove of and object to—many a woman has lost a good divorce case by just such weaknesses.)

During that summer I spent much time on the beaches with Ruth G. going out in the morning for a picnic supplied by her with her liquor, and in her car. . . .

Forty-seventh Street was quite a street—gangsters, murderers, bums, drunks, gamblers, broken down actresses and actors—down and outers of every class or strata of society found their way to 47th Street. Pimps and fairies mingled with the whores, racetrack touts, taxidrivers of very questionable repute, Chinese, Japanese, soldiers, sailors, niggers, Filipinos, Marines, newspapermen—all up against it, hiding out—the drunks were legion.

If you preferred to sleep in the daytime and to stay up all night, Forty-seventh Street before the war was the place. The lights glared there all thru the night—not only was there the reflection from the gay white way always overhead (half a block away) but the hotel lights and signs that were 47th Street's own, announcing the wonders of each tavern's delights or of oriental foods or Chinese laundries, glittered and gleamed from sunset to dawn. I loved it— I was drawing $25 a week for expenses and entertaining—that

369

meagre sum paid for my rent, for my food, for my liquor and for my women—life was something then.

I bluffed my reports—I had to.

I got up late every day between 3:00 and 4:00 in order to check in.

All night long the street teemed with activity—when the saloons closed the drunks sat on the steps (of the old brownstone rooming houses) and screamed and swore and fought till dawn. Brutal brawls would take place in the wee small hours of the morning—swearing and cursing they would fight and roll in the gutter, women and men, men and men, women and women (the women were the worst).

The police never seemed to bother very much. They brawled and beat one another and fucked as they rolled in the gutter—with or without clothes as the case might be. The daughter of a prominent physician—he wealthy but she a drunkard—would swizzle until the "dumps" put her out screaming—then with an extra bottle of fire-water bribed from some bum she would sit up until dawn night after night—in bedraggled rags, upbraiding the rats who surrounded her, eager for a few extras drams of her alcoholic poison. She would curse them and defame them and feed them liquor in return for their admiring attention.

Life flowed thru that street at its height from midnight to morn—drinking, screwing, brawling—men and women, their pagan emotions bare for all to see unashamed, unabashed—no inhibition on that "drab" (by day) and tawdry glittering by night street.

It might have been an outcast haunt in Shanghai, for food, lodging, liquor and women were cheap there—and sometimes one would be killed.

One night I ran into a very shabby fellow—dejected depressed, listless, and a bit dazed—hardly recognizable— He was loafing in front of one of the creep houses. The last time I had seen him he had been a spry snappy active young assistant Vice-President of the Bank of America in charge of that institution's Southern Correspondent bank.

At the bank he had always been well groomed and attractive—vital and immaculate.

He had been let out when the National City absorbed the Bank of America—then had come the crash of '29. Banks had failed all over the country—there had been a superfluity of banking men and business-getters—there was no place for him. He stood the degradation—the failure—as long as he could—then he committed suicide.

Men having failed in life or on their way up from the depths of humble surroundings somehow seemed to find their way into the

47th street "Maelstrom"—some never got out—some sank further into the oblivion of the bowery slop houses or the Bellevue Alcoholic ward or the City morgue or potters field.

Some merely stopped there on their way down the toboggan. Coming down, they cushioned there and picking themselves up, rose again to a proper place in the sun—others just gave up.

Some went up and then returned as adversity overcame them once again—some never descended so low again. Those that climbed back were mostly men.

Women when they go down down down to the depths of poverty and depravity or become dope fiends or alcoholics, seldom redeem themselves and reclimb the social economic ladder.

The ravages of time—the trials and tribulations—the worries and cares tell on women sooner than on men, leaving a devastating and irradicable scar—women show their misery physically more plainly than men. Their vitality, their virility generally lessens faster with the years than with men.

During the summer months not only were there fights and brawls to keep up the hubbub, but jute boxes, the small string instrument orchestras, the little tavern dance bands, the broken down piano players, the vocalists that huskily rasped out their bawdy tidbits for a glass of grog, a crust of bread or a night's lodging—in order that the visiting firemen and their lady friends of questionable character might be amused.

It all added up to life as she was lived on New York's tawdriest street—47th between 6th and 7th Avenue. That was my home from the middle of June until the middle of August 1936.[1]

There was enough going on at night to make you forget your own troubles and to keep you up until you fell off to sleep near day break.

Watching the men register at the desk and ask for a girl or register with a stray street walker who was always a sight. Men are just as shy in New York about their screwing (the would-be cosmopolite and sophisticated of the big city) as the country yokel, miner or farm boy from the hills of Nevada visiting a crib for a lay. Their entrances are just as nervous and nerve wracking and their exits as embarrassed—and they are hot as hell when they enter, agitation personified—and they all wonder as they depart why they bothered, what the hell had been the necessity—worried for fear they may have gotten a dose—and why hadn't they stuck by their old woman or their steady.

Even the regulars, who were cheating on somebody and came

371

every week on a certain night, were always just a little bit timid—a little ashamed—as they made their arrangements with poker-faced Dave C. for the sexual festivities of the evening. Even the half potted were bashful.

Vice ungarnished is dull and uninspiring and as every whore or madam knows once a male has shot his load remorse sets in and he wonders why he took the trouble. Then the cunt stands cold before him unadorned and shorn of the glitter and glamour of a stiff prick illusion—he might just as well have used the knot hole or a bit of vaseline or putty thinks he, and maybe it would have been just as well or better. . . .

I had gotten behind in my rent at the St. Margaret a matter of six or seven weeks. Dave, (the night man), or Leonard, (the day man), never spoke to me about it, but one day the new owner asked me if he could have a little something on account. I had just had my expense money raised to $35 per week payable every 15 days—and so I announced that I not only would pay him a little something on account, but I would pay up my entire arrears and move out. That meant an immediate search for a new place. Sunday was the day—I read *The New York Times* furnished room and furnished apartment want ads—I checked those I thought would be desirable and sallied forth afoot.

At 904 Park Avenue two flights up in the rear I found a large combination bed room and living room with kitchenette, bath and dressing room—it looked out on an attractively furnished garden—summer tables, colorful umbrellas, swings, flowers, a little pool with fish, etc. and backed up on the Todd Hunter School.

James S., former head of the National City Bank whose wife was Fifi S.—whose girl friend was Flo Leaves of the Indian Guide divorce case fame—owned the house. It adjoined his palatial home on the northwest corner of 79th Street and Park Avenue—the rent was $50 furnished, with linens, until October 1st then $50 unfurnished—Melba had all the furniture so I had no choice about a furnished or unfurnished place.

I was favorably impressed—upon leaving I noticed a very beautiful woman in a dressing gown at the door of the ground floor apartment. She apologized and said she thought I had rung her bell—she was the tenant with the garden apartment. I discussed the apartment house with her and she invited me in, offered me a drink, etc. That decided me—what with a neighbor like that, life should be very pleasant—her apartment was attractively furnished—her living room had a large piano, and her furnishings were all smart and expensive.

From the mailbox or doorbell I found that her name was Harriet S.—before I got back to the St. Margaret I tried to telephone her but her phone was private (non-listed) so I sent her a screwball sentimental wire and some flowers and asked her to phone me which she did about 8:00 o'clock—she invited me back and I came arunnin'— we had a bit to drink—Harriet was quite tight and quite decollete.

She excited me so I spent the night—she had an attractively appointed bedroom and bath, and a full size kitchen and dinette well stocked—she was amusing, full of fun, gay and carefree—and loved to fuck.

The next day I rented the apartment and moved—kissing the St. Margaret goodbye. Tommy B. helped me move and Ruth G. loaned me her car to save cab fare, etc.

All my life I have had a weakness for a home, a place to cook, to entertain—I've always preferred entertaining at home more than going out to night clubs, restaurants, etc. Meals at home mean much more even when I have to cook them, serve them and wash the dishes and clean up afterwards.

Harriet S. was a former Ziegfeld beauty of the bygone days —she was a lot of fun. . . .

That was when Park Avenue was a junk pile—a haven for goats and tramps—it was but an open cut and the New York Central and the New Haven roads burnt coal for steam in their locomotives. . . .

Being free I met many new and attractive women—although I was hampered by a lack of cash. . . .

The incidents were not worth recording in detail. There were others that I have already mentioned and still others that I will discuss as I go on. . . .

I sometimes wonder why I pound this out—I doubt if you will ever read it or if anyone will ever have the fortitude to wade through such a mass of personal junk.

Recently I have been going to funerals of certain friends—something you never do until you have passed the half century mark—and the futility of it all weighs in upon you whether you attend an orthodox Hebrew service, Romanist, Presbyterian or what have you.

Then I listen to people yap who have gone in for science, astrology or mysticism.

Heard the arguments of those who believed in reincarnation.

For myself I do not believe that the set of the planets at the time of our birth has anything to do with our dominant characteristics.

If there were anything to such fancies, it would have to prevail at the time of conception—not after the egg is set and the child has reached the sufficient development to step forth on its own.

Nothing can affect the human's mental processes at that time—it must occur at the time of the blending of the two bloodstreams that produced the fertile egg—so astronomical effects at womb ejection are meaningless.

I seriously doubt if there is any hereafter—except as parents live on in their children and their children's children until the third and fourth generation.

Just as the fruit of the tree fertilizes the tree—unless the fruit is removed and commercial and synthetic fertilizers substituted—so the human goes back into the soil, in the flesh or as ashes—and makes in either case excellent fertilizer for crops to feed his children and his children's children—or being civilized, we waste that fertilizer because of fanatic rituals embraced by man in the various sects that abound the world around. . . .

You cannot deny nature's plan of checking development—we will always have in nature our feasts and then our famines—water will not run up hill unless forced by man using a greater energy than the flow of water—then you can only force it up—it will not run up of its own volition—and after you force it up it will quickly seek its own level.

You cannot waste without wanting—we here have wasted our re-sources and manpower for eleven long years, and now the nation wants—except for the war plant workers (who are but viciously overpaid draft dodgers) and yet the war workers want, too, because their ill gotten gains will not buy them the things they wish for since they are nonexistent, for Mr. Roosevelt did not permit us to accumulate in times of plenty.

When we had much, our stocks of cattle, pigs and grain and cap-ital were wantonly destroyed by the New Dealers until our National Granary was nearly empty.

It is tragic to see a great nation that developed free enterprise and individual initiative—a nation which was founded to such a great and unlimited degree to escape the embitterments of nationalistic clashes, cramped economy, religious prejudices—surreptitiously embrace all the false and misguided tenets and prejudices of the embittered and warring peoples of the world at the colossal sacrifice of our own blood on the field of battle and the destruction at home of the very institutions

374

that we diligently and painstakingly built to get and keep away from the European mess.

If we are to give the people of the world all our resources every time they go to war they will always go to war and our standards of living will always be lowered by the amount that we raise theirs.

We are suckers for honeyed words—the mental process of the masses the world over is low—the people of China, Russia, Japan, Italy, Germany, England and the United States are fall guys for catch phrases and grinning dictators.

Hitler murders a few thousand jews who had tried to take over the life of the German people, so he is a beast—Stalin exterminates millions of Christians but he is a great hero because after several years of desperate fighting with our Military supplies, our tanks, ammunitions, arms, airplanes and food (much of which he cannot use) he is able to drive the enemy (a former ally in rape) out of his own country.

The jews objected to Hitler's extermination program—the Christians were docile about Stalin's massacre of the Russians.

We were propagandized, pushed and shoved into the war by the jews on the side of the murderer of Christians who had by stealth been trying to undermine and destroy our government and our way of life.

Russia, where the standards of living had fallen as low if not lower than in China, was held before us as a great ideal to be obtained.

The jews were at the bottom of it all—they were the real agitators —for war and the overthrow of our constitutional government.

When war finally came—where were the jews? In hiding—using every kind and known type of subterfuge to avoid the draft and getting away with it. . . .

Today we have rabble rousers who are the leading inciters for their own political benefit—in order to perpetuate themselves in office —encouraging the jews to follow their sect line—having the negros front for them on the question of race discrimination.

I can remember when I courted Jewesses—loved them and fucked them—most jewish women are well trained in cock sucking— both the married women and the young girls.

When I had my own office I was scrupulously careful never to show religious prejudice—in fact, I didn't have any—I had as many jewish girls as Christians working for me.

Well I must get on with my story—but every so often I find it necessary to blow off about the jews—they are such mean petty stinkers—and yet there is little to add to the detailed dissertation I indulged in somewhere back when I started that section of my letter, so I will

375

return to the subject matter at hand—my life in 1936 as I recall it.

I gave a party on my birthday that year at 904 and another in December the day Edward the VIII abdicated—I need not go into the details of Wallis Warfield's love affair here as you know them better than I do.

You have read from your Aunt Virginia's diary how those girls, Virginia Page and Wallis Warfield and Emily Merryman got around together—what (as silly youngs things) they thought of the then Prince of Wales—how they eavesdropped at the head of the stairs in your grandfather's house at 941 North Calvert Street to your father's wooing of your mother, and their comments thereon—and how years later I was unable to recall Wallis Warfield the debutante but always retained a vivid recollection of Emily Merryman, the other one of the trio—who was the first girl to kiss me at the wedding after your mother and I had been joined in holy wedlock. . . .

The sex life at 904 was so rampant that I have a hard time getting around to my other activities. . . .

The bankruptcy had cleared a few debts away and for a time I was in the clear but the farm soon got me down. While it was run as a corporation and worked as such people were always trying to get around the company at me or suing the company—then when I lived at 2 Beekman place I ran into heavy debt trying to get by with Melba and the children and their schooling on a nickel—and keep going— there were the bills from the West Coast hotel and my travels for Borah etc.—they had a way of sneaking up on me—people were always inadvertently telling my creditors of my whereabouts, and the process servers were forever on the search. It was a useless performance but harrowing to me—I have for the most part lived the life of a hunted man, of a criminal at bay—I knew they couldn't do anything to me— I had not stolen—but I was always getting threatening letters from lawyers and investigators and being hounded constantly by process servers, many who perjured themselves so that judgments would be taken without my knowledge and I would find myself in contempt of court for failure to answer summonses in supplementary proceedings which had never been served—but the process server had falsely sworn to having served me in order to collect his fee with the least amount of trouble.

For years I have been judgment proof—I have had nothing that could be attached—I have earned little yet always they are after me. It hasn't been a happy state of affairs—and has given me what some might call an inferiority complex.

If it had not been for the adoring adorables to bolster my deflated ego I would have expired long ago. To always be expecting such unpleasantness is in itself depressing, disturbing and mentally unhealthy —in fact it affects everything and everyone about you adversely.

Then the trips to court—waiting, waiting, waiting for your case to be called. . . .

[My father rented an apartment on 83rd Street with Tommy B. and then attempted to sublet it at a higher price to create some income.]

Peg H. of 43 West 85th Street and then 307 W. 76th Street was quite a woman—she had two kids and was trying to keep going by renting apartments—she lived with the children in one room in the house at 43 West 85th Street near Central Park West—Peg came to look at the apartment for a client.

Peg spent several nights with me at 83rd Street both when Tommy was there and away—I gave her $25 to get her real estate brokers license with.

I didn't know what it cost then but she got something for herself out of it. I helped her with small sums for food for the children and we had a lot of fun—she was a wonderful fuck, just built for screwing—enough animation to give her ass to you with lusty thrusts— and she loved it—and so did I.

When she came the whole world could know it for all she cared and she would let out a snort that was something—while she was holding on she had a grip that was nobody's business—and her flood was something. Her first name was Margaret but she liked to be called Peg.

We spent a good deal of time together that month and it helped to get over the bumps—I received three different deposits on that apartment that failed to materialize—they all dropped out—some wanted their money back when they decided they weren't going thru with the deal—but I was relentless, I needed the dough. I never saw a place where so many wanted it on first inspection and then backed out after other members of their family would disapprove.

When renting one or two rooms you have only the individual who is going to live in the place to contend with—but when you rent a seven-room apartment, their mama and papa and the seven little dwarfs all have to be considered—to say nothing of the sisters and the cousins and the aunts. . . .

The stories of those negotiations would fill a volume. That was a tough neighborhood and we were handicapped not having a phone —we didn't turn on the electricity, we had only the gas that came with the rent, we used candles and were out most evenings—there are a few sections of New York that are so unpleasant. . . .

Four or five bucks, sometimes three a week, would get a room in that area. There were higher priced ones, and suites or front rooms for the whores—street walkers—the massage artist—the dancing parlors etc. where every variation of intercourse known to man was indulged in. . . .

Christmas rolled around and found us very low in funds—Tommy and your father. I had bought presents for the Ettl children and Joe Lilly's, and for Melba's—she and the children were living at 14 East 60th Street and she was sliding by with work at Sonia's now and then, and help from the girls—Morgan twins. . . .

Tommy was contributing a couple of dollars for his room so he had the room with the brass bed—I slept on the floor.

After selling the plates and brass lamp it occurred to me that the parlour (or living room) furniture might have a value, so I called in a half dozen antique dealers to make offers—two were enraged that they had been called to look at such junk—one offered $75 cash to take it out at once—then I asked $250—another went to $125. Then I was sure I had something—finally one fellow who started at $100 came up to $200 and I let him have it—in a weak moment, I let Melba have half of it for the children—then I bought a folding wire spring bed arrangement on 9th Avenue & 43rd Street for five dollars and took it home in a cab—so that got me off the floor—but Peggy still preferred the floor to the springs, for her fucking—and I think she had something.

During the morning, we got together a meagre breakfast. Peggy came over during the day with a bit of holly and her ass—that left Tommy to the daily paper. For Xmas dinner we went to Stewart's Cafeteria for a couple of bowls of soup and some vegetables, bread and butter—we had a buck between us and we spent 60¢ of it—that was a low point Xmas for me. The only bright spot had been Peggy and her tail—and that had its drawbacks when you took in the surroundings and knew her condition.

After our repast at Stewarts we returned to 83rd Street and slept it off.

The next day a Christmas card from Elise arrived with a $10 bill attached. It was a welcome Xmas present, but it would have been more welcome before than after Xmas—then we could have had a real feed.

It was not a novelty for Tommy—being a bit of a rum hound,

he had frequently found himself broke on Xmas day from imbibing too much the night before—but Xmas 1936 was a very sober one, both before, during and after.

I suppose a handout at the Mills Hotel or the Municipal Lodging might have been worse.

1936 had been quite a year—much activity—income from nothing to $750 per month and down again—visiting with the mighty, living with the derelicts all in the same year, sometimes in the same month or week.

Man is certainly an adjustable creature—to climate, to adversity, to riches—there hadn't been, I can truthfully say, a dull moment in 1936.

In the middle of August riding downtown in the subway to have lunch with Joe L. and the other commissioners of the City Government, I caught sight of a lovely thing. I looked and she looked—she left the train at Grand Central. It was the East Side of course, and she headed north by East—I followed—to hell with the Commissioners—they would have done the same. I caught up with the strikingly attractive damsel and she didn't object—seemed she was headed for the Beaux Art Apartments where she had a very nice layout—it developed she was going home for a mid-day repast—she was selling offset printing to some of the large steamship and railroad companies.

I fell like a ton of bricks and instead of eating, we screwed. She was "Bobbie Lee" from Savannah, the daughter of a Georgia cop—she was lovely to look at and wonderful to screw.

She soon became a court favorite, giving G. a close race for number one position in my affections. The only trouble with Bobbie was that she had two or three old guys from Georgia who had made good in New York in a big way, who took her out wining and dining, and to the theatre, dripping with orchids—among her devoted lovers she numbered Bedeaux of International fame—the guy who was going to bring the Prince of Wales to America, but didn't.

Bobbie was a frequent visitor to 904 on her nights and afternoons off. She had a bungalow in the foothills of New Jersey—I was going out there for Thanksgiving with her when I learned you were coming thru—so I took her to the train in Jersey and returned to meet you. I had a habit of introducing her to all and sundry—while I was still tied up to Melba (which was safe)—as my third legal wife to be. . . .

And so I pass from 1936, the year of ups and downs, mostly

downs—sex life rampant—I kept my pecker up sexually that year.

Borah—women—California—women—real estate—women— the Republican National Convention—women—Melba's divorce proceedings—women—Mary Pickford—and whores of every degree —William Randolph Hearst—women—public relations—women— an inheritance—women, women, women—and Ruth G.—that was a fast moving year and little change.

And so I turn that page in my life to 1937—and that was an even more turbulent year.

1937

1937 came in with a struggle—alleviated in small part by my real estate deals on the apartment at 904, where I was getting $35.00 a month profit, and the apartment at 83rd Street, which was rent free—I was still in litigation over the Provident Loan account with the Whit Organization, and I was unable to get anything substantial from my inheritance from the Lucy Ward estate.

1937 saw Melba the vocalist with Vincent Lopez's orchestra at the Astor Hotel—saw me move from 83rd Street on the 19th of January to the Ritz Carlton where I remained until the 19th of June, when I moved to the apartment (furnished on 82nd Street East) where I remained until October 1st, when I moved again, this time to the Vanderbilt Hotel and from there I took my apartment at 6 East 37th Street.

That was the year in which Ruth G. was quite a bit on the wane—that is the year that we fell for Jerry Worthing, the actress who had played at Hanover—that was the year I visited Lydia Locke at Yorktown Heights, that was the year that I met Ellen Niehaus, the German refugee, and fell for her—that is the year I gave a party in the kitchen of Joe Pani's Merry-Go-Round on the day when the Hindenberg blew up at Lakehurst, May 6th.

That was the year that Harriet S. and the cat woman were

having a big time of it—that was the year that Ruth G. and Mabel Baron visited me at the Ritz Carlton, where they had cocktails with Joe L. and myself in my apartment while the movies were being shown—that was the year that the vitriolic Margie K. was in my life.

That was the year that I opened my own business, W. Ward Smith & Associates—that was the year that I discovered the Provident Loan were not seeking publicity when they engaged the Whit Organization and subsequently Ward Smith & Associates, but were in fact, seeking a contact with the Mayor, in order to amicably adjust their differences with him, and when that was accomplished they no longer needed me. . . .

That was the year that the Missing Persons Bureau claimed that Melba had been seen in California, with the missing Judge Crater—when she was singing at the Astor all the time—and which Harold Fowler finally straightened out.

That was the year Melba and Esther S. had an affair at the Ritz—Esther was Lopez's secretary and mistress at the time—that was the year that I had charge of the publicity for the First National Trailer Show.

That was the year that I established agents for my Publicity Bureau all over the world—that was the year I fell for Sylvia Randolph (A Canadian Jewess)—that was the year that I obtained signatures (5,000) petitioning me for a candidate for Councilman under proportional representation (I only needed 2500)—I didn't file because the expense seemed to be prohibitive.

That was the year I met Margaret M. who afterwards played such an important part in the life of Tommy B., that I met and fell for Lorell P.—and that I became enamored of Norah Anderson, the painter, sculptress and dancer—that I made fudge for my Christmas presents—that Ruth G. sent me the turkey from Gristedes. . . .

[My father here lists the names and addresses of thirty-nine women with whom he had affairs that year.]

That was the year that I got high when my teeth were to be extracted and was charged with disorderly conduct (case being dismissed thanks to political influence).

That was the year that I tried to bring Paul and Bob Moses together for the purpose of having Paul tell Bob he didn't know what he was talking about in connection with trailer space at the World's Fair (purpose publicity for the Trailer Show). That was the year that Gypsy Rose Lee was a flop when she appeared at the Trailer Exhibit.

This was the year that I had my famous art [photograph] collection of the feminine beauties that had been in my life, prominently displayed in my apartment at 6 East 37th Street, Apartment 5-D.

This was the year that Lorell P. was going to decorate my bathroom with exotic paintings, but a boyfriend and the Mary Elizabeth candy store blower or air-conditioner prevented.

And it was just at the last of the year, between Xmas and New Year, when you were returning to Dartmouth, that I first met Berenice Holloway—but that little story will have to wait to be told mostly in 1938. . . .

After renting the apartment and settling matters with the Provident Loan, I moved to the Ritz Carlton Hotel—where, because of the poor times, I was able to engage, as you may recall, a fairly large room and bath for the nominal sum of $4.50 a day, payable weekly. . . .

Probably the most important event of that December was unexpected—and at the time I am sure that you never anticipated that my life would be so affected by an event as minor and as innocent as occurred on the evening you phoned me from the station enroute back to Hanover, after spending Christmas at Baltimore.

If you remember, as I remember, you were returning to Dartmouth before the holidays were over in order to undertake some special work, or maybe you were just tired of provincial Baltimore.

Just before you called, Ruth G. had telephoned me—it was after dinner—her husband then had gone to a prize fight or something, and she had an urge to be with me—I too was eager for her. Hardly had I agreed to meet her and hung up the phone, when your call came thru—so I immediately cancelled my date with her. You came over to 37th Street and we visited together between your trains.

We chatted for quite a while about this and that, the future of the nation and the world—then we ambled off to the station—and that was to eventually change the course of the life I was then living.

In November, December '37, I had seen a great deal of Benjamin Hanft at the 37th Street apartment but I hadn't been able to get anything going from the standpoint of productive activity. I bought a portable typewriter, a copy of *Webster's Unabridged Dictionary,* and a *Columbia University Encyclopedia* and settled down to writing, frugal living and intensive loving—definitely on the promiscuous side—but we're coming to that shortly now—and before we do, I want to finish off the serious side of 1937.

Arriving at Grand Central Terminal, we strolled down to your car, or Pullman, and we put your things away in your berth, and then we returned to the platform for final goodbyes. As we stood there talking, my eye caught and your glance followed a very smartly turned out female of the species (attired in a short Kolinsky fur jacket) coming down the platform. We struck a bargain—if she boarded the train for the North she was to be yours—if she didn't board the train, but was merely there to say goodbye to a departing passenger, she was to be my game.

She passed us, unnoticing our very existence—and headed for the forward cars. Up near the end of the platform she was joined by another girl and several men—we watched them and discussed them—then the cry was "all aboard"—the men boarded the train, the girls remained on the platform. You stepped into the vestibule of your car and as it gained momentum, closed the door—we had said our goodbyes. We had been talking about Charles Meredith and the Little Theatre movement—Charles was in town—you had been eager to meet him—for a moment you had been undecided whether to change your reservation and stay over, or return to College, as you had originally planned—you finally decided to go on. As the train moved out, you tried to call a message to me—it had to do with Meredith, and your plan to write him—in order to get what you were saying, I had to sprint alongside the moving train.

Now the girls had turned—they were walking back. As I jogged by, keeping up with you, a facetious observation was half mumbled, half spoken in jest—then I waved a fond paternal farewell, and turned in my tracks back to the station. I hadn't gone far, and it did not require many rapid steps for me to overhaul them.

The girl I coveted was on the offside from me and disinclined to enter into conversation—the one nearest me was not in the least reticent.

The girl in the Kolinsky coat—the one you and I had spotted and staked our imaginary claims on—was reserved—she did not enter into the light banter between her girl friend and myself as we strolled back down the platform to the station. In fact, it was not until we were in the center of Grand Central that we got around to introductions—to which I paid, as usual, little heed (mistakenly, unfortunately—a bad slothful habit—always a handicap)—I then suggested that we have a "drinkee."

I had about 40¢ to my name—enough for a taxi to 37th Street and that was all—but there behind the bar I had the grog.

The girls accepted my invitation (thinking, as I was afterwards informed, that I was taking them to a new place. I was—but it was my own, private—not public).

When we alighted from the cab they expressed some surprise, when I escorted them into the self-operated lift they were convinced that all was not well—at the door to the apartment, when I searched for my key, the girl in the Kolinsky balked, but her companion, by that time, consumed with curiosity, and being a bold piece, was determined to go thru with it, and see the inside of the den of iniquity—and she succeeded in breaking down the resistance of the girl in the Kolinsky.

When we got into the apartment, the bold one asked for cigarettes, and I, having no money, it was rather embarrassing. She finally got it thru her dumb head that there were to be no cigarettes at 37th Street that night—so she decided it was time to go, much to the relief of the shy one—so they both departed after a giggling conference in the bathroom—before leaving for their homes, unescorted by men account of my lack of cab fare, cigarette money, etc.

The bold one gave me her name, address and telephone number for the book—the retiring lass (who had a very seductive way of nonchalantly handling her lanky limbs) was disinclined to furnish details about herself—but I had picked up enough from the conversation while the girls were at the apartment to make it possible for me to get the quiet one's phone number from information, but not correctly enough to find it in the book for myself—we will come to that shortly however.

Little I realized that night that the entire course of my future was to be so definitely altered—not without a struggle—and that I was to become another personality molded into the pattern of a "Berenice Holloway design."

June 6th, 1944:—3:45 A.M.—It's D-Day! When I came downstairs I noticed in the darkened Huylers candy store the outline dimly silhouetted of a man and woman—they were loving there in the dark —so I strolled down the street and when I strolled back again it was to see a white girl and a negro boy in fond embrace at the door—they looked up and strolled up the Avenue—he with his arm around her shoulder in fond embrace—they noticed me watching the amorous tableau and waved a greeting—defiant—some might say the degeneracy, the perversity of it caused my prick to rise—well, thought I,

384

this is the new era, the new decade—the crossing of the races black and white, the mingling of men and women of all colors, creeds, nationalities the world over—that's what fighting produces—that's the debris in the wake of war.

At that very minute men were being cut down by withering fire, blown to pieces by the ground and aerial bombings, the bombings beneath the ground or the water's surface, and from the skies above, as they raced ashore to the beachheads of France to destroy an Aryan who had hoped and planned for a superior white race (by the complete extermination of the Semitic scourge from the face of the earth). Hitler may have had the right idea, whereas our monstrous semitic and negro loving dictator may well have been all wrong—only posterity will be able to record that fact long after we have gone.

Those were my observations, my thoughts, my activities on that momentous occasion as the hour struck—H-Hour, D-day.

Now back to the past. . . .

Ruth G. had been away most of that winter in Florida (1937) and I found that I got along much better without her than with her. Despite my promiscuousness—my screwing all over the place—I was able to attend to business better—I always do a better job when fucking the field than when tied up to one dame, legally or otherwise. Discovering this, I decided to ignore Ruth on her return—but that only worked for a short while. . . .

Girls! Girls! Girls! All types, sizes and shapes. All colors and creeds—the Ritz drew them like flies to molasses. After the Ritz, it was the penthouse in the walkup that attracted the wenches—then the Vanderbilt Hotel and finally the conveniently located studio on 37th Street off the Avenue, in the heart of New York's commercial center just down the block from J. P. Morgan's on the Southeast corner of Madison and the National Democratic Club on the N.E. Corner of Madison Avenue. . . .

One evening, as my sojourn at the Ritz was nearing its end, and the pile of bills in the Hotel safe deposit box was getting lower and lower, Tommy B. phoned—an old girl of his, a bit passe— in her late sixties but still with substantial funds—a typical continental cosmopolite who maintained an elaborate salon in Paris. . . .

Julie Batchelder, the old bat—Tommy's gal of the evening had an old battle axe in tow—currently known as Lydia Locke—a former aspirant for Metropolitan Opera honors, so she said.

Tommy not wanting to discourage Julie's desire to provide a

festive occasion—food and liquor at no cost to himself—sought to please Julie by getting me to make up the foursome. Altho I was short of cash, I wasn't much interested and didn't care to have old dames buying meals for me.

However, I agreed to assist him in whatever nefarious plot he was up to, and which inevitably was—as it was in this case—an effort to inveigle large quantities of alcoholic stimulant without any expenditure of cash on his part.

Lydia was fat and fifty and must have weighed over 250 pounds —a loud, boisterous, domineering and unattractive whore with a filthy tongue who dwelt entirely on sex and sex perversions—Lydia swore like a trooper, and the uncomfortable part about those old gals was that they always insisted upon going to the smart, quiet places where they were their loudest. Being extravagant guests and tipping lavishly, managements reluctantly put up with them in dull times— now one of the old gals is dead and the other is dying.

During dinner it was decided to go to the Merry-Go-Round to see Melba—it would be noisier there and they would be less conspicuous then at the Old Bijou where we dined, much to my embarrassment.

One of Lydia's greatest claims to fame was the fact that she had either inherited or received large alimony or settlements running into millions from five different husbands—she had been accused of murdering two of her spouses, and had stood trial and had been acquitted in at least one instance.

While I painfully shoved her about the floor at the Merry-Go-Round, she suggested a weekend at her estate in Westchester, and it was an estate—in fact three estates—a stupendous place at Yorkshire Heights—three mansions—one of them her former husband had built for her and lavishly furnished—another built by a previous owner and one she had recently completed for herself in widow-hood.

As part of the new house, she had a very beautiful music room or organ hall more like a private chapel, adjoining the main house— just why one with a career such as hers behind her, should have felt in need of such an inspiring sanctuary, I was never able to fathom, but she had it built herself and she had installed a most valuable organ.

She enticed me—she lured me—with a luscious description of a teen age voluptuous illegitimate niece of hers—so I accepted, protesting all the while that my real interest in going up was Lydia, and that was why I was going.

386

My tenure at the Ritz being on thin ice, I decided against taking one of my largest suitcases for the weekend in order to avoid any suspicion of a contemplated getaway—instead I purchased for $5.00 a petite overnight case of real leather, it was goodlooking—smart—it is now in storage at the Willard Hotel in Washington. . . .

Lydia met me at the station in a big chauffeur driven limousine and enroute to her main house, pointed out the construction work that was going on—mainly the erection of a dwelling for her sister and a sister's illegitimate child (girl), both of whom she continuously denounced but with the most abusive but artistic vituperation.

Lydia had an adopted son of her own for whom she professed great affection—how anyone ever let her adopt a son, I do not know.

I was given a very charming guest room and private bath which connected with Lydia's sumptuous suite.

At dinner the sister, the niece and a girl friend appeared—there had been much drinking at cocktail time, and the meal was very fullsome and festive.

After a cordial or two, we all retired to our respective quarters— there had been a good deal of suggestive by-play during the evening which indicated that there was no question in the minds of any of those present but what was expected of me for the remainder of the night.

While I was undressing, in fact just as I was about to slip on my pajamas, Lydia opened the adjoining door between our rooms and standing there in a fluffy lace pink georgette crepe negligee—over a flesh colored chiffon nightie—all of which tended to make her appear even larger than she was, but it did give her the somewhat lewd appearance of a madam of a whore house who was not adverse to a diddle herself occasionally with a preferred client.

I was drunk and the picture excited me—as usual my god damn cock stood up and pleaded for a screw—she crossed the room to my bed, threw her arms around me and suggested that I come in her room—the bed was larger there and more comfortable—greater resilience.

I got in her bed with her—it was comfort personified—I loved her—fondled her and removed her nightie. She had taken off the negligee when she had climbed in under the sheets, which were quickly thrown back—what a gross but voluptuous sight she was stripped— her nude body was in rolls—in fact rolls upon rolls—like inner tubes piled one above the other, only her rolls were a pinkish white instead of the usual tube gray or red.

She had covered her body with scented powder—the bed sheets

and her hair were scented with seductive perfume—I think Lydia was the largest and oldest female I had ever fucked—her flesh was soft and flabby—it sounds revolting yet it was exciting. The wench knew all the tricks of the trade and she used them—her tits were so large that I fucked her between them—she sucked me off—and when I finally shoved my cock into that cow-cunted bitch, I shot one hell of a wad. The novelty, obscenity of it, got me—she loved and wiggled her fat ass all over the place.

I stayed with her all night—we would fuck and suck—oh yes, I went down on her during the night—she loved that. We played with one another and each other—we slept only a little—she always wanted more—by morning she was suggesting matrimony, offering to turn over everything she had to me if I would marry her.

The next day was Sunday. We arose late—after breakfast in bed—then Lydia took me for an inspection trip of her entire property. She wanted to sell some—she thought I might help her to do that—she had grandiose schemes for the balance of her estate and she suggested that I might be interested in managing that for her.

Her proposals were many and frequent and varied. She kept a crew of men, laborers, artisans working Sundays as well as weekdays and she drove them with a firm determined hand, with all the ability, the capability of any road boss or construction gang superintendent— she was a hard task master—she knew what she wanted and she intended to get it, and the most for her money.

She set a very lovely table and we had about completed the Sunday midday meal when her broker, a fellow by the name of Shaskan who had finally married his mistress, the little girl who had come to my father's office many many years before with a Miss Maurer—I had interviewed Miss Maurer and hired her.

Shaskan's wife was with him, as well as another couple whose names escape me at the moment. Shaskan had been a partner of Hamilton P.'s and a notorious bucketshop operator.

We drank mint juleps and again we made a tour of the property, followed by more mint juleps—then it was suggested that we should go swimming in Lydia's lake—as Shaskan's wife and I ambled home from one of the inspection tours, in a slight stage of alcoholic inebriation.

The suggestion was received with gusto—and we all prepared for the bath in nature's best. Lydia, the most playful of the group, was a nauseating sight to behold in her 250 lbs. plus, but S.'s wife was

388

a most delectable morsel in the nude and well worth the effort and discomfort of a dip in the cold still lake, while the early Spring mosquitos did their best to make a meal of the occasion.

After the dip there were more drinks to warm the cuddles—then the uninvited guests departed. Somewhere along the line of the afternoon's drunken conversation, I had expressed a liking for spaghetti with Italian sauce, which caused Lydia to proclaim that she would take herself to her kitchen and prepare my evening's repast for me herself.

This caused great confusion.

When the hors d'oeuvres were served I discovered, much to my delight, that I had some tuna fish on my plate—being tight and with my weakness for Tuna Fish, when it was passed the second time, I rudely took a second helping, then to make matters worse, I asked for more. This incensed Lydia who assumed that I would lose my appetite for the spaghetti she had prepared if I ate so much tuna fish—she remonstrated with me, ordered the butler to remove my plate and I, asserting my independence, and my fearlessness of her domination, became embroiled in a hideous and violent row with the bitch in which she finally ordered the butler to fetch her gun—she was determined to have her way—I was determined to have more tuna fish.

Knowing her propensities for murder and her reputation for a light finger on the gun, I excused myself—ostensibly to go to the can, actually to phone the State Constabulary—which I did over the extension in my bedroom. I requested them to send a cab for me from Ossining and to accompany the cab themselves—this they agreed to do.

Unbeknownst to me, Lydia suspecting that I was up to something had lifted up her extension—and had come in on the conclusion of my arrangements with the State troopers, catching just enough of the conversation to become aware of what I had done.

Whereupon she broke out in hysterical remorsefulness and shedding voluminous crocodile tears and screaming undying devotion implored me to spend the balance of the night, and go down in the morning.

How I packed I'll never know—but I did—and the troopers and the cab arrived in the midst of the peak of her hysteria. With the aid of the State Police I drew myself aloof from her fond embrace and lustful clutches, and departed. As I drove off, her sentimental feelings suddenly turned to vile denunciations.

Arriving at the station with my police escort, I found that I had an hour to wait for my next train. By this time my appetite knew no bounds, but the hour was late and the local eating emporiums were closed—but I bethought me of my friend the Warden of the State Prison, Sing Sing—but a stone's throw from the station—and his full larder—and thence I directed my chariot (taxi).

The Warden—Lawes—was then living in his new mansion outside the prison walls—it had been designed like the new death house, the new cell box, etc. and approved for construction during Governor Miller's administration, and my approving signature had been affixed to most of the plans on account of one of my ex-officio duties.

No one was about on the ground floor when I entered—I called and no one answered. As drunk as I was, I was able to recall the general plan of that ground floor and so I took myself to the kitchen without further ado—but to my great dismay I found the huge refrigerator of that great exponent of Criminal Reformation padlocked and sealed, against the prying hands of the trustees of the much heralded honor system.

During the commotion, the children's maid or nurse appeared on the scene, but she had no key—the "trusty" cook had that—then came the guard. By that time, like the moronic inmates of most of our prison cells, I had given vent to my predicament and pronounced my own opinion of an Honor System so successful that the Warden had to padlock his own icebox.

In my own inimitable scrawl with my little lead pencil on the white enamel icebox door—

Years later Lawes professed never to have seen the pungent epithet I had penned thereon.

The guards had stealthily removed my potent remarks in the wee small hours of the morning. The Warden, I forgot to say, was in the City giving his weekly Sunday broadcast to the nation on the penal problems of the day.

An exhibitionist at heart, eager for the public praise, and the cash commensurate therewith, he was everlastingly during his regime at Sing Sing, writing, lecturing, broadcasting, with the material he constantly obtained in his post of trust, as Warden of Sing Sing Prison —for which he was amply and substantially compensated by the taxpayers of the Empire State.

Disgruntled I returned to the station, caught my train and enroute to our Fair City, regaled all the paying customers of the New York Central Line with my opinion of a Warden who had to padlock his own icebox and then had the audacity to proclaim the virtues of the Honor System far and wide.

[Included here is a portion of a letter from my father to Ruth G. recounting one of my visits to New York.]

Needless to say I told [Page] all about you—he approved—he is for you for his next step-mother—wants to meet you—likes your picture—anxious to go to Russia—Thank God I have a liberal son.

Apparently the latest college slang in this modern age which horrifies most parents, I understand, is SHIT—it even jolts me—and I don't think it very effective, but there it is—

Ever hear of RAT FUCKING—well I hadn't either except to make more rats—but at Hanover that means the raiding of the students rooms on one floor by the students from another floor—the boys go in groups of eight or ten—turn everything upside down in the students rooms—even fire buckets of water are employed to make the wreck complete—that's progress—

At the schools of higher education (our American Colleges)— RAT FUCKING—My, my, what a lot Page will have to tell the boys at Oxford besides the beautiful women of America and the C.I.O. . . .

East 82nd Street loaned itself to fornication.

I had a large livingroom with fireplace, kitchen, and then a sleeping room or porch on a setback, which afforded a nice roof garden, plants, etc.—off the livingroom was a spacious bath—the girls liked that—and I could see into my bathroom from my sleeping porch.

It has always excited me to watch a woman piss on a pot—then when they lift their skirts to wipe their ass or powder their cuzzy, it has stood my cock on end.

A Miss Freeman—who worked in the Museum of Art—rented me the place furnished for the summer from late June, July and August to early September—she only got one month's rent out of me in advance and she made the mistake of leaving her phone connected.

I hired a French maid—to clean and cook three meals a week or whenever I gave a party—French maids are so understanding.

Ruth G. was the first to visit me there—she took sun baths on the roof afternoons and screwed me on the bed on the sleeping porch —the first few weeks she found it handy to run in often—then she got out of hand—she was living around the corner on 83rd & Fifth Ave. . . .

That summer I knocked up Ruth for the fourth or fifth time to add to my troubles—while she always paid the freight on such oper-

391

ations, she raised hell about it—and as I have said before I never knew whether I was the father or her husband—I liked to think I was the fertile one. . . .

Harriet S. was still living around the corner at 904 Park Avenue and frequently dropped in for a drink or a screw. Harriet had found an old girl friend living in the basement of a renovated apartment on 80th Street—next to the famous Todd Hunter School for girls—the old dame had a weakness for cats. Harriet took me to call on her— Harriet was fascinated—the old dame would get a little tight and then flop on a couch in her livingroom, pull up her skirts and the goddamn cats would crawl all over her, lapping at her cunt—until she would go into a spasm and come—much to the delight of the felines.

It was quite a sight to watch—I got so hot watching that I took my cock out and Harriet sucked me off.

Betty C. had taken up with an octoroon that season—Betty always had some good looking younger girls in tow—Betty went in for them and they for her.

Ever since the fall of 1936 when Betty got a peek of my cock while glancing up the stairway at 904—saw the damn thing erect thru the slit in my chinese mandarin robe—she had been clamoring for a ride on my prick—in fact, she had been so impressed that she had sung its praises to all and sundry, far and wide, and she had made up her mind that she would feel it inside her.

I could think of no valid reason for denying her that great pleasure—so I invited her to dine and to bring her current slightly colored female amour along.

After dinner we got down to the purpose of the meeting and all disrobed. Betty nearly swooned as she fondled and caressed my big cock—she couldn't stop loving it—the nigger went to work on Betty first—they had quite a time of it. Betty just couldn't let go of my prick—she kissed it as the nigger kissed her—and I came inadvertantly all over Betty's face—then I peed on her and then on the nigger as they lay together—but my cock, to Betty's great delight, wouldn't go down—a bad habit it has always had—deflation being in the case of my prick much slower than inflation.

Much to her annoyance I put on a condom and screwed the mulatto—and kissed Betty as I did so—after that fuck, the old instrument was still standing erect, and Betty was still begging to be laid.

While Betty was washing the piss off her little body, I put on another condom and went after Betty when she got back on the bed.

When she discovered that I had on a rubber her annoyance was complete—the first time she objected, mildly—but when I laid her the second time with the rubber still on, her protestations were angry. She wanted me in the raw—she wanted to feel the hot load come within her—she wanted it all. She was such a drunk and rounder that I felt I shouldn't—that it was too great a chance to take. I tried to fool her and sidestep but she would have none of it—in a fit of violent temper she refused to screw again if I wore a condom—and since I wouldn't take it off she dressed and left in a huff—as I gave her girl friend one more—and that was the end of Betty for me. . . .

The 82nd Street apartment had proved a most enjoyable recreational center for me in the metropolis, that summer.

On September 23rd, I moved from 82nd Street to the Vanderbilt Hotel to be near my office and the trailer show.

In engaging girls to do secretarial work for the council campaign, I was careful to select Jewesses, Irish Catholics, etc. A particularly attractive girl that I put on at the time was Sylvia R.— Melba figured I had designs on her from the start and she was right.

Sylvia was a good worker—loyal and attractive—young, luscious, and not averse to being fondled—and to playing with the boss's cock. She began at first by jerking me off—then she would go down on me in the office—she kept me in white heat most of the time. We were very busy and often worked late at night—she was always the last to go home—she had a Jewish boyfriend who called for her frequently—and Ben H. (a Jew himself) who was working with me at the time warned her against Jews, said they had no respect for Christian girls—but she went on seeing him—and playing with me.

I was falling for her like a ton of bricks—thought I might like to marry the gal—G. was slipping more and more into the background.

I dined Sylvia every night that fall—in the office or out.

While at the Vanderbilt I ran across Florence M.—she was staying there too—and we managed to be together several times— but it was stale. Outside of Florence, I only had one chambermaid in my Hotel room and a girl on the same floor whose name escapes me —but I still saw Nancy O.—Della and Anita S.—so as not to sluff off in my screwing, political campaigns or no.

After the trailer show was over and I had withdrawn from the councilman's race, I had upon the constant urging of Nancy and Ruth, decided to have my teeth fixed—my bridgework and remaining teeth were in bad shape—the teeth were rotting and the heavy gold bridgework was afloat—nothing to anchor to. Morris Maltzer, the lawyer, gave me the name of a Jew friend of his, a dentist—a young fellow in the neighborhood named Berke. Berke said I should have all the uppers out, so the deal was made and I gathered together the dough for the job on a down payment.

It was to be done in the evening—I thought I was too busy to have the work done during the day. The evening of the appointment with the dentist Ben H. asked me to sit at the press table—free liquor and food—at some Jewish benefit he was running at the Biltmore. I went there for a few drinks and a plate of soup to fortify me for the extractions, but I lingered too long—when I reached the dentist's office he had gone to attend some lecture where he instructed others.

So I returned to the banquet and the free liquor—the dinner over, I did the rounds of Greenwich Village on my own with special attention to the Lesbian places—about two o'clock in the morning, I headed north, drunk as a lord, woke up Tommy and proceeded to some drinking den of his.

We ordered liquor for ourselves and a couple of whores—we got their addresses—the drinks were slow in coming and I got into an altercation with the proprietor and departed without paying for the liquor—by that time of night, most places were closed (a few days later Joe L. and I called on the whores and Joe screwed one of them in the kitchen five minutes after he arrived—and then nearly died of remorse and fright) so we went to the Kit Kat Club. The doorman was having a row with a departing guest on the sidewalk over a cheque and didn't see me—the doors were barred and they wouldn't let us in. This annoyed me and when a cop appeared out of nowhere —they always do around those places—Tommy quickly and quietly disappeared as he always did when trouble was afoot and left me alone.

I strolled off by myself after some strong statements about the cop not attending to his job on his beat.

The more I thought about the cop's neglect of duty the madder I got—and so I engaged a taxi to trail the cop when he returned to his post and tour—which was to try the store doors along Third Avenue to see if they were locked.

Now the cop knew that the Kit Kat Club was violating the law —the precinct officers knew it and the divisional inspector of the Police Department must have known it.

I followed the cop for half a dozen blocks up and down Third

394

Avenue hurling critical charges at him—finally the taxi driver sold me the bill of goods that the cop had a family and kids and to let up on him—so we drew up alongside again to call it quits and go home. I am in my cups and use the wrong salutation in calling him over to the cab (there must have been some southern blood in him because his response when I finally hailed him with a friendly "you old son of a bitch—come over here" was to jump on the running board of the car and order the taxi driver to the 51st Street House)—my second trip in seven years.

I was booked on a disorderly conduct charge (but the Kit Kat Club wasn't closed)—after getting in touch with Joe L. and Stanley H., the Mayor's Tax Commissioner and Secretary, I was permitted to go my own way, being booked as William W. Smith, with instructions to be in the 57th Street Magistrates Court in the morning.

Being highly excited and greatly upset, I took myself at 5 AM up to Nancy's—she was enraged at my calling at that hour without phoning first—her profitable lover might have been there, she said—but being Irish and sympathetic by nature toward anyone in trouble (real), she let me crawl into bed—she got me up again at 8:30 and giving me breakfast, sent me to the Vanderbilt to shave and change my clothes and take a bath.

When I arrived in Court I found the Mayor's chief clerk—he visited the judge and when the case was called, the cop said I followed him up and down the Avenue calling him names. I said I had merely been pointing out his duty as I saw it—the Judge admonished me to exercise greater discretion in my choice of language in addressing officers of the law, and to avoid harassing them while doing their work and dismissed the case.

There had been no bail set or finger printing etc. that time. I was released on my own because my friends were in power and they could trust me to show up—in fact I didn't even get a lawyer to represent me. . . .

A week later I went to the dentist again on a Saturday night and had all my teeth—top teeth—removed and a plate inserted at once. As the novocaine wore off the pain increased so I went to a newsreel —I got thru that—but after I got back to the hotel I took the plate out—and even using a mouth wash of salt and water and stuffing with swabs in my mouth, I damn near bled to death.

During the night I spit up quantities of blood and when I finally dozed off, after taking many aspirin tablets (4), I awoke to a very

395

bloody pillow and bed—the dentist pooh-poohed my predicament over the phone.

When I phoned Ruth about it, she called her brother and he urged me to insist upon seeing my dentist—I was in pain and the bleeding wouldn't let up—the sight of all the blood made the hotel maid ill—the towels were a sight.

I was weak but managed to get into my things with the aid of a bell boy and get myself around to the dentist. He finally succeeded in clotting up the opening and the bleeding was under control but it took days for me to fully recover and several months before I could wear the plate with any degree of comfort.

As I said before, I moved from the Vanderbilt on October 24th, 1937 to the studio apartment at 6 East 37th Street, apartment 5-B.

And there I started to dictate at home—that brought Sylvia over to the apartment—and gave me a freer opportunity to woo her.

When I was closing 904 Park Avenue, after my lease was up and the doctor had moved out, I heard a prospective tenant for one of the other apartments express interest in the decorations of the apartment he had been looking at and asked Wilford (the janitor) about them—he told me and that roused my curiosity so I went up and looked at the artwork for myself. Over the mantel in the living room was a very fine sketch or oil painting of a Chinese mandarin—it was painted on the wall—it was beautifully executed.

I wandered into the bathroom and found the walls and ceilings covered with the most exotic and ethereal nudes—the work was excellent, but again it was permanent. I asked Wilford who had done such fine work and he announced that it had been done by the beautiful wife of a Jew lawyer who had lived there.

That aroused my curiosity further and I got him to give me the lawyer's name and office address—some weeks later I had Sylvia phone the Jew's office—she explained to the lawyer that we had some art work for his wife, so he gave her address to us. I did nothing about it until I moved into 37th Street—then I bethought me of those nudes for my bathroom—so I had the girl call the wife and explain that I had a commission for her to do some painting for me. Her name was Lorell P.—she had not been married to the Jew—she had only been living with him.

When she arrived at 37th Street, Walter P. was there—I thought it best to have a third party present—she brought a girl friend with her—I don't recall the friend, but Lorell was quite the loveliest thing I had seen in years. I fell for her hook, line and sinker. I told her what I wanted—she said she would submit sketches—and would do the work for $50.00—after a drink or two she departed.

Several weeks later she phoned that the sketches were ready. I invited her to dinner—it was a Sunday evening—she accepted. I had my Chinese boy prepare the meal—I wore my robe—the lights were low—the setting set for seduction. When the hour arrived she phoned to say she had a cold—it was raining—should she send the sketches —I said by all means. Her boyfriend—a jealous kid, the son of Madam Burenilla, a dress designer—arrived, announced himself below, was invited up. The hall door at 37th Street, as you may remember, had a peep hole in it—I could look out and see who was outside, but they could not see in—so I had a good look at the gent. The chink opened the door—I was fully dressed by then, and went out to greet him—took the sketches, thanked him and sent him on his way, without inviting him in—then I slipped back into my robes, as I had called up Ellen N. as a substitute to eat the meal and fuck—and she was due.

Not long after that Lorell came over herself—we talked about the work—she got tight—we fucked and fucked.

While Lorell had a lovely body—she was a bit phlegmatic—she was lovely to look at and wonderful to touch. She was modeling for evening dresses for a house firm; that was the beginning of a fine friendship that lasted many years—one you yourself once met up with—and found a bit difficult and complicated.

I offered Lorell my apartment—tried to get her to come in and live with me. But altho low in funds, she had other plans at the time and when she was ready to it was too late, for I had married another by that time—life is like that—but more about the beautiful Lorell later.

I bought this typewriter while there [on 37th Street]—on time (a dollar down, a dollar to come). The trailer account was still dragging on unpaid.

I bought a big dictionary and *The Columbia Encyclopedia* on time too, and prepared to bring this letter up to date.

Before closing out 1937, I shall try to take up 1938 on a more serious note—altho the wave of fornication that engulfed me at the Ritz carried me thru the days and nights at 82nd Street and at the Vanderbilt and then on to 37th Street and continued on thru to 1938 —the forepart, January, February and part of March—and then I married again.

Sexually 1937 had been quite a year for an old buck of 44.

Before leaving 1937 to posterity—for better or worse—I want to add that these fornicating orgies referred to were not the only ones.

Frequently the girls mentioned came to see me time and again and my only reason for not mentioning the encores is that repetition or recounting is as dull and as unexciting as many of the return engagements were—after the first few encounters of the quivering bodies one settles back—in fact, falls back upon a series of variations to keep up the spirit and alive the fire.

There were other girls who failed to make an impression or to leave behind either a pleasant or unpleasant recollection—and there was the usual amount of masturbation always indulged in—just to keep in form. . . .

In this day and age a man's word is no longer his bond—the only thing that counts is his accumulation of material things or temporary fame, regardless of how attained—by hook or crook. Men and women of America, in fact, men and women the world over, have but certain very fundamental urges or desires—they are food for the body, a shelter to sleep in, and sexual relations—and those are the prime forces that activate all mankind.

True, the New Deal, for its own selfish reasons, has tried to substitute an equitable even distribution of goods in equal amounts to all citizens, and not having succeeded in doing so in the United States, desires to do so the world round. As they have not succeeded at home, they will not and cannot succeed abroad.

Nations just as their peoples are economically and politically selfish—and we seem destined for many generations if not for many centuries, to go on living in a world where "grab all" is the principal motivating force in the individual, in the group, in the nation—wherever it be on the sphere.

I could go on at length elaborating on this theme, which is fundamentally the law of the survival of the fittest, but I am anxious to take up 1938, and I must be on with the past, rather than continue to discuss the present and the future, and so, I say Adieu to another hectic year, 1937, in the pursuit of life, love and happiness—and lust.

1938-1939

To begin—1938 was especially eventful because it marked the beginning of my third matrimonial venture, and a revolutionary change in my mode and manner of existence.

The New Year was ushered in—during a period which, for me, was most precarious financially—altho that was not a new, a novel, or unusual situation.

I was in hot water at 6 East 37th Street, Apt. 5-D, over my rent—when I moved in. I had been given a month's concession so that my rent was paid up to December 1st—then when they constructed the air-blowing system right over my head, and used my apartment and my balcony as a runway and scaffold for their construction materials, I raised particular cane.

Aside from my marriage to Eve, which I will go into shortly, I was involved in the tapering off and concluding of my affair with Mrs. G.

In the first months of 1938 I was greatly enamored of a sculptress, dancer and painter by the name of Delores—and of a successful milliner by the name of Anita Andre—and Edwina Powell, Charlotte T., Alice B., Gladys Lafler, Dunn, Graham de Ryder (the Maid of Melvale) and several others.

I circularized all my friends that year in connection with my Public Relations business, emphasizing what I had been able to do with the Trailer Show, and pointing out that I was able to give them publicity anywhere in the world.

I made a bid to get the Publicity Account of the Chinese Government, and also to make a deal to get planes and fliers for them. . . .

I also submitted a plan to obtain publicity in the metropolitan press for the Republican candidate for United States Senator from New Jersey—which was a plan to set up a Publicity Office in the City of New York for the candidate in order to cover the New York papers with large circulations in the Eastern end of New Jersey (the New York commuting area of that State).

399

I gave a big party at 37th Street in February, and I gave a big party at Sutton Place that year, after I was married—but most of the time was taken up with Eve's illness and the readjustment of our lives, which had been considerably altered by our marriage—it was a trying period from that standpoint, and how we ever succeeded in working out a solution that was feasible, I will never know—but more about that anon.

1938 should not take long in the telling—there was more difficulty with my mother-in-law, with my brother-in-law, with my new sister-in-law, and the period of adjustment was a tough one.

In order to save my financial situation, I resorted to my old trick of sub-letting. . . .

After I moved up to 61st Street, into the furnished room, across the street from the private home of my old friends, the George Washington Cavanaughs, I became a bit morose and at midnight on the 31st of January, I sat down and wrote the following dribble to Ruth G. —I set it forth here to show you my irrational state of mind at the time—what a mentality such as mine can sometimes indulge itself in.

RESOLVED BETWEEN JANUARY-FEBRUARY MIDNIGHT 1938

Dearest Darling Ruth:

I have set the date—St. Valentine's day—February 14th, 1938.

I will sell my furniture on the 13th—put my books and papers which are nearly ready now in storage, under Page's name—and set forth never to return alive.

You no longer love me—what brought the change about I do not know—fear of abortions may have done it—I am told that will kill any urge or love.

I have glorified you—worshipped you—loved you dearly—still do—you are all there is of life to me—

If I could have believed that success for me would have in the end meant you—then I could have gone on striving—

Your readiness to hurt me—your eagerness to find any excuse to condemn me and to go out with others—

You denouncing me for things I have never done while you yourself have been unfaithful in thought, has been too ludicrous for words. . . .

By nature I am affectionate—I have wanted you to come to see me—if I couldn't go to you—to talk to me—be near me—if you didn't want to love—well, you could have had your way—but you might have come to 82nd Street and here—

400

I cannot take it—one doesn't commit suicide on the spur of the moment—

I am going away where it will create no commotion—

I have resolved to relieve you of further annoyance or embarrassment—you will have no more telephone calls—no one waiting at the door. . . .

I don't know what effect my going out will have on Page, I doubt if any—

There is no one that will give a damn—no one that will ever miss me.

How you could have treated me the way you have, after all we were to one another I do not know.

Our lives have been so different—I was born with a silver spoon in my mouth—brought up to believe that I was a superior sort of person because of my parents and their parents and their parents, and the position they had always occupied in the community—only to be bumped and bumped and bumped in the hard school of experience. . . .

No one ever likes you except for what they hope they can get out of you—at least that has been my experience—

No one has ever liked me for myself.

When I was young I was brilliant, or at least people thought I was, and I went ahead rapidly—everything I touched was successful—I was constantly in the public eye—and then time caught up with me. . . .

Now what do you think it does to me—not to have a home—to have to live here alone—in this cold room with little light—so cold it's hard to write—

Have you ever gone for days without food—saving for someone you loved, only to get your face slapped—well, I have and the pangs of hunger are not the most enjoyable in life.

To satisfy your own selfishness your own wilfulness—you have crucified me time and again—broken my spirit, humiliated me beyond words—I have taken it—suffered—because I loved you so—

No, I won't follow you to Florida—I will go elsewhere to my death—

I wanted so for us to have a child—I felt—I always felt you knew so much about all things but me—that you had an uncanny shrewdness about business—that with you beside me I could have recovered the lost ground and gone on to greater heights.

But I was wrong—your passion has really been to set me down—

Well, it won't be for much longer now—

You probably will hold yourself aloof even from a little kiss goodbye.

God, it's cold in here—and so my sweet, my darling girl when I have passed into the great beyond—don't think of me too harshly —try and think of the few happy blissful moments when we were near and close and supremely happy.

As you drive by Trinity—occasionally give a glance to the hill that rises there from the Riverside—and remember—remember— and think what I might have been—what we could have been together as the silver threads slipped in amongst the gold—and blow a kiss—a tiny little kiss from those pretty lips across your lovely hands and fingertips to me—your lover who gave all he had to give— but couldn't take it.

When I go out—you, as I close my eyes, will be with me in my dream world—but no longer will I be around in your real world to worry and harass you—

So Ruth—my Ruth—my only true love—be sweet to me these last few days—I won't mention this again—I am sober—my mind is clear—my life empty without you—the future blank—old man Reaper awaits me and the sod at Trinity is ready for me—goodbye my love—your Wardie—in life so it will be in death.

Sometimes when I write this crap about myself I get restless—my head binds, it doesn't ache. I feel as if I will never get it done—how futile it all is—I feel as if I might go quite mad—the effect is very great—it all must be gone over—but then it probably never will—you may never see it anyway.

Shortly after I moved to the room on 62nd Street I telephoned Berenice Holloway.

She was living at 24 West 59th Street, which was just around the corner from my room. . . .

I had but a nickel left and with that I wished to purchase a can of Campbell's soup—they were a nickel a can then. I also wished to phone B. H. So, I put the nickel in the slot first, dialed the operator, told her I had gotten the wrong number, had the nickel returned, and was duly connected—for the first time she answered the call herself, and she invited me to come around and call that evening—I accepted the invitation.

I purchased the can of soup, took it to my room, cooked it, consumed it.

Then I went over to 59th Street—Ann H., the girl who was with "B" when I met her, was spending the evening—in fact, she had been there for dinner, as had Mr. and Mrs. Eric Atterbury. Mrs. Atterbury was the former Marguerite Preece, daughter of Godfrey Preece, the well known polo pony dealer—Eric was an Australian, had been a stable boy, jockey and trainer. . . .

Tiring of my chit-chat, Ann H. and the Atterburys departed—this annoyed B. H., as she did not wish to be left alone with me. After they left, I ambled on in my own dull way, skipping around in general conversation and going into greater details about La Brossie, the fellow who had worked for me in Florida—La Brossie, a waiter for us at the Sands Point Casino, and at the Melton Point Casino at Rye, had married a wealthy widow by the name of Celept. . . .

Berenice Holloway was not inclined to be affectionate, seemed only interested in a conversation. I remained an hour or so, then after having had my timid advances rebuffed, I departed for my garret room.

The apartment on 59th Street was furnished in excellent taste—antiques predominated—it had charm and comfort. After sizing the place up I decided that mother and daughter were probably living on an income of approximately $100 a week—but that's where I was wrong.

My many interests had kept me busy the forepart of January—my funds had become limited and I couldn't get about much. I was unable to entertain, so I only called once or twice on the phone after that until!—

On Sunday the 13th of February I had a date with Edwina P.—I was still on 62nd Street—she lived on 55th Street between Lexington and Park, one of New York's loveliest streets.

While I was with her, a former beau broke in on us. He was as attentive as hell—he didn't even sit down. He borrowed ten bucks from Edwina and then invited us both to have cocktails with him at the Waldorf—we refused—Edwina was planning to see her elderly Englishman, and before that we were going to take the dog for a walk—and anyway she saw no reason to go drinking on her own money.

As we strolled along 57th Street I noticed two smartly dressed damsels approaching from Lexington Avenue—they were walking east to west—as they drew nearer, I recognized my "Kolinsky" girl friend of the Grand Central Station episode. It was the first time I had seen her and her compatriot since the evening I had called in January.

One of the most disconcerting things about trying to reach Berenice Holloway (after I met her in December) early in January, 1938, was the fact that in order to talk to her on the phone I always

403

had to run the gauntlet of some uppish female before I could be connected with her—obviously, a ma bent upon discouraging all callers for her daughter was answering the phone.

We all exchanged pleasantries on the street, and after I left Edwina at her boy friend's, I called Berenice from Genay's apartment that evening—the Genays lived on the 58th Street side of the house, and that Sunday night I was showing Ira and Georgette along with Harry M. and his wife V., my "dirty movies"—Ira had gotten hold of a projector for the occasion—I had seen the "dirty pictures" so often myself that I was rather bored with them, so while they were running I went in and called up Berenice and chatted with her at length—she announced that she was leaving for the coast next day—St. Valentine's day—I asked her if I could call—she was busy packing—but she said I could. However the pictures took longer than I anticipated and by the time they were through running it, it was too late for me to drop in, so we postponed the visit tentatively until her return from the coast.

When I went home that night I sat down and scribbled a valentine message on a piece of yellow paper which I took around to her apartment (so that she would receive it before her departure)—she contends that she never took the message contained therein seriously. She thought it fiction not fact—and to this very day says that had she known it was fact and not fiction, she would not have left for the coast.

The valentine read as follows:

WARDIE

I have

> Law suits to the right of me
> Bills galore to the left of me
> Process servers in front of me
> Judgments in back of me
> No food inside of me
> No job in sight of me
> Only old clothes to cover me
> No place called home to me.
>
> My money has flown from me
> My wives have all gone from me
> My children are lost to me
> My best friends have forgotten me
> Only one woman interests me
> And she says she is going West from me
> So there is no one to care for me.

404

My debtors don't pay me
My landlord is after me
The hock shops dispair of me
My best years are back of me
But a few years are ahead of me
Living is lonely for me
And that's all that is wrong with me.

My mind hasn't left me
So that's why there's hope for me
For that's really
Wardie.

She sent me a picture post card from Palm Springs that raised my hopes.

She was due back on the 14th or 15th of March in order to sign her income tax papers. On that day I called on Bob Ripley ("Believe it or not") at the New York Athletic Club, for the purpose of inducing him to reconsider [a] proposal for his personal publicity.

We did much drinking in his room and as we drank, we denounced the two semitics that had played important and perhaps destructive (although they themselves contended constructive) parts in our lives—the two Ruths, G. and R. . . .

On my way to visit Berenice Holloway I stopped at a corner drugstore to purchase a small can of "Fastteeth" to hold my ("Woolworth's") plate in. It had gone through quite a bit of hard work that afternoon and evening, what with the drinking with Ripley and the heavy chewing at the Genay's dinner table—the plate wasn't much of a fit anyway. . . .

After I . . . crossed over thru the passageway from the 58th to 59th Street side of the house, I poured the powder on the plate to hold it fast. Then I entered the 59th Street hallway and had myself announced.

Mrs. Holloway had not returned with her daughter, so we were alone.

Most of that evening was taken up with the discussion of Miss Holloway's trip to the coast and the heavy rains and washouts in California. After a number of Scotch and waters I left around one o'clock in the morning, after a most discreet evening, for discretion had appeared to be the better part of valor in that instance. I was intrigued—she was different—I was impressed—I liked the girl, strangely I respected her.

405

I was back at 37th Street by that time and was using my telephone liberally, especially when I found I had someone new to listen to my telephone prattle which went on by the hour—I remember one occasion when I was cooking a rice pudding, we got into a considerable discussion as to the proper procedure to be followed in baking same. She had one idea, I had another (they have never been reconciled).

She had a maid and she ate many of her meals at home—she invited me to come to dinner that Friday and I accepted—in fact, I always easily accepted any invitation to dine in those days.

For the other guests at dinner, she had a Mr. & Mrs. Edward Rutt that she had met in Bermuda—Mrs. Rutt was an employee of the J. Walter Thompson Advertising Agency. . . .

That night I left after dinner when the Rutts left—but I merely walked around the block and came back again. I stayed late and talked much—I thought—I hoped I was making a good impression. My interest was rapidly mounting. That night as I departed I bravely ventured a "peck on the cheek"—and to my amazement didn't get slapped.

On Sunday she called and invited me to drive out on Long Island with her and Ann H. for skeet. I wanted to go—I longed to go—but I didn't have the cash for drinks, for shells or for meals or gas—and I had a tea date with Anita Andre and a girl friend of hers and a dinner date with Walter Piel. But she said I could call after dinner which I did. That night I kissed her and talked marriage—I was bolder.

Then I invited her to have dinner with me several nights later.

It wasn't very successful—I had sent my carving knife to be sharpened—it was late in arriving—the dinner was over done and the meal was anything but appetizing—the roast beef was cooked to a frazzle. She was a slow drinker, taking a considerable time to consume a long drink of Scotch and water, and we had lingered long over the alcoholic consumption.

That evening I gathered that she was in some way gainfully engaged in some business in midtown—I hadn't paid much attention. She hadn't discussed it to any degree, in fact she had avoided all discussion of her activities—but she had given me her office phone number. Then the next day she came to lunch as she had been shopping in my neighborhood. I continued to talk of marriage—my desire to remarry, etc.

The following day or on the evening of Friday of March 25th I dined with her alone at her apartment.

Her sense of humor was intriguing me, there was that indefinable something about her that attracted me. She was smartly dressed—I liked her eyes, her good manners, her intelligence, and her integrity—she carried herself well and handled her legs in a most seductive fashion—her good food pleased me, her sexual naiveness captivated me. I knew nothing of her family, except that her father was dead, that she had a mother who was visiting her sister in California, and that her brother, altho a year below you at Dartmouth, was a year older than you.

She was obviously well born, well bred, well brought up—I was reverting to type—in my youth I had see-sawed between sluts and ladies, and in middle age I had hung in the balance with bitches (charming)—Melba and Ruth and Florence. Now I was swinging back to a woman of refinement and culture.

Her maid was not much as a fashion plate, but she was an excellent cook, the food left nothing to be desired, and was beautifully served on a charming service.

We talked about life and the future—I had always leaned a bit to career women—I had been keeping house as a bachelor for nearly two years. I was fed up—she seemed to be the answer to an old man's prayer. We drank a lot—it was Friday night.

As the night wore on, I explained to her that my Valentine message had been sincere, that it genuinely reflected my plight—that my condition had not improved to any measurable extent in the interim—that it still was serious on the financial side.

I truthfully painted the picture as black as I could—but for some unknown reason, all my life, people have discounted my contentions of adversity and poverty—they have always steadfastly refused to admit of my dire straits. That has been one of the crosses I have had to bear, no matter how shabby my appearance, it has been almost impossible to convince anyone of my straitened circumstances, even when they were at their lowest ebb, and she also refused to take my statements seriously.

That night I popped the question—I was amazed when she concurred in the suggestion—in fact it took my breath away. It never for an instant occurred to me that she, or any woman for that matter, would consider for one second entering into such a contract with an old reprobate in my plight—she didn't seem to be the type to do such a thing—but she fooled me. She accepted.

We sat up late discussing what to do—it was agreed that we should be married the next day, Saturday, March 26th, but there were complications, serious complications where I was concerned. It was

407

3 or 4 o'clock in the morning before we realized the hour and then she panically decided that it wouldn't do to have me depart at such an indecent time, so I remained the night thru, forming plans and preparing for an early start.

My total cash assets consisted of several dollars in pocket—I explained I couldn't buy a ring, engagement or wedding and she produced her grandmother's to meet that contingency. Then she ordered her car for 8—I had an idea for some unknown reason, that it was a dilapidated Model T—instead it turned out to be a Sporting Convertible Buick Coupe, with gayly upholstered seats of red leather.

We had breakfast, hastily gotten together, and then I went to 37th Street for a change of linen.

While she waited below, I phoned Joe L. and told him of our plans; both he and the Public Library explained that Elkton, Md. was out as a quick marriage spot—the Maryland laws had been changed, said they—the Library suggested Alexandria, Va. for a wedding that day. Then there was the question of getting a copy of my divorce papers in the action of Melba vs. me—they were in Rockland County, at New City, the county seat—so we headed there, after I had changed my shirt, shaved and parted my hair.

We crossed the George Washington Bridge—reached the Courthouse and while she waited without, I went in and got a copy of the final papers in the case. We needn't have bothered or taken the time, as they were not needed.

While waiting for the papers to be made out, I phoned Walter Piel and Ben Hanft, collect (my funds were low—I had had to pay the bridge toll and the fee for the papers—and when I had finished and returned to the car, I had but 40¢ left to my name).

I had fumblingly tried to explain my financial difficulties and I was getting panicky for lack of funds—I was all for going South on the Jersey side, but my fiancee feeling that the time was short—it was noon by then—felt we should cross the bridge—thence down the West Side Drive to the Holland Tunnel and back to Jersey again. She was insistent so I had to brutally bare my financial predicament—I had no money left for the license, clergyman, etc.—the car was gassed sufficiently for the trip.

To ease my embarrassment, never at a loss in a spot, she was quick to produce a $50 bill and gayly announced there was plenty more where that came from—so we stepped on the gas for Alexandria.

At Plainsboro, we grabbed a bite at the Walker-Gordon Lunch Room and telephoned her maid—she would not be home for dinner

408

that night. Then on we rushed—thru Camden and Newcastle we sped—at Elkton on the outskirts, as we flew past at 90 to the hour, we spied a sign "Marriage, License, Clergyman." A man was sitting there —he waved solicitously—I jammed on the brakes—we backed up. He offered to arrange the ceremony for a fee—I questioned him at length about the law—he said it was in abeyance—held—pending a referendum that would take place in the Fall.

He wasn't convincing and neither were we—for he finally decided that we had been married some time and were merely pulling his leg. Since time was short we hastened on, and as we reached the town of Elkton, the streets were filled with criers before every house eagerly soliciting matrimonial business for the dilapidated dominies inside—we pulled into the driveway of the most pretentious dwelling in sight, at such an angle as to hide the car's New York license plates from the eagle eyes of the steerers—then I entered and made a deal— $5.00 for the dominie, $2.00 for the license fee, $3.00 for the steerer. We drove around the corner to the Court House or Clerk's Office— there were several couples there in line ahead—a girl sat at a typewriter with a continuous manifold sheet on a roller typing out the necessary license documents—the questions and answers were simple —documentary proof of divorce unnecessary.

With these technicalities dispensed with, we re-entered the car which had been parked in front of the fire house all the time and returned to the clergyman's home—three or four couples waiting were shifting about in the stuffy waiting room, anxiously awaiting their turn.

It was a beautiful spring day, the first touch of Spring was in the air—the bride-to-be could not stand the stuffiness of the waiting room or the people, so we waited on the porch—and as we waited we noticed that the Clergyman in bidding goodbye to each bride and groom shook their hands with his shrivelled "mit"—that was too much for the expectant bride—she announced flatly that she would have none of that handshaking performance.

When our turn came we went inside. It was an ugly uncouth room, the furniture and fixtures were shabby and worn, the place smelled dank. I gave the Clergyman's assistant $5.00, she crammed it in a desk drawer full of bills, then they stood us in the center of the floor, on a worn-out bit of carpet, and proceeded with the Baptist Marriage Ritual.

When he reached the following part in the service: "Then Adam took a bone from his side" and etc. I could hardly contain myself, it

409

struck my fancy so—and when he added "And then he made Eve," I determined to nickname Berenice "Eve" and told her so—Berenice was too long and formal—her friends called her "B" which I thought too short and frivolous, and so Eve it was. We were given a pamphlet commemorating the occasion and set forth on our way—on the porch it was necessary for Eve to turn a complete circle in order to avoid the shrivelled handshaking performance of the Dominie—but he got her anyway.

We went immediately to the local Telegraph office where we wired you that Percy Holloway was your uncle, and wired Percy that you were his nephew—then we set forth for Philadelphia and New York.

We decided not to stop in the City of Brotherly Love but to try and make New York for our wedding repast—by the time we reached Trenton, we were tired and decided to stop for a champagne cocktail —I think Eve really wanted to pee. When she returned from the Little Girl's Room, I sensed that something was wrong—for the second time on my nuptial night my bride was unwell—your mother was the first.

Then we headed North for New York where we went to the Ambassador for our bridal supper and champagne—the bill was $20.00 there and when they gave me change for a $50 bill they short-changed me $20.00—wedding night or no, I squawked and they made good.

From the Ambassador we went to the El Morocco, the Stork Club, Ceruitti's at 121 E. 54th and several other night spots—by 3 o'clock in the morning I was driving down Broadway thru all the red lights regardless.

I took my new bride home to 37th Street—and in the conventional superstitious manner, well known to many a man and a maid, carried her across the threshold and deposited her within.

That was to begin a new era, or a new episode, or a new reign in my life; the reign of Eve—much of it you know—some of it you've heard—a great deal you are vaguely aware of—and of most of it you are not aware.

It was not until we were homeward bound that I actually learned what Eve's activity was in life—and what her income ($20,000 annually)—and she claimed that it was not until then that I fully disclosed the story of my "Woolworth's" (false teeth).

I was glad to have Ruth G. definitely behind me and nearly out of my life—that had been an unhealthy, unprofitable and impossible affiliation. I was happy in my choice—I was glad to be able to put the Jews out of my life—from a close personal association standpoint.

We were headed and destined for a turbulent beginning, for a hectic and trying period of adjustment—which in the first few months and years nearly wrecked our venture many times.

Eve's father was an Englishman, Charles Holloway—Eve's mother was half Irish and half Anglo-Saxon American—Mrs. Holloway, before her marriage, had been Berenice Evans, the daughter of Katherine Garrett and Thomas Peachey Evans. Thomas Peachey Evans was of old American lineage, stemming from the prominent Peachey family of Williamsburg, Va. (the old Peachey homestead still stands—restored by Rockefeller money—on the village green). The Peacheys were distinguished citizens in the Colonial days of Thomas Jefferson. A sketch of that family which is of considerable historical interest follows. They survived the Revolution and the Civil War:

Two of Eve's uncles, her mother's brothers, were famous Virginia horsemen—Lee Evans having at one time in his early youth been Master of Hounds of the Warrenton pack. Percy Evans another uncle, was the first master of hounds of the Middleburg Hunt—Percy was killed riding Association owned by Temple Gwathmey at the United Hunt Steeple Chase at Belmont Park in 1916.

For many years, Lee Evans owned a stable that he raced on the flat—he also trained many winners. Blockade was once owned by him before he became the famous three-time winner of the Maryland Cup—Lee had raced him on the flat and he wasn't much good at that.

Eve's grandmother owned a large place at Warrenton which was only recently sold by her uncle who was supposed to have kept it intact for his nieces and nephews. The Evans and Holloway families were well known in the horse world—Eve's first cousin, Sidney Holloway, being one of the outstanding trainers in the country, both of gentleman jockeys and of horses.

Having lived in a horse family all her life, Eve was never much interested—but as I look back over our short courtship, I remember being quite thrilled when I learned that she only rode side-saddle—I have never liked women riding astride—in the first place, it requires a much greater degree of horsemanship to ride side-saddle and in the second place, it is much more graceful—too few women have mastered the art in recent years, but then, riding is rapidly becoming one of the lost pleasures of life, except for a few Semitics in the large industrial centers, who were never intended for anything but the back of an ass.

Eve had had part of her schooling at the fashionable country school of Madame Boulliene in Warrenton.

As a little girl she had evidenced great interest in clothes and had made dresses for her own dolls and the dolls of her friends and her sisters—she dressed dolls for little marionette performances, and then as she grew older she made things for her schoolmates, appearing in the amateur theatricals—sewing, design, cut were a passion with her then, and have been a passion with her always. She is always fashion conscious—she loved clothes and her grandmother being a woman of considerable means, from time to time, spent large sums on her wardrobe.

When I met her, she was thirty-five years of age, had never been married, but had crossed the Atlantic Ocean on an average of four times a year, for a period of 8 or 9 years, spending much time in Paris, but also visiting other parts of the Continent—her trans-atlantic crossings were the bright spots in her life.

En route to Elkton, a thought that troubled her most was whether or not we would have anything to talk about after we were married, if, as the years marched by, we might not run out of conversation— well, for the last six and one-half years that fear has proven to have been unfounded.

Part of her life was spent in Virginia, part of it in Washington, part of it at Westbury, Long Island, and Great Neck.

She was no Broadway, or cafe society glamour girl—she had nothing in common with the bizarre—she was and is conservative— a bit aloof, with a degree of shyness, rather becoming in any female. To many she would appear prim and proper—but what many men fail to realize is the fact that the prim and proper female invariably makes the best wife, the best mistress, the best courtesan.

Eve has never forgotten how I arrived home on 37th St. on our wedding night slightly in my cups from too much champagne—I proceeded to take Ruth G.'s picture and smash it to bits on the terrace, frame, glass and all, tearing the photo to pieces.

The next day I wired her, Stanley H. and others, informing one and all of the sudden change in my status—matrimonial—the wire to Ruth never reached her because of an error on the part of the Telegraph Company.

From Miami, Ruth again, against my wishes, had gone to Havana, instead of returning to New York—largely in defiance of me, so I was doubly glad to be able to abruptly and finally strike her off the list.

412

Sunday afternoon we phoned Melba and I introduced her over the telephone to her successor—she was flabbergasted, she couldn't believe and wouldn't believe that I had ventured forth again and with another. Somehow, she seemed to have believed that altho she had divorced me, she still had me at her beck and call—her emotional tears were audible over the phone—she could not contain herself—Tom B. told me she called on him (hysterically) for confirmation.

None of my friends had ever met Eve—none of them had ever heard of her—I had kept that wooing strictly to myself—I had not bandied her name about.

We also called Ann H. to tell her of the news—she obviously was annoyed, and so great was her annoyance, that from that day forward, a friendship of many years standing between Eve and Ann came to an abrupt end—"piqued" I think they call it—because the other girl got the man.

Eve didn't like the 37th Street apartment, she wanted me to get rid of it—her mother was still away and she felt we would be much more comfortable in her own home. All the furniture she had paid for, she was paying the rent and for the maintenance and upkeep of the place—she had the maid there and the facilities for keeping house—she could see no reason why they shouldn't be made full use of.

In a moment of great weakness, still under the first blush of my bride's charm, I capitulated—and that was my first great mistake. The psychological effect of returning to her apartment was bad—it was bad in the eyes of her friends, more so than in the eyes of mine—but it didn't create the right impression anywhere—it made her master of the house.

Sunday evening, we called you and Percy at Hanover, only to learn that you, with great tact, according to your own statement, when Percy had told you that his sister had always paid for his education, his board and keep and was putting him thru college, and then asked you if you thought her marrying of me would make any difference on that score, you glibly replied: "Yes, I think it will—if I know my father, he thinks men should earn their own way thru life and pay for what they get themselves—the hard way." That upset Percy no end and eventually enraged his Ma—it was true, but had been better left unsaid.

After talking to you both, we then called California, to inform the Mater. I had never met her—she had never met me—she had heard nothing about me from anyone save what her own daughter had casually mentioned, but when Eve called her full of joy and over-

413

flowing with happiness, her mother received the news coldly—irritated and annoyed that her oldest, the family provider had ventured forth.

When Eve introduced us over the long distance phone, she was cold and distant, almost to the point of rudeness—there was no sound of welcome in her voice, no greeting of heartfelt congratulations—she resented her daughter marrying and marrying in her absence. For years she had interfered with her daughter's life—she had embarrassed her (because of an inherent weakness) on crucial occasions—she had pointedly discouraged courtships of any kind—she was almost a pathological case as far as Eve was concerned. To her, Eve assumed the form, and had for many years, of the provider—of the head of the household—she looked upon her daughter as a woman looks upon her husband, the breadwinner. Her reaction to our marriage was that of a wife who had just learned that her husband and provider had run off with another woman. She was bitter—she never got over the blow—she never forgave.

You could almost feel Mrs. Holloway recoil to the news over the Long Distance phone—it was a hell of a slap in the face. We were both very happy and bubbling over with enthusiasm for the great adventure that lay before us—we were eager to proclaim to all and sundry the union that had taken place, and Mrs. Holloway's reaction placed quite a damper upon our enthusiasm—it was as if someone had dashed a bucket of cold water in our faces. It took us some time to recoil from the shock of that reception.

We had moved back to the apartment Eve and her mother had been sharing on 59th Street, which as I mentioned was a mistake. I had concurred in her suggestion—I hadn't wanted to definitely oppose at that moment, but that's where I was wrong.

There is little doubt that had we set up housekeeping regardless of how cramped the quarters for two on 37th Street, the first three years of our married life would have been smoother, there would have been less opposition on the part of Eve's family to overcome, and it would have placed me in a much better light with everyone. But we couldn't see that then, we weren't concerned with what others thought —we were only concerned with ourselves.

[In 1938, not long after his marriage to Eve, my father discovered he had kidney and bladder stones that necessitated an operation. He decided that the operation would probably be fatal and made arrangements for his death.]

During the heat of our recent campaign, I discovered a certain

414

amount of pus and blood and foreign matter in my urine. I had been rather suspicious for some time that all was not well—for from seldom having to take a leak except in the morning and then at night, I had to piss frequently—and it was not always a satisfactory stream —sometimes a mere dribble or drip drip drip. I mentioned the details to the family doctor who brushed the symptoms aside with a statement that men as they matured got that way.

The condition was so obviously wrong that I went to see another doctor, who after giving me some sulfa drugs for a week or so without correcting or reducing the amount of foreign matter, took pictures of the "innards" only to discover a well developed stone near the kidney and a large stone in the bladder—a condition that obviously had existed for some time—for years in fact.

It will necessitate two operations—front and back—to remove the stones. These operations, cause unknown, are often successful, but there is always the possibility that they may not be and that brings me to a few minor points in connection with what may be my "grand finale."

I face the eventuality of what may come in perfect calmness, for I have gotten much out of life.

I shall not have time to complete this letter insofar as bringing it up to date—it matters little whether I do or not—for nothing in this life individually really matters to anyone but ourselves.

I shall not be able to proof-read the first copy from my first original draft—I have gotten too far behind for that.

I shall endeavor to put Eve's affairs in such state that they can be carried on without too much difficulty—at any rate they are largely matters of tax disputes with the Federal and State Tax Departments.

I shall leave the genealogy part of this letter for the files of the New York Genealogy Society—anyone experienced can review them and then complete them if they wish to.

I shall not apologize for those things that Society would undoubtedly consider I should have done differently than the way I did them.

I shall not apologize for my conventional sins of so-called omission.

If I had my life to live over again it would probably be led the same way.

If you ever take the trouble to read this letter, which you probably won't, you will discover for yourself what my real weaknesses were—you will determine from your lights what you think I should have done rather than what I did. . . .

People must be accepted for themselves—for what they are as they are—and the best must be made of them as they are, accepting them for better or for worse—they cannot be remade, they were cast at conception and once cast a man cannot be remade. . . .

My great regret in going will be the leaving of Eve alone—I of all those she has ever known have understood her better than anyone —I have admired her rare qualities, her loyalty, honesty, forthrightness, humor and genius—and have revelled in the temperament that has accompanied her extraordinary abilities. She has been a rare and a fine woman among women, she has been a great wife—no man could ever have asked for more—she has given me the love and devotion and understanding that few men are ever privileged to know —and from my experience of women, I know whereof I speak.

She has been generous beyond words in heart and deed—she has sacrificed, she has slaved—but always for others rather than herself. I have loved Eve and literally worshipped her as I never believed I could continuously love and worship any woman. My life with her has been superbly happy. To truly love and be loved, to understand and be understood, and to enjoy a real companionship is the zenith of the happiness and tranquility on earth that I have known with Eve.

Leaving Eve is the only regret I will have—because I have lived my life.

Alice B. upon her return from one of her coast to coast promotional tours for *Vogue*—in January 1938, to be exact—she was with her family in California for Xmas 1937—invited me to dine with her in her apartment at the Beaux-Arts and to see the colored movies she had taken on her trip. Much of the picture showed her tacky parents and their frightful Los Angeles bungalow.

That performance was our after dinner entertainment—home movies of our loved ones are always a bore to others even when well done.

During the showing of the pictures the maid cleaned up the apartment and the kitchenette.

The show over, there was the usual polite chit-chat for a respectable period and then the other guests departed.

The maid following shortly thereafter.

That left us alone—and my prick got hard.

The moment had come to strike, if Alex Ettl was to have his curiosity appeased—if he were ever to know if Alice were still a virgin or not.

Alice was a willing—yea—even eager subject.

I fondled her on the sofa—kissing and pawing her.

I caressed her cuzzy—and showed her my stiff cock.

Now Alice loved her comfort—she liked to do things nicely.

Many of the apartments at the Beaux-Arts on East 44th—she lived at 310—were fitted with "in-a-door" beds—and hers was one of those.

As I said, Alice liked her comfort—so she, sensing hopefully what appeared destined to occur, upped and opened the doors on the bed closet and pulled the bed out and down—not my cock—that was to come later.

By that time she was in an alarming state of disarray and I knew that Alex was right and Dorothy (his wife) wrong—for Miss B. was no longer acting like a maiden virtuous. In fact she was nearly nude.

She was a tiny delicate thing—flat chested, small tits—my "piece de resistance."

In a jiffy—in fact as she was lowering the bed—I slipped my coat and shirt off, dropped my pants and drawers down all in a heap on the floor—I never was one for wasting time when it came to exhibiting "my manly form" in the nude.

She quivered and shook like a leaf as I stripped her completely and laid her out on her "in-a-door" bed.

She feigned shyness—she wanted to get under the covers.

She professed great ignorance of the sexual ways of a man with a maid or vice versa.

Whether she was "pulling my cock" or not I do not know.

I told her many things she may or may not have known—but I enjoyed the telling—it excited me the more—that may have been her innocent purpose. It pleased me to be a teacher, it helped whip me into a white heat of passion—her cunt was as tight as a virgin's.

But she wasn't a virgin. Alex had won conclusively—for years he had wondered about his wife's college chum.

Alice had had an ardent lover in her life for some years but that had fizzled out.

She was a strange woman. Men often ask women how they compare with other men as lovers—if their cocks are as big or bigger than the other fellow's—they always hope theirs is the biggest, the longest or the thickest, if not the prettiest.

Women seldom ask you how they compare with other courtesans or whores—but Alice wanted to know how she was doing, how she compared with other women as a lay.

I gave her the build-up—and putting a pillow under her tiny ass, fucked the living daylights out of her.

She never protested or opposed when I went down on her and lapped her cunt—she willingly sucked my cock—she let me "frig" her in her ass hole—she was a glutton for it all.

Her only concern seemed to be her fear of getting "knocked up" and she would rush for the "douche" each time I shot my load inside her.

All in all, Alice was a good lay—it was a pleasant evening and when I finally departed I wired Alex in Florida that I had rung the bell five times—and that I hadn't been the first. . . .

Norah A., a former model of Harry M. (in his bachelor days Harry really was a commercial artist or illustrator for magazines like *Collier's* or big advertising agencies), was a show girl of some renown —she was a red haired beauty with plenty of fire and "it."

In addition to her modeling and dancing she was a painter and sculptress—from February 28th to March 15th she held an exhibition of her paintings and other work—a one-man show at the Delphic Studio, 44 West 56th St.

Harry M. had taken me to her preview—enroute Harry grew so nervous contemplating the meeting with his former model and love that he literally broke out into a sweat with the perspiration rolling down his face.

The work of hers that I liked best was her "Sphinx Moderne" (in plaster).

Norah had some circulars printed, announcing her showing, and I mailed a lot of them out on my personal mailing list—this was a gesture for the purpose of ingratiating myself—she had a natural bent for publicity and her showing got her a lot of feature articles that attracted the Hollywood scouts.

Remember you saw her dance semi-nude one night in the Greenwich Village Inn under the name of Delores.

After her showing was over, she came to dinner with me at the 37th Street apartment and spent the night—she was an exciting screw —boy how she could lay it on the line.

Just at dawn as I was pounding hell out of her belly I noticed her bust, tits, face and rumpled hair in the early gray light that was creeping in thru the window.

Her poised lips, her disheveled hair, her firm and projecting breasts were a startling replica of her "Sphinx Moderne" in plaster.

418

Then the truth flashed thru my mind—she had but modeled a self-portrait of herself in plaster—of her exotic disarray following a good working over (sexually)—she looked for all the world like a temptress from Hades.

She was the lay of lays—one of the best fucks that ever crossed my threshold. She put everything she had into each and every thrust of her lovely body and we both came and came and came until we were completely exhausted—we literally screwed the whole night through.

It was a one night stand never to be repeated—I doubt if it ever would have been the same.

In less than two weeks' time I had married again and that was that—I never saw Norah again, except the night with you and then one night when Eve and I went down to the Greenwich Village Inn to see her show. That night she borrowed Eve's silver fox cape to be photographed with Earl Carroll—the picture was printed in some Broadway sheet and she had a part in Carroll's West Coast night club Revue.

Lorell P. has a luscious body—but was a phlegmatic screw. Her drinking, her oversexed conversation, her filthy, but clever sketches—all roused me greatly.

Whenever I would meet up with Lorell, for luncheon or what have you, she would draw dirty pictures on the menu—frequently of monkeys jerking off or fucking or sucking beautiful nudes.

Lorell was never much of a talker—but she could "draw well," "write well," "drink not too well," and fuck passably—and her body was lovely—she was insidious rather than active.

I would see her from time to time after I married Eve—whenever Eve was lunching with someone else.

One Saturday when Eve had gone off for the day with her mother, brother and girl friend, I had luncheon with Lorell at the Crillon. We got a bit high—Lorell always preferred to drink her meals—during luncheon she told me of her uncle and his wife, how they were both after her—so during the afternoon, we went up there —they had an attractive apartment—the uncle was treasurer of a large and well known woolen firm.

All was well for the first hour or so—then as the drinks took hold, the Aunt and Uncle both became amorous—I, myself, had felt the glow of the liquor and the call of the cunt.

Her aunt-in-law especially resented the obvious affection we were at that moment feeling for one another.

The uncle as he got hotter and tighter became edgier and edgier.

Then as night fell and I went to phone Eve, that I was detained —the sparks began to fly.

I was drunk by that time—showing my cock to Lorell every chance I could get, or whenever the Aunt and Uncle were out of the room snarling at one another.

I was defiant of Eve—because she had left me for the day and made no bones about it—in fact I told her off in no uncertain terms— what Eve said and did is something else again—she packed her things and moved out—women never learn not to leave their men.

Then I went back to Lorell.

While I was on the phone, both the Uncle and Aunt went after her.

When I returned to the room I entered into the spirit of the occasion and between the three of us, we literally stripped Lorell bare—this seemed to appeal to her perverted tastes, but in the fracas, the Uncle became very jealous of his wife and me—insults followed insults, then we started slugging—that brought Lorell to her senses.

She interceded before anyone was killed—and whispering she wanted to go home and to bed with me, pulled on her bedraggled clothes as I adjusted mine—and we departed as the Uncle slumped to the floor in a drunken stupor.

When I got her home we stripped—and indifferently she let me fuck her whenever I wanted to the rest of the evening.

Lorell had good taste in clothes, dressed smartly and would have made an excellent designer or artist—a keen sense of satire— only liquor and sex always got in her way.

I heard from Lorell some weeks later—she was drunk and called me up to speak her mind. Her drunken tirade was an upbraiding of me for being a pimp—she blandly announced that I had married Eve only for her money or large income—that I didn't love her—that I was a skunk—that I was fucking around with other women. Lorell was so closely allied with the dress business that I didn't want Eve to know who it was—I never told her because she liked Lorell and Lorell grew to like her, as all who know her do—I said it was a friend of Ruth G.'s, because Eve had answered the phone. . . .

Eve was not experienced in the ways of men and women— marital—nor did she know much about "preventatives"—douches, etc.—and the method of self-administration of same.

420

The night of our wedding, she was embarrassed by nature's monthly call.

Well, that had happened to me the night I married your mother so it was no novelty.

That meant a week of abstinence with a bride as unsophisticated sexually as Eve.

We had been married for almost a week when the coast appeared clear—we had a very passionate affair—in fact, Eve was, without doubt, one of the most responsive, if not the most responsive, affectionate and lovable women I had ever known—her emotions knew no bounds.

Her sexual naiveness captivated me.

Her good food pleased me—but above all her sense of humor and her good mind enthralled me. She was smart, had nice eyes, an excellent mind—a quick, clear, thinker, entirely devoid of bunk or hokum—she was frankness personified. She had had a hard life of bread winning—been kicked around by her family—but she held her head high—she was always to the manor born. . . .

An idea as to how naive Eve was sexually—we were married for over a year before she knew that a "hard on" was not my permanent condition—for my prick was always stiff. . . .

[A few months after his marriage to Eve my father had his final meeting with Ruth G.]

I met Ruth and we drove out on Long Island around Westbury—she was all wrought up—we fought, screwed in the car, out in some field, tore at one another—her clothes were literally in shreds—our faces and bodies clawed and black and blue.

I explained to Eve that my condition was due to a fist encounter with Willie Burns, an old school chum who owed me some money—that we fought over the debt and she should see him. I never saw Ruth again after that except on the street or in restaurants—but not to speak to—I talked with her from time to time, over the phone, for a while, but that was all.

How Eve and I ever survived the rows at 400 East 57th I will never know.

One night I was so drunk and violent that when she locked herself in the bathroom I smashed the panel in to get at her—another night she foiled me by putting on my suit and sitting in the tub—in order to turn the shower on her I had to wet my suit.

I frequently talked of suicide and wanted to make it a double.

All in all it was a tempestuous summer—trying to reconcile our

421

separate ways of life and a conglomeration of weird friends—mine more so than hers.

How she survived—how she lived through it, stuck it out, I will never know.

But we came up to the 1938 finale and the beginning of 1939 much more reconciled than we had been at any other time since our marriage.

It had been a tough row—but we had taken it and were coming through.

The course of true love did not run very smoothly. In addition to several brawls, which we indulged in when drinking heavily, there were many fights about finances, etc.

Eve was forever slipping away to visit with her mother and I resented that—I resented her mother not coming to the house—I resented the way her mother was defiling me and talking about me to all and sundry behind my back. I frankly didn't care much for Eve's brother—I had not met her sister, but I had glowing tales told me about that young lady and her supposed charm. . . .

Into that tense situation, Percy projected himself one morning— I was stretched out on the chaise-longue, promoting my candidacy for Secretary to the State Committee when Percy arrived—I wasn't dressed—Eve was lunching with Ann H. at the Algonquin—I didn't stop talking. . . . I continued to talk, hoping that Percy would leave with Eve when she went to keep her luncheon date—but he didn't.

Some words followed, and I knocked him down on the bed— altho he was taller than I am and younger, he was lighter. When he attempted to rise and continued to struggle, I held him down and choked him—when I finally let him up with the understanding that he would . . . leave the house at once, he proceeded as soon as he was on his feet, to start the argument again—once more I knocked him down and I picked him up by the collar, and literally threw him out of the apartment.

The thing that enraged me the most about the whole proceeding and the reason I threw him on the bed and choked him, was the fact that when we were slugging it out he (with his shoes on—I was bare-footed) proceeded to kick my shins and tried to step on my feet— altho I only had my underwear or shorts on, I chased him down the hall and threw his hat after him, as he ran into the freight elevator.

I called Eve at the Algonquin and she was terribly upset, blaming me entirely.

We battled it out all summer at 400 East 57th Street, which was a dirty, dusty place at best—more than once we separated, sometimes for a few hours, and then once Eve went home to her mother for several days, before a reconciliation was effected. . . .

1939 was in many respects all in all a pleasant year for me. There was little to mar the tranquility of our marital status other than the usual mother-in-law difficulties.

We rented a little house at Mill Neck, Long Island, on the Burdick's property—it was a little too close to their home for complete seclusion, but it was nestled on the edge of a thickly wooded section which kept it very cool in summer and protected it from the worst storms in the Winter.

The rent was only $35.00 a month and from January to June, we used it primarily for weekends; then we sublet the Sutton Place apartment to a little number known as Tony Van A. She sported a car and chauffeur and a little dog—her references were prominent bankers, businessmen and investors. Eventually it became obvious that her profession was one of the oldest in the world—the most widely and universally practiced—her angle I suspect was flagellation—the status with her customers, high—she was versatile in the ways of a maid with a man, professionally. . . .

In January of 1939, we set forth by car for Florida. . . .

[My father describes their visit to the Breakers at Palm Beach.]

We strolled out on the hotel parapet overlooking the ocean after dinner (formal) in the moonlight. We ensconced ourselves on a cushioned settee in a dream world. The setting was perfect—Eve, the moonlight, the glittering ocean, the palm trees, the soft music floating out from the hotel alive with its multitude of lights. Without exception, in addition to her physical attractiveness, Eve was the finest woman I had ever known—able, with an excellent mind, far above the average. She was a woman of sterling character—brilliant, in fact, a potential genius, if not actually one. She was generous beyond measure—a fine sense of humor. It was always a joy to be with her.

Eve truly graced Palm Beach.

It was a perfect setting for her.

We sat there in complete silence for a long time—the silence only comprehended by two souls completely akin—then we talked of life and love and all the sweet nothings that make life "for two" so heavenly—at times we were very very much in love—at least I was and I suspect it was mutual.

Eve was a vision in her evening gown—I was proud of her,

proud and thrilled to be seen with her, to have it known that she was my wife.

It was not until we finally arose to stroll along the walk that we became aware that we had been sitting in a puddle left by a gardener when watering the plants—our tails were wet. We had been so absorbed with one another, with the spell of the place, that we hadn't noticed before that the cushion was very wet.

That was tops for me at Palm Beach for all time—heavenly contentment—perfect bliss. . . .

1940-1941

[Shortly after his marriage to Eve my father began negotiating to develop tung oil plantations in Florida. The great bulk of tung oil, a vital ingredient in marine paint, was imported from China and Malaysia and my father tried to persuade the various governmental agencies responsible for military procurement to underwrite a vast program for producing tung oil (made from the nuts of the tung tree).

One of the principal obstacles to this ambitious plan was the fact that it takes at least three years for tung trees to begin to bear and the war might well be over by that time. My father, nonetheless, spent much time and a good deal of Eve's money trying to bring off the tung oil deal. What might be called the Great Tung Oil Delusion was my father's last fling, a demonstration for his new bride of his energy, his initiative, his numerous friends in high places. From the point of view of impressing her it was eminently successful. Eve was charmed by the whole venture, the conferences, letters, phone calls to important officials, the studies, the pages of statistics, the mustering of evidence and arguments on behalf of tung oil, the conviction that tung oil was a vital product, critically needed to keep America strong. To Eve my father appeared a brave and resourceful David battling against the Goliathlike bureaucracy. The tung oil caper enabled my father to overcome the stigma of being a kept man. It was a play in which the leading character was the heroic entrepreneur trying to save his country. To be sure he never prevailed upon the government to make him a millionaire—I suspect he never really expected it to; although it has probably made many no more able or worthy adventurers millionaires—but he did demonstrate his talents, so to speak. These high-level negotiations made the dress business look like small potatoes by comparison. That, at least, is clearly what Eve believed.]

1939 had proven to be for me a year of marking time—I hadn't accomplished much, in fact I hadn't accomplished anything at all—there hadn't even been any outside female or sex interest to occupy any of my time. . . .

1940 was to bring forth a variety of activity, none of which produced from the financial standpoint. . . .

By 1940 Roosevelt, aided and abetted by New York's demagogic little Mayor—the would-be Napoleon, Fiorello H. La Guardia, variously known as "The Little Flower," "Butch," "The Big Hat," etc.— had stirred up religious hatred to a white heat.

The Jews were all yelling for us to go in and beat up Hitler (that is, they wanted the Christians to do the fighting making sure to keep well in the background themselves, far from the actual fighting) altho they had been strangely silent when the Russians were destroying millions of Gentiles.

Lindberg and his "America Firstists" were cutting quite a figure. "Slim" had put his finger right on the Semitic sore point—their rabid insistence upon our making war upon Germany on account of the way Germans were treating the Jews was revolting.

Our military men who were in World War I were astounded with the capacity the Germans were showing in the early days of World War II as individual fighters—their initiative and resourcefulness in open formation dumbfounded the military experts, who thought the Germans could only operate in mass formations as wholly knit machines.

[1940 saw the acceleration of the war in Europe. One of the consequences of the German invasion of Holland was the problem of Dutch refugees. Through his friendship with Van Loon, which had been to a degree revived, my father undertook to act as Executive Director of the Queen Wilhelmina Fund, a fund collected to aid Dutch refugees. My father was largely responsible for the success of the fund-raising campaign.]

We had sublet our apartment to a Mrs. Barber and her daughter because Eve wanted to be with her mother at Manhasset, where she was recovering in Eve's house (her mother was recovering from the

425

operation on her hip following the fracture from the fall), in the latter part of 1940.

A day or two before we were to turn the apartment over to the sub-tenants, I was taken down with a severe attack of the Flu. I couldn't remain at home, so Dr. Sanford had me removed to the Roosevelt Hospital where I was given a semi-private room without any other patients because I was contagious.

Having hospitalization, I was able to spend a week there without any cost except the doctor's bill. It was inconvenient for Eve, who was living out at Manhasset, and it wasn't a very merry New Year for me—altho the nurses who were very attractive, and the orderly who was bi-sexual (and gloried in the fact that he was married to a prostitute, a street walker who brought him in a tidy sum each night) did everything they could to amuse me and make my stay interesting— and that they did.

The floor orderly came into my room on New Year's Eve (ostensibly on duty) and talked and talked—he told me (he was very young and illiterate) that his wife "hustled"—fucked—for part of their living—he made very little. He told me how he watched her with her customers thru a crack in the wall of their room—how it excited him—how he would come, watching them—then after the customer had departed he would be so hot that he would lap up his wife's wet deck and then "frig" her himself.

His tall tales of his wife and her lovers and his part in the sexual goings-on at home plus his conversational revelations about his al- leged fucking of the nurses got me hot—noticing thru the sheet that I had a hard on, he put his hand in under and felt my stiff prick— then taking a great chance (anyone might have come in) he opened his fly and showed me his big tool—it was quite a specimen. I took it in my hand and caressed it as he played with me—then he went down on me—I couldn't resist or hold back—I was too hot. I came in his mouth—then I jerked him off—I thought he would never stop coming.

I gave him a couple of bucks for his pains—it was worth more, but he was only accustomed to small sums.

The next day, New Year's, the nurse who came to bathe me was a lovely lass, short, red-headed, full of vitality, vibrant—she was not one of the regular floor girls—she was up from the "public ward," relieving for the holiday.

The regular nurses when they are giving you your bath in bed (your sponge bath) when they come to your tool are supposed to give you the washrag to wash and wipe your own prick—but that gal didn't—she washed it herself. At her bath manipulations of my cock, the old rod stood up—she toyed with it—her waist or uniform was cut low—I could see her tits when she bent over me and I was in a white heat. In a flash I slipped my hand up under her dress, felt her damp cuzzy—boy, she was hot—then I played with her teats. I could hardly keep from coming—when she bent over me she let her bubbies pop way out and then she rubbed them against my cock—my fingers were working way up her hole—she liked it up the "arse" hole as well as the cunt. She went down on me, and did I come—I gave her everything I had as she came on my fingers—she had a luscious cunt to finger fuck.

I never saw her again—she went back to the Public Ward the next day and I left the hospital shortly thereafter.

My regular day floor nurse lived around the corner in a two-room flat with another nurse. I called on her several times—she was a fair fuck—I never got to her in the hospital, but in her room it was different. Once when I found her roommate also at home with her we had a threesome—nurses are hot numbers.

Driving Eve into town every day left me sort of footloose with nowhere to go but park and sit in the car until I met her for luncheon, for I didn't have an office, so I rented a small apartment on the south side of 27th Street. . . .

When I arrived at the new house, I found the landlord—he showed me a nice clean room on the first floor up, rear, at $6 per week—a new bath that was shared by three—a fireman who wanted to get away from his nagging wife; a girl who worked in the Metropolitan Life. The front apartment on the same floor had a bathroom and kitchen—that was $35 per month.

I talked it over with Eve and took it. It gave me a place to work on my papers and follow up Tung Oil. I got out all my old pictures of girls, many in the nude—covered the walls with sketches and pictures—I hung the lovely sketches that Lorell P. made for me, the series of the nude beauty having an affair with an ape—one showed the monkey sucking the girl—then fucking her—then jerking off—and then the girl going down on the monkey—she always promised to do one of the monkey fucking the girl between the tits. . . .

The landlord had a French cleaning woman who got quite a kick out of the pictures. Nearly every day she would come into my room while I was there—I would be lying around in the nude—she liked to suck me off—she started in by playing with my cock. The first time she came in my room when I was there I was dressed and she talked about the pictures and looked at them carefully—I got stiff, and felt her ass, then I slipped my penis into her calloused hand —she was coy at first—then I got my balls out—then dropped my pants and got my hand first on her teats, then her cunt—she jerked me off. I don't think she had to do much jerking—I came all over the floor and wall—that delighted her.

The next day I had a robe on when she came in—then I dropped it off—my prick was stiff (it had been just in anticipation). That day she stripped after a little coaxing and sucked me off—after that I never had anything on when she came in to clean—since I seldom slept there, all she had to do when she came in was to play with me. I never fucked her—fear of a dose, I guess. Now and then she would bring in a mulatto girl late in the afternoon—a girl who worked in one of the other houses up the street—they would suck one another off as I jerked off all over them.

Whenever Mrs. H. became too difficult I spent the night. Sometimes Eve would stay there with me but it was not comfortable for two—and then I never knew what would turn up.

Eve and I frequently lunched in one of the Armenian or Turkish restaurants.

On the South side between Lex and Third Avenue near the Theatre on 27th Street, there was a private dance parlor—one of those two-room jobs—walkup and dance, belly rub and fuck—also another favorite of mine on Lexington between 30th and 31st and one on 34th St. and Lex.

They always turned the music on as a blind. The fee was $1.00— for that you could come in your pants while you danced—rubbing your cock against their cunts, you could watch yourself in the center of the room before a long mirror. There was always a long mirror— so you could accidentally pull the girl's skirt up from the rear, slowly but surely, until her ass was bare. For $2 they would jerk you off or suck you—for $3 you could fuck them (I preferred to be jerked off or sucked off—thought it safer from disease).

There was always a couch in the next room for the pupils to rest on or fuck on. Eventually most of those small places were closed by the Mayor.

The girls were hot numbers—when you were new to a place they made some pretext of teaching, but not for more than a moment or two—then they would come in close and rub their cunts against

428

your cock. Mine was always hard in expectation—they never wore much, in fact nothing but their light thin dresses which you could look thru and see the outline of their legs all the way up when they got between you and a light—which they always did. Their flimsy dresses were of black silk mostly. Times were not so easy then—women did anything to get by and there were plenty of lovely girls in the business—today they give it away—they make so much at anything.

Usually by the time you got their asses bare in the mirror, you were ready to come in your pants—or take it out and come all over the floor or in their mouths.

I wrote about these places on the upper west side of town when Joe L. and I used to visit many of them along Central Park West and the side streets.

Just writing about those places gets me hot—I wonder if it's the memory of them or just thinking of the lovely creature who will type this out for me, that makes the damn prick stand up and wave at me —I frequently come just writing about my recollections of those days.

The girl in the room next to mine was a bit on the heavy side—she liked my room too. Ann was good for an occasional workout nights, when I was there alone—and nothing better offered.

The couple that moved into the front apartment were in show business—when the husband was on the road, we would have matinees —she was a swell lay. I picked her up by laying in wait for her to put out her swill.

In a gin mill on 34th Street near Lex. I met up with a telephone operator of the Associated Hospital Service of New York. She worked for David McAlpine Pyle who was head of it—she lived in a room in the apartment house above the saloon.

I took her to my room quite often at night—on one occasion I took pictures of her in the costumes that I brought back from Paris— they are in this file—she was also on the plump side—I cut out the background so Eve wouldn't recognize that room if she found them. She liked having me fuck her so much that she was forever calling me at 27th Street.

A few other nondescript lays came and went—I wasn't exactly idle—all told my three months stay on 27th Street was pleasant from many angles.

On July 15th, 1941 Eve and I set forth determined to learn more about Tung Oil. We headed for Louisiana and Florida to inspect existing groves. In New Orleans, after we had washed up, removed the dirt and grime from our persons, I took Eve over to Antoine's for dinner—none better the world around—the gourmet's delight. Nowhere on the face of the globe can such gastronomic delights be found as there—Bouillabaisse, Huites en coquille a la Rockefeller, Pompano en Papillote, Pommes Souffles, Frogs Legs saute demi-Bordelaise and Louisiana River Shrimp.

While introducing Eve to the wondrous edibles of the place the manager gave us a copy of their centennial souvenir—1840 to 1940.

The Souvenir contained a list of notables that had wined and dined there during the years—with comments by some of them—some such were Irvin S. Cobb, Will Rogers, F. D. R., Cal Coolidge, Alf Landon, Herbert Hoover, O. O. McIntyre, H. L. Mencken, George Sokolsky, Julian Street, Ethel Barrymore, Katherine Cornell, Fiorello La Guardia, Helen Morgan, Hendrik Willem van Loon, Lawrence Tibbett, Eddie Cantor, Justice Felix Frankfurter, Cornelia Otis Skinner, Lucius Beebe, etc.

Eve was scanning the list of distinguished guests who had supped at that "fine board"—men like Theodore Roosevelt, William Howard Taft, Marshal Foch, John J. Pershing, Gen. Smedley Butler, Admiral Byrd, Henry Wallace, Harry Hopkins, J. Edgar Hoover. . . .

Reading thru these long lists of great and near to the great, she came to the list of authors, columnists and artists: Heywood Broun, Sherwood Anderson, Thomas Wolfe, Archibald MacLeish, Stark Young, Will Durant, Rube Goldberg, Drew Pearson, Quentin Reynolds, Francis Parkinson Keyes, Alexander Woollcott, Sinclair Lewis, and lots of others—and to her surprise came upon the name W. Ward Smith in the forefront of that list. At first she couldn't believe her eyes, then light dawned (shadows of the *Nomad* days) when she read my name off, I thought at first that she was trying to be funny—just putting it in herself—but when she showed it to me, I was indeed pleased—it did much for my ego.

That I had not won or deserved the right to be in such company little mattered—there it was for posterity to gaze upon—and that called for another bottle of champagne. My exuberance was complete—I loved Antoine the more, if that could be.

All my life even when in school I had longed to write, to express myself, my thoughts, my opinions thru the written word—to report in writing so that others reading could understand what I had to say, what was on my mind. I wanted so much to be able to express myself in writing on current affairs, domestic, international or what have

430

you—Heywood Broun, F. P. A. Kenneth McGowan, Mark Sullivan, Walter Lippman, Bill McGeehan, F. F. V. (Frank Van de Water) were my early envies—how I wanted to be able to do what they were doing.

In latter years, Westbrook Pegler and Hugh Johnson held my envy—Hendrik Willem van Loon, Konrad Bercovici, John Gunther, William O'Donnel, George Skolsky; I have always wanted to write editorially or a column—I have never wanted money very much, enough to cover the bones, and persuade women to let me make love to them, and for a bit of pub crawling now and then—but that's all.

At the same time I have longed for the society of gentlefolk without doing anything to warrant my getting it or holding it if I got it—for all my life I have defied conventionality and have forever shocked my friends or fought with them when I felt they were not doing or thinking as they should. In theory, I recognize the right of everyone to do as they damn please altho few can (do as they damn please).

Back to New Orleans—dinner over, Roy Louis Alciatore the grandson of Antoine Alciatore (the founder) showed Eve thruout the place and all the treasures therein—principally menus of famous banquets and special occasions—and that too called for another bottle of champagne.

The hour was getting on, so we departed—very pleased with ourselves—at least I was. . . .

Eve has a definite aversion (which I have never been able to break her of or to overcome) to public demonstrations on the lewd or sexual side of life—she is the antithesis of Melba in that respect. In public and before others—even in her own home—Eve is still, after more than 8 years with me, a prude—privately, alone with her hubby, she exudes sex and is curious as hell about it all and will say and do anything almost—her reactions are healthy and when she lets her hair down it is always a surprise and a thrill. . .

One night in August when I was in Washington on Tung Oil, Percy (H.) drove me out to Ft. Meade to see you. He was working with Eastern Air Lines (in operations) at the time—he was living with Cecil Moore (Dartmouth '40) in Washington.—Cecil was in the ticket selling end. Cecil was engaged to a girl flyer in Eastern reservations named McKenzie—Percy to Ann Loughlin, a girl from Smith living with her family in Montclair.

In addition to Cecil, the Goldberg boy (son of Rube) who had changed his name to George came along. They were all jelly cake

431

when we dropped in on you and saw your setup and found you were a sergeant—the *Baltimore Sun* has just given you quite a writeup in its issue of August 21, 1941. . . .

I couldn't help but recall, as we sat there and chatted and had a drink, that day back in May when I had first called on Oscar at this same home of his in Arlington—and how he had said, as we lolled and chatted on his back lawn as the children romped and played, that the other side would have to start the shooting—and how he had suggested, in answer to a question of mine—that it might be started in the Red Sea by the Germans firing on some American ship carrying war supplies to the British. And I wondered then (Dec. 7th) if Oscar hadn't been dragging a red herring across my vision that May day and if he hadn't known all along that it would be the Japs—and had been really thinking of the Japs in the Pacific instead of the Germans in the Red Sea. Maybe he had said the Red Sea as a blind.

In May I said that to have a munitions ship blown up in the Red Sea wouldn't arouse the Americans enough to go to war—even after the second World War, we sat by and calmly watched the satellites of Red Russia shoot down American air ships and kill American flyers.

There never was any doubt in my mind but that Roosevelt knew that he could eventually jockey the Japs into attacking us—his State Department knew it—every Army and Navy officer who had ever been in the Orient knew it—and Roosevelt's family were very familiar with the Far East.

If I had anticipated it for twelve years prior to Pearl Harbor—certainly the Roosevelt gang were aware of the danger, but they didn't want to stop it, they wanted it to happen—everything I ever heard firsthand or have read or observed, has convinced me that they were yearning for an attack and doing everything possible to bring one about. The Germans wouldn't fall for FDR bait, for they remembered the first World War.

The Japs grabbed the bait and the Roosevelt Brain Trusters had their wish fulfilled.

Roosevelt's place in history is questionable—he will be there, but he will still stink for his infamy and his betrayal of his own country for a few fleeting moments of world glory and power. . . .

The following days were hectic—Washington was a beehive of activity. Inadequate guns were mounted on roof tops—supposed to be anti-air craft—and men were posted at the bridges and guns mounted there—many of the guns were dummies set up to fool the enemy.

432

Then a rumor came thru about noon that German planes were roaring down the New England coast bound for New York. I tried to reach Eve to tell her to stay indoors—I couldn't get her on the phone, she had gone out to lunch early. The telephone wires were jammed—I was frantic, worried to death about her—sirens screamed about New York and Washington and other cities. I had rented a radio—it was on full blast—people everywhere were paralyzed—but Eve in New York went about having her lunch, doing her chores and ignoring the excitement and confusion. I finally got her but only when she got back to her office after lunch—by that time the all clear had been sounded or announced—nobody knew what it was all about—so confusing—the signals hadn't been properly worked out and anyway it had been a false alarm.

I knew your outfit was returning from manoeuvers and I figured that you would be at the Fort Hill Reservation by Monday night—you being north bound from the Carolina mountains to Fort Meade.

That afternoon, (December 8th) I travelled South to meet you. I picked up a GI on the way down—he was part of the regular garrison at Hill. Every bridge south of the Potomac had a detachment of soldiers guarding it—but I wasn't stopped.

When I reached Hill and let the boy off, they wouldn't let me in the front gate—the boy, however, had told me of a way to get around to the rear of the reservation where you all would probably be—the only reason the kid had given me any hope at all of getting in the front way was to get a ride all the way—but he had tipped me off, so I backtracked and groping around in the dark, found my way thanks to the aid the friendly boys along the way gave me.

To me it all looked like a tangled mess—but that encampment that night with its glowing fires, its mass of equipment and the black outlines of the men as they were silhouetted against the fires, was one of those impressive sights that being seen for the first time and then never again leaves a deep imprint on one's memory. It was a usual sight for you and the others and must have become quite commonplace for you as the years rolled on.

Those hot blazing fires in the pits with the iron rods across them surrounded by company groups keeping warm and chatting until the time to move on came, were a great sight. When you stepped out from the group around your fire in that crisp cold air and we walked over to the car together, it was for me the clicking of something long desired. I married young so that my son—my oldest—and I could be close companions, much closer and nearer of an age than my father

433

and I had been in our camaradarie—but it was never to work out that way for me except on a handful of occasions. The blame?—who is there to judge impartially—perhaps I had been too selfish, too impetuous—whether it was all my fault or not, I do not know.

What I had always wanted most—and that too was no doubt a selfish egotistical parental yearning—I was never really to have consecutively, and that may have been just as well at the time for you. In fact, you would have been better off had you broken away entirely from your mother's influence from college on—you were making headway then as an individual—you continued to be yourself at Camp James and in the Army and when you married Eloise—but then you slipped back to those provincial surroundings in which you had been submerged so many adolescent years.

I think men and women are the better for developing themselves —free from their parents' ways, customs and influence—children so often not only look like one parent or the other, but favor one or the other parent in speech, mannerisms and the approach of life. It's an insoluble problem.

While it may have been better for you that my plan to have a close pal-ship and understanding with my son did not materialize, it would have been better still if you had gotten away and stayed away from your mother's apron strings. That by virtue of the circumstances and the worldly comforts it affords, and the emotional chords that have always been so adroitly played upon, you will never be able to decide objectively and then do.

I kept the motor running and the heater on that night—in a convertible job, that does not keep you hot as toast, but it takes the chill off. As you will remember, we got in and settled down to a long talk about your future in the reflected glow of all those roaring fires along the hillside and in the flat—as far as we could see in the dark.

The immediate problem was whether you should go to Officers Training School or not—it seemed that there wasn't much difference between the pay of a Top Sergeant with wife and 2nd Lieut.—so why wait for a commission, why not marry Eloise immediately? At that time if you were married, you couldn't train for a commission.

I argued as earnestly as I could (without irritating you, I hope) for officer's training—first and foremost as I told you, your standing in civilian life afterwards would be vastly improved, especially at the war's end if you came out with a rank (later in life, it doesn't matter much, but at the start it does).

434

Second (a thought I did not give voice to), it would postpone your contemplated marriage to the blonde nugget from the Carolinas. I myself had rushed into so many legal and extra legal affiliations with the female of the species on account of an impatient prick (a stiff tool knows no conscience) that I was fearful for you. When you get hot you lose all perspective and balance, and never weigh the many factors that must of necessity enter into any union if it is to be successful and enduring.

I didn't want you to make a snap decision and be sorry afterwards. I have made snap decisions in such matters and had them successful (Eve, for example)—and then on the other hand, my marriage to your mother was not a hasty decision—ours was a long drawn out engagement that, after marriage, ended on the rocks—all of which disproves my own and the accepted theory in such matters. But nevertheless, as all men know and you yourself have so aptly said, before you get your tail, you think you cannot survive without it, and then after you have had it, you wonder why you bothered.

The professional prostitutes and the demi-mondanes have known all about that feeling thru the ages—that is why they get the five bucks on the mantel beforehand. That's why there has to be something more to marriage than a good screw—all kinds of women can get your cock to stand up and keep you hot for their pussy or their mouth or tongue, but you must have similar likes and dislikes in most cases to last—or else one must dominate the other and the other like to be dominated. Mutual interests are essential if the marriage is to be on an equal basis —with some, the "small fry" are the binding factor, but that is frequently not enough.

Then, too, I felt that if you held off there would always be the chance of your meeting someone that had been reared the same way that you had, that had had the same advantages—someone you would not have to train, that you would not feel superior to. I felt that you should have a taste of marital bliss before going overseas if you were to go—and it was a sure thing almost then that you would go.

Promiscuous tail on the curbstone satisfies for the moment, but the home brew has, as your ma once pointed out to me, many advantages—you don't have to get up and go out or home in the cold of night—some may let you stay till morn—and the possibility of venereal disease is considerably decreased.

Finally, but reluctantly, you came to the conclusion that you should try for a commission—it was a wise choice.

Another point which I did not mention to you and never did,

was the concern I felt about your going into action—you had had such bad luck as a kid, cutting your face on the scrap basket, your lip on the sleigh, hurting your leg, your colds and many minor things (that I never heard about)—that I feared you would get in action and get hurt—and you did. So I wanted to delay or postpone the inevitable as long as it could be postponed—and going into officers training was one way of delaying you. Another was when you were made an instructor—that was done for two reasons, your ability and my request.

I assume that your mother was also urging you to train for a commission—but you were hot pants to get married.

I knew what you had been up against as far as girls in your own immediate circle were concerned—it is difficult to find them with intelligence, hot pussies and social standing—they seldom have all three. Some have sex unbridled and social position, some are heavily sexed and brilliant, some are stupid and sexy, and many of the better brought up ones are stupid, attractive and cold or have been brought up to keep their cunts in a chastity belt or kotex pad (this latter class are becoming fewer and fewer)—nevertheless, I hoped you might find an intelligent sexy gal in your own sphere.

You sure were lovesick—and the glasses that you used to gaze upon your bride-to-be with were of the rosiest hue—how you sang her charms as you saw them, to all and sundry. Her artistic merit defied the art critics—a great painter not in the making but who had arrived, flawless—a brilliant intellect that had struggled upward and forward against adversity (a la "Honest Abe"). All this you saw with your own eyes and much more—and that was as it should have been and was.

One should never extol their own wares—for what one man sees in a woman, another never does, and they think you nuts for your raving and vice versa. What one woman sees in a man another woman never does—so both men and women should keep their enthusiasm to themselves.

After midnight the orders came to move out of Camp Hill and we said adieu—you agreeing to apply for officers training, I agreeing to stand by you in your love venture.

I watched the wagons roll away as the embers glowed, faded and then were smothered out—then I too drove away. I passed your motor-cars on the highway north of Fredericksburg and I sped back to bed down at the Willard in Washington.

That had been a night of nights for me, my son—one which few

436

fathers ever know, for few are in my boots—and that too is just as well and I hope that you may never be on such terms with your son (if you ever have one and I expect you will) that one night will mean so much—or that in your lifetime there will be other wars and men going.

In frankness I must admit that there is more than an excellent chance for more and bigger and more devastating wars to come within your life—yea, even maybe within my own—however short the balance of that may be.

I have always admired you, Page—admired your work at Dartmouth, your work afterwards and your work in the army especially at Fort Benning—I was always in close touch with your record there. I have not always agreed with your economic thoughts and your philosophy of life—but I have respected your opinions and your right to hold them, and even your right to choose whomever you pleased as your legally wedded wife.

That we couldn't see eye to eye after your wife decided that Baltimore held more for her than New York I always regretted—I never compromise with my beliefs—and I didn't expect and couldn't expect and wouldn't have thought anything of you if you had not taken the stand you did beside the woman you married, for better or for worse.

On the way to the church she told me of her intentions and her ambitions—I hope for your sake and for your daughter's sake, that she attains her objectives—they were large, and time causes shrinkages.

My admiration for you has never waned no matter what our personal relations have been—I yearned in my youth to be and do many of the things you have done and been.

I had been actively interested in the America First movement—most of 1941—attending meetings in Washington (addressed by the La Follettes) with Eve at the National Theatre.

I had been opposed to our involvement in World War I and definitely opposed to the second venture—the futility of it all was always too apparent. Our job was to be an arsenal of defense, armed to the hilt on land, on the sea, and under the sea, and in the air—to keep abreast of any possible combination that might be employed against us if not ahead of the other fellows—leave them alone, sell them for cash, no lend-lease or lease lend—it would have been expensive, but dirt cheap compared to what we have wasted in resources in these last two years.

437

The America Firsters held a large mass meeting at the Manhattan Opera House on 34th Street—their first big one in New York. Walter Piel had bought a box—we couldn't get near the front entrance, the crowd was so dense. Lindbergh and Senator Walsh (of Mass.) were the speakers—John Flynn presided. When we couldn't get near the front door, we went around to 35th St. to the stage door —the crowd was thick there but we outwitted the "mounties" who were riding human herd and got Mimi and Eve in with us. Inside we bumped into Joe Boldt—you knew his brother at Dartmouth—he was an active official with the committee, sort of an aid to Flynn, and with much pushing and shoving reached our box an hour before the show opened.

What a mob that was—the Irish who hated the English—the communists who were all for keeping us out until Hitler and Stalin tied up—the Germans who didn't want any interference with Hitler —and just plain Americans like Lindbergh and myself who didn't personally and for historical reasons believe in foreign entanglements. I had been opposed all my life to involvement in European conflicts.

Walter Piel (he had been a naval officer in World War I, a flyer for the Navy when they only had box kites, and an aide to Byrd— was a violent America Firster) gave the America First organization large sums of money and was almost pro-German in his excitement. His mother and father were born in Germany and they had large holdings of property there—that naturally raised the question of whether his opposition to war was not really based on his tie with the fatherland thru birth. I think it made him more violent—he was conscious of that interpretation of his position.

I liked Lindbergh and I had always been a great admirer of John Flynn, the chairman of the New York County Committee of the America First Committee. I enjoyed that evening—Walsh, Flynn and Lindbergh were all excellent speakers.

For my part I wanted to do all I could to keep us out. I firmly believed then that involvement in Globular warfare could only mean the eventual destruction of our Republic—the lowering of the standards of our way of life—where every man had a right to worship, speak, think, write or fuck as he pleased and to seek riches or be a bum.

On October 30th, 1941 the America Firsters held their biggest rally of the anti-war movement—this time at Madison Square Garden. . . .

[Edwin] Webster gave a supper party or buffet party after the

438

meeting in his house across the way from 30 Beekman place at #35 Beekman Place for the speakers of the evening and some of the more active workers and the big subscribers. It followed the Garden meeting—Senator Wheeler, Senator Clark, Cudahy, John Flynn, Lindbergh, Michael Strange (former wife of John Barrymore), Walter and his wife, Mrs. Finerty, Dorothy Bayer, Sophia Pinckney, Tommy Brodix came along with Eve and myself.

Eve told Lindbergh that she had seen him in Tiffany's in London some years before and he remembered having been there, said he had been having a watch fixed—he was able to recall the incident because it was the only time he had been in Tiffany's in London.

When I talked with him I recalled the first all air transcontinental flight to California—and the fact that I had been on it and that he had been at the Newark airport when we set off on that inaugural journey—we also chatted about the trips he made thru the West prior to World War I when he piloted his father from town to town in their four wheel jalopy.

Lindbergh was affable and friendly, he mixed easily—Wheeler was a bit grouchy, tired, irritable—Senator Clark was very pleasant, Flynn delightful. . . .

December 7th abruptly ended the anti-War activities of the America Firsters. Theirs had been a glorious but losing fight against the monster, the evil one in the White House who was set upon a venture which eventually brought the entire world to its knees in complete economic and political disaster.

The country was opposed to war—the President knew it—he knew the American people would never enter another world war of their own free will unless they were attacked—that's why he longed and prayed for the attack that came so obligingly for him on that fateful Sunday morning of December 7th when the Pacific Fleet lay huddled together like a lot of duck decoys in Pearl Harbor. The great White Father had gotten his wish—he had baited the potential enemy in—he tempted them as he goaded them and they bit and bit hard, but it was a terrible thing for the people of America—it humbled them before the world and dragged them down to such depths that they may never recover their old standards for generations to come.

Morally they were degraded and economically they were shorn for the fleeting moment of glory of an egomaniac—the vain commander-in-chief who knew so little of military tactics and less of world power politics, yet who was so frequently envisioned as the wise one who knew all and who time and again not only betrayed the blood of the youth of his nation but as a traitor to his sworn oath, again and again bartered away the economic wealth of his people for a few vain moments at international confabs. .. . .

1942-1946

Before getting into the serious side of my activities during 1942, I am going to talk about me—thoughts on my thoughts—and then to mention several things that have occurred this year, which I may never get around to report. I did some of that sort of thing in 1943, and again in 1944, when writing out the happenings of many years previous.

To begin with, I am commencing to suffer from a feeling of frustration—I do not know whether that's brought about by the failure of my many undertakings these last few years or whether it's because I have dropped all active interest in the details of political manipulation, plus the fact that the work of restoring the old house at Sagaponack has now reached the point where it takes very little time or effort.

Maybe I have remained actively married too long to one woman —yet I am devoted to Eve.

It may be a combination of all these things and many others that I am not aware of—it may be traceable primarily to the fact that Eve has been producing successfully, while I have been solely on the receiving side. Or again, it may be due to the times—the much greater effort that has to be put forth in order to accomplish only a small part of what it was so simple, so easy to accomplish when I was much younger—perhaps it's just old age.

I'm puzzled at times about myself—my weaknesses—I wish I knew what it was that made me weak. . . .

I wonder why I slip, and when I slipped, and how I slipped— wherein I failed. I would have so much enjoyed the activity of it all—

action on a large scale, on a wide front, involving big movements of men, has always appealed to me.

I know I lack staying qualities—stick-to-itiveness—I tire easily, I get fed up, I get bored with most everything I contact—I suffer from great fatigue when I haven't been doing anything to fatigue me, and when I do things that would wear down many men, I feel no fatigue. . . .

It was pleasant to live when we didn't have foreign wars to pay for, or totalitarian governments to support—when we were taking care of ourselves and letting the rest of the world take care of themselves—when we were minding our own business and not permitting outsiders to butt into ours.

When we had no income taxes—when men could buy what they pleased and pay whatever they felt they wished to pay, and could sell what they bought for what they chose to ask without any government interference. The government did not come into your home or your office and tell you what to do or how to do it, and then tax you for doing it—you hired men and fired men, paying them what you thought they were worth, and they worked for a day's pay.

My father worked six days a week, and frequently on Sundays, when he was a younger man, and as he grew older, he always worked six days, sometimes leaving a little earlier on Saturday afternoon—frequently going to his office Sundays for a few hours. To my knowledge, he never took a vacation—I am sure that he was none the worse in health, in wealth and spirit. As a matter of fact, the important thing in life is regularity. Daily repetition of the activities of the day before. It's a fallacy to say "that all work and no play makes Jack a dull boy." . . .

Human beings are oddities in their thinking en masse—they are prone to follow false prophets to their own detriment, always seeking something for nothing—they rally to the slightest suggestion that something may be obtained for nothing, without effort, without ever weighing the possibility or probability that it is not within the province of mortal man to fulfill such alluring promises.

Men, of course, are forever making promises amongst themselves which they know to be impossible of fulfillment and have no intention of fulfilling at the time they are made—they make them primarily to attain some personal end or gain. . . .

There was a time in the history of this country when the peoples' concept of government was that the Government was a creature of the people. Today in the United States of America and in most parts of the world, the people have become the creatures of the governments they themselves have created by one false move or another. Individual freedom and the right to live one's life as one should is no longer the right of man on the North American continent or the world around, with but few exceptions.

The Marxian dialectic which regards man as a biologic creature serving the ends of the state has succeeded in setting up a tyranny over the mind and spirit of man in many parts of the world—the ultimate of this doctrine is the totalitarian state controlled either by one despot or by an elite oligarchy the world around.

Men for generations feared the privation of old age, so in their youth they worked and slaved and saved, so that they might not end their days in the poorhouse over the hill—they saved for the rainy day, for illness or adversity.

Today, when the worker diligently labors from a quarter to 80 percent of the fruits of his labor is taken from him, in order to provide for those who have not produced or saved for their old age or adversity.

For myself, fear has always been upon me and will always haunt me—fear of the unknown, dread of the known—and while I am capable of rationalizing the predicaments that others find themselves in, I have never been capable of rationalizing my own predicaments sufficiently to comfort or console myself.

In the translator's introduction to Kierkegaard's *The Concept of Dread* he said first "know thyself" (in that effort I have also failed W.W.S.), and he continued:

> Dread is a desire for what one dreads, a sympathetic antipathy. Dread is an alien power which lays hold of an individual and yet one cannot tear one's self away, nor has a will to do so; for one fears, but what one fears, one desires. Dread then makes the individual impotent, and the first sin always occurs in impotence—apparently, therefore, the man lacks accountability, but this lack is what ensnares him.

Kierkegaard was certainly much concerned with sin and the dread of sin, and in his gropings gave expression to many truisms as I see life and thought.

> That human nature must be such that it makes sin possible, is, psychologically speaking, perfectly true. If one were to think it, sin

442

would become man's substance. It is easy for cunning common sense to escape the recognition of sin.

Hereditary sin is so deep and dreadful a corruption of nature that it cannot be understood by the reason of any man, but must be recognized and believed by the revelation of the scripture.

The account of the first sin in Genesis has, especially in our age, been regarded rather carelessly as a myth—sin came into the world by sin.

Pelagianism lets every individual, unconcerned about the race, play his own little history in his private theatre.

Dread is a sympathetic antipathy and not an antipathetic sympathy.

Sinfulness is not sensuousness, but without sin there is no sexuality, and without sexuality no history.

I would say that learning to know dread is an adventure which every man has to affront if he would not go to perdition either by not having known dread or by sinking under it. He, therefore, who has learned rightly to be in dread has learned the most important thing.

If a man were a beast or an angel, he would not be able to be in dread. Since he is a synthesis he can be in dread, and the greater the dread, the greater the man. This is not affirmed in the sense in which man commonly understands dread as related to something outside a man, but in the sense that man himself produces dread.

He who is educated by dread is educated by possibility, and only the man who is educated by possibility, is educated in accordance with his infinity.

The dread of poverty, the dread of unfavorable publicity, the dread of discomfort, the dread of disease, the dread of violence and physical suffering are compelling factors in the life of man—with many the dread of sin, as sin is understood, by those who dread it most, is often mitigated by the belief that there can be atonement.

The times or the age we live in moderate or increase our fears—without fear, man would grow fat and useless—and die.

My antidote for fear is sleep (it's my opiate) with my head under the pillow and the sheets piled up high—mayhap a childish hangover. . . .

I delay, postpone the issue. In my youth, I met the issues head on, but now I avoid them. I procrastinate maybe—and I wonder if that is not a serious fault. I frequently delay in order the better to marshal my defense, never my offense—but then, I seldom am on the offensive these days.

Eve meets any issue head on. . . .

I have a hard time accepting the world as it is today. Naught I do can change the present or the future the tides of destiny have set—the world I knew and heard about at the turn of the century is the world I could have favored most, but that is not to be again—there will be other times, but not those times, and so it has been ordered since the beginning of time and so it will ever be.

Aristotle accepted the world as it was—happiness was for Aristotle man's chief purpose and to have it a man must have a certain amount of worldly goods, a certain amount of good fortune—that is not Hedonism—Aristotle distinguished between pleasure and happiness.

Reason—but there are times when one can reason for others, but not for oneself—yet "The highest good is the life of reason."—Aristotle. . . .

"The happy man, the virtuous man, is the man who steers midway between the two shoals that threaten on either side to wreck human happiness. In every act, in every thought, in every emotion, a man may be overdoing his duty, or underdoing it, or doing it just right."—Aristotle.

You, my son, are inclined to overdo. . . .

With me, it has always been too much or too little—never in moderation. . . .

William James—need I tell you of him—well, I seem to fit into his "tough-minded" grouping, being Empiricist, sensationalistic, materialistic, pessimistic, irreligious (much of the time, altho very religious in early youth—I still have occasional lapses), Fatalistic, Pluralistic, sceptical. You lean to the "Tender-minded" gauging from the little I know of you. I suspect that you are Rationalistic—I know that you are intellectualistic, idealistic, whether you are religious or not I wouldn't know—I should say that you might be a free-willist—I have been a touch that way myself at times—monistic, maybe yes and then maybe no—time will tell. Dogmatical—a touch. . . .

Truth as I saw it and as you practiced it was what caused our separation—fundamentally—what colored Eloise's vision of truth was the difference between what the Pages of Ruxton and the Smiths of 30 Beekman had to offer materially. . . .

444

The futility of it all, the stark futility of human striving and aspiration—it appalls—the search for the true truth, so purposeless when one atomic bomb may destroy the universe. Today, we should live only for today, getting the most out of each and every minute. Tomorrow—for there may be no tomorrow.

The wastefulness—the uselessness—of all this effort of words to you—but it gives me momentary expression—occupies idle hands and helps the girl a bit who transcribes it all—otherwise it is wasted wordage.

It is not easy to see ourselves as we appear to others—our adulation of our own self-portrait is hard to dispel even when we eavesdrop and hear a much less pleasing, nay even unpleasant version of our deeds and thoughts—even an unbiased description of our physical appearance can come as a shock to our vanity. To evaluate oneself no higher than one's neighbor evaluates one is not so simple of accomplishment, but our own evaluation may be a truer one than another—especially of those seeking to be in our good graces, who only reflect the picture that we most like to see.

We, for our part, are always seeking what is not.

What ails me—my greatest comfort is sleep?

I worry and fret and stew about all manner of things—seldom outwardly, but everlastingly inwardly. So I sleep 8, 10, 12, 14 hours a day. And yet I well remember in my youth my sleep was often nil —an hour or two a day and sometimes not that. When troubled or beset, then to the bed I would go and sleep myself out of my dilemma.

I have no objective in life—I do not seem to be able to find a mark to shoot at—I weigh the pros and cons of all possibilities and finding the cons usually well in majority, I dismiss the object of my speculative interest. I see men venture into commercial, industrial life, yea, even political life, without the slightest knowledge of the pitfalls, the procedure involved, and no appreciation of their own limitations or availability for the task involved—like babes in the woods. Yet in their very naiveness, they succeed where others skilled and aware, fall by the wayside—so many gain by merely venturing. It sometimes makes you stop and ponder about the human race—it's certainly to the opportunist and not to the well prepared or trained education—bah! It's more often a greater hindrance than a help. . . .

Not only is sleeping one of the pleasant sensations of man, but eating is a pleasant indulgence—and crapping is the most enjoyable relaxation. Fucking has them all beat for there is nothing like a good straight screw—provided all the preliminary variations of perversity have been indulged in—the H'ors d'oeuvres so to speak.

As to food, I like to cook—soup is my favorite—waffles—beef —particularly steaks over a charcoal fire outdoors—mashed potatoes —saute—scrambled eggs—vegetables—puddings—Fudge—griddle cakes—oatmeal—but soup, that's what I like best to do. . . .

And now you have a son as well as a daughter to guide thru the formative years of life—you will probably apply to your homelife, your wife and your children, a code of conduct contrary to that which you understood to have been mine.

I, for one, choose to believe, as I have often said before, that you are the better for having attained what you so far have attained in life, without reliance upon aid from your father. Had I chosen a different course than I have, and had I been sufficiently successful financially to maintain my family in the style to which it was thought by some they should have been maintained, I would have been prone to extend myself in providing lavish comforts and entertainment, particularly during the formative years—thereby offsetting harsh disciplinarian tactics, which I most certainly would have employed in the rearing of my sons, if their upbringing had been entrusted to me.

A great fault in my makeup was developed by the knowledge and assurance that I always felt while they lived that I could rely upon my parents in the way of material aid and assistance when confronted with adversity or in need, and on my wives and mistresses when my parents were no longer available for me to lean on.

I feel that you and your brother escaped spoiling to a degree in the household at Ruxton, altho pampered and raised in a most provincial atmosphere, with all the limitations that that pampering and provinciality imposed. Don't pamper your children—make them earn for themselves that which they desire most as they go thru life—do not raise them in a provincial atmosphere, whether it be scholastic, commercial, financial, political, economic or industrial. . . .

[Eloise, a few months after our marriage at Fort Benning, Georgia, went to New York to take up a scholarship she had won at the Art Students League. On one occasion she called my father and asked him to cash a ten-dollar check for a friend of hers. This request touched my father on a very sensitive nerve—his financial situation and available credit. He asked Eloise who the hell she thought he was—Henry Mor-

446

genthau (then Secretary of the Treasury). She hung up the phone. Soon afterwards she gave up the scholarship and returned to Columbus, Georgia, where I was a mortar instructor at the Infantry School.]

On November 3rd, I wrote you as follows:

November 3, 1942

Lieutenant Charles Page Smith
36 Fox Avenue
Benning Park,
Columbus, Ga.

Dear Page:
Your wife's insolence Friday night was inexcusable—I told her I had talked with you and was about to give her your best, when she curtly stated that she was not interested—that she had had a wire from you.

I heard that Eloise and Richards had had quite a time of it while he was here—apparently she greatly enjoyed visiting the sophisticated haunts of New York's Cafe society with him—so didn't subject him to any of her petulance—she had always led us to believe that she didn't like those places.

Her failure to drop in or phone to say goodbye to Eve and myself would have been unpardonable from the most illiterate hillbilly—her cousin Ruth, who appears to have had about the same upbringing and background, seems aware of the simple amenities of life—so Eloise must know better.

On the way to the wedding, Eloise said she was going to ignore the Baltimore attacks on her and win her way into the Ruxton family —she stated that if anything happened to you, that she and any off-springs she might have by you would be entitled to your share of the so-called "Page fortune." I told her I didn't think it would run to very much, but of course it would be more than could ever be looked for from me.

Knowing there is little to be gained from us financially, may account in part for her rudeness—frankly, it was noticeable that as soon as she definitely decided to curtail her visit and no longer had any use for the little hospitality we might be able to extend to her, her strange attitude was accentuated.

Not being an art critic, I would not venture to pass judgment on any art work or to come to any conclusions from the criticisms of others. I was simply amazed at the wide difference between her report of the criticism of the critics and the statements made to me.

I trust that there is enough at stake in Baltimore for her to

447

try and make a special effort to be polite to your family and your friends. . . .

My only regret in connection with my communications regarding Eloise is the fact that I permitted Eve to prevail upon me to delete from my original communication the things Eloise had said about me to Usui [a Japanese picture framer]. I have always felt I should have let you have that straight from the shoulder as well as telling you how she planned frankly and avowedly to get her share of whatever wealth she considered the Pages to possess, and that declaration as I may have mentioned before, she made en route from the hotel to the chapel, the day she married you—maybe it was all youthful enthusiasm a bit on the naive side. . . .

I have kept very carefully your communication dated January 3rd, 1942. It should have been 1943, because that was when you wrote it. You were not married in 1942. What always amused me about that communication was the fact that you never bore any resentment over the things your grandmother and your mother wrote about your then wife-to-be—they were pretty harsh. They were tough on Eloise and tough on her family and when I say tough I mean tough, because they were things which she had been born into and could not help, whereas, no matter how humble one's origin may be—there is no excuse for purposeless untruths.

You seem to feel that I should have shown greater patience and understanding of her conduct—I understood her conduct perhaps even better than you. I knew what she was interested in and what she was striving to attain—Baltimore held greater promise than New York—I have been confronted with the stupid lies of the female of the species many times in my life. In that respect I can think of only one gal, however, who was in a class with Eloise and that was Morris V.'s fifth wife, a little vitriolic redhead from California. She was 18 when she married Morris, who was 45 at the time. Russell Patterson couldn't trust her, but he fell in love with her—and for a time deserted his wife for her—he used her on the cover designs for *Ballyhoo* that made him famous. The truth wasn't in Lyle V. but men adored her and worshipped her, fought over her and squandered their time and money on her.

I gather that Eloise greatly improved under your mother's direction, but then only recently, in fact, this winter, I heard that all was not well and that she and your mother were not in complete harmony. I think that's unfortunate.

448

Lest you forget, the following is your letter of January 3rd, 1943:

January 3, 1942

Dear Father—

I'm returning your Christmas present of the ten dollars and under separate cover the books you and Eve sent us for Christmas. I am sorry to have to do this. The fact is that after the things you wrote about my wife I would have very little dignity if I would still accept gifts from you.

I've heard both sides of the unfortunate misunderstanding between you and Eloise and I feel that for a man of your maturity and worldly experience you showed a surprising lack of patience and understanding. However, this is beside the point. We both appreciate what you and Eve have done for us. Eloise was particularly upset that Eve should have received any impression that she was rude or unpleasant to her in any way because she has only the most pleasant memories in regard to her. We hold no rancor and no bitterness, but in view of the things you wrote me and your general attitude, I think it better for us to sever relations.

Sincerely,

/s/ Page

I do not know whether or not I ever sent you my letter of January 7th in reply to your letter regarding the 1942 Christmas gift—I seem to be in possession of the original, but just in case I didn't send it, I am inserting it here because it still clearly states my position and attitude in the entire matter:

January 7, 1943

1st. Lt. Charles Page Smith
36 Fox Avenue
Benning Park
Columbus, Ga.

Dear Page:

The Christmas money you returned—has been used to pay the Officers' Club bill, which you failed to take care of with the money that I sent you for that purpose.

It was interesting to get your letter confirming the severance of relations. Interesting because of what you had written me about the letters your mother, your brother and your grandmother had written to you and your then prospective bride— As I recall it, your mother was so ashamed of the union that she deliberately misled people as to the date of your wedding, so that she wouldn't be embarrassed by questions about your wife at Virginia's nuptials—that conduct you said you would never forgive—but in no time, to my surprise, you both were crawling back to Ruxton—kowtowing—"without dignity" and Eloise was boasting about it, and proudly displaying the gifts of jewelry that had been bestowed upon her from that quarter. Could it be, as Eloise pointed out on her wedding day, because the stakes for you both are high at Ruxton?— I had hoped you had more character than that.

It is difficult to comprehend how your wife could have failed to have been aware of her conduct up here, because it took such a decided change—toward Eve and myself—after she determined we could be of no further use—. I suspect she never behaved that way at Ruxton—I would have been tolerant, had I for one instant thought that she didn't know any better and wasn't aware of what she was saying or doing—There was nothing that Eve or I ever did that in any way warranted her impudence to us—.

Yes—our relations have been broken for some time, and will continue to be broken until your wife has apologized for her unspeakable behavior and has the common decency and courtesy to thank Eve for her hospitality. . . .

Perhaps my world-wide experience, with men and women, makes me in my maturity, discerning, critical and exacting.

I don't like deceitfulness and lieing for any purpose, whether by you, your wife or your mother— Unfortunately, you have been placed in embarrassing positions because of the Ruxton attitude. In the long run, however, I think you will find it better to take a position, frankly and openly,—as to what you want and intend to do—and stand by it. It was distressing to learn from you that you had prompted your wife to lie to me, and to lie to your mother.

In my old age—I am selective—emotionally, I do not approve of Premiers, Presidents, Diplomats, Politicians or little girls and boys who do not tell the truth, or who try to mislead people for their own selfish ends.

When I find someone lieing about me to others, and then lieing to me about others—I call a halt. . . .

Philosophically, I don't give a damn, for none of it makes any difference to me— As a matter of fact, only your egotism is involved —your pride and dignity at stake—Wasn't your dignity also at stake at Ruxton, after they had depreciated your wife to all and sundry?— or wasn't it?—

As for actuating reasons, they are sometimes diametrically opposed points, but as to facts, there are always two sides—the true and the false.

Every man should stand up for the woman of his choice, right or wrong— There is no doubt about that—altho there is nothing to

450

prevent his trying to polish off a rough stone—particularly if it is a precious one and worth it.

I have had enough experience with husbands and wives to know that when either one or the other is told the truth about the other, the friendship of both is lost. Nevertheless, as your father, I could foresee that if Eloise continued unchecked, it would be a serious reflection on you, and I told her so,— For a long time I sought to avoid the issue headon, because of the effect it might have upon her. I hoped it could be approached obliquely—but in the end, I was forced to be thus candid and frank with you for your own good. . . .

There should be no rancor nor bitterness between a father and a son, nor between a mother and a son, nor for that matter, between parents—living together or separated— Invariably, parents are primarily interested in the welfare and future of their children—true, their interest is usually a matter of personal egotism in wanting their images to always appear to the best advantage and to achieve the greatest possible success and honor in life.

As you have so aptly said, there is no reason for rancor or bitterness—there is not even a misunderstanding—all that is involved is the question of the behavior of a little girl who happens to be your wife, and my prerogative as an elder, to approve or disapprove, of unbecoming conduct—

I wrote you purely in the hope that you might gradually be able to bring about a little more respect for veracity and greater consideration for the acknowledged amenities on the part of the woman who bears your name.

Some prefer a world of fantasy—unreal, and thrive on lies. I happen to be a realist, believing the truth and trying to respect the rights of others who do likewise. It has always been my contention that while in Rome, one should do as the Romans do. I don't think it is a bit smart to be rude and crude in utter disregard for your fellowman. . . .

Love is blind, and that is as it should be, or there would be no mating season. I always thought I knew more than my father about women and things—but I lived to learn that he knew best—but that sage discovery was not made until he was under the sod in Trinity. . . .

If my dignity had bothered me—the way your dignity seems to bother you—I never would have gone along with your wedding plans, and cooperated the way I did— Now think that over. Minor things I can overlook, but obvious intentional rudeness, should be checked whether aimed at you, at Eve, at me, or anyone else.

Eve has always been devoted to you, and always will be, and

that goes double for me. We liked your wife—we put up with a lot from her on account of you—but her latter day manners, her petulance and her unspeakable conduct were unpardonable.

It's your bed—you are the one to straighten it—clean it—or lay in it—and lying in it is usually the easiest.

And so! Me lad and lassie, adieu— May the world treat you well, right or wrong, and may you conquer it and yourselves.

Your devoted Father,
/s/ W. Ward Smith

When we decided to take the apartment at 31 Beekman Place, we put an ad in the paper, in order to sublet our 30 Beekman Place apartment furnished.

As usual, the *Times* brought results—there were many inquiries, due in part at that season of the year, to the desire on the part of commuters to take up residence in New York on account of the gasoline shortage. . . .

I made the deal for the apartment with Vivienne L. . . . She was living at the Hotel Royalton at the time, and I took her to the Algonquin bar, where we discussed the apartment and her guarantors—then the next time I took her to lunch at the Algonquin where we ran into Konrad Bercovici, and others connected with the publishing and writing game. . . .

There were many who wanted the apartment, but none who had the appeal that Vivienne L.—when I escorted her from the Algonquin back to the apartment to check it over, she gave in without any resistance—let me undress her—she played with my cock—loved to suck it—I figured that she was laying the town so I rubbed my cock with vaseline and put on a rubber—then I greased that. I hate the damn things—they always fit so tight and are so hard to get on— but she kept playing with my balls and my prick kept good and stiff —she was a pretty good fuck—she really loved it.

On one occasion when I came over to see her and her friend about something in the apartment—they received me in the nude. They were running around naked—that was too much for me—I went down on one while I fucked the other.

Whenever they came over to pay the rent, they would have little on under their outside dresses—I would pull up their skirts—open their waists—kiss the tits, play with their cunts while they would jerk me off or go down on me right in the doorway of the apartment.

Eddie Ballou used our Garden for a cocktail party of his own,

452

and as luck would have it, I got into our tiny bathroom with two of his women guests. It wasn't my party, so I had a good load aboard—one girl was on the can—she pissed on my hand, while I finger-fucked the other one—then the girl on the toilet sucked me off while her friend played with my balls—just as I came, Eddie and a beau of one of the girls came pounding on the door—it was all over then—so we came out a bit distraught.

We had a little vegetable garden, as well as a flower garden, and a grill over which we cooked our steaks, when dining in the garden—we bought some garden furniture and had many very delightful parties out there on the banks of the East River, amidst the soot of the passing boats and the dust of the dirty city. . . .

I made some interesting studies in the back yard of the Hollywood models that I dressed in some of the old Parisienne costumes that Melba and I bought in Paris in 1929—then I made one with a girl in her bathing suit, holding samples of Tung Oil in various interesting positions in her hands, between her legs, etc.

One such picture made it appear as if the girl had a pencil between her legs. I could watch them undress and get into their costumes thru the mirrors or the bathroom window without their knowing I was watching. When I helped them tighten up or adjust their clothes I would feel them all over—I usually took the models' measurements first, and that gave me a chance to feel their thighs and tits —I would have a hard on—fix them a strong drink and then, when they undressed, go to work on them.

I paid them five bucks an hour, took their pictures in the back yard, and laid them in the livingroom. They were easy—one time I got two together—they were living together and loving one another. They were hard to approach, but when I got a few drinks into them it was simpler—then I encouraged them to love one another as they undressed—I got undressed too, and watched—and laying close to them on the sofa, jerked off as they went down on one another—they were hot babies and they loved it—no time for me, but how they could lap up one another's cunts and ass holes—to say nothing of the way they played with their tits.

I get a stiff prick as I write about it—memories about such things are that way. I suppose I will end this by jerking off or fucking the maid in the rear end.

One of the models that I favored that summer was a blonde—platinum blonde—she was quite lovely, but a bit hard.

The models would come to my office at 101 Park Ave. for

inspection—that was largely filling out an application—then I would measure them—then I would eliminate—the ones I selected I would have come to 31 when I was sure Eve was out of the house—around eleven in the morning—the sun was just right then.

1947

Times are returning to normal, the stock market is declining, Republicans have been elected in a landslide across the nation—there are plenty of rooms in the Washington Hotels—the cabinet maker and repair man solicit your business—the District of Columbia is saturated with empty cabs—the dining car waiters on the railroad trains are courteous (and serve you quietly and decently—no more throwing things at you and rushing you out)—the parlor car porter polishes your shoes as you approach your destination and brushes the dandruff off your coat collar—he even cleans your hat—gentle folk are to be found riding in the Pullmans again once more properly clothed—Jews, in the Washington parlor cars are now few and far between, for their false god (FDR) no longer holds sway in the nation's capital.

Congress being out of session also improves the calibre of the riders. The niggers are still crowding the air-cooled, thank God, day coaches on the Baltimore-Washington route, almost 25% black—the trains are departing and arriving on their right tracks and once more generally are on time. And "Whitman's Sampler" chocolate candy is again openly displayed on the local druggist's counter. . . .

The Van Loon funeral set off a line of thought—made me reflect upon my own fruitless life—the narrowness and ruthless selfishness of my fellow man in his battle to survive.

I may never finish this or get caught up—so I will let my thoughts wander here a bit lest when I come to where they should be put down I will no longer be here to do so.

I have scanned the rituals of the many sects—I know the dogma of my inherited faith—I well know the transitory nature of our daily life, and that the only certainty is death—that we have no control over our creation or extermination (except in a case of suicide, and I rather wonder whether that is as premeditated as we are prone to believe). . . .

People are forever planning and having their plans go asunder. Mine always do—just as death lurks stealthily around the corner—as Old Man Reaper shadows us from the cradle to the grave.

All there seems to be to life (and it is a maddening thought to some) is the material existence we know.

When life ceases to exist and passes out of the body, we then could make excellent fertilizer—but that would destroy the mystery of many sects.

That is really all we are good for after death—fertilizer. . . .

There are times when I seem to exist in cycles—perhaps I am inclined to over-sensitivity—nothing has ever come to me that I have ever sought, outside of women, no job I have ever wanted has been mine, nothing that could have benefited me materially has ever materialized—when I have been the instigator, in my own belief.

Whenever I have worked without an objective for the sheer love for what I was doing—and without compensation—things have come my way.

For example: I never sought the job of Secretary to the Governor—my real interest at the time was in the transportation facilities of the City, State and Nation, and occasionally I harboured a slight thought of being a Public Service or Transit Commissioner—when such thoughts occurred it was never the salary that occurred to me, it was the work that appealed.

But such notions were easily dismissed, for I was well aware that I never possessed the political qualifications (the Republican Party was not indebted to me).

The Secretaryship came out of a clear sky—the appointment to be Associate Chairman of the Small Loan Division of the Treasury Department came in the same way. More recently the small, petty honors—unremunerative—by the lively little local Republican Club were entirely unsolicited.

I was made head of the Actors' Fund, Endowment Fund Campaign thru no solicitations on my part—the "Hoover for President" activity was not of my own determination—W. S. S. was the doing of Karl Behr aided and abetted by Guy Emerson, as was the Mitchell parade.

The Preparedness Parade (World War I) was my father's idea—he thought there should be a Lumber Trade Division. Schuyler Meyer drew me into the 15th Assembly District fight—the banks on Long Island, were an idea of Father's—the Whit Organization, Joe Lilly's. . . .

Life is full of contraries. FDR has a pleasing, yes, delightful personality and charm—acquired, of course. Developed over years—but economically, he is unsound and his advisers crackpots—he is a stubborn, dictatorial egoist, as lacking in administrative ability and sound business sense as he is overdeveloped with cultivated charm.

Our Governor—Dewey—is an upstart—a cute, sly, arrogant, ruthless, dictatorial, inflated egotist, a relentless slave driver obsessed with his own importance, and resigned in his own mind to the fact that he is a man of destiny. If elected President of the United States he would be as uncompromising and dictatorial with Congress and his Party as F.D.R. He is not a false-face like the President—he does not feign at charm in order to accomplish his purpose—he is direct in his ruthless dealings with his fellowman, whereas the President is always oblique and two-faced. Then too, Governor Dewey would bring, if elected, to the National Administration new blood with which to prime the rundown machinery—advisors and counsellors whose ability far exceeds anything the Democrats have ever had to offer in the National field.

Perhaps and in fact, I believe that for men to succeed in the highly competitive game of politics or in business or in finance or in commerce, or in industry, that they must be ruthless and heartless, and concerned only with their own destiny—dedicating themselves completely to their objectives and to hell with all and sundry along the path that they must tread to reach their destination.

I haven't been so gaited—perhaps that's why my existence has been so useless to myself and to my fellowman—why I have wasted and dissipated what I have, if I have anything.

If there has ever been anything in the balance that I have instigated myself or that I have wanted, the scales have always dropped against me.

And yet I cannot complain, because I have had much out of life, in a general sort of way—my senses have been appeased in many ways—perhaps my interests were and have always been too diversified. . . .

Americans are getting tired of being taxed to poverty in order to pour vast sums into the empty European pit, only to have the re-

456

cipients of our bounty thumb their noses at us and seek by devious means to overthrow our form of Government, change our way of life, and reduce our high standard of living to the low levels to which they have been so long accustomed and from which most Americans' ancestors fled to escape the inequities of.

And so I come with these few observations on things current in 1947 to the end of the more or less colorless activities of 1943, as far as my personal existence was concerned. . . .

It used to be the movement of merchandise—the movement of precious metals—the movement of current invisibles—the movement of invested capital—the movement of temporary credit. Now it's the movement of the bowels that counts most.

AND THAT IS ALL FOR NOW

Afterword

The letter did not end; it stopped. It stopped, perhaps only co-incidentally, with the reconciliation of Eloise and me to my father and Eve—at whose initiative I cannot now recall, certainly without those apologies my father had insisted must precede any healing of the breach. It was ratified, typically, by a great effusion of Christmas gifts for the children and handsome presents for ourselves.

There was visiting back and forth; my father and Eve to our old tenement-building apartment in the Cambridge semislums. Eloise and I and the two children, Ellen and Carter, and then a little later, Anne, went to Sagaponac or Bridgehampton, once for the road races (which went past the front door) and once, as I recall, for Christmas, during the years I was in graduate school. Then later, after the Bridge-hampton house had been sold for a large profit and my father and Eve had bought a farm in Stowe, Vermont, to Stowe and, in the last decade of his life, to Greenwich, New York, a small town near Saratoga.

My father's fortunes in this period were entirely dominated by Eve's professional life as a dress designer. In the middle fifties she left or was fired by Leonard and Levine. Her violent anti-semitism may have gotten too much for them to tolerate or she may simply have gotten tired of the nerve-wracking demands of the "rag business" and decided to extricate herself. In any event, she developed a line of knit twine handbags, placemats, and shoes which were farmed out for fabrication to the wives of, for the most part, French-Canadian farmers. My father undertook to sell the bags to fashionable women's stores and gift shops. He also ran a small dairying operation with a dozen or so cows and, typically, feuded with the natives, protesting the quality of workmanship done on the original improvements to

458

the farmhouse he and Eve had bought and fixed up, much as they had restored the Sagaponac house, leaving bills unpaid and swearing vengeance on anyone who provoked his wrath. Vermont and upper New York State farmers are a tough and resourceful breed. On one occasion a disgruntled creditor got a lien placed on my father's Buick. It was locked in his garage pending payment of a bill for plumbing and for several months he and Eve commuted from Stowe to New York by train and bus.

He had a measure of revenge during a dry time for cows. When his and his neighbors' animals went dry, my father loaded his dry cows on a truck in the dark of night and carried them across the border to Canada where he got freshened cows that were giving milk. Thus surreptitiously he replaced dry cows with fresh ones and was delighted when word reached him that his fellow dairymen were thoroughly baffled by the milk tanker's report that Smith's cows were giving three hundred pounds of milk a day.

As he had earlier at Melvale, my father entered energetically into the not wholly unfamiliar role of farmer, albeit part-time. My impression was that the woven twine venture—Stowecraft it was called—was not an especially flourishing one. Certainly it did not permit my father and Eve to live in the style to which they had been accustomed when she was a topflight dress designer. After three or four years of knitted twine, Eve found another designing job in New York. They took an apartment in the city and bought the weekend and vacation house in Greenwich.

After I left graduate school and we moved to Santa Monica, where I took a position at the University of California at Los Angeles as an assistant professor of history, our contacts with my father and Eve became infrequent. My father called on the phone three or four times a year for long, rambling conversations, usually about politics, and when we moved to Santa Cruz with the opening of the new campus of the University of California in that community he and Eve visited us. There were presents at Christmas, though on a far more modest scale than formerly and on those rare occasions when we saw each other, there was much reminiscing and many references to the letter. He professed pride in my career and my modest accomplishments but he never really gave the impression of being interested in me as a particular person although he abounded in sentimental references to me *as his son*. The same was true with Eloise and his grandchildren. He tried to impress them with *him* but he showed little capacity to enter into their own rather interesting personalities.

459

One felt that they, like my wife and I, had little reality for him. He could not engage any of us, son, daughter-in-law, grandchildren as people distinct from himself; we were all like extras in a play in which he (and to a lesser extent, Eve) were the stars. Or perhaps we were more like the scenery, the stage set itself, sounding boards, more or less inanimate auditors of his monologues.

Eve was delighted with him. In her eyes he was a person of infinite charm. She never tired of hearing the endless self-glorifying stories that so bored others—what he had said or written to Mrs. Roosevelt; how he had put La Guardia in his place, and told off that slob Hoover. She thought him a great wit, a brilliant intellect, and an enthralling conversationalist. She reveled in his power over headwaiters, in his imperious manners, and even in his violent and abusive temper. She thought him the handsomest man alive and never ceased to marvel how she—an ugly old maid—had managed to capture such a paragon.

My father, for his part, knew which side his bread was buttered on. He had been down too many times not to know up when he saw it. He attended faithfully to her needs. He squired her about with his great air of importance, demanding special courtesies and attentions for her, flagging down taxis while less imposing figures waited, getting the best tables, the best accommodations, the best service, and, not infrequently, paying for it all with a rubber check, because, despite the fact that Eve had what was, for the times, a very substantial salary, they always lived beyond it. The check-kiting, the false bank accounts, the pseudonyms, the subpoena servers did not cease with his marriage to Eve.

He shared the cooking (he had always had a penchant for cooking), got up every morning and prepared a simple breakfast for her and served it to her in bed, paid the bills and, for the most part, spent the money.

Although, as he himself observed, Eve had no interest in kinky sex, she resigned herself to his obsession so long as it was not flaunted in front of her or her friends. She and age eventually tamed him. The fires were banked, the ravenous sexual appetites diminished.

I remember being startled when, some six or seven years after his marriage to Eve he said to me, very casually, matter-of-factly, "I've gotten very fond of Evie." Indeed, he came, I would say, so far as he was capable of that uncertain emotion, to love her. Or perhaps he only became accustomed to her, which in itself is not to be taken lightly, men and women being what they are.

Eve I always liked. There was a directness about her that was appealing. I suspect that almost anyone who does a craftsmanlike or craftswomanlike job is in a measure redeemed by it, made more human or more real by it. Thus Eve always seemed more real to me than my father. She was tough and capable with an energy as vast as my father's, but one that was clearly focused. Her political ideas were simplistic. She accepted unquestioningly whatever my father said about politics and enthusiastically shared his anti-semitism, but she had a sense of humor and a body-wracking, hiccuping laugh that was infectious. She smoked incessantly and drank too much but she preserved my father from such grim fortunes as can only be imagined.

When he died quickly and easily of a heart attack in his seventy-fifth year, life was over for her. She did not wish to live. He remained for her the most wonderful, the most gifted, handsome man she had ever known. She began to drink incessantly. She visited us in Santa Cruz, two years after my father's death, still hopelessly bereaved, skimping along on some hidden savings and social security, but stubbornly refusing financial help. The night before she was to return to the house in Greenwich, which had become her permanent home, she broke her hip; the rumor was, dancing on a piano in a local bar. Her hip was set; she went from the hospital to a convalescent home where she could be near the doctor and get proper therapy and she turned the home upside down, smoking like a chimney, smuggling booze in, refusing to be quiet and tractable, steadfastly unwilling to behave like an old lady with a broken hip. One home virtually ousted her and in the one to which she was transferred I was constantly being appealed to to speak to my stepmother about her raucous and undisciplined ways.

Her drinking imperiled the mending of her hip. In fact she didn't care whether the hip ever mended or not or, indeed, whether she lived or not. Finally, still rebellious, she insisted on flying back to Greenwich. My daughter, Anne, accompanied her and got her settled. Kind neighbors attended her and a practical nurse cooked and kept house. Three months later she called a cousin of my father's in New York and told him that she had decided to blow her brains out (her brother and sister had both been suicides). While he was still remonstrating with her, she got a shotgun, went out on the porch, placed the gun against her head and pulled the trigger. She died some seven or eight hours later.

The principal riddle of my father's life was his obsession with

461

sex. I always saw it as, in part, a consequence of his life in New York City. To me the city simply was (doubtless because of my association of my father with sex and with the life of the city) a sex-saturated environment. One was surrounded by women out of context, so to speak. They were not perceived, as one brushed past them in the streets, in crowded places, saw them on buses and above all, of course, on subways, as wives or mothers or people imbedded in some particular, defined social situation, but as mysterious, alluring sexual creatures, each seeming to promise a blissful assignation. That my father should have been so eloquent on the subject of what might be called "subway sex" seems significant to me, because of all the places one encountered women in New York, the subway was the most sexually suggestive if only because of the press of bodies stimulated by the motion of the train. It was one of those odd encounters of extraordinary if transient intimacy, in which the modern city abounds; eyeball-to-eyeball contact, body contact, olfactory contact that was at the same time outside of any normal context of social relationship. It was probably safe to say that people have never encountered each other in this fashion before in history. At the same time the experience of the subway was novel enough for my father's generation so that all these sensations, the potency of which was dulled for later generations of subway riders by custom and habit and by the deterioration of the stations themselves into noisome hellholes and the trains into foul vehicles of unpredictable velocity, were fresh and powerful. I believe that the fact that the subway was "underground" contributed to its sexuality; it was underground that dark and desperate acts had always been performed. The word itself suggested illicit affairs.

The city streets also, particularly of course in the Broadway area, reeked of sex, and it is clear that this atmosphere both excited and disgusted my father—one of the most vivid parts of the letter is his description of the area in the midforties off Broadway where the hotels St. Margaret and Coolidge were located; and what an irony that those seedy fleabags, those multistoried dens of iniquity, should have had those particular names!

In the mythology of small-town America, to which for perhaps unfathomable reasons I feel so close, the city has always been a symbol of sin, evil, and wickedness. It was where the country boy went and lost his money and his virtue, returning shamefaced to the town, possessed by guilty secrets. Thus my father's sexuality was, for me, and I am sure for him as well, intimately connected with the city. I have always been aware, as a consequence, that I could not live

462

in a city. It would produce and, in those brief times when I am in cities, has produced in me an unbearable sexual tension.

Conversely, when my father lived, however briefly or intermittently, in rural communities and small towns, his obsession moderated, grew less feverish and intense, more general—and for very good reason: the opportunities were infinitely less, and those women encountered belonged, for the most part, to some kind of social context that lowered the sexual temperature.

The problem also remains for me of my father's preoccupation with what were once called sexual perversions (and are today referred to as "kinky sex"), oral and anal sex, voyeurism, et cetera. The portions of the letter recounting these episodes were, frankly, most troubling to me both because I found them offensive and because they will offend many readers, among them people whose good opinion I value. I would have preferred to omit them on a variety of grounds. They could have been omitted without in any way diminishing the predominantly sexual character of the letter and of my father's life. We are told by many self-proclaimed experts on sexual matters that there are no such things as sexual perversions, that everything we enjoy doing we should feel free to do. The perversions are, as this argument goes, only in our minds. I did not retain such accounts in the letter because I accept this argument. Rather, I left them in because I felt that they had a conclusive psychological importance in the story of my father.

Some years ago Norman O. Brown praised "polymorphous perversity," the indulgence in every form of perversity, the tasting of all forbidden pleasures, descending into the depths in order to come out on the other side purged of the sexual anxieties and hang-ups accumulated over centuries of repression. My father ran that course and although I saw no signs that it freed him from anything, it seems to me it is part of the record, so to speak.

And what of the women who gave themselves to him with such abandon? What of them? What did they see in him? Certainly the aura of sexuality. And what else? The pure, simple, unadulterated, uninhibited power of sex, sex so much obscured, repressed, even maligned by the proper world. Did it need—did sex need—its pioneers, its explorers, its radical advocates? Was my father really an innovator, a precursor of the sexual revolution, a type which, appearing well in advance of its time, must suffer obloquy and chastisement by a society whose mores have been so flagrantly defied? Was he, like the Marquis de Sade, forced by the prudishness and hypocrisy of society to ex-

463

tremes of degeneracy? Or was he simply in the vanguard of the coming sensate culture, a forerunner of a general decline in moral standards?

I can only see him as a victim rather than a precursor. But yet, the story is clearly more complex than that. My father became pure act; from his violent disembodied rages to his reckless spending of money and semen, he tested the limits of man as a creature of self-gratification.

Sexual encounters were, for my father, I believe, an effort to overcome fear of death, to assert his own masculinity, which he confessed often to doubt, and, finally, I suppose to exercise a particular skill—an expertise—on which he prided himself.

I see my father as a victim, in part, of the transition from a prudential to a sensate culture (to put the matter in a rather fancy way), that is to say, nineteenth-century America had believed above all in control, in control of one's emotions, appetites, money, semen. Controlled, calculated, prudential behavior—what has been summed up as the Protestant Ethic of thrift, piety, and hard work—was the ideal and even, perhaps, the norm. George Washington was the hero of that consciousness because he was for his admirers a man of iron self-control. Tears or any excessive display of emotion were considered to be weak, effeminate qualities. The emotionalism of women was in sharp contrast to the "control" of men. My father grew up in the time when America generally, and the great metropolitan centers in particular, were on the verge of what has been called a sensate culture, a culture in which the immediate gratification of one's appetites and desires was replacing the old prudential behavior. The new ethic was the ethic of cheerful consumption rather than of saving, reserving, suppressing, storing away, retaining. To spend money, even money one didn't have and had to borrow, was to be a good American, to stimulate the economy, to keep cash circulating. Increasingly, money and semen were to be spent, not retained. There were already prophets of the new ethic that were eagerly read by those in the know—Freud himself, in a way; Havelock Ellis, Edmund Carpenter, the Englishman who advocated orgies and bisexual experience for sexual release; and, nearer home, Margaret Sanger, only part of whose message was birth control, the other being uninhibited sexuality and open marriage. My father read these authors and numerous others and became an enthusiastic advocate and practitioner of the new sexual freedom. He demonstrated, in his own life, what happens when control breaks down. He was, like a figure on the crest of a breaking wave, never

464

really in control. One thus searches in vain for some clear point at which it was possible to say, "If only here . . . If he had only done this instead of that. . . ." He was like a skier skiing out of control, a surfer riding an impossible wave to an inevitable wipeout, a racing driver headed into a suicidal corner too fast. A curious combination of themes and forces converged in him—exploitive capitalism, the American success ethic, social ambition, the trend toward what the late C. Wright Mills called fictitious personalities, figures created by the media, the rise (or appearance) of national names and personalities, famous people, and the tireless promoting of them by newspapers, magazines, and radio. Promotion. Selling. Quick fortunes. Promotion, for instance, implied advancing something not particularly worthy on grounds other than the intrinsic merit of the thing itself. Besides promoting things an ambitious young man was expected to promote himself. In my father Horatio Alger joined forces with Casanova.

His violent rages provided another clue. I could not understand how these rages could be so transient, one moment furious shouting, the next smiling amiability. Rages that would have left me shaken for a day had they possessed me, passed from him as readily as the reflections of clouds on water. But the rages were like the sexual explosions. They never, or rarely, touched anything central *in him*. Perhaps that was why he so often doubted the reality of his own experience.

In a document as lengthy as my father's letter, what he has omitted may be as important as what is included (or, in some cases, more important). For instance, in the account of his brief period as Secretary to Governor Miller, the pages telling of the events that led to Miller's firing him are missing. There is only one specific reference to his feelings in that part of the letter. Much later, writing in a suicidal mood, my father recalls his temptation to kill himself when Miller told him that he must leave his administration and he speaks of the time as one when he reached the nadir of despair. I believe that, remarkably candid as the letter is, my father could not bear to allow his original account of that event to pass into my hands. That surely is a measure of the horror of the experience for him. There were some things that even he could not bear to tell, or, if he told them, could not bear to leave as part of the record of his life.

My father seldom speaks of *his* father in the letter and what he does say is in the nature of conventional filial piety. He describes him as handsome, honest, hardworking. It is clear enough that my father's mother—Honey—and aunts were much more important to him than his father or uncle, although Uncle Gov, with his yacht, seems to have made a strong impression. My guess would be that my grandfather held my father to a very strict standard, made a great deal of his weaknesses and was furious over his frequent lapses. I suspect that my grandmother and her sisters, on the other hand, spoiled him outrageously and that he came to feel a certain contempt for his mother as a consequence. Certainly, my father's letters to his mother, written after his father's death, are not pleasant reading. They are condescending and admonitory, asking for money in many instances and rebuking her for being selfish and complaining too much.

Then there are the frequent references in the letter to being a coward. In referring to his failure to enlist in the army at the beginning of World War I (and to his efforts to avoid being drafted), he speaks in an almost offhand way of his cowardice. He had flat feet and was thus ineligible on physical grounds. But he mentions that just the thought of being shot at made him sweat with fear. His conviction that he was a coward seems to me to be related to his sense of the unreality of his own life. The philosopher, J. Glenn Gray, in his book about men at war, *The Warriors,* speaks of the cowards that he encountered in the army during World War II as men with little ability to relate to others. "The coward," he writes, "does not know the sense of a common effort and a common fate," [and] "has, unfortunately, not gained in its place any strong individuality or any full awareness of self. . . . The coward's fear of death stems in large part from his own incapacity to love anything but his own body with passion. . . . The inability to participate in others' lives stands in the way of his developing any inner resources to overcome the terror of death. . . . The coward, unrelated to his fellows, has an insufficient hold on life and is not in charge of himself or his fate."

I quote the passage at some length because it seems to me to provide an important clue to that sense of unreality that seems to have obsessed my father at many periods of his life.

If cowardice and the inability to love are, as Gray suggests, closely connected, they are often associated with the need to suffer and inflict pain. My father, I fear, enjoyed inflicting pain and suffering on others but he also needed to experience it himself. For instance, his virulent anti-semitism did not prevent him from having a number of affairs with Jewish women whom he professed to love

466

passionately while at the same time disparaging them in the letter.

I believe that it was because he could not love that he continually degraded what is called too loosely "the act of love." Each violent and perverted sexual encounter was, in its own way, a plea for love. Although my father wrote constantly of loving, I could never find in meetings with him, in his treatment of others, or even in the letter itself, any evidence that he was truly capable of that emotion. Did he have some haunted, unarticulated sense that if, like the monster in a fairy tale, he could find someone to love him, he would become a splendid prince and was I, above all, the one from whom he hoped for release from that grim prison of unlovingness? Who, long before I was an actor in his life, refused him love? Or said or did something that made it impossible for him to love?

Another indication of my father's determination to punish himself and others can be found in his lifelong propensity to break off highly valued friendships on some startlingly trivial pretext. The case of Hendrik Van Loon is typical. His friendship with Van Loon was, among all his friendships, the one most treasured and featured. There are dozens of affectionate letters back and forth between the two men. My father bought literally hundreds of copies of his books to give to friends and relatives and Van Loon dutifully autographed all of them. My father applauded Van Loon as a genius, gave him in his "rich year" a handsome gold stopwatch from Cartier, and bombarded him with advice as to how to advance his career. Then because Van Loon did not instantly produce a Christmas card to be sent out from Melvale (my father wanted it done in three days) he wrote him a bitter, vitriolic letter declaring the friendship at an end.

While his relation with La Guardia was not a particularly close one, it was obviously one that my father prized. Again on some utterly inconsequential issue my father wrote him one of his "kiss-off" letters. He wrote many angry, vituperative letters, of course, to people that he did not know or knew only casually. He did know Hoover and he had been one of his earliest and most enthusiastic boosters; in time he became one of his bitterest detractors and wrote a long, denunciatory letter to him. Judge Robert McCurdy Marsh, who he had declared to be like a second father to him, who stood by him through a number of legal scrapes and embarrassments, and who managed his divorce from my mother, was written off by letter and physically assaulted. Poor Walter Piel, Harry Millar, Tommy Brodix, his drinking and whoring companions, all eventually got the kiss-off though in some instances there were eventual reconciliations. And me, the designated recipient of the fabled letter, his son and heir, because of some ridiculous contretemps with my wife, he wrote me an insulting letter, to which, by his own admission, I could only have properly reacted by anger and indignation, by a breach in our relatively recent and rather shaky relationship. So to punish and be punished was clearly a deep-seated need. It stemmed, I believe, from the same basic feeling of unreality that lay at the heart of so much of his behavior and, indeed, of the letter itself. The past was always more real to my father than the present. The past could be arranged and rearranged, recounted and reviewed, in a measure controlled, while the present had to be experienced, often in very excruciating ways, and the future, full of terrors and anxieties had, in some manner, to be neutralized. A classic way of neutralizing the future is, obviously, to be obsessed with the past. He tried to overcome the terror of the dream, of nullity, by striking out, by seeking to evoke the reassuring response, by what I can only understand to be strange cries of anguish, even in the midst of the most furious sexual debauches. Only in these moments when he was gripped by sexual ecstasies did he feel himself to be in touch with the fringes of reality. The physical violence, the verbal violence, the sexual violence, the suicidal moods, never really suicidal, always playing at suicide, too cowardly by his own account to really confront so final and desperate an act, all these come to one point: "Tell me that this is not a dream," or, conversely, "Waken me from this nightmare, and tell me it is a dream."

For me, the most appealing episode in my father's life was the Melvale venture. The mad energy with which he plunged into the undertaking, his impatience, his determination to reshape the whole environment in less than two weeks in order that he and Melba might celebrate Christmas in their new quarters was completely in character. He fantasized a country Christmas and, like a sorcerer, made it come true. He waved a magic wand and, presto, there was a farmhouse rebuilt even to the chimneys. One can be sure it set rural tongues clacking all over the county. No wonder he was called the Baron. Moreover, he was no gentleman farmer; he got dirt under his fingernails, he planted cabbages, pitched hay, picked apples, plowed fields, took his produce to market, immersed himself in the arcane lore of rural life, made the farm a kind of universe from the center of which he, now Farmer Smith (as opposed to Politician Smith, Businessman Smith, and all the other half-formed and discarded Smiths), dispensed homely rural wisdom to anyone willing to listen. On one level he must have known it was only a charade, a play that would soon be over. But on another level he played the part with a furious gusto which I find irresistible. Was that really his problem? Was he, in fact, a kind of earth figure, a creature so elemental that only when he touched earth could he touch reality and like Antaeus, gain fresh strength? Was he at heart a son of the soil whose powers were perverted by the alien atmosphere of a city that drew him back time and again like a magnet?

Certainly, his relationship to his city was a central fact of his life. He lived in the city, certainly in the thirties, by his wits and instincts, like an animal in the forest. He was aware enough of the ambiguity of his own feelings to see his constant travels as efforts to escape from the place where he was so essentially rooted, the place, most acutely, of his triumphs and defeats. I believe each of us has a destiny, dimly perceived though it may be, unrealized though it may be. It is a fate appropriate to our capacities—healing us and reconciling us to the world. The lucky ones discover it; the others pursue it. Perhaps it is just the current romanticism of "loving the earth" but I would like to think that my father's protean energies were meant to be rooted in the soil, in the common, consoling earth, and that, for a moment, he perceived this and entered into that realm with the instinct that he was coming home. Although he never again took up conventional farming, he never gave up a rural *pied-à-terre*.

One point that cannot perhaps be sufficiently emphasized was the ability that my father displayed in the various political and financial ventures that he undertook. Literally thousands of pages of the letter deal with these undertakings and one cannot, I believe, fail to be impressed by his remarkable organizational abilities. He was unsparing of himself and others in his efforts to achieve a particular goal: aid to the Jews, funds for the Actors' Memorial, War Stamps, Hoover's or Lowden's or Landon's presidential campaigns, Florida real estate, tung oil, the Queen Wilhemina Fund, the Mexican Tourist Bureau, the Anderson Air-Conditioner, the National Trailer Show, on and on. Certainly energy and intelligence, those usual guarantors of success, were not missing. But his extravagance, not simply in a specific financial sense, but in a total sense, his inability to contain or master his vision or his appetites brought everything eventually to nought.

One thing I wish to make as clear as I can. I have no illusion

469

that in these efforts to account for my father's strange temperament I am in any real sense "explaining" him. I would be untrue to my own perception of human life and historical process if I left the impression that my father's life could, in any clear and final way, be explained in terms of some combination of psychological traits. I am not a psychoanalyst; I do not even believe in the efficacy of the science. I believe that it is far too often used as a form of reductionism—that is to say, the reduction of the infinite and ultimate mystery of human life and experience to a set of superficial formulas. Yet some degree of understanding (on the notion, perhaps, that to understand all is to forgive all) is necessary, or at least it is necessary to struggle to achieve it, and this, particularly, in the case of someone as closely connected as one's own father. Thus one moves from the specific acts and events to some general principle that will make clear a pattern, a connectedness, between the specific acts and events, so that they do not appear to be merely discrete, unconnected. Thus one gropes, inevitably, I suspect, for a theme, a principle, a perspective which will enable one to break free of the tyranny of the particular and gain a broader understanding. Having at least tentatively identified such themes one comes back to the particulars at least partially freed from them. I believe that the only substantial use of what might be called, loosely, psychological insights is that they increase and extend the range of our sensibilities; they make us aware of elements of character that we might otherwise scant or overlook entirely.

What I am trying to say is that if I were to rest on an amateur's (or even a professional's) psychological profile of my father I would have in the process evaded my real responsibility, which I understand to be reconciliation. Thus, whatever might be said about the particular persons and the historical forces—the milieu—that helped to shape his character, my father remains what he was very conscious of being—a sinner. And that is, in simple fact, what we all are, in the view at least of Christian orthodoxy. I am certainly very conscious that that is what I am. It is not, therefore, up to me to "forgive" my father—that is God's business. It is as a fellow sinner, on a somewhat less imaginative scale, that I can perhaps encounter him most sympathetically. Indeed, I suppose it is only so that I can escape a note of self-righteousness in regard to my father, a note which I am conscious of having had to struggle against throughout this undertaking, a note which I am sure affected, or infected, our relationships during his lifetime and of which he can hardly have failed to be aware.

To his dying day, my father remained obsessed by sex. In conversation he was as tiresomely repetitious about sex as about politics. But he did not need, after his marriage to Eve, to find verification or to seek reality exclusively in sex. Or, apparently, to search any longer for his son. And so the letter ended; from the record of a continuing journey, it became a legacy. One wonders if, in the twenty years between its abrupt ending and my father's death, he ever thought of destroying it. Such an impulse would, I suppose, have been suicidal. All then that would have remained of Ward Smith would have been the rapidly fading memory of a rather garrulous old man preoccupied with sex. There are plenty of those around.

The last thirty years of my father's life belonged, in a sense, to Eve. She was the reality principle in my father's life. His relationship with my mother was doomed from the beginning. Melba was a co-conspirator in his fantasy trip. Eve was the first person to attach him, at least to a modest degree, to the real world. He had reached out for her like a drowning man, reached out to this gawky, homely old maid and she had saved his life. She had loved him so much that she could not bear to live without him. So that unlikely match had turned out, after all, to be a classic romance. The sordid affairs and desperate expedients were finally absorbed in the last act of a drama of romantic love.

After my father's death when I returned to Greenwich for the funeral, I was relieved, as much for Eve's sake as my own, to find that I could weep for him. But I listened, with a kind of embarrassment, to her describing a man I did not know, the paragon, the "greatest."

I felt, aside from the perhaps too easy tears, the same detachment that I had always felt in regard to my father. I could not really mourn. I felt no sense of loss; indeed, none of the emotions a son might be expected to feel upon the death of his father. I did not even feel the fearful sense of my own mortality that seized me at my mother's deathbed three years later. Only a kind of nullity, an emptiness, a slightly apologetic sense of being unable to summon up emotions appropriate to the occasion.

My father's account of the night he searched me out at my division's encampment on the A. P. Hill Military Reservation in the piney woods of Virginia where I was on my way back from army maneuvers in North Carolina is, for me, the most poignant passage in the letter. Pearl Harbor had just been attacked. It was one of those strange moments in which world history and one's own personal history converge. I had met, on maneuvers, a young artist who I was determined should be my wife. In the light of that miraculous, staggering fact and the peace and certitude that the knowledge of it as ordained and irrevocable brought with it, I had little concern for anything else. The bombing of Pearl Harbor was of significance only as it might affect my prospective marriage. I do not even remember the encounter that was so important to my father.

Reading about our meeting in the letter, it seemed to me that the key to that document lay there on the page, so obvious that it was hard to see how I could have missed it. Perhaps I was so accustomed to the myth of the son's search for the father that I was insensitive to the equally powerful theme of the father's search for the son. The letter was the agent or instrument of my father's search, his effort to attach himself to an archetypal human role and thus introduce a principle of reality into his world of fantasy.

Small wonder I could not comprehend all this during my father's lifetime. He pursued me and I fled the emotional attachment that he at least thought might have saved him. The playing of the traditional roles of father and son which he sought so tirelessly I resisted with every instinct of self-preservation as long as he lived.

And then, after his death, his final stratagem came into play. He called once more to me beyond life in that vast, interminable, problematical letter, so repugnant and so compelling—a kind of plea or curse, a last petition for acceptance and understanding, for reconciliation.

So I am disposed to say: "Father, I read your letter and I have tried, after my fashion, to answer it. I accept your life, sadly misspent as it has always seemed to me to be. I have discovered a principle of reconciliation in Eve's love for you, her own Adam, fallen and redeemed. I am willing to be your son and acknowledge you at last as my father. I find I can weep again for you, better tears than those brief, bewildered ones I wept at your death. And weep, as well, for myself. I hope that is enough."